THE SECRET LANGUAGES OF IRELAND

WITH SPECIAL REFERENCE
TO THE ORIGIN AND NATURE OF

THE SHELTA LANGUAGE

partly based upon Collections and Manuscripts of
the late

JOHN SAMPSON, Litt.D.

*Sometime Librarian of the University
of Liverpool*

by

R. A. STEWART MACALISTER

Litt.D., LL.D.

*Professor of Celtic Archaeology, University College
Dublin*

D1610427

CAMBRIDGE
AT THE UNIVERSITY PRESS
1937

But, when he pleas'd to shew't, his speech
In loftiness of sound was rich;
A Babylonish dialect,
Which learned pedants much affect;
It was a party coloured dress
Of patch'd and py-ball'd languages:
'Twas [Irish] cut on Greek and Latin
Like fustian heretofore on sattin.
It had an odd promiscuous tone,
As if h' had talk'd three parts in one;
Which made some think, when he did gabble,
Th' had heard three labourers of Babel;
Or Cerberus himself pronounce
A leash of languages at once.

'Hudibras', Part I, Canto i.

To

THE MEMORY OF
JOHN SAMPSON

CAMBRIDGE
UNIVERSITY PRESS

University Printing House, Cambridge CB2 8BS, United Kingdom

Published in the United States of America by Cambridge University Press, New York

Cambridge University Press is part of the University of Cambridge.

It furthers the University's mission by disseminating knowledge in the pursuit of education, learning and research at the highest international levels of excellence.

www.cambridge.org
Information on this title: www.cambridge.org/9781107671508

© Cambridge University Press 1937

First published 1937
First paperback edition 2014

A catalogue record for this publication is available from the British Library

ISBN 978-1-107-67150-8 Paperback

CONTENTS

INTRODUCTION

The main portion of the following work is based upon a random collection of loose sheets, letters, manuscript notebooks, pencilled scraps of paper, and printed matter, along with a box of dictionary slips into which their contents had been systematically, but incompletely, distributed—relics of the industry of the lamented John Sampson, known to all as one of the greatest of the world's authorities on the Gypsies, their origin, history, manners, customs, folklore, and language. This material was placed in my hands by Miss Dora Yates, the Secretary of the Gypsy Lore Society, and Dr Sampson's colleague at Liverpool and literary executor.

The history of the discovery of Shelta by Charles Godfrey Leland, of its acquisition by Sampson in the slums of Liverpool, and of its scientific study by Kuno Meyer, is set forth below, in its proper place. From the manuscripts put at my disposal, it appeared that the preparation and publication of a book, the joint work of these three scholars, had been projected. Little actual progress had been made with it; but something of its intended scope was indicated by a number of notes and 'schemes', as well as by some fragments which were published, after Leland's death, in the *Journal* of the Gypsy Lore Society.

So far as possible, I have followed the lines laid down in these 'schemes'; but as there are several, differing among themselves, I have felt free to follow what seemed to me the most convenient arrangement of the material. In the original plan, Shelta, the discovery of which was the special occasion of the projected book, was to come first, the other 'secret languages' following. But on chronological grounds the order here adopted seemed preferable. Most of the chapters are at least vaguely adumbrated in the notes of Sampson and his colleagues, though next to nothing had actually been written of any of them. The chapters on 'Cryptology', 'Hisperic', and 'Vagrants' are not included in any of the 'schemes'; but they are of importance for a complete statement of the subject, and I have therefore added them on my own responsibility. On the other hand, a chapter on 'The Secret Language in ancient Irish Art', which Leland appears to have written, and to have valued highly, is not forthcoming. It has a special mention in every 'scheme', but the manuscript is missing. Among the collection of fragments, however, there was found a sheet written in the handwriting of the late Margaret Stokes, to whom it had evidently been submitted, and who criticized it very severely. On the whole, the disappearance of this manuscript is probably no very serious loss.

It was at first intended to include in the chapter on 'Hisperic' an analysis of the Hisperic texts, as well as a complete edition, now practically ready for publication, of the imperfect but important glossary Harl. 3376 in the British Museum, which contains much Hisperic material, but of which less than half has been published. But it soon became evident that the volume would thereby be made unreasonably large; this part of the material has therefore been reserved for a companion volume.

I had not worked long over the collections before I found myself compelled to adopt views regarding the origin and age of Shelta differing from what would have been advocated in the book projected by the original authors. After consultation with Miss Yates (whose sustained interest, ready helpfulness, and valuable suggestions throughout the progress of the work I gratefully acknowledge) I have determined to treat the problem in my own way, and to speak throughout the book in my own person. It is a delicate matter to modify the views of men who can no longer speak for themselves; but I feel confident that the reader who weighs all the available evidence will agree that though there is some early material embedded in Shelta—this is shewn in the 'Summary', with which the work concludes—the language in its present form does not possess the high antiquity which its discoverers, not unnaturally, claimed for it. It is no more than right to acknowledge that doubts of this antiquity were first suggested to me in conversation by my colleague Dr Bergin, long before I had any anticipation that this work would come my way.

When a musical aspirant submitted to Moscheles a funeral march which he had composed on the occasion of Beethoven's death, he drew down upon himself the caustic comment: *My friend, would that you had died, and that Beethoven had written the march!* As I dip my pen to sign an 'Introduction' that should have been signed by Charles Godfrey Leland, John Sampson, and Kuno Meyer, I can forefancy a reader saying something of the same kind.

R. A. S. MACALISTER

1936

CHAPTER I

OGHAM

I. The Testimony of Caesar

Gaius Iulius Caesar, the arch-destroyer of Celtic civilization on the Continent of Europe, is nevertheless the writer of antiquity who has preserved for us more valuable details about that civilization than all the rest put together. Every study of Celtic Religion begins with a passage from *De Bello Gallico*, wherein the chief gods worshipped by the Gauls are enumerated; an important passage, though requiring some caution in making use of it. Every study of Celtic Literature begins with another passage from the same history (Book VI, chaps. xiii, xiv) wherein the author speaks of the druids; and from this rule our present investigation is not exempt. These chapters have been quoted so often, that it might be supposed that every possible minim of juice had been squeezed from them long before this: yet we shall find it profitable to remind ourselves of what Caesar has to tell us, on the subject with which they deal.

Two classes of people, he says, among the Gauls, are held in especial honour—druids and *equites*. The druids are concerned with matters of religion, and with the conduct of public and private sacrifices. A great number of youths go to them for teaching; and they—presumably the druids, not the youths, but the sentence is ambiguously worded—are held in high honour. They decide almost all judicial cases, public and private, criminal and civil—questions of inheritance or of territorial boundaries, for example. Anyone who refuses to accept their decision is punished by excommunication from the sacrifices. This is the heaviest of all their penalties, for he who is put under such a ban is made the object of a drastic boycott—thus we may render Caesar's words, though naturally he could not anticipate the transcendencies of modern civilization so far as to use this particular terminology.

One of the druids holds chief authority. When he dies, his successor is elected by vote, if there be no one marked out for the vacant office by supereminence in dignity. Sometimes, however, competition for the office becomes so hot, that they contend for

M S L

I

it by force of arms. At a certain season of the year they assemble in a sacred place in the land of the Carnutes, regarded as being the central point of Gaul [and in modern times believed to be the site of Chartres Cathedral]. Hither comes everyone who may have any dispute, in order to have it decided.

It is supposed that their teaching was discovered in Britannia, and carried thence to Gallia; even yet those who wish to understand it in greatest perfection journey to Britannia for instruction. As druids are exempt from military and fiscal services, these privileges attract many students, who go of their own accord, or are sent by their parents. It is said that they learn by heart a great number of verses, and that some spend as much as twenty years in this discipline. They do not consider it right (*fas*) to commit these verses to script, though in almost all public or private matters they make use of Greek letters. I suppose, adds Caesar parenthetically, that this is either because they desire to guard against the vulgar becoming acquainted with their mysteries, or because they are afraid of weakening their students' power of memory, seeing that much of this power is lost by trusting to written notes. He concludes with a few vague notions about the subjects of the druidic teaching—the immortality of the soul, the stars and their motions, the world, the size of lands, natural philosophy, and the nature of the gods. On these matters, we read, the druids hold disputations and impart instruction to youths.

Thus far Caesar, who next proceeds to tell us about the other honourable class, the *equites*. There we need not follow him; in the two chapters which we have paraphrased he has given us sufficient food for thought. He has introduced us to a caste of functionaries, semi-religious, semi-judicial; who preside over ritual ceremonies and courts of law; who are held in high honour and enjoy high privileges; who are expert in the traditional theology of their people, in natural philosophy as it was understood at the time, in astronomy, and in all such matters; who endeavour by disputations to enlarge the knowledge which they possess; and who impart that knowledge to schools full of pupils. These pupils come for instruction, often from a distance and even from beyond the sea; for though there are schools in Gaul, those which are most frequented are in Britain, where, it was believed, the doctrines of the druids were first formulated.

Instruction in the schools is conveyed in the form of verses, dictated to the pupils and by them committed to memory; for a religious tabu—such is the implication of the word *fas*—forbids both teacher and taught to commit them to writing. And in this drudgery many pupils spend as much as twenty years.

Let us consider what this implies. Suppose that the pupils were allowed two months' annual holiday, which is probably liberal: in other words, let us for arithmetical convenience keep them at school, 300 working days in a solar year. Then, if they learn no more than ten lines of poetry in the day, they will have acquired a total of 3000 by the end of the year, and in twenty years they will be masters of 60,000 lines. This is considerably more than twice the united lengths of the two Homeric epics. Even if they learnt only one single line *per diem*, they would have assimilated matter roughly equal in amount to the first ten books of the *Iliad*: if they enlarged their daily task to thirty-five or forty lines, they would in the end possess, stored in memory, matter equal in extent to the prodigious *Mahābhārata*.

As we have no information upon the average rate of work, we can come to no definite conclusion as to the magnitude of the literary material imparted to the students. But on any theory, if we accept the premises, we must conclude that it was of very considerable bulk. And there is no obvious reason why we should not accept the premises. Caesar had ample opportunity for learning these three superficial facts, which were probably common knowledge—that the druids taught screeds of verse to their pupils; that these verses were never written; and that the instruction often lasted twenty years. It is unlikely that he had any information as to the contents of the poems, or their literary quality: they may have been impressive hymns or epics; they may have been mere mnemonic doggerel. The carefully guarded secrets of a druidic freemasonry would not have been communicated to Caesar, a hostile alien: it is significant that when he begins to tell us what the teachers taught, he drops into hazy and obvious generalities. [But see *post*, p. 31.]

No other source of information in antiquity supplements Caesar's testimony with details of any value. Diogenes Laertius, in a passage undeservedly quoted at least as frequently as Caesar's chapters, says something about the druids teaching their followers ' to worship the gods, to do no evil, and to exercise courage'.[1]

[1] *Vit. Phil.* introd. § 5.

Canon MacCulloch, whose very useful book on *The Religion of the
Ancient Celts* treats Caesar's testimony with more than a spice
of scepticism, says (p. 304), 'If the Druids taught religious and
moral maxims secretly, these were probably no more than an
extension' of the three excellent precepts just quoted. But surely
the pupils must have been very dull if they found it necessary to
spend twenty years in assimilating such rudimentary morality,
however extended: and it is not obvious that any body of initiates
would suffer harm in prestige or otherwise by committing to
writing these copybook platitudes. If those who repeat the quotation from Timaeus would take the trouble to refer to the original
passage, they would find that it is the most casual of *obiter dicta*,
devoid of all authority, and professing to do no more than to
express current notions about the Celtic druids and the Indian
gymnosophists. It is just as worthless as contemporary notions
about Freemasonry among those who (like the present writer) are
not in the secrets of the craft, and so cannot by any possibility
know what they are talking about. Incidentally, we must describe
it as a mere fatuity to imagine a Celtic 'triad' as underlying the
threefold maxim stated by Timaeus.

Let us therefore return to Caesar; let us now consider for a
moment the prohibition of writing. Caesar's speculations as to
the reason for this are not convincing, though they possess a very
real secondary value. It is certainly true that, other things being
equal, a memory which has never known the crutch of pen and
paper is stronger than one which relies upon these supports. But,
apart from the moral conditions imposed by competitive examina-
tions, the external memory of a notebook is superior to the
memory which is the gift of nature. The former is permanent, and
is always available for reference: the latter is liable to fluctuations
due to ill-health, advancing age, and so forth. Regard for the
student's power of memory was not a sufficient reason for the
total prohibition of writing. The alternative suggestion, that its
purpose was to guard against the vulgar becoming acquainted
with the mysteries, is much more to the point: in all ages the
medicine-man has surrounded himself with an aura of occultism,
which establishes and safeguards his powers and his prestige. We
learn, in passing, from Caesar's theory that if the druidic teaching
had been written down, and if the writings had fallen into the
hands of the vulgar, the vulgar could have read them. Writing
was no learned monopoly: Caesar implies that it had to be pro-

hibited by those interested in maintaining the secrets of their order, just because it was cultivated with some freedom for secular purposes.

If, in these modern times, we can improve upon Caesar's guesses, it is because we know of analogies with which he was not acquainted. Writing is a secular art, used for profane purposes: those who have inherited religious faiths and formulae from an unlettered ancestry have an instinct that this novelty profanes sacred texts. Religion is conservative. Candles seem more suitable than electric lights as illuminants for churches. Solomon must build his temple without the touch of iron,[1] then newly brought into use—a metal against which, even yet, supernatural beings are alleged to feel repugnance.

The first enthusiasts for Islâm were reluctant to write down the revelations of which their prophet had been the medium—did not he himself make a proud boast of illiteracy? They fixed them with pen and ink only when they discovered that within a single generation wars were thinning out the human repositories of the tradition, and moreover that the treachery of human memory was introducing intolerable variants into the divine words. To this day, according to strict orthodox views, the book dictated piecemeal by Muḥammad must be multiplied by hand, or, at most, by lithography: the secular mechanism of the printing-press is unworthy of a duty so exalted. To this day, translation of the book into any language other than its native Arabic is looked upon, to say the least, with disfavour. To this day many—even Turks, to whom Arabic is a foreign language—burden themselves with the tremendous task of committing the whole of its interminable monotony to memory.

India presents a yet closer analogy. We hesitate before citing the august canon of the *Rig-veda* in connexion with Caesar's druids. We recall only too vividly such cautionary tales as the tragedy of the frog who sought to emulate the ox. Before pursuing the analogy, we must safeguard ourselves by disclaiming any knowledge, or any theory, as to the literary value of the druidic traditions. They may have soared with Homer or with Pindar: they may have grovelled with the incredible people whose inspirations adorn the provincial press. In any case this question is irrelevant, so long as the druids themselves were satisfied with their inheritance. Comforting ourselves with this assurance, let us examine the Indian parallel a little further.

[1] I Kings vi. 7.

In the *Rig-veda* we have a *corpus* of lyric poetry, the work of a succession of sages, roughly equal in quantity of matter to the Homeric epics, and essentially religious in character. Its composition extended over several centuries, some time in the latter half of the second millennium B.C.; and for nearly a thousand years it was transmitted by oral tradition only, although for much of that time writing in one form or another was freely practised. These hymns 'are largely mythological...[they] enable us to see the process of personification by which natural phenomena developed into gods...one poet...wonders where the stars go by day....The unvarying regularity of sun and moon, and the unfailing recurrence of the dawn, however, suggested to these ancient singers the idea of the unchanging order that prevails in Nature.'[1] This is not unlike Caesar's statements, for what they may be worth, as to the subjects of druidic teaching.

Indeed, the analogy—a frog-and-ox analogy if you will—is so complete that it cannot be ignored. The druids must have had a canon of traditional hymns, at once the instruments and the subjects of instruction; and must have preserved them in memory because they were too sacred to be committed to the Greek letters used for secular purposes. We shall have something more to say about these Greek letters presently.

This Indian analogy now leads us a step further. Human language changes with changing generations, even in these latter days, when the printing-press exercises a steadying influence. On the other hand, the iron discipline of a sacred tradition resists all such linguistic innovations. I remember hearing a minister of religion, during the European War, in an extemporaneous prayer, offering a petition 'for those who ascend into the heights of the air, or descend to the depths of the sea'. Evidently he shrank from the utterance, in an act of worship, of such modern words as 'aeroplanes' and 'submarines'! Language, on the popular lips, is in a state of constant flux, and before many generations have passed, it parts company with the stereotyped language of hymn or of ritual. What meaning does an English bumpkin, in his heart, attach to such phrases as 'trumpets and shawms', 'to lie in the hell like sheep', or 'to grin like a dog' which he encounters periodically in the Church recitation of the Psalter? What would a Roman guttersnipe have made of the Litany of the Arval Brothers? With these and similar analogies before us, we may

[1] A. A. Macdonell, *A History of Sanskrit Literature* (London, 1900), p. 67.

doubt whether a Gaulish youth, packed off by provident parents to a British school that he might acquire knowledge which in years to come would exempt him from military service and taxation, could have understood without a commentary the very first lines that his new preceptors caused him to recite.

It was so in India. The Vedic literature of necessity accumulated around itself a vast body of explanatory material, as advancing time increased its obscurities. Ultimately, the language of the Vedas had become so completely divorced from any current vernacular, that it became in itself a subject for special study; and thus the mountainous erudition of the Indian grammarians gradually came into being.

Likewise, the students in the druidic schools would have found their hymns more or less unintelligible; just as an Englishman without preparatory study finds an Anglo-Saxon document or even Chaucer unintelligible. This helps us to understand why the curriculum extended over so long a time. The pupils were not like Sunday-school scholars, learning off by heart easy and popular hymns. Rather were they like French schoolboys, whose master makes them learn odes of Horace off by heart: we say 'French' because it makes the analogy closer, seeing that French and Latin are essentially one language at different stages of evolution. It is no illegitimate straining of the imagination to reconstruct the process of the teaching in such a way as this. The master first repeated a line, or a quatrain, or whatever was regarded as the unit of verse. The students repeated it after him till they were perfect in pronunciation and intonation. The master then analysed it, explaining its grammatical structure word by word, and setting forth its meaning and the truths, or supposed truths, which it was intended to convey. When he was satisfied that the pupils had assimilated his teaching, he proceeded to the next section of the composition. In this slow, laborious way we may suppose the sacred canon to have been passed from generation to generation.

Grammar, therefore, must in some form have been an important subject of study in the schools; and when the pupils left, they possessed, among their other acquisitions, a mastery of what was virtually a new language. Scholars of the Middle Ages had Latin for a second language. Latin franked them over the whole world of learning: in Latin they could discuss high problems in theology, science, and what not, undeterred by the risk of giving away injudicious secrets to unlettered eavesdroppers. So a druid, fresh

from his schooling, wheresoever in the Celtic world he might find
himself, could shew, among his other credentials, a mastery of an
ancient speech, known only to those of his own order. And to
everyone who has a secret to keep, be he the most exalted am-
bassador or the most disreputable gangster, a secret language in
one form or another—an official cryptographic code or an arbitrary
and irresponsible *argot*—is as necessary as the elementary needs
of the body.

II. The Testimony of Irish Literature

Though Caesar is speaking more particularly of the druids of
Continental Gaul, he makes it clear that the educational system
which he describes was current over a wider area. He points,
indeed, to Britain as the original source of the teaching, and as the
centre where it was still to be acquired in its fullest perfection.

Statements like this must not be forced to carry more weight
than they can bear. The most that we can derive from Caesar
is, that in his time it was believed that Britain was the region
in which the doctrine originated. How far was that belief justified
in fact? Popular beliefs are so frequently wrong, that they must
always be corroborated by some responsible authority before they
can be accepted.

On the other hand, we may admit that the teaching might well
be less contaminated on an island, protected by its marine bul-
wark from foreign influence, than in the open area of a continent.
This, however, does not imply a concession of the claim of Britain
to having originated the druidic doctrine: and when we look to
see if Britain has any corroboration of Caesar's statements to
offer, we meet with disappointment. The scanty and obscure
literature of early Wales tells us little or nothing to the point, and
the field is confused by the antics of 'neo-druidism'. Tacitus and
Dio Cassius tell us something about the sacred groves of Mona,
and the worship of an otherwise unknown goddess Andrasta, but
these matters, interesting though they may be in themselves, are
here of no special importance.

Caesar makes no mention of Ireland in this connexion. The
omission may, however, be apparent rather than real. In his
condensed description—which was never meant, and should not
be taken, for an exhaustive treatise—it may be that 'Britannia'
includes 'Hibernia'. If it appears that the testimony of Irish

literature follows along lines parallel to those of Caesar, we may reasonably infer that this was actually the case, and that the druids in Ireland taught in the same way as their brethren on the Continent, and belonged to the same philosophical freemasonry.

We must, however, bear in mind that neither the later Roman authors, nor the Christian editors through whom we have received the surviving fragments of Irish literature, had any temptation to accord fair treatment to the druids. In Gaul, druidism was the chief unifying force: without its influence, the divided, often mutually hostile peoples of Gaul would have yielded much more easily to Roman arms. In Northern Europe, druidism was the chief obstacle to the extension of Christianity. In both cases, therefore, what we know about the druids has been transmitted by their enemies.

By a fortunate chance, however, the two hostilities have taken different forms, which cancel each other out. The Romans held up their hands in a horror pestilentially Pecksniffian, which ignored the ghastly orgies of the Colosseum, as they spoke of the monstrosities of druidic human sacrifices. After all, these sacrifices were little more than sanctified judicial executions, for the victims were usually criminals; and though disgustingly cruel, they were humanity itself in comparison with the hell-begotten abomination of Roman crucifixion. But the Romans admit, notwithstanding, that the druids were reverend personages, held in honour by their own people. When we turn to the Irish writers, we find little or nothing about druidic sacrifices, human or otherwise: but they delight in putting the druids into awkward or undignified positions, or in representing them as mere jugglers or buffoons—reminding us of Aristophanes and his outrageous caricature of Socrates. Thus the two adverse testimonies are in flat contradiction each of the other; yet they converge, almost against their will, in a corroboration of the truth of what we are told of the more honourable sides of the druidic functions.

We are not writing a book on the druids, and we therefore make no exhaustive analysis of the references to the druidic order to be found in the extant fragments of Irish literature. For our present purpose it will be sufficient to set one or two passages side by side with each statement of Caesar, so as to shew the similarity between them.

The druids were held in especial honour. This is the case in the Irish documents, though to recognize the fact we have often to

'read between the lines'. The writers do not tell us this in so
many words: but they permit us to see lay-folk (kings and com-
moners alike) paying regard to the druids. They are the power
behind the thrones of the former: they dominate the minds and
the lives of the latter. Throughout the sagas of the Ultonian
cycle, for example, the druid Cathub 'pulls the strings'. He is the
adviser of the great king, Conchobor mac Nessa; to his decisions
the king himself submits. In like manner the druids of Loiguire
mac Nēill, the king of Ireland at the time of St Patrick, direct and
advise their master in his dealings with the new teacher.

As an interesting illustration of the form in which these and
similar traditions have come down to us, take the following, from
the life of St Senān.[1] Before the saint was born, his mother, a
peasant woman, entered an assembly in which was a druid. The
druid rose, to do her reverence. Forthwith the whole assembly
rose, 'for great was the honour which they had for the druid at that
time'. But the story goes on to say that when the druid had thus
paid respect to a peasant, they ridiculed him; whereupon he
explained that his respect was offered, not to the mother, but to
the great saint whose birth was to be expected. Sift out from this
story what is obviously unhistorical: the druid's foresight, and
his reverence for a future champion of a rival creed—and what
remains? An understanding between author and reader that an
assembly would not remain seated while a druid stood, 'for great
the honour which they had for the druid'. Our good hagiographer
has tried to 'dis-harm' this damaging admission by telling us of
the assembly's laughter at the druid's supposed *faux pas*. But
even here he confesses more than he imagines: he makes a tacit
admission that it would have seemed impossibly absurd for a druid
to condescend to perform an act of courtesy to a peasant woman.

The druids were concerned with matters of religion, and with the
conduct of public and private sacrifices. This testimony is confirmed,
for Gaul, by Diodorus Siculus (v, 31): but so little has been allowed
to survive in Irish literature bearing upon the pre-Christian religion, that we cannot point to any description of a ritual act of
worship in which the druids take part. In the arts of magic and
divination they are adepts: they interpret omens, reveal hidden
truths, utter spells, and perform sundry miracles. They are, in
fact, the medicine-men of the communities which they serve; as
such, we need not hesitate to assume that the duties involved in

[1] W. Stokes, *Lives of Saints from the Book of Lismore*, ed. Stokes, line 1875.

the performance of religious celebrations would be committed to their charge.

A great number of youths go to them for teaching. We may quote here the famous story of the interview between St Patrick and the daughters of king Loiguire: it is told in the *Vita Tripartita Patricii,* and is of considerable antiquity. We need not trouble ourselves here with the details of the colloquy, but we note that these maidens were at the time under instruction, at the hands of the druids of the royal seat at Crūachu. If girls were sent for instruction to druids—which must have been unusual—we may infer that boys would likewise enjoy that privilege. In the life of St Ciarān, from the same hagiological collection as that which we have already quoted,[1] there is a variant of the Senān story which contains the same ideas—a druid, appearing to pay honour where it was not due, and getting himself laughed at. In this case the druid heard the noise of a carriage, and told the boys who attended upon him to see who was travelling in it, 'for that is the sound of a carriage bearing a king'. The 'king' was the unborn saint: the boys saw no one but the peasant mother, and ridiculed their master. Once more we may expunge as obviously un-historical the druid's prophecy, his expression of obeisance, and the mockery of which he is made the victim. He was attended by a number of lads—presumably his pupils. He had to ask them who was in the carriage, therefore presumably he was blind, and must have imparted his teaching by oral instruction.

The druids decided judicial cases. Here at first sight we en-counter a discrepancy. The Irish texts seem rather conspicuously to avoid putting a *druī* or 'druid' in the place of a judge or legal advocate. These functionaries are usually called *brethem* 'judge' or *file* [dissyllable], a word which for want of a better equivalent we must translate 'poet', though in doing so we must empty the English word of most, if not all, of its natural associations. 'Weaver of spells' is, perhaps, a more accurate equivalent: the *file* was much more magical than literary in his duties. The chief poet (*ārdfhile*) of a king was no mere poet laureate. He was a personage who was believed to possess supernatural powers, which it was his business to exercise on behalf of the king whom he nominally served. We say *nominally* served, for we often are uncertain which is to be regarded as master and which as man.

But this was the function, or one of the functions, of the druids.

---

[1] *Lives of Saints from the Book of Lismore,* line 4013.

The druids were not likely to tolerate rival magicians at the royal court, so we must infer that the druid and the *file* were different aspects of one and the same official.

Let us take a peep at a law case which was transacted at the court of the great Ultonian king, Conchobor mac Nessa, who is said to have reigned just before the beginning of the Christian era. It is described in a glossarial note inserted in the law tract called *Senchus Mār*.[1] We read that down to this time the privileges of judgement had been the monopoly of the *file*-class. It fell out that two sages went to law in the matter of the right to possession of the robe of office of another, by name Adna, who had shortly before solved the riddle of existence. The two claimants were Fer Chertne and Nēide, the latter being son of the late Adna. And as they respectively pleaded their cause they spoke 'in a dark tongue', so that the chieftains standing by were unable to understand them.

'These people', they complained, 'keep their judgements and their knowledge to themselves. We know not the meaning of what they say.'

'That is only too true', said the king, 'and an end must be put to such a state of matters. Henceforth every man must have a fair share of justice; the *file*-people must not have any more than what is due to them.' That king Conchobor so much as conceived the possibility of breaking the *file* monopoly marks him out as a great man.[2]

In these disputing *file*-people we must see the druids, secret language and all. In this respect also the evidence of Caesar is valid for Ireland as for Gaul. The Christian writers were unwilling to represent the chief exponents of a hostile paganism as sitting in the seat of justice, especially as St Patrick himself did not hesitate to retain the services of a *file*, Dubthach maccu Lugair by name, when he was faced with legal trouble.[3] We,

[1] *Ancient Laws of Ireland* (Rolls Series), vol. i, p. 18 f.

[2] Some tenth-century charlatan who knew this story has endeavoured to reconstruct the dispute, in a composition called *Immacallam in 'dā Thūarad* ('The Colloquy of the Two Sages'). The text will be found, accompanied with the tentative translation which alone is possible, but which is quite sufficient to set forth the nature of this production, in *Revue Celtique*, vol. xxvi, pp. 4 ff. The disputants are shewn to us, seeking to confound each other with obscure allusive kennings and other literary vices; but (except for some otherwise unknown words) there is not much in the composition bearing on the question of a secret language. Most of it is mere childish affectation; and the influence of Christianity, which it quite evidently displays, sufficiently proves its spuriousness.

[3] *Ancient Laws of Ireland*, vol. i, p. 6.

however, need not share their qualms. We have found our druid-judges, and we have heard them speaking in a language which even kings and chieftains could not understand.

A man who refused to accept their decisions was punished by excommunication. As we are told so little about the normal religious rituals of paganism in extant Irish literature, we cannot expect to find evidence of any such rite of exclusion therefrom. But the consequences of offending a druid are always represented as being of the direst. Examples of this might be multiplied almost indefinitely; as one single illustration, we may recall how the Ultonian king Mongān hardly dared to maintain the accuracy of his own version of an historical incident, against that set forth by his own court *file*, although he had first-hand knowledge that his version was correct.[1] Perhaps we may look in this direction to explain the remarkable phenomenon of 'blotches on the face' and similar disfigurements, appearing after an offender has been cursed, bespelled, or satirized by a druid.[2] As we recall the many strange instances on record of the influence of mind upon matter, we hesitate to assert the impossibility of the curse of a man, to whom superhuman powers are attributed, producing physical effects of the kind upon a superstitious layman. But it is more probable that the expression is to be understood metaphorically. One blighted with such a curse became in the eyes of his fellows a moral leper, a *katharma*, to be shunned as though he were infected with physical disease.

One of the druids held chief authority—as Dubthach maccu Lugair, mentioned above, is described as 'chief *file* of Ireland'. *When he died there was often a contention for the vacant seat*—we have just been reading what looks like the report of such a contention. No doubt Fer Chertne and Nēide would have been quite ready to go to war to settle their dispute, just as no less a person than Colum Cille, the apostle of Scotland, is said to have gone to war because the king of Ireland decided an arbitration against him.

At a certain season of the year they assembled at a sacred place, supposed to be the central point of Gaul. The great assemblies of Ireland, held at various seasons of the agricultural year at places of established sanctity, were among the most important elements in the religious and secular life of ancient Ireland. They were held

---

[1] See the story in Meyer and Nutt, *The Voyage of Bran*, vol. i, pp. 45–52.
[2] Here again examples might be multiplied: the story told in O'Curry, *Manners and Customs of the Ancient Irish*, vol. ii, p. 217, is as good as any.

for ritual purposes, doubtless to ensure fertility in the fields and cattle-byres; and at the same time were used as convenient occasions for the promulgation of laws, the settlement of judicial cases, and the conduct of horse-races and literary and musical contests. One of these assembly places was the Hill of Uisnech, in the modern county of Westmeath, which was believed to be the exact central point of Ireland.

We repeat, that we are not writing a book on the druids. We have contented ourselves with setting down, more or less at random, a number of illustrations which, when read in connexion with Caesar's chapters, lead us to the conclusion that the druids in Ireland differed in no essential respect from those of Gaul. They were alike members of one and the same organization, whose influence was not confined to any one region. This being so, we may infer that they possessed the same literary heritage. From Caesar's evidence, we have drawn the conclusion that the druids in Gaul must have had at their service, in the language in which this literary heritage was composed, a means of communication known to no one, however exalted, outside their own circle of initiation: though we have no means of ascertaining what this language was, and indeed find no means of verifying our conclusion in Classical literature. This verification we found, when, unseen spectators from a century then far in the distant future, we took our place in an Ultonian court in or about the first century B.C., and watched the indignant perplexity of the king and his courtiers. Their druids had discovered, and were making a practical exposition of, the great maxim which has made and unmade more empires, and upset more applecarts, than any other: Language was given to Man, to the end that he might conceal his thoughts!

III. What was the Druids' Language, and of what Nature was the Traditional Literature?

In or about the year 560 a dyspeptic British monk, by name Gildas, writing in the safe retreat of a French monastery, produced a pamphlet called *De excidio Britanniae liber querulus*, which has had the unmerited good fortune to be the earliest extant native authority on British history. In this book he made a vitriolic attack upon the contemporary rulers of his country, whose crimes, he told them, had brought the Saxons upon them as instruments of divine vengeance. Among the princes at whom he rudely protrudes his tongue was Voteporius, or Voteporix, king of the Demetae, the people who lived in what is now Pembrokeshire: and the only thing of real importance which we learn from Gildas about him is, that he was alive, and advancing in years, when the book was written about the middle of the sixth century A.D.

Towards the end of the nineteenth century the tombstone of this ruler was discovered, at a place called Llanfallteg, on the border-line of the modern counties of Pembroke and Carmarthen. The stone bears two inscriptions: one in Latin, VOTEPORIGIS DEMETORVM PROTICTORIS, giving the king's name in its Brythonic form; and the other in Ogham letters, translating it into Goidelic for the benefit of the Irish colonists who continued to speak their ancestral language, VOTECORIGAS.

The names in ancient Celtic inscriptions are almost invariably in the genitive case, some such words as 'grave', 'stone', or the like being understood to complete the sense. In this name, the genitive of the Ogham form is expressed by the external suffix -AS. Before the extant beginning of written literary Irish, as we have it in glosses of a century or two later, this termination had shed, first its -S, and then its -A, in colloquial speech. But if the Llanfallteg inscription truly represents the colloquial speech of its own epoch, these changes could hardly have had time to take place and to become completely established, when the glosses began to be written—for the latter represent a literary tradition that was already old and stereotyped, where the grammatical conventions of the Ogham inscriptions are absolutely lost. Moreover, if the inscription were as old as the -AS genitive would suggest, the writer would hardly have made the mistake of representing the Brythonic P by 'c'. He should have written the very different letter Q, which is never confused with c except in late and degenerate examples of Ogham writing. We find only one conclusion open to us. 'VOTECORIGAS' is a piece of what the lamented H. W. Fowler called literary 'Wardour-street'. The writer of the inscription had endeavoured, with incomplete success, to write the name in a form older than the time to which the known date of Voteporius obliges us to assign his monument.

We chose this inscription as a text, because it can be dated with sufficient exactness from external evidence. There are many others which do not possess this special advantage, but which shew something of the same characteristics. These are scattered throughout Ireland, being found in greatest abundance in the southern counties; they also appear in the parts of Wales where Irish colonists settled. They are certainly in some form of the Gaelic language: but linguistically they are quite irreconcileable with the oldest extant monuments of Irish literary composition, which date back at least as far as the sixth century. In orthography, in the accidence of substantives (we have no material for saying anything about the verbs), they reveal a stage of the language, centuries removed, philologically speaking, from that of the earliest MS. literature, although historically they are not separated from the MSS. by any great stretch of time; the latest inscriptions, in fact, overlap with the earliest MSS.

The inscriptions make use of letters—Q, V, Ng—unknown to the MSS. They have a wealth of inflexional desinences, evanescent or altogether lost in the Irish of the oldest MS. sources. It is hardly an exaggeration to say that the linguistic gulf which separates the MSS. from the inscriptions is as great as that which separates a page of *La Chanson de Roland* from a page of Classical Latin.

These differences are not much more than a matter of orthographical tradition. The English word *bought* is no longer pronounced with a rough guttural (**boχt**), as it still is in some parts of Scotland: but the *gh* remains in its spelling as a record of the time when it was actually so pronounced. The Goidels, for whose benefit the king's name was written as *Votecorigas* on his monument, are not likely to have *spoken* the syllable '-as', when they had occasion to mention his name in the genitive case. Their ancestors at some time then remote in the past would have done so: but the case-endings had been first slurred and then dropped, as speakers found that they could understand each other perfectly without them. When we find in one district, or even in one cemetery, stones, apparently not differing greatly in date, bearing an ancestral name rendered here *Dovinias*, and there *Dovinia*, it is reasonable to infer that the *s* had ceased to be of practical importance. It could be retained or omitted according to the taste and fancy, or the energy, of the engraver, or to the space available on the stone. It was a mere fossil of speech, like *gh* in *bought*—a word often spelt *bot* in bill-heads, and in that form ugly, but intelligible. If the *s* had retained its ancient importance as a sign of the genitive case, it would have been carefully inserted wherever a name to which it belonged was to be expressed in genitive relationship.

We are thus introduced to a language which, in comparison with that of the oldest manuscript Irish, was highly flexional, and had a well-established and more or less stereotyped orthographical tradition totally different from the manuscript tradition. At the time when the inscriptions were cut, this inflexional language, as a spoken tongue, was dead; the peculiar forms used in the inscriptions are archaistic survivals. The archaisms are not always philologically accurate. Sometimes names are declined with wrong case-endings: we have already seen a phonetic confusion between C and Q, which would never have happened in the time of the living language. The tradition is no longer healthy, and is rapidly heading for dissolution.

On the other hand, such complicated forms of declension could not have been maintained at all, even with the imperfections and inaccuracies which it is possible to detect, unless some literary tradition had been in existence, to transport them from the ancient and forgotten speakers who used them in their daily conversation, to the inscription-writers who used them merely because 'it was the thing to do'. 'Bought' would be written in some such way as *bawt* if English were only now beginning to be written for the first time: the inscription-cutters would never have known or cared anything about these case-endings, much less written them, if their inscriptions had represented the first effort ever made at writing down the Gaelic language. It is absolutely necessary to postulate an extensive *literary* tradition, accompanied with elucidatory grammatical study, if we are to explain the phenomena of the inscriptions.

But this is just what we have been seeking: and now we begin to suspect that in the language of these inscriptions we catch the last echoes of the language of the druidic literature and of druidic instruction. *This* is the secret language which perplexed the court of Conchobor: there is no need to look for any other. The language of the traditional Druidic literature was Old Goidelic —which, as has already been hinted, bears much the same relation to the earliest Irish of the MSS. as Latin does to mediaeval Italian or French.

Very slight differences in a spoken language are enough to cause a measure of perplexity such as Conchobor suffered. It is not easy (*experto crede*) for one who has grown up amid the English of the Irish Pale to understand instantaneously the English of the Cambridgeshire peasant. The difference between the literary affectations of the learned poet-judges, and the colloquial conventions of the illiterate chieftains, need not have been much greater than the difference between the French of the simple-minded Monsieur de Pourceaugnac in Molière's lively comedy, and that of the physicians who persecuted him, to produce the mysteries which irritated the Ultonian court. I once knew a family of children who had contrived a private language of arbitrarily modified English words, which they spoke fluently, to the complete bewilderment of their elders.

This, then, is the conclusion at which we arrive. The ancient inscriptions of Ireland and of Wales represent the end of a literary tradition, absolutely different from the tradition which, for us, is inaugurated by the earliest extant Celtic glosses and other literary fragments. These two traditions overlap, but do not intermingle. The one descended from a remote past of the language; the colloquial speech, contemporary with its scanty extant records, had parted company with it. The other is a development of that colloquial. It is rooted in no literary antiquity: its beginnings are merely explanatory notes, designed to help students, whose vernacular was colloquial Irish, to understand words and sentences in Latin texts. The Church has introduced a new literature: for the moment, Latin is the only admissible literary language. Druidism is waning, but it is still a force to be reckoned with: its literature, with its pagan associations, is to be discouraged; and the archaic language which is its vehicle, must perish. But, as it disappears, a few 'die-hards' write it upon the tombstones of their friends.[1]

The inscriptions of which we have been speaking are written in a peculiar alphabet, to which is given the name 'Ogham' (in Old-Irish spelling *ogum, ogom*), a word of uncertain etymology and meaning. This alphabet consists of groups of strokes, from one to five in number, arranged in various positions about a central stem-line: and five other characters, a little more complicated, which, in the mediaeval MSS. where we find the alphabet set forth, are interpreted as diphthongs, but which more often

[1] For further details on the subject of the foregoing paragraphs, consult E. MacNeill, 'Notes on the Distribution, History, Grammar, and Import of the Irish Ogham Inscriptions', *Proceedings*, Royal Irish Academy, vol. xxvii, section C, p. 329. *Idem*, 'Archaisms in the Ogham Inscriptions', *ibid*. vol. xxxix, section C, p. 33.

than otherwise have a consonantal value in the inscriptions. The alphabet, as usually written, is as follows:

The third letter is always called 'F' in the Irish MSS. which give us particulars of the alphabet; but for philological reasons, here irrelevant, the old value of 'V' must be restored. In the inscriptions the sign 'Ea' must have a guttural value, which it is convenient to express by 'K'; 'Ia', in the few cases where we find it in practical use, is *always* to be interpreted as 'P'. 'Ae' is used only once, in a scribble on the margin of a MS.; and there the context shews that it must be interpreted 'SC', 'CS', or 'X'.

The reader has only to jot down a few sentences in this alphabet to convince himself that it can never have been used for any extended literary purpose. The short inscriptions which we possess are the longest documents which could in reason be expressed by these laborious and clumsy letters—their very monotony would deaden all literary inspiration!—and even such inscriptions often extend along the whole length of a tall pillar-stone. But the Ogham letters are quite suitable for spelling out words and sentences by means of finger-signs. The number of the groups of scores, from one to five, irresistibly suggests the hand and its fingers. All these letters, including the group of complex characters at the end of the row, can be made with one hand or with both, held in various attitudes, and with as many fingers outstretched as may be required.

Evidently this is a convenient device for secret communication. I have some knowledge of the common 'deaf-and-dumb' manual alphabet, but I am without skill or practice in its use; and it would be impossible for me *ex improviso* to follow a rapid conversation between two expert deaf-mutes. Two druids communicating by finger-signs such as these, in the presence of an illiterate or

semi-illiterate audience, could 'conceal their thoughts' in perfect
security; they could even secretly contradict what they were
saying openly, by word of mouth! There seems to be no reasonable
explanation for the invention, and continued existence, of an
alphabet so childishly unpractical, other than that it was originally
intended as a manual sign-alphabet, and that its use as a script
was secondary and adventitious.

'Childishly unpractical', certainly. But when we examine it
critically we see that its construction is very far from childish.
There is learning behind it. Its inventor knows the difference
between vowels and consonants—indeed, it is the only European
alphabet which resembles that wonderful monument of phonetic
analysis, the Devanāgarī script, in keeping those groups of sound-
symbols apart. Moreover, the vowels are arranged in a phonetic
order of tone-colour, as in this diagram:

Again, the consonants shew some rudiments of classification.
They are divided into groups, of which one is headed by the labial
B, another by its corresponding nasal M. The rest of the B group,
L, V, S, N, is composed of continuative or vowel-consonant
sounds; the next group, headed by the spirant H, contains stop
consonants—the dentals D, T side by side, the guttural C and
the closely related labio-velar Q side by side. The M group contains the sonant guttural G and its nasal Ng side by side, and
also Z, R: these two likewise have some superficial relationship,
for in certain circumstances, at least in modern Irish, the letter R
has a 'Z' colour in its pronunciation. There can be no doubt that
the Ogham alphabet is the contrivance of a grammarian, or, at
least, of a phonetician.

But not even a grammarian could invent a manual sign-
alphabet unless he were already able to spell. Like all other
cryptographic systems, Ogham must be founded upon some pre-
existing alphabet. Endeavouring to identify this, it is natural
to think first of the alphabet with which Imperial Rome endowed
the world; and it is usually assumed that this was the foundation
of the Ogham cypher. The presence of Q in the Ogham favours
the assumption: but there are some very troublesome difficulties
in the way. Our grammarian must have made a selection from
the Roman letters: what principle did he follow in doing so?

Why did he burden himself with Z and H, which are never used in any inscription (except in some late adaptations of the Ogham script to the alien Pictish language, found in the region of the Picts in Scotland)? Why did he trouble to differentiate between U and V? or to introduce a sign for Ng? Why did he leave F and P out of his scheme, which, though rare, were sometimes wanted? These questions at least suggest the possibility that we may have to look elsewhere for the origin of the alphabet.

Let us recall Caesar's statement that they—the druids—in secular matters make use of *Greek* letters: and let us remember also that 'Greek letters' is a vague expression, covering a long period in time, and a considerable range of epigraphic evolution. We have to bear this in mind when reading Caesar, in other passages beside that set at the head of this chapter. Army lists were found in the Helvetian camp written in Greek letters (*B.G.* I, 29): the druids habitually used Greek letters: yet Caesar, writing a despatch from the land of the Nervii, used Greek letters to guard against its being read if it were intercepted (v, 48). It is admittedly possible that Caesar wrote to his correspondent in some pre-arranged cypher involving the use of Greek letters, though naturally he would not share the secret of its construction with his readers: but even though the Nervii may have been an especially barbarous community, who forbade the entry of foreigners, the proceeding seems hazardous. Experience teaches us all that, disregarding the demands of courtesy, it is unwise to discuss secrets in an out-of-the-way tongue, trusting to luck that none of the bystanders will understand it: there was every chance that some one would be hanging about the Nervian headquarters who could undertake to spell the letter out.

The extant epigraphic evidence indicates that Gaulish inscriptions from the South of France are written in Greek letters, because the Gauls in that region learnt to write from the Greek colony at Massilia;[1] those from Northern Gaul are in Roman characters, except on coins, some of which carry the Greek alphabet further north than the lapidary inscriptions. A few Gaulish inscriptions from Northern Italy are in the script which the Gauls there learnt from the Etruscans. There is no *a priori* impossibility in maintaining that it was the Greek alphabet rather than the Roman which afforded the foundation upon which the Ogham script was constructed.

[1] On the use of Greek by the Massiliotes, see Strabo IV, i, 5.

The alphabet of the ordinary grammars will not serve, however, if only because it does not possess a Q. But the Greek alphabet once included that letter: and if we examine the varieties of the Greek alphabet which contain a Q, we shall discover with surprise—it certainly surprised me—that there is one which in its selection of letters is to all intents and purposes identical with the Ogham alphabet.

This version of the Greek alphabet is scratched upon two vases, found respectively at Formello near Veii, and at Cervetri, the ancient Caere. They are assigned to about the middle of the sixth century B.C. Facsimiles are accessible in various textbooks, such as Roberts's *Introduction to Greek Epigraphy*, vol. I, p. 17. The letters upon the vases are reversed (according to modern European practice), and the script proceeds from right to left: it will be sufficient to represent them here conventionally:

ΑΒΓ ΔΕϜΖΗΘΙΚΛͶΝ⊞ΟΠΜϘΡΣ ΤΥ†ΦΧ

a   b   g   d   e   v   z   h   t^c i   k   l   m   n   x   o   p   š   q   r   s   t u x′ p^c k^c

The letter H denotes the *spiritus asper*, not the vowel η. All students of the history of the Greek alphabet know that the parent Phoenician alphabet bequeathed to its Greek progeny an *embarras* of sibilant riches, and that the five letters Z, ⊟, M, Σ, and † were far more than were needed to express the sibilants of Greek. The last of these early disappeared altogether, though it lingers in the Formello-Cervetri alphabet. M (=*sh*) persisted for a little longer, but it ultimately ceased to exercise any phonetic function; in the form ⋊ it maintained a foothold, but as a numerical sign only.

Let us expunge the evanescent † from the Formello-Cervetri alphabet: we should find it gone if we could discover a similar graffito of the fifth century. Let us imagine a druidic scholar of that later time adapting the twenty-five signs that remain as instruments for the expression of his own language. We are not to suppose for a moment that the prohibition of writing, in connexion with the sacred oral literature, implied a total exclusion of the art in other connexions. Caesar, in fact, states the exact contrary: 'in all other matters they make use of Greek characters.'

Our scholar takes the alphabet as it stands, with one modification—a modification for which there are plenty of precedents. It

often happens that when one community borrows a script from
another, it gives new values to letters that would otherwise be
of no service. The Greeks did so, in adapting the Phoenician
alphabet to their own use: finding a new use, as vowels, for
some signs which originally represented consonants peculiar to
the Semitic languages. Our druid had no use for M (*sh*): but he
felt the want of a symbol for ŋ,[1] and adapted for the purpose
this otherwise useless character. The expedient was presumably
suggested by the external resemblance of the letter to NΓ, or the
Greek convention ΓΓ.

Let the reader now copy out the Greek alphabet as set forth
above, omitting ✝, writing *c* for *k*, and substituting ŋ for š as
the equivalent for M. Let him then turn back to the Ogham
alphabet on an earlier page, and take each letter in order, striking
out the corresponding Greek letter in his copy. After he has gone
through the first four Ogham letter-groups, he will find that in
each alphabet he is left with five letters. He will also not fail to
notice that these letters have a close similarity in outward form;
this has been shewn on p. 19, by writing the Greek letters above
the Ogham signs to which each corresponds.

The *Ea* sign is identical with **X**. The *Oi* sign, plus the section
of the stem-line which its loop encloses, is identical with **Θ**. The
equation of the *Ia* sign to **Π** is especially interesting. Let the
reader make an imitation of the Greek letter **Π** by stretching
the thumbs in a line, apposited at the tips, and protruding the
first two fingers of each hand at right angles to that line. He will
find that the slightest pressure on the thumb-tips will cause the
fingers to fall into the cross position of the Ogham letter. This will
not happen if the index fingers only are stretched out: but we
may suppose that the fingers were doubled to prevent the correspondent from reading the symbol as D or L. The *Ui* sign resembles **Φ** written cursively (φ). The *Ae* sign should be a cross
of 3+3 lines: it has been made into 4+4 simply on account of
the physical difficulty of keeping three consecutive fingers outstretched and doubling up the others.

Thus, all of the peculiar letters which form the fifth Ogham
group are merely equivalents, as nearly as can be conveniently
represented by the fingers, of the residual letters of the Caere-

[1] As it is convenient to represent a single sound or a single letter by a
single equivalent character, we shall in future represent the Ogham Ng
by the usual phonetic convention ŋ.

Formello alphabet. A mathematician might possibly be able to calculate the chance against the exact coincidence of these two alphabets being altogether fortuitous: probably it would be a figure as far on the way to infinity as any non-mathematician could desire.

This comparison leads us to the further inference that in the so-called Ogham diphthongs, the consonantal value, for which we have no MS. authority but which we can infer from the ancient inscriptions, was primary; the vocalic value, which monopolizes the mediaeval manuscript alphabets, was secondary. The Greek values of these letters would be of little use to Celtic writers. The sound of ☰, on the few occasions when it had to be used, could be represented by ΚΣ just as conveniently as by the clumsy sign in the Formello alphabet. The sound of *p* (**Π**) is eschewed in Goidelic: that it appears in Brythonic, as a development of the Indo-European *q*, is beside the point, for the Ogham script is not associated with the Brythonic branch of the Celtic tongues. The three characters Θ Φ Χ, when the druids took over the alphabet, were still true aspirates (t', i.e. *t+h* as in *pothook*, and so for the rest), not the fricatives which they became in later times (as *th* in *moth*, etc.). As such, they were of no use either to Celts or to Latins, and if used at all by the Celts they must have dropped the aspirate and become mere doublets of T, P, K. In the inscriptions Χ is indistinguishable in its use from C (= K);[1] the other two 'aspirates' are never used at all as consonantal signs, except possibly in some of the Scottish Pictish inscriptions.

When the 'druids' first borrowed this Greek alphabet, they did not necessarily disturb the original order of its letters. But a body of teachers, whose duty it is to secure the preservation of an oral literature, must pay close attention to phonetics. The Indian grammarians did so, and the Devanāgarī script is the monument of their industry in this department of study. The Jewish Massoretes did so, and the huge elaboration of vowel, accent, and tone-marks in the Hebrew Bible testifies to their zeal for exactitude in reproducing traditional pronunciation. The less elaborate, but still punctilious notation superimposed upon the fundamentally consonantal script of Arabic, especially in the rendering of sacred texts, is analogous both in intention and in achievement.

---

[1] On Gaulish coins the name PICTILOS is sometimes written PIXTILOS and also, apparently by a misinterpretation of the c, PISTILLUS. See Blanchet, *Traité des monnaies Gauloises*, vol. I, p. 135.

To return once more to our 'bought' analogy. We pronounce it *bawt* in current speech. But if we attached a religious importance to maintaining the pronunciation of words in the English Bible exactly as it was in the days of Wycliffe or of some other early translator, we should be obliged, in such sacred connexions, to say *boχt*; and we should be compelled to invent a special symbol for the guttural sound, which English has discarded, and to train our theological students in pronouncing it. To preserve a traditional literature against the inroads of linguistic evolution calls for a study of phonetics no less than of accidence and syntax: and this involves a phonetic classification of the symbols by which the sounds are expressed.

We need not suppose that the analysis of the sounds of this traditional druidic language, and the adaptation to them of the Greek sound-symbols, was all the work of one man, or even of one century. Whatever may have been the steps of approximation, the final form of the letter-order seems to have been as follows:

CONSONANTS	continuatives	Λ N F	
	sibilants	Σ Z P	
	gutturals and velar	Γ M (=ng) K Ϙ	
	dentals	Δ T	
	labials	B μ	
	spirant	H	
VOWELS		A E I O Y	
SUPERFLUOUS LETTERS		⊞ Θ Φ X Π	

Obviously this is not a perfectly scientific arrangement, but it is creditable: and we now proceed to shew that such an arrangement must be at the basis of the alphabetic order of the Ogham cypher. The inventor had to find symbols for fifteen consonants, five vowels, and the five superfluous letters: the five fingers, coupled with these groups of fives, would suggest a symmetrical arrangement—five rows with five letters in each. He had already the two bottom rows before him, in the table printed above: to head the other three rows he took the three letters which precede them, thus:

```
B  *  *  *  *
μ  *  *  *  *
H  *  *  *  *
A  E  I  O  Y
⊞  Θ  Φ  X  Π
```

and filled in the gaps with the remaining consonants in order, just as they come in the foregoing scheme:

B Λ N F Σ
μ Z P Γ M
H K Ϙ Δ T
A E I O Υ
⊞ Θ Φ X Π

This was the first approximation to the alphabet, and it lasted long enough to establish for it the native name B-L-N (in Irish, *beith-luis-nion*), which it maintained in spite of subsequent changes.

An improver altered the vowel-order from the traditional alphabetic to a stricter phonetic arrangement. With it he shifted all the consonant groups. It looks as though the alphabet had been conceived of vertically rather than horizontally—associating together letters with the same number of scores, rather than those with scores in the same position. The effect of this change (which did not affect the otiose superfluous letters) was as follows:

B F Σ Λ N
μ Γ M Z P
H Δ T K Ϙ
A O Υ E I
⊞ Θ Φ X Π

A further shift brought the consonant group with long scores to a position next to the vowel group with long scores—reversing the μ and the H groups in the above table. This accentuated the inconvenience of trying to distinguish between these two long-score groups when represented by finger-signs: an inconvenience at least sometimes evaded by giving to the superfluous consonants the sense of the vowel just above. And it will be noticed that the figures have a chance resemblance to one another in their Greek forms. ⊞ is something like A; Θ like O; Φ like Υ; X (especially when it is written in the form \v/, as it actually is at Cervetri) is like E, and Π like I. Thus it comes about that these letters are provided with vowel or diphthong values in the manuscript tradition, and their true, but unnecessary, consonant values are forgotten.

Finally, and after Caesar's time, the druids abandoned the Greek for the dominant Roman letters. All bilingual Ogham inscriptions are accompanied by Roman, never by Greek letters, and no trace suggesting the continuance of Greek letters appears to have survived. This induced a slight shift in the B group. F (*digamma*) was now represented by V, as was also the vowel V; it was convenient to have the now identical letters represented by signs which used the same number of digits. This had the further advantage of bringing the related sounds S and Z into the same relative position, each in its own group. About the same time, probably, the extra characters, which had become alternate vowel-signs, were rearranged into a symmetrical order. The cross characters, like the linear characters, are placed in the order of the number of fingers required to make them, two, four, and eight: and then the two loop characters are alternated with them. This is the proper order, as the tract on Ogham in *The Book of Bally-mote* makes clear: following an old mistake, which goes back at least as far as the time of General Vallancey, printed books often transpose 'Ia' and 'Ui'. In this laborious way the alphabet seems to have finally attained to the order of letters set out at the beginning of the present discussion.

All the foregoing argument may seem fantastic, over-elaborate, and far-fetched to the reader. But it explains, better than any other theory that I can hit upon, certain facts that call for explanation; and it explains them completely. These facts are:

(1) The letters of the Ogham alphabet are exactly the same selection as the letters of the Formello-Cervetri alphabet, allowing for the early disappearance of +, and giving a new value to the otherwise useless M. No other alphabet can have been used as a basis without forcing us to assume an arbitrary selection of letters, which does not actually correspond to the needs of the Ogham writers.

(2) Five letters of the Formello-Cervetri alphabet proved by experience to be superfluous; but being in the alphabet they were allowed to remain there. The Ogham symbols representing them are as close as may be to a manual reproduction of the original forms of those letters.

(3) The Ogham alphabet certainly betrays the work of an inventor with some skill in phonetics. Its Irish name indicates that for some time after its first invention its first three letters were B-L-N. The separation of the vowels and consonants, the arrangement of the vowels in a phonetic order, and the vertical or horizontal juxtapositions of letters having cognate sound values *cannot* be accidental.

(4) The Ogham alphabet is associated in its inscriptions with an archaic form of the Gaelic language artificially preserved, and appears to be based on a form of the Greek alphabet. According to Caesar's testimony, and to legitimate deductions that can be drawn from it, the druids had an archaic language, artificially preserved; and they made use of Greek characters.

These are facts, not theories; and the explanation given above, which may now be summarized, fits them exactly.

(1) An early form of the Greek alphabet, current in some parts of Italy, was borrowed by the druids in Southern Gaul for the purpose of writing (though not of writing their sacred texts), probably some time in the fifth century B.C.

(2) The letters of this alphabet were rearranged on a phonetic basis, to assist students in learning to pronounce the sacred texts with the necessary exactitude.

(3) The alphabet called Ogham was invented on the basis of this phonetic rearrangement, for the *sole* purpose of secret communication by means of manual signs. It was never intended to be written: its use as a script probably began in short private messages, nicked on slips of wood and sent from a druid to some colleague at a distance—the nicks representing the outstretched fingers. It is to be noticed that this involved the restoration of the original vowel-signs. The new vowels, based on the superfluous consonants, were convenient to frame with the fingers, but troublesome to nick upon wood. They are rare in the inscriptions.

We must not confuse the druidic adaptation of the old Formello-Cervetri Greek alphabet with the later adaptation, to which reference has been made already, of the ordinary Greek alphabet by dwellers in the region of Massilia. This was a perfectly independent process, and the two alphabets were quite distinct, though both of them could be described as Greek. The Formello-Cervetri alphabets are written, as we have seen, in a reversed form, and run from right to left. It is conceivable that this is why Caesar felt safe in writing his secret correspondence in Greek characters: these, being penned in the ordinary way, from left to right, would look like *Spiegelschrift* to a native scholar who happened to get hold of them; and Latin, written in Greek letters which seemed to be turned the wrong way, might have been quite a sufficient puzzle. We need not infer from the use of Greek letters that the druids were skilled in the Greek language. The druid Diviciacus seems to have known no language but his native Gaulish, and Caesar had to communicate with him through an interpreter. On the other hand, the scholarly Celt who, appropriately enough, instructed Lucian[1] in the nature and attributes of the god Ogmios, was not only acquainted with Greek but had some familiarity with Greek literature.

Our conclusion is that the druidic language was archaic Goidelic. It is in archaic Goidelic that the Ogham writers of Ireland endeavour to express themselves: and there is no reason to endow the druids with more sacred or secret languages than one.

'Ogham', says the treatise on the subject which we find in *The Book of Ballymote*, 'was put together by Ogma Sun-face, son of Bres, son of Elada.' This conducts us into august company. Whatever the author of the treatise may have supposed, there is no shadow of a doubt that Ogma was originally a god. He was one of the Tūatha Dē Danann, the numerous pagan gods of the Goidelic people, whose complicated *theogonia*, euhemerized into a bald string of genealogies, is made into an 'invasion' of Ireland in the history of the country concocted and taught in the native schools. It scarcely admits of doubt that Ogma is to be equated with Ogmios, the god of eloquence, whose gospel the learned Celt preached into the unresponsive ears of Lucian; and what Lucian tells us—and it does not read like one of that ingenious scoffer's fabrications—is enough to shew that he was a god of the first rank of importance.

But what did Ogmios or Ogma invent? Surely it did not require the intervention of a god to invent the puerile Ogham *alphabet*! But a *language*—that might well have been the gift of a god to his particular votaries. The druids or their students may have speculated on how this difficult speech, which they acquired with so much toil, and which was so exclusively their special possession, came into existence. It would have required more philology than we can credit to them, to have realized that it was merely an obsolete form of the common talk of the *profanum vulgus*. That a god had endowed them therewith would be the most easily evolved of aetiological myths; and it would have the advantage of increasing the reverence in which they held it, and the care with which they preserved it. We suggest that 'Ogham' (however we may choose to spell it) originally meant *the language*. 'A stone written in Ogham' meant an inscription in *the language*. But as

[1] Lucian, *Heracles*, 1 ff.

the language was expressed, on such stones, in a script-adaptation of the finger-signs, the expression first became ambiguous (just as the Devanāgarī character may be loosely called 'the Sanskrit alphabet') and finally veered toward the significance of 'a stone written in the finger-script'. So the word Ogham became a name, not for the Proto-Goidelic cultivated by the druids, but for the secret alphabet which first began to be written down, just when it, and the language, and, indeed, the druids themselves, were passing off the stage.

The literature of the Ogham language, as a whole, is lost for ever. But we possess a poetical composition which may very well be one of its hymns: and we have some hints as to its contents and its limitations.

The poetical composition is a wild spell, said, in the tale of the landing of the 'Children of Míl', who, for the synthetic historians of early Christian Ireland, represent the latest incomers, to have been chanted by their chief bard, Amorgen, as he set his foot on the soil of Ireland. That some such spell should have been uttered on such an occasion is only to be expected. To set foot in a strange country was indeed a terrifying experience. Its unknown and savage inhabitants, human and animal, would be formidable enough; but worst of all were its unknown gods. The foreigners with whom the king of Assyria colonized the ravaged city of Samaria were devoured by lions because, they believed, 'they knew not the manner of the god of the land',[1] and they were assuredly not the only strangers who attributed misfortunes which befell them to a like cause. Spells and enchantments to avert the terrors that awaited them were an absolute necessity, if an invasion was to have propitious consequences. We need not have any doubt that Amorgen actually sang such spells, in the old story which the historians worked up into a literary form. But we may very reasonably question whether the chant which they have put into his mouth was the spell which he actually sang. It is quite inappropriate to the situation: and a garbled version of it appears in Welsh literature, in a totally different context. The story in which it there occurs is a late hotch-potch of tattered shreds and patches, professing to narrate the mystical early history of the bard Taliesin. In the course of the story the child bard is made to utter a poem, narrating his transformations in previous existences: and this poem is obviously a translation into

[1] II Kings xvii. 26.

Welsh of as much of the song of Amorgen as the compiler could remember.

What, then, is this song of Amorgen? It is a hymn, setting forth a pantheistic conception of a Universe where Godhead is everywhere and omnipotent. This interpretation has been challenged: but it still seems to me to cover the sense of the poem better than any other. What we have is, of course, only a translation, possibly an expurgated translation, into the colloquial Irish of the Christian historians, out of the druidic 'Ogham' speech: doubtless it has lost something in the process, but it is still not without a measure of sublimity. Of this, we feel, the Christian writers were conscious; amid all the wreckage of druidic tradition, they were unwilling to let it go; and to avoid all risk of the charge of disseminating paganism, they forced it into the incongruous association where we now find it. God speaketh: and this is what He saith:

> I am wind in the sea,
> I am wave of the billows,
> I am sound of the sea:
> I am an ox of seven fights,
> I am a vulture on a cliff,
> I am a tear of the sun [=a dewdrop],
> I am fair among flowers,
> I am a boar,
> I am a salmon in a pool,
> I am a lake in a plain,
> I am a word of knowledge,
> I am the point of the spear that fighteth,
> I am the god who formeth fire for a head
>   [=giver of inspiration].
>
> Who maketh clear the ruggedness of a mountain?
> Who telleth beforehand the ages of the moon?
> Who telleth where the sun shall set?
> Who bringeth the cattle from the house of Tethra?
>   [Tethra=the ocean: the reference
>   is to the stars rising from the sea.]
> On whom do the cattle of Tethra smile?
> What man, what god formeth weapons,
> Singeth spells.... [Is it not I?]

The last line or two are very obscure and corrupt, and need not here detain us. As we read a poem like this, we cannot but feel that it is a very suitable preface to the hymnary of a philosophical school: and, like the opening chapter of the Kur'ān, or like the

Apostles' Creed in Christendom, such a composition might well
have been used, not merely in the studies of druidic pupils, but
in the liturgies of public religious functions—such functions as
that from which recalcitrants were excommunicated. Knowledge
of its contents would thus make its way outside the druidic
schools: was it of this hymn, or of what he had been told of the
contents of this hymn, that Caesar was thinking, when he
wrote that the druids taught of the stars and their motions, the
world, the size of lands, natural philosophy, and the nature of the
gods?

But the canon was not confined to philosophical hymns. There
was an historical canon as well. A list is preserved of the stories
which historians were expected to know, and to be able to recite
when called upon, at feasts, assemblies, and what not. Some of
these stories are still extant, in more or less late prose versions;
many are totally lost; of a number of others, the general lines
can be recovered from chance allusions. They were 350 in number;
250 'principal stories' and 100 'subordinate stories'; and they
were classed under the headings of destructions, cattle-raids,
courtships, battles, tragical deaths, voyages, etc.

The list of stories, which might not be diminished—for a complete knowledge of the whole was a necessary qualification for
the historian—and to which, apparently, no addition was permissible, was not, like the catalogue of a seaside circulating
library, an index to the amusing fiction available. Otherwise there
would be no point in its rigidity. Though, as we have it, the list,
and the use made of the list, have undergone modifications due
to the incidence of Christianity, it is the end of a tradition, going
back into far older times. It is a summary of the historical section
of the druidic canon.

The hostility of the Roman emperors brought druidism to an
end on the Continent. Whether or not their teaching was more
perfectly preserved in Britannia (and Hibernia?), we may be
certain that the cutting-off of the supply of Continental students
was a heavy blow to the schools: and the growth of Christianity
effected in no long time a complete breach in the tradition. For a
time there appears to have been a sort of working compromise
between the disciples of Christ and those of Ogmios. We have
even memorials in the Ogham character of a bishop, a presbyter,
and a deacon, as well as of other persons whose Latinized names—
Sagittarius, Marianus, Amatus—suggest that they were Christian

ecclesiastics. But, quite apart from the impossibility of a permanent pact between Christianity and paganism, the druidic system was doomed by the democratic appeal which the new religion made.

In Ireland, for example, Christianity gave an opportunity to the servile classes: aborigines whose masters, first Celtic-speakers and then Teutons, had reduced them to vassalage. These, the hewers of wood and drawers of water, had no share in druidic learning, such as it was. But they had a very considerable share in the shaping of the then colloquial dialect of the Irish language, and in making complete the already wide breach between the spoken tongue and the traditional 'Ogham' literary language. For when conquerors force upon a people a language which these do not speak by nature, the conquered will inevitably mould it to the phonetics and idiom of their own tradition. Servants, to whom the new language is foreign, will impart their contaminations to children under their charge; and thus the blunders of the unlearned will filter into the upper strata of society. This is what has happened to English as spoken in Ireland: it has assumed an Irish intonation, phonesis,[1] and syntax, even on the lips of persons of education. It is what is happening now, by a curious turn of the wheel, to the artificially revived 'Irish' of the present generation. The spelling has been 'simplified' to make it easy for people who originally learnt to spell on an English basis; and speeches and writings are riddled with adaptations of English words and idioms. Very probably certain of the peculiarities which the Irish language displays are due to its coexistence for some time with another, older speech, spoken by the *majority* of the population; ultimately, however, ousted, because Irish was the language of the classes that held the monopoly of domination.

To these unlettered aboriginal folk the monasteries opened their doors—or some of them at least: there were exceptions. These people had to be taught, and means of writing the colloquial language had to be improvised, rather than naturally developed. The traditional spelling of the older language was utterly unsuitable to the new, so far had the two travelled apart. No doubt the ecclesiastical authorities did not, at first, contemplate the literary

---

[1] Perhaps I should apologize for this word, which dropped unconsciously from my pen. I find it branded as 'not naturalized' in the *Oxford Dictionary*. But it is not without its usefulness, and I venture to let it remain.

use of any language but Latin; but gradually the familiar vernacular made its way. Good stories were either translated out
of Latin, or were modernized out of the old Goidelic tradition;
thus step by step, a new Christian Irish literature came into
being, and the older language, the heritage of the druids, fell into
oblivion. It is to the time of overlap, in which the druidic learning
was gradually coming to an end, that most or all of the extant
Ogham inscriptions are to be assigned. 'We're giving up Romani
very fast,' said a strolling knife-grinder, of whom we shall hear
later: 'its a-gettin' to be too blown.' In his own idiom he was
echoing a complaint that we might have heard from an ancient
druid. 'There is no use talking our secret language, making our
secret signs, if our pupils change their religion, and so emancipate
themselves from the vows of secrecy which safeguarded our
monopoly' would have been the substance of the druidic complaint.
'Our symbol-alphabet is useless now, as a secret: let us keep it
as a magic benediction for those who die in our faith and obe-
dience.'

But the language did not wholly die. There is a strange story
to the effect that Colum Cille, who was a man of literary enter-
prise, came on a visit to the dwelling of a scholar named Longarad.
Longarad hid his books, so that Colum Cille could not see them;
whereupon the indignant saint uttered an imprecation against
them, putting upon them the curse that never again should they
be of any use to anyone.[1] And the biographer adds that the curse
was fulfilled: 'for the books are still extant, but no man reads
them'. Why was Longarad so churlish? What was wrong with
the books? When a hagiographer dips his hand into the lucky-
bag of folklore, to find miracles with which to trick out the lives
of his heroes, that is one thing, and we take his statements in the
spirit in which they are offered. But when he assures us in so
many words, 'These books are even now in existence, but they
cannot be read', that is quite another matter. We are bound to
accept what he tells us, unless we can prove that some contemporary weighed it in the balance and found it wanting. The story
becomes crystal-clear if we suppose these books to have been
relics of the ancient learning and of the ancient language. Longarad
had a pardonable pride in possessing them—a pride, however,
tempered with uneasiness. Was it quite right to own these pagan
things? Would Colum Cille approve of them? Might he not

[1] *Martyrology of Oengus*, ed. Stokes (Henry Bradshaw Society), p. 198.

perhaps order them to be destroyed? No bookman would take the risk! So he kept his books, and they endured for a season after their owner had joined the druids in the world of shadows. And those who pored unintelligently over their mysteries consoled themselves for their want of comprehension by fashioning this myth of a saintly curse.

Even then, if they had got hold of the right man, they might have learned what was in the books. The tradition of the language still lived on; the last we hear of it is so late as the year 1328. The so-called *Annals of Clonmacnois* tells us that in that year there died a certain 'Morish O'Gibellan, master of art, one exceedingly well learned in the ould & new law, siuill and canon, a cunning and skilfull philosopher, an excellent poet in Irish, & an excellent eloquent & exact speaker of the speech which in Irish is called ogham, in sume, one that was well seen in many other good sciences: he was a Cannon and singer in Twayme, Olfin, Aghaconary, Killalye, Ednagh Downe [Tuam, Elphin, Achonry, Killala, Annaghdown] and Clonfert: he was officiall and common Judg of the whole Diocesses, & ended his dayes this yeare.'

In estimating the eulogy of this Admirable Crichton, we must make some allowances. The original text of the *Annals of Clonmacnois* is lost, and the book is known to us only by a MS. English translation, in a queer Pepys-like style, made in 1627. The MS. of the Irish text was in many places injured and barely decipherable, and we know not the translator's qualifications for the task which he undertook. His work does not read like what a translation of any other volume of Irish annals would be, and we suspect that it is a free paraphrase rather than a literal rendering. The Irish text was compiled some time after 1408, the date of the last entry, and therefore something over eighty years after O'Gibellan's death. We have no information as to the authority here followed by the compiler, or as to the qualification of that authority to adjudicate upon O'Gibellan's accuracy and fluency in 'the speech called Ogham'. The *Annals of Ulster* and of *The Four Masters* both record O'Gibellan's death, but say nothing about this special accomplishment. Certainly a man of such diverse interests might have thought it worth his while to acquire some knowledge of the ancient speech; and he might have had access to books, like Longarad's, to help him in studying it. But this story of a fluent speaker of 'Ogham' in the fourteenth century reminds us only too vividly of the meeting between Lamartine, on his Syrian travels, and a worthy who claimed to be the only person in the world able to converse in ancient Phoenician. When Lamartine very naturally asked where, in the circumstances, he could find a partner for his colloquies, he drew himself up impressively, and replied: '*Monsieur, j'en fais des monologues!*'

It is convenient to speak here in terms of Ireland, where the "Celtic" tradition has been most perfectly preserved; but it should not be forgotten that "Celticism" is there an altogether exotic growth. The "Irish" language is, in Ireland, the monument of the most savage and bloodthirsty invasion which that country ever suffered—the raid of the brachycephalic horde who swooped on her in the middle Bronze Age, coming doubtless out of the land now called England, and impelled by a lust for the gold-fields. They had few virtues: later, but still contemporary, authority (Strabo) describes them, with some reserve, as cannibals. Like other cannibals, in Central Africa and in the Southern Seas, they were excellent workers in metal. In the second La Tène period they were subdued by an iron-using immigration, also questing gold: the ethnological evidence that this new people, who established a dominant aristocracy, was of Teutonic blood, is absolutely unshakable. Their use of native women, however, had the result, normal in such cases, of preventing their Teutonic tongue from ousting the Celtic, which had already "dug itself in".

Claudius (A.D. 41–54) issued decrees expelling druids from the Roman Empire. Ireland, now reduced to some sort of order by its Teutonic masters, could have afforded them an asylum. This combination of Celticized Teutonic patrons, and cultured refugees who could not but have absorbed some veneer of Roman civilization, is just what is wanted to account for the literary and juristic efflorescence which subsequent centuries witnessed in Ireland. Quite possibly all Irish tales about druids, dating from before the decrees of Claudius, are backward projections of conditions actually produced in the country after, and as a consequence of, those decrees.

CHAPTER II

CRYPTOLOGY

Cryptology may be defined as the art whereby two persons, A and B, interchange a communication, while withholding its purport from a third person Z,[1] who has cognizance of their means of self-expression. This may take the form of speech (overheard by Z) which may be secret (*a*) because the language is unknown, or (*b*) because the words are used with unknown meanings; gestures (observed by Z, consciously or unconsciously); or writing (accessible to Z). There are thus apparently four varieties of the art, which, sacrificing in some measure euphony to convenience, we may call cryptoglossy, cryptocheironomy, cryptolaly, and cryptography.

Cryptoglossy. Here A and B speak in a language unknown to Z. The language used may be some actual but little-known tongue; or an artificial jargon, slang, or argot. This method of secrecy has three drawbacks: it cannot be concealed from Z that A and B are talking secrets, which he is not allowed to share; proper names are not easily disguised, though in the circumstances of the communication it may be most important to do so; and Z may actually be acquainted with the language, unsuspected by A and B—such improbable coincidences have a disconcerting way of happening.

Cryptocheironomy. Here A and B communicate by a pre-arranged code of manual (or other) gestures. Card-sharpers, members of secret societies, etc. make much use of this method of secret conversation; the gestures may be so insignificant as actually to escape the notice of Z. If A and B communicate by means of the deaf-and-dumb alphabet, assuming it to be unknown to Z, they are practising this branch of the art. The Morse Code, Army Flag-signals, and the Ogham alphabet, in its original use as a system of finger-signs, are further examples.

---

[1] We shall use these symbols throughout this chapter—A and B for the initiates, Z for the person excluded from their secrets. They need not necessarily denote single individuals, but may stand for groups of any number of persons.

Cryptolaly. Here once more A and B communicate by speech, but in this case they do not use a language assumed to be outside Z's competence. On the contrary, they utter words and sentences which Z understands perfectly, but they import into them a pre-arranged abnormal meaning of which he is unaware. The really impressive performances of trick 'thought-readers' offer excellent illustrations of Cryptolaly. At these displays, A borrows from Z a watch, keys, or anything else available. He puts questions about them to B, who is so placed as to be unable to see them; and B answers the questions correctly. The answers, of course, are latent in the questions—in their numerous possible nuances of choice and order of words, or of intonation: A and B are merely making mechanical use of a pre-arranged code, in which long practice has made them expert.

Cryptography. This, it is needless to say, is the use of the almost countless varieties of secret forms of writing: or else of inks specially compounded to remain invisible till treated with the appropriate reagents.

That Cryptology, in its several branches, was extensively practised in Ireland is shewn by a very valuable tract to which we made a passing reference in the preceding chapter, covering folios 167 δ 14 to the middle of 170 *verso*, of the late fourteenth-century MS. called *The Book of Ballymote*, in the library of the Royal Irish Academy. A facsimile of the tract will be found in the Academy's publication of the great codex in which it occurs, pp. 308–14; others will be found in the *Journal* of the Royal Historical and Archaeological Association of Ireland, Series IV, vol. iv (1874–5), p. 202 [with a transcript of the text and a translation]; in Brash's *Ogam Inscribed Monuments of the Gaedhil* (1876); and in Calder's edition of *Auraicept na n-Éces, the Scholars' Primer* (Edinburgh, 1917), p. 272 [again with a transcript and translation, which supersede the publication of 1874].

I have called this a very valuable tract, in the full knowledge that an altogether different opinion has been passed upon it by many scholars. *Wertlose Spielerei* is one of the less severe judgements that have been expressed about its contents, *in toto* or in detail. For this the author of the tract cannot altogether escape from blame. He must have had a disorderly mind, and he threw out facts as he happened to find them, without troubling to marshal them in any logical or intelligible way. But though we may judge his methods harshly, we cannot so summarily dismiss his matter.

His book must be taken as a serious treatise on secret methods of communication.

We can shew this best by a rearrangement of the material. Calder's edition makes it unnecessary to reprint the text as it stands; but if we adjust its contents so as to follow a logical classification, its real importance will become much clearer. Even without such a study, however, we might well pause before dismissing the tract in disdain. The nature of the volume in which it is found almost compels us to treat it with respect. This is a sober compilation of learned matter, historical, genealogical, and so forth, contained in an enormous book of vellum, each leaf of which, at a guess, might have cost half-a-crown's worth of money in our current rate of exchange. It was intended to be a permanent record of facts deemed to be of importance. If it was subject to the inevitable limitations of knowledge, or of critical judgement, which hampered the scholarship of its time, that was not its compiler's fault: and it is incredible that after writing some 300 pages of such material, he should suddenly begin to waste valuable folios with childish fatuities of the 'A was an apple-pie—B bit it—C cut it' order. Even before we begin to read, we must come prepared to find a statement, serious in intention, of what was accepted in mediaeval times as *facts* about Ogham writing, its origin, and its use.

To us, Ogham letters are known as the characters in which certain ancient epitaphs are cut upon stone—the two or three surviving inscriptions on other materials scarcely count. But if we could transport ourselves back to, say, the fifth or sixth century, we should find that these tombstones were a mere by-product. At the time when the alphabet was in actual use, its employment as an instrument of magic, as a code of manual signs, or as a cryptographic form of writing on wood or on wax, would be of far greater importance.

Probably the magical use of the script was the most important of all: but it is of the least significance in connexion with the subject of the present book, and we may dismiss with a word or two the little that the author of the tract before us has to say about this aspect of the matter.

It begins with some particulars about the invention of Ogham, doubtless enshrining traditional beliefs, but here unnecessary to discuss. It then tells us that the first thing ever written in Ogham was seven strokes cut on a birch rod, which warned the mythical hero Lug mac Ethlenn that his wife would be carried off seven times to fairyland unless she were 'protected by birch'. The story has become worn down to an unintelligible fragment, but it displays to us a practice of nicking messages upon message-sticks, which could be interpreted by the *illuminati*. Two forms of divination by means of Ogham are also described in the course of the tract, called respectively *Mac-ogam* and *Bas-ogam*.

Mac-ogam ('Son Ogham'). I cannot fully understand the description of this device, and I suspect that the compiler of *The Book of Ballymote* did not understand it either. But in outline it is a method of determining the sex of an expected child, by some sort of cryptographic jugglery with the name of the mother, or of a previous child if there has been such.

Bas-ogam ('Palm-of-hand Ogham') is laconically and ungrammatically described in Latin, thus: i.e. *manus aliam percutit lignorum*. This probably means that a number of pieces of wood, variously marked, were thrown together, and one of them was picked out at random: the answer to the question propounded being given by the mark on the selected piece.

Certain arrangements of Ogham characters, or of characters resembling them, in circles or squares (74, 75, 76, 83)[1] are also magical or mantic in purpose. They do not appear capable of being adapted to the service of cryptography.

The remainder of the tract can be rearranged under the three heads, Cryptocheironomy, Cryptolaly, and Cryptography. Cryptoglossy is outside its scope.

Cryptocheironomy is only slightly touched upon: but particulars are given of two of the means by which the Ogham gestures were performed. We are told of *Cos-ogam* and *Srōn-ogam*: *Cos-ogam* ('Leg Ogham'), in which the gesticulator uses the ridge of his shin-bone as the Ogham stem-line, and forms the letters with his fingers on the two sides; *Srōn-ogam* ('Nose Ogham'), in which he uses the ridge of his nose in the same way. It is evident that the first of these could be used conveniently by a person seated or squatting, the second by a person standing.

Before we go into what the tract has to teach us of Cryptolaly, let us look back at the Ogham alphabet printed above (p. 19) and remind ourselves of its essential character. The author of the tract describes it in verbiage needlessly, though perhaps inten-

---

[1] These numbers in brackets are the reference numbers in the margins of the facsimile plates in Calder's *Auraicept*.

tionally, obscure. There are twenty-five letters, divided into five groups, of which four are formed by means of short scores, from one to five in number, depending from a central stem-line: the fifth group is composed of slightly more complex characters. It is important to notice that by the time of the compilation of the tract a few modifications had taken place in the values assigned to the characters. V was now F; Z is always represented by a MS. abbreviation or compendium for St; and the fifth group has completely lost its consonantal values (though some hints in the body of the tract shew that this has not been wholly forgotten) and is transliterated by diphthongs. In the subsequent pages of this chapter we shall use the terminology of the following table:

The B group formed of B scores, representing the letters B L F S N
  ,, H group   ,,   H scores,   ,,   ,,   HDTCQ
  ,, M group   ,,   M scores,   ,,   ,,   MGƝStR
  ,, A group   ,,   A scores,   ,,   ,,   AOUEI
  ,, diphthong group, representing the letters Ea Oi Ia Ui Ae.

We must now observe further that these letters are named acrophonically, after trees, as who should say

    B for Birch
    L for Larch
    F for Fir

and so on. [*These names, and similar names that we shall have to give presently, are not translations of the Irish: they are corresponding English names, chosen because they happen to begin with the appropriate letter.*]

We may pass over a classification of the trees, with speculations on their relative 'nobility'; after which we come to two lists of *Bríathar-ogam* ('Word Ogham', Calder, pp. 276–89), each of them stated to be the invention of an ancient sage, who is named. These are two sets of twenty-five other names for the letters, not necessarily acrophonic, and of a fantastic fashion. It would be futile to spend time over the far-fetched attempts which the author of the tract makes to explain them: we content ourselves for the moment with noting the bare fact that they are two lists of names for the letters, differing from the ordinary tree-list in that they seem to be quite arbitrary, both in construction and in application.

Then comes a number of other name-lists, which, however, are less arbitrary, in that they form definite *groups* of things.[1] These lists are of two kinds. The first, like the tree-list, are acrophonic. Thus we have

Linn-ogam ('River-pool Ogham'), an alphabetical list of rivers, as Barrow, Liffey, Foyle, etc.

Dinn-ogam ('Fortress Ogham'), a similar alphabetical list of famous fortresses.

Ēn-ogam ('Bird Ogham'), as Bittern, Lark, Falcon, etc.

Dath-ogam ('Colour Ogham'), as Blue, Lake, Flaxen, etc.

Cell-ogam ('Church Ogham'), an alphabetical list of famous churches.

Ogam Tīrda ('Agricultural Ogham'), an alphabetical list of agricultural tools.

Rīg-ogam ('King Ogham'), an alphabetical list of kings.

Nāem-ogam ('Saint Ogham'), a list of saints.

Dān-ogam ('Craft Ogham'), a list of arts and occupations.

Biad-ogam ('Food Ogham'), a list of foods.

Lus-ogam ('Herb Ogham'), a list of plants.

There are also lists of jargon words (Calder, nos. 26, 78–81) which appear to be alternative names for the letters.

In the second category there is an individual name for each *group*, the letters being distinguished as one to five individuals of that group. This is a makeshift; it would be impossible to compile, in these groups, complete acrophonic lists. Thus, in *Daen-ogam* ('Person Ogham') the B group is represented by one, two, three, four, five *men*: the H, M and A similarly by groups of *women*, *warriors* and *lads* respectively. Slightly different is

Muc-ogam ('Pig Ogham'), in which the letter-groups are named after swine of various stages of growth and different sex, and the letters in each group are distinguished by *colour* (one-score white, two-score grey, and so on with black, saffron, and blue). This, however, is unique; the other alphabets of this type are formed numerically, like the *Daen-ogam* given above. They are:

Another *Daen-ogam*, of women: one to five *women, hags, maidens, small girls*.[2]

Ogam uscech ('Water Ogham'): one to five *rills, weirs, rivers, springs*.

---

[1] Calder, pp. 288 ff.
[2] The diphthong group is ignored in all of these alphabets.

Con-ogam ('Dog Ogham'): one to five *war-dogs, greyhounds, shepherds' dogs, lapdogs.*

There are others, scattered through the cryptographic lists, and constructed in the same way:

Os-ogam ('Stag Ogham'), *Arm ogam* ('Weapon Ogham'), *Muc-ogam* ('Pig Ogham'—the author has forgotten that he had given this already), *Ogam n-ethrach* ('Ship Ogham'), and *Ogam cuidechtach* ('Company Ogham'), in which the letters are classified as *priests, warriors,* etc.

But surely, the impatient reader will exclaim, all this is mere 'A was an apple-pie' childishness! He will not be the first, by a long way, who has thus criticized this ancient compilation; I did so myself, before I came to understand its purpose.

To explain that purpose, let us recall what we have already said about the drawbacks of Cryptoglossy; that the use of a strange tongue *ipso facto* arouses the suspicions of Z, the man (or men) to be kept in the dark: and that even if he does not understand the language spoken, he will catch at the proper names. Supposing that Z's name is Cormac, and A has to say to B 'You must kill Cormac', or perhaps 'Cormac proposes to kill you'. Then in Z's ears his own name will stand out in a Dead Sea of unintelligibility, and he will realize that he is being spoken of in a way unfit for publication. Beyond doubt such drawbacks were recognized, as the fruit of actual experience.

But now let us suppose that in some way—by an imperceptible gesture or otherwise—A makes B understand that he proposes to speak in 'fruit-ogham'. (There is no such alphabet in the Bally-mote list, but that is no reason why it should not have been in use, as well as many others.) Then he may say something like this:

I was told that a man in Italy has succeeded in grafting cherries upon olive-trees. This encourages me to go on with my experiments in crossing raspberries and medlars. But I am surprised that the Italian did not rather try apricots, which are so much nicer than cherries.

To the bystanders he will appear to be talking in a visionary way about orchard cultivation. But B will attend to nothing but the names of fruits, and when he has spelt out Cherries, Olives, Raspberries, Medlars, Apricots, Cherries, and has understood what word their initials make, the fate of Cormac, whatever it may be, will be sealed.

If A and B talked about nothing but fruit, Z would once more become suspicious. In a long and serious colloquy it would be essential to alter the alphabet from time to time; and that is why our author has piled up all these apparently pointless variations on the theme. The second group of alphabets has to be helped out with finger-signs; when A speaks of war-dogs and holds out four fingers, B will understand the letter S. Anyone who has been present at one of the 'thought-reading' performances, referred to above, will have no difficulty in believing that expert practitioners would be able to ring the changes on a number of alphabets in the course of a single conversation: and would completely baffle unauthorized hearers, even though these might have reason to suspect that the conversation contained matter which did not lie upon the surface.[1]

The genuine communication might have been of the gravest importance: the actual words which reached the ears of Z might have been frivolous or even silly, like the fruit-absurdities imagined above. Incidentally it suggests itself as a subject of curious speculation, whether these apparently foolish conversations had anything to do with the development of the idea that the druids were mere buffoons. However that may be, it may be claimed that this explanation of the apparently childish varieties of alphabets in the Ogham tract vindicates its author from the charge of being a mere nitwit, who wasted precious parchment on futilities.

It is suggested that the chief purpose of these alphabets was to conceal proper names: certain devices called *Caechan-ogam* ('Blind Ogham') and *Losc-ogam* ('Lame Ogham', Calder, pp. 294–5) seem to have been invented for this very purpose. The explanation of their use is, however, not lucid, and I admit my inability to follow it.

CRYPTOGRAPHY occupies the remainder of the tract: and this portion of the work consists of a large number of more or less mechanical variations of the Ogham alphabet.

The Ogham alphabet is itself an essentially cryptical alphabet, and was doubtless originally invented for cryptical purposes, for it *certainly* could never have had any extended literary use. But by the time when it began to be used for monumental inscriptions,

---

[1] The purpose of the letter-names *which are meaningless jargon* must be to conceal proper names by spelling them out when A and B are talking in a language, real or artificial, unknown to Z.

which were presumably intended to be read, the secret had leaked
out, and the alphabet in its simple form could no longer be used
for cryptical purposes: the monumental inscriptions on stone
assuredly are *not* cryptograms. Hence it became necessary,
when secrecy was required, to disguise the Ogham in various
ways.

Some of these disguises, *to us*, look like mere puerilities. *We*
know the rule of 'the most frequent letter' and can decipher, for
example, the silly secrets of the agony column with very little
difficulty. But it does not follow that an unauthorized intruder
in 'Ogham' times would enjoy our facility. It is quite likely that
these simple modifications would prove very baffling, in an age
where the arts of reading and writing were but little cultivated.
Only the most verdant of agony-column greenhorns would now
imagine that he could keep his sentiments to himself by moving
the letters in which he expressed them forward one step (writing
B, C, D, etc. for A, B, C, etc.) or three steps (writing D, E, F,
etc. for A, B, C, etc.). And yet such rudimentary devices were
enough for the private correspondence of Augustus and of
Iulius Caesar respectively.[1] Some of the eighteenth and early
nineteenth century Irish manuscripts contain cryptograms
in which arbitrary symbols are substituted for the ordinary
letters. At first sight these look as mysterious as Etruscan,
but a few minutes' contemplation is usually enough to unriddle
them.

On the other hand there are a few examples of more elaborate
disguises. There is an Ogham cypher written on the margin of
the Ballymote tract at present under consideration; and another
in the margin of *The Book of Fermoy*; and I confess that the second
of these has beaten me, and that I should certainly not champion,
contra mundum, my views about the first. We shall return to these
presently.

In any case, having now (as I hope) shewn that this tract is
to be taken seriously, it will follow that the author thought it
worth his while to place these alphabets on record, *because experience had shewn that they were effective*, for the purpose of
concealment for which they were designed.

Of the two kinds of cryptography, the use of cyphers and the
use of invisible inks, only the first is known to our author. The

[1] See Suetonius, *Diuus Augustus*, 88; *Diuus Iulius*, 56.

forms of cypher specified by him may be classified under the following heads:

   I. Anagrams.
   II. Confusion by means of arbitrary insertions.
   III. Tampering with the form of the stem-line or of the letters.
   IV. Substitutions.

   I. Of *Anagrams* the simplest example is (15) *Ogam uird* ('Order Ogham'), in which the letters of a name are written in the alphabetical order of the Ogham alphabet—as when the name *Bran* is written BNRA, or *Labraid*, BLDRAAI. This is a device described by the grammarian Maro, of whom we shall hear in the following chapter: he gives examples of whole sentences written in this way, as when he writes *spes Romanorum perit* thus: RRR.SS.PP.MM.NT.EE.OO. A.V.I. Of course such a cryptogram could not be resolved, in any reasonable time, on account of the enormous number of permutations that would have to be tried: but the anagram of a single word is usually not difficult to elucidate—it is indeed a common feature in the popular crossword puzzles.

   Once more, it is suggestive that the examples given are personal names; it was probably to conceal names in a communication that the device was invented. If the correspondents A and B had serious business with *Labraid*, then BLDRAAI would be fairly clear to both of them, but its obscurity would be sufficient to puzzle a third party.

   (18) *Gleselgi*, a word that seems to mean 'the track of the hunt', is another Maronian device. It consists in separating and interlacing the syllables of two names: thus *Fethnat* and *Segnat* may be written FETHSEGNATNAT.

   Nathair im cenn ('A serpent round a head') is not strictly an anagram device: rather does it belong to the 'arbitrary insertion' group. It may, however, be mentioned here as, like the two preceding devices, it is used for obscuring personal names and not for longer messages. The name is written backward and then, starting with the initial (which comes at the end of what is written) it is written forward. Thus the name *Cellach* is written HCALLE-CELLACH.

   Two forms may be mentioned here which will hardly fit under the other heads. The first of these is (31) *Ogam romesc Bres* ('The Ogham which bewildered Bres'). This consists in writing the name of the letter for the letter, as though one should write

Alpha-gamma-alpha-mu, etc. for 'Agamemnon'. The name of this cypher is explained by a story to the effect that a message thus concealed was given to the ancient hero called Bres as he was going into battle, and he lost the battle because he was distracted by trying to read it!

Cend a muine ('Head in a bush') and *Cend fo muine* ('Head under a bush') are variations of a reverse form, in which, if a syllable in a word is identical with the name of any letter, the letter is written for the syllable: thus *ruis* is the name of the letter R, so MAEL-R may be written for *Mael-Ruis*. In 'head in bush' the suppressed syllable is the first of the word, in 'head under bush' the last.

II. The following are the varieties which come under *Confusion by Arbitrary Insertions*:

(45) *Ogam lēni dā rēib* ('Shirt-of-two-strokes Ogham'), with a vertical A score between every pair of letters.

(58) *Ogam ebadach* ('Ebad Ogham'), with the mark X (the name of which is *ebad*) between every pair of letters.

(37) and (39) *Ogam maignech* ('Enclosure' or 'Sanctuary Ogham'), with a score between every pair of letters of the group to which the first of them belongs. Thus (let us say) the word LOC would appear in this form:

L : O : C :

⎧(65) *Ogam fordūnta* ('Shut-in Ogham').
⎪(68) [unnamed].
⎨(71) *Loc-ogam* ('Place Ogham').
⎩(72) *Fiaclach Find* ('Find's toothed Ogham').

In principle these are all alike, differing only in detail. They consist of writing the message straightforwardly, but confusing it by enclosing each of the letters in a frame. The difference between the varieties lies in the shapes of the enclosing frames.

(66) *Nathair fria frāech* ('Serpent through the heather'). The message written in ordinary Ogham, and a wavy line drawn, which runs alternately above and below the successive letters.

III *a. Tampering with the form of the stem-line.*

   (i) Suppressing it.

(55) *Ogam dīdruim* ('Ridgeless Ogham'). In this form the stem-line is not drawn. In a forgetful moment the scribe of the Bally-mote book actually drew the line before he realized that he should not have done so, but he took care that his letter-scores should not reach it. Even the long scores, which ought normally to pass through the line, he interrupted in the middle, to let his stem-line pass through without touching them.

   (ii) Changing its shape.

(52) *Cenn debtha* ('Head of quarrelling'), in which the stem-line is bent up into a sort of 'Wall-of-Troy' pattern. This would be a very confusing cypher for the inexpert, and possibly disputes about the meaning of the message might account for its enigmatical name!

   (iii) Dissecting it.

(1) *Aradach Finn* ('Finn's ladder'). A short *vertical* stem-line for each separate letter. Crypt-runes were constructed in this way, and these may possibly have been suggested by Ogham cyphers thus written—just as the end-to-end arrangement of ordinary Runic letters occasionally found (called by Stephens 'sam-runes') appears to be suggested by Ogham letters on their stem-line.

(24) is a variant of this, in which the stem-lines are made to radiate like the spokes of a wheel. This is another method for disguising proper names. The example chosen is again CELLACH, and there are seven spokes. A mark like the head of a north-point in an architectural plan distinguishes the spoke containing the first C, where the reader begins: he follows the remaining six spokes in a clockwise direction.

(2) is another variant of *Aradach Finn*, like the preceding 'wheel' unnamed in the tract. Here there are two parallel horizontal lines: the B letters depend from the upper line, the H letters from the lower: the remaining letters each on independent vertical stems intercepted between them.

   (iv) Multiplying it.

(4) *Ogam Trēdruimnech* ('Three-ridged Ogham'). Three horizontal lines, the B group on the lowest, the H group on the topmost, the other groups on the central line.

(6) *Lad-ogam* ('Millrace Ogham'). A variant of the last, in which the B group is transferred to the central line of the three,

and there are no letters at all on the lowest line. Its function would be to divide successive rows of letters from one another.

(5) *Tre-lurgach Find* ('Finn's three-shanked Ogham'). Three horizontal lines, with the letters distributed among them, thus:

B S D Q Ŋ A E Ia	on the top line
L N T G R O I Oi Ui	on the middle line
F H C M St U Ea Ae	on the lowest line

(7) An unnamed variety of the last, with a slight difference in the distribution of the letters.

(8) *Cethardruimnech Cruteni* ('Cruitene's[1] four-ridged Ogham'). Four stem-lines, B on the lowest, H on the topmost, M and A as long strokes crossing all four.

(9) An unnamed variety of the last: four stem-lines, B on the lowest, H crossing the two lowest, M crossing the three lowest (vertically), A crossing all four. The diphthong group is included in this alphabet; the first character is on the lowest, the second, third, and fourth in order up to the topmost: the fifth is also on the topmost line.

III*b. Tampering with the external form of the characters.*

(17) *Ogam adlenfid* ('Letter-rack Ogham'). A single score of the appropriate shape, with as many strokes at the end of it as there are scores in the letter indicated, thus:

B L F..MG Ŋ &c.

The strokes are at *both* ends of the long scores of M and A.

(40) *Brec mor* ('Great speckle'). A single score of the appropriate shape followed by as many dots, less one, as there are scores in the letter indicated: the dots in a horizontal row, thus:

B L F.. M G Ŋ &c.

---

[1] These names presumably belong to the real or mythical inventors of the alphabets to which they are attached.

(49) *Brecor beo* ('Living speckle'). A variant, in which the rows of dots are vertical.

(51) *Ogam Dedad* ('Deda's Ogham'). A single score of the appropriate shape, with as many short horizontal strokes running out of its right side as there are scores in the letter indicated, thus:

B L F..M G Ŋ &c.

(53) An unnamed variant of the last, in which the short strokes run through the parent score.

(56) *Ogam focosach* ('Footed Ogham'). This is an elegant variety rather than a cryptical device. There is a dot at the end of each score.

(50) *Cend imresan* ('Head of strife'). The B and the H scores slope like the ordinary M scores: the M scores are shaped [, the A scores], and the scores of each letter of these two groups nest into one another.

(61) *Taeb-ogam* ('Side Ogham'). All scores beneath the stem-line: B thus ╱, H thus ╲, A thus |, M thus ∧, the scores of each letter of this last group nesting into one another.

(62, 63, 64, 67, 69, 70, 73). These are all similar variants, the scores being of different shapes (zigzag, etc.) but in number and disposition following the ordinary arrangement of the alphabet.

(19) *Crad cride ecis* ('Vexation of a Poet's heart'). A rectangular (or, in the case of the M group, rhomboidal) figure laid down in the appropriate position with regard to the stem-line. From the end away from the stem-line there project as many tips of scores as are needed to define the letter, thus:

B L F..M G Ŋ

(13) *Ebadach Illainn* ('Illann's Ebad-Ogham'). A series of X figures laid on the stem-line, for B and H letters: the B scores on the lower left-hand limbs, the H scores on the upper right-hand limbs. The M scores represented by lines shaped like mathe-

matical integration-signs (∫), with a diagonal line running across them. The A letters are of the usual form, but with an X drawn across each. [The 'integration-sign' form of M letters appears elsewhere, as an elegant variant, in the alphabets in this tract. In actuality it is found in Pictish Oghams in Scotland, but there it represents vowel-letters.]

(12) In this unnamed alphabet, the scores of the B and H groups are brought to both sides of the stem line, thus:

0	1	1	2	2		1	1	2	2	3
1	1	2	2	3		0	1	1	2	2
B	L	F	S	N		H	D	T	C	Q

L–D and S–C being differentiated by slight variations in the relative positions of the component scores. The M group is formed of scores of this shape C, the A group of scores like this Ɔ.

(57) *Ogam ndedlaide* ('Separated Ogham') appears to be similar, though it has been misunderstood by the author or his copyists. It is said to be so called 'because the fifth letter is severed' from the groups; i.e. the first group consists of four letters only, BLFS, and so for the rest. This, however, is not so: the setting-out of the M group shews us the proper form of the alphabet, which the scribe has bungled. The last score of each letter is represented as a short score—in the B group above the stem-line, in the H group below the stem-line, in the M group sloping above, and not reaching to, the stem-line, in the A group vertical above, and not reaching to, the stem-line. Thus the following is the form in which the B group should be set out:

BL F S N

(The Ballymote scribe has omitted the B, and has shirked the problem of transliteration.)

(34) *Ogam ar abairtar cethrur* ('Ogham called "Four-man"'). This might be represented among the substitutionary cyphers which we are to analyse presently, but as the letter-order and number of scores is unchanged it is rather more appropriate here. It uses the letters DTLF to represent the four groups, and each

of these characters is written as many times as the letter represented has scores, thus:

  s, four scores in the B group, is written DDDD,
  d, two scores in the H group, is written TT,
  r, five scores in the M group, is written LLLLL,

and so for the rest.[1]

(48) *Coll ar guta* ('C for the vowels') is similar to the foregoing. Here the consonants are written as in the normal alphabet, but **C, CC, CCC, CCCC, CCCCC** (in Ogham scores) is substituted for the vowels.

[A cypher of this kind, in ordinary Irish letters, was a favourite plaything among the scribes of eighteenth-century MSS. I have a fragment of a MS. on the Ogham alphabet, with directions for writing *Ogham Coll* ('C Ogham') and *Ogham consoine* ('Consonant Ogham'). In the one, the vowels are represented by **C**'s, just as in the Ballymote alphabet: the diphthongs are also represented by **C**'s in various positions, thus:

          ◡   ⌐   ⌐⌐   ⌐⌐   ⌐
         ea *oi* *ia* *ua*[sic] *ae*

In the second, combinations of consonants are written for the vowels and diphthongs, thus:

          BH DL[*sic*] FT SC NQ̈ MM PP LL BB CC
written for *a*   *o*   *u*   *e*   *i*   *ea* *oi* *ia* *ua* *ae*

A later owner of the book has written the name Tomās ua Conchubar [*sic*] into the pages in the two cyphers, thus (the first is not quite correct):

          Tccmcs   ⌐⌐   Cccnccccbcr
          Tdlmbhs   bb   Cdlnchftbhbhr.]

IV. *Substitutions.*

  (i) Two or more letters written for one.

(21) *Ogam accomaltach* ('Conjoined Ogham'). BL written for *b*, LF for *l*, and so on. This reappears at no. (59) under the name *Ogam Feiniusa* ('The Ogham of Feinius'): a proof that our tract is a compilation from at least two earlier sources.

---

[1] Here, and in the description of substitutionary alphabets, the letter *that is actually written* is represented in CAPITALS, the letter *to be understood* in *italics*. Thus ⦀ is T; but we shall presently see an alphabet in which it is to be read *ng*.

(22) *Ogam emnach* ('Twinned Ogham'). Each letter doubled.

(43) *Sluag-ogam* ('Host Ogham'). Each letter tripled.

(37) *Ogam maignech* ('Enclosed Ogham'). The first letter of the group to which any letter belongs written after it: thus BB, LB, FB, SB, NB written for *b, l, f, s, n*: HH, DH, etc. for *h, d*, etc.

(ii) Reversals.

(33) *Cend ar nuaill* ('Head after pride (?)'). The letter groups reversed:

NS F L B Q C T D H R St ꝺ G M I E U O A
written for *b l f s n* *h d t c q* *m g ŋ st r* *a o u e i*

(38) *Fraech frithrosc* ('Heath (?) reversed'). The whole alphabet backward, *including* the diphthongs:

Ae Ui Ia Oi Ei I E U O A R St ꝺ G M etc.
written for *b l f s n* *h d t c q* *m g ŋ st r* etc.

(36) *Rind fri derc* ('Point against eye'). The alphabet backward, *excluding* the diphthongs. The scribe of the Ballymote MS. has carelessly forgotten to reverse the letters of the A group, which here stand for the letters of the B group.

(iii) Interchanges of the letter groups.

(42) *Ogam imarbach* ('Contending Ogham'). The H group written before the B group, the A group before the M group, and the letters presumably substituted correspondingly, though the writer does not definitely say so, thus:

H D T C Q B L F S N A O U E I M G ꝺ St R
written for *b l f s n* *h d t c q* *m g ŋ st r* *a o u e i*

(46) *Ogam sesmach* ('Steadfast Ogham'). The four groups inter changed in this order:

M A B reversed H reversed
written for *b h m*   *a*

(iv) Interlacements of the letter groups.

(41) *Ogam cumusgda* ('Mixed Ogham'). The B and H groups interlaced, and the M and A groups interlaced:

B HL DF T S C NQ M A G O ꝺ U St E R I
for *b l f s n* *h d t c q* *m g ŋ st r* *a o u e i*
as we may presume, though (as in *Ogam imarbach* above) the scribe does not say so.

(44) *Ogam ind co ind* ('End-to-end Ogham'). The A group reversed interlaced with the B group, the M group similarly with the H group:

B I L E F   U S O N A   H R D St T   ŊC G Q M
for *b l f s n*   *h d t c q*   *m g ŋ st r*   *a o u e i*

once more, by presumption.

(35) *Ogam buaidir foranna* ('Outburst of rage Ogham'). All the five groups interchanged, the first letter of each group standing for the B letters, and so on, thus:

B H M A Ea   L D G O Oi   F T Ŋ U Ia etc.
for *b l f s n*   *h d t c q*   *m g ŋ st r* etc.

(47) *Gort fo lid* ('A coloured garden'). A variant of the last, in which the diphthongs are omitted:

B H M A L   D G O F T   Ŋ U etc.
for *b l f s n*   *h d f c q*   *m g* etc.

(v) Other forms of substitution.

(60) *Ogam indiupartach* ('Fraudulent Ogham'). The letters moved on a step, so that

L F S N H   D T C Q M   G Ŋ St etc.
stand for *b l f s n*   *h d t c q*   *m g ŋ* etc.

(16) *Ogam ar a mbi aen* ('Plus-one Ogham'): one score added to every letter. It resembles the last, substituting six B scores for *h*, six H scores for *m*, and so on.

(32) *Ogam dedenach* ('Finals Ogham'). The last letter of the ordinary name substituted for the letter. Thus S (the last letter of *ruis*) would be written for *r*, and L (the last letter of *coll*) for *c*. A bad alphabet, for as several groups of letter-names end in the same letter, decipherment would be ambiguous. But it might be very useful, as in other cases, for concealing from prying eyes a proper name known to the correspondents.

(14) *Ogam Bricrend* ('Bricriu's Ogham'). The letters formed of equal vertical strokes, one to twenty in number.

(vi) Cumulative figures.

{
(3) *Luth-ogam* ('Hinge Ogham').
(11) *Run-ogam na bfian* ('Secret Ogham of the Warriors').
(54) *Insnithach* ('Interwoven').
}

One description will serve for these, although in external form they are quite dissimilar. The principle of construction is the same

in them all: the five-score letter of each group is represented by
an arbitrary character which consists of five strokes, or to be
more accurate, can be built up by a succession of five operations:
and the five successive letters of the group are represented by the
gradual accumulation of these operations. One specimen will
suffice as an illustration:

B L F S N

In addition to these more regularly formed symbols, there is a
considerable number of fantastic characters, incapable of classification or analysis, invented to represent various combinations of
letters: they are possibly the syllabary of a system of shorthand.
There is also, at the end of the tract, a little collection of foreign
alphabets. The 'Egyptian alphabet', so called, can be seen without
difficulty to be a very corrupt form of the Hebrew alphabet. The
'African alphabet' is less easy of identification. The 'Foreign
alphabet' is a badly drawn Runic alphabet, the native names of
which are added to the characters.

Thus we see that although the purveyors of mysteries did not
advance very far in the science of Cryptography—there are many
forms in modern use of which the tract shews no conception—yet
they carried it far enough to puzzle their own contemporaries,
which was all that was necessary. And the two cyphers following
shew that they could set nuts sufficiently hard even for posterity
to crack.

The first is written in six lines of *Ogam Bricrend* in the lower
margin of the page of *The Book of Ballymote* which bears a description of this form of cypher. Here the letters are denoted by short
equal vertical strokes, 1–5 in number for B to N, 6–10 for H to Q,
11–15 for M to R, and 16–20 for A to I. To decipher the text
requires patient and monotonous counting of the groups of scores,
which are separated by dots. In the text before us, after writing
out seventeen letters in this toilsome way—as far as SASA in
the first line—the writer suddenly changed, from groups of strokes
separated by dots, to groups of dots separated by strokes; and
he continued in this form to the end of the cypher. In the absence
of evidence to the contrary we may assume that this change of
form does not imply a change in the construction of the cypher.

The first three letters, UES, will be sufficient to shew what the cypher looks like:

||||||||||||||| · ||||||||||||||||| · |||| ·

U   E   S

(18 strokes)   (19 strokes) (4 strokes)

While the last three letters, A I R, will serve as an example of the latter part:

|················|······················|················|

A   I   R

(16 dots)   (20 dots)   (15 dots)

I have counted through these tedious letters on three separate occasions, and, admitting slight doubt as to the number of scores or dots in one or two worn places, I can make of them no more than the following unintelligible sequence:

$\dot{\text{U}}$ E S G $\frac{\text{I}}{\text{E}}$ S $\dot{\text{L}}$ E $\dot{\text{B}}$ I N $\dot{\text{I}}$ M S A S A $\dot{\text{C}}$ O $\dot{\text{O}}$

F $\dot{\text{B}}$ $\dot{\text{H}}$ E $\dot{\text{G}}^1$ O ꞥ E R E ꞥ I N

Q I ꞥ N U $\dot{\text{S}}$ A D E O C $\dot{\text{D}}$ $\dot{\text{S}}^2$

$\frac{\text{G}\ \text{L}}{\text{St}}$ I $\dot{\text{M}}$ $\frac{\text{D}}{\text{FS}}$ $\dot{\text{U}}$ I N N T E S G^3

S S $\dot{\text{B}}$ $\frac{\text{L}}{\text{V}}$ U S T T B E S L U S A G C

Q $\frac{\text{N}}{\text{BS}}$ G O L U S A I R

There is a tiny, sometimes barely traceable, 'tick', over the letters here printed with a superposed dot. I thought at first that these might be word-separators: but I concluded after careful consideration that they were nothing more important than, so to speak, marks of approval, made by the original writer or by some other, after checking over the cypher with the text on which it is based, and finding it satisfactorily correct.

This interpretation, if we may accept it, gives us some much needed encouragement. It is disconcerting to find that the application of a cypher alphabet to a composition, ostensibly written in that alphabet, produces nothing but gibberish: and we are tempted to conclude either that the author was very inaccurate

---

[1] Tick over the G doubtful.   [2] The final DS doubtful.
[3] The final SG worn.

in setting out his strokes and dots, or that he was perpetrating an elaborate practical joke upon posterity. But we cannot legitimately take refuge in either of these easy hypotheses, until we have exhausted all the other possibilities.

The first means of approach which occurred to me was to take the composition as a double cypher, or the cypher of a cypher. A sentence is obscured by changing its letters on some substitutionary scheme: and then the *substituted* letters are represented by the new symbols. Any one of the letter-shifts specified in the foregoing pages, or any one of countless other possibilities which are equally admissible but do not happen to be mentioned, might have been applied to the original document. Thus we might represent

B L F S N—H D T C Q

by the symbols   1 2 3 4 5   6 7 8 9 x

but having previously, and for greater complication, interchanged the B and H letter groups, we should have to interpret '8' as meaning F, and '5' as meaning Q.

But to this there is an almost unsurmountable objection. I counted the frequency of each individual letter,[1] and obtained the following result:

B L F S   N H D T C Q M G Ŋ Z R A O U E I
4 5 1 13 6 1 3 3 3 2 2 6 3 0 2 5 5 6 8 8

eighty-six letters in all. Having obtained these figures, I took a number of Ogham inscriptions, of which I had accurate copies; and eliminated the words of relationship which, as they occur in almost every inscription, would give an undue advantage to the letters composing those words. Having thus obtained a consecutive series of 516 Ogham characters (six times the number of characters in the cypher) I counted the distribution of the several letters, with the following result:

B L V S N H D T C Q M G Ŋ Z R A O U E I
17 26 15 23 47 0 19 26 37 7 17 27 1 0 24 80 34 30 36 50
[24 30 6 78 36 6 18 18 18 12 12 36 18 0 12 30 30 36 48 48]

The lower row of figures, in square brackets, is six times the figures for the cypher. The comparison is not altogether fair, as the Ogham inscriptions are exclusively personal names; and as

---

[1] Taking the *upper* alternative in the ambiguous cases as printed above, which is always the more probable.

these are in the genitive case, the letters forming the genitive case-endings must be unduly preponderant. The case of S is the most remarkable discrepancy; another is A; and these may be thus explained. But on the other hand, the vowels maintain their preponderance in both, and the rare letters H, Z are rare in both. And if we set out the letters in the order of relative frequency, we shall find that, with a few exceptions, the two rows will agree fairly well, the difference in the character of the documents being quite sufficient to account for any deviations.

Occurrences	0–20	21–40	Above 40
Cypher	ZFHQMRDTCIꞐ	BLAONGU	EIS
Inscriptions	ZHꞐQFBMD	SRLTGUOEC	NIA

We infer therefore that there has been no letter-shift; and that the cypher must be taken as it stands.

With all diffidence, and with a full appreciation and acknowledgement of the fantastic appearance of the hypothesis, I suggest that in this queer scribble we have a note of some magical abracadabra, a mumbo-jumbo liturgical formula, which had somehow fluttered out of the dark recesses of paganism to the feet of an owner of *The Book of Ballymote*. The curiosity interested him, and he did not wish to lose it; but from some superstitious scruple he feared to place it on record in readable characters.

When we look back at the cypher, we remind ourselves that the first line of writing is set forth in strokes, except the final letters COO, and that the remaining five lines are set forth in dots. We note further, that the letters written in strokes, whatever the words which they form may mean, are pronounceable, and have a metrical sound:

uésgislébin ímsasá

Looking a little further, we find in the second and third lines groups of letters that form words with a similar rhythm, and rhyming with the above:

góꞑeréꞑin qíꞑnusá

with the less tractable *coofbhe* separating the two rhyming formulae. Then comes *deocds*, and then what appears to be a third line:

glímduínntes...béslusá

with *gssblustt* inserted in the middle; then *gcqn*, followed by *gólusá*, completing the rhyme, and finally *ir*.

The interpolated 'words' are partly unpronounceable; and in this they shew affinity to another formula, or group of formulae, that has already been long familiar. In one of the early stone structures at Glenfahan, west of Dingle, Co. Kerry, there was found a slab bearing a cross, some rude ornament, and an inscription in Ogham letters, not cut, as usual, on the angle of the stone, but on an incised stem-line, reading LMCBDV. A bead of amber, long preserved in Ennis, and traditionally possessing magical qualities, which passed during the nineteenth century through the Londesborough Collection to the British Museum, is similarly inscribed LMCBTM (reversed). Formulae of the same kind, even more obscure, are cut in some cryptical variety of Ogham on a slab at Aultagh, in East Carbery, Co. Cork. These rows of letters may conceivably be the *initials* of liturgical formulae, chanted by the subordinate officials, in response to the versified 'words of power' uttered by the arch-druid. The unknown words would make the whole ceremony extremely impressive, though unfortunately we cannot write the ritual out in full:

℣ 1   UESGISLEBIN IMSASA!

℟ 1   *c.o.o.f.b.h.e.*

℣ 2   GOƉEREƉIN QIƉNUSA!

℟ 2   *d.e.o.c.d.s.*

℣ 3   GLIMDUÏNNTES—

℟ 3   *g.s.s.b.l.u.s.t.t.*

℣ 4   —BESLUSA!

℟ 4   *g.c.q.n.*

℣ 5   GOLUSA!

℟ 5   *i.r.*

If this explanation be right, it is something to have recovered even so much of a druidic liturgy. If it be wrong, and some one else hits on a better one, I shall be the first to congratulate him and to accept it. I guarantee nothing but the accuracy of the transcript, which I have checked and re-checked. I do not, however, undertake to stand surety for the accuracy of the original scribe; if *he* has made any mistakes, I do not see how they are to be detected and remedied.

The disturbing psychological effect of gibberish like this, even in these materialistic days, is illustrated by a curious story to

which Miss Yates has called my attention.[1] It is to the effect that
a certain Greek gypsy entered a café in Cardiff, where he scraped
acquaintance with a commercial traveller and 'talked to him with
lightning rapidity in a foreign language mixed with English, until
the victim fell into a stupor, lost his power of resistance, and lent
the gypsy £36 that was in his wallet. The latter made some
pretence of telling the bagman's fortune, returned the notes, and
went out leaving his dinner uneaten; and the traveller, when he
had recovered and could count his money, found that £17 was
missing.'

Naturally it is not legitimate to form a theory like this and then
to play with the text in order to make it more conformable thereto.
But it may just be permissible to notice that if the scribe had
accidentally left out a single dot in each of the letters E S at the
end of the third versicle, the reading would be GLIMDUÏNNTIN,
which would make the rhyme and the rhythm both perfect.

The second of the two cyphers is written in the lower margin
of a page of *The Book of Fermoy*, or, rather, of a fourteenth-century
text of *The Book of Invasions* which has been bound into that
volume (folio 5 *verso*). Here is a facsimile of the text, which is

[a bne n eadhht   rg u goŋmn gtuilt geanbs I I]
               ?   ?

very difficult to make out, owing to the injudicious use of gallic
acid as a reagent in a more careless generation. What form of
cypher it may illustrate, and what it may mean, I have been
unable to discover. These rudimentary mystifications are even
yet effective: the Ogham tract is not such a *wertlose Spielerei*
after all: and its compiler, in the blunt language of the market-
place, was not such a fool as he looked!

Under the heading Substitutions, no. IV above, it was noticed
that nos. (21) and (59) are identical. *Muc-ogam* is also repeated
twice, and there are several cases of alphabets with very slight
differences between them. This all points to the conclusion, indicated in the place referred to, that our tract is a combination of
two independent lists of cryptographic alphabets. It is possible
that the seemingly arbitrary presence or absence of the diphthong

[1] *Journal*, Gypsy Lore Society, Series III, vol. xiii, p. 130.

group is essentially a result of this conflation, alphabets with these extra signs belonging to the one list, those without them belonging to the other. Unfortunately this question cannot be worked out in detail; for though in some cases the scribe has left no room for doubt that his alphabet never possessed the extra characters, in other cases, where he has been pressed for space, he has contented himself with writing part of the alphabet and an *et cetera*, which leaves us uncertain as to how it originally ended.

The foregoing chapter does not profess to discuss any more of its subject than is relevant to the matter before us. The whole theme of Cryptology in Northern Europe would take us far afield, and would oblige us to contemplate the cryptical Runes at various places such as Rök in Sweden, Maeshowe in Orkney, and Hackness in Yorkshire. The Hackness cryptograms are especially interesting[1] as they have clearly been contrived by someone familiar with the Ogham character and its capacity for variation. His invention is, however, quite different from any of the cyphers enumerated in the Ballymote tract. It might have some bearing on the present study if we could solve the riddle: but it still holds secure the secrets, committed to its keeping long ago.

[1] A discussion of the inscription by the late Professor Baldwin Brown and the present writer will be found in vol. vi of Professor Brown's *The Arts in Early England*, pp. 52 ff., with several illustrations.

CHAPTER III

HISPERIC

Like the beginnings of all great movements, the beginning of Christianity in Northern Europe is wrapped in deep obscurity. It is a history from whose opening chapters many pages have been torn, so that the narrative cannot be followed consecutively. Everyone is free to fill the gaps as he will: and as everyone, whatever his theological prepossessions may be, appears to be able to draw comfort from what he finds there, we may reasonably infer that all such restorations are subjective rather than objective.

We are not here called upon to deal with insoluble, or, at any rate, unsolved problems of Church history. Who were the 'Scots who believed in Christ' to whom, according to Prosper Tiro, Pope Celestine sent as first bishop the predecessor of Patrick, Palladius? Whence did they receive their Christianity? We do not know: nobody knows: and all the answers are mere guesswork. Did the heresiarch Pelagius come forth from Britain or from Ireland to rock the Church of the fourth century? Some say the one, some say the other: nobody knows. When we arrive at Patrick himself, we are on surer ground; for he has left us what may be called an autobiographical homily, from which certain facts of his life and activities can be established. But, like Gerontius, we

—fain would know
A maze of things—

on which he does not condescend to enlighten us.

Patrick was a great saint of God. His own writings are enough to tell us that. Though he laboured under grave educational and other disadvantages, he was a skilful organizer: this also must be admitted by anyone who makes a close study of the relevant literature. But he could not accomplish the impossible; and one impossible thing would be for a missionary to *convert* to his teaching, within his own lifetime, an entire population, scattered over 32,000 square miles of difficult country. We italicize the word 'convert', because we wish it to be understood in the radical sense which alone is of any real value in missionary work. The type of event in a general election, invariably and incomprehensibly described by journalists as a 'landslide', is never an indication of a change of heart in the voting Demos: it is merely the result of a puff of wind playing from an unexpected quarter upon that most unstable of all weather-cocks, and the first by-election which follows inaugurates the inevitable reaction. A political conversion without a change of heart, a religious conversion without a change of heart, are alike worthless: they merely denote a superficial and temporary instability, for of all things the human heart is among the most difficult to change. It is a safe rule, that the more spectacular the apparent success of a mission may be, the less likely are its fruits to be permanent. At best it will establish a sort of compromise, a syncretism of the ancient faith and the new. That this actually took place in Northern Europe, the many survivals of well-worship and similar cults remain to this day to witness. Patrick left Ireland on the road to Christianity; but unless 'the Scots believing in Christ' who preceded him were much more numerous than we have any authority to suppose, the Pre-Christian beliefs and practices must have been still vital and active when he rested from his labours. Manus O'Donnell, who in the sixteenth century compiled from older sources a life of Colum Cille (St Columba), expresses these truths in the following picturesque language: 'Now that most noble and honourable mill, Patrick, working and grinding by the rich water of the graces wherewith God had endowed him, ground the men of Ireland and her women. Yet so rough and intemperate were the Folk at the beginning of the Faith, that he could not choose but leave much dirt and tares in the wheat.'[1]

We hear very little of clashes between the rival religions. Patrick himself met with occasional persecutions, though his greatest troubles seem to have come from the ecclesiastical authorities, his superiors, who might have been expected to strengthen his hands. One Coroticus made a murderous foray on a group of his catechumens: an event which hardly counts, for this person does not appear to have been a native Irish prince. In short, as has been indicated in the first chapter, for a time the disciples of Christ and those of Ogmios seem to have settled down into an easy mutual affability.

[1] O'Donnell's *Life of St Columba*, ed. O'Kelleher (Illinois, 1918) p. 16.

Druidry, however, was in any case doomed. Ireland, a land outside the Roman empire, was its last sanctuary; under Roman auspices it had been suppressed, and its exponents were thus deprived of the support which, in happier days, had come from their membership of an omnipotent freemasonry, efficient over a considerable area of Europe. In the Ogham inscriptions the old learning was flickering out. Christianity advanced, and *pari passu* druidry receded: and as it ebbed, Christianity entered into the possession of its vacated seats.

Notwithstanding the adverse criticism of D'Arbois de Jubainville,[1] quoted with approval by Roger,[2] we cannot altogether set aside the connexion which Alexandre Bertrand sought to trace between the monastic establishments and the preceding druidic colleges.[3] Not in the crude form in which Bertrand states it: there is nothing druidic in the institution of Christian monachism *per se*. But the more we search for the early history of the various monastic establishments scattered over Celtic Ireland, the more does the conviction grow that most, if not all, of these were situated in places which had already possessed sanctity of some sort in pre-Christian times. It is here that we must deplore the loss of many precious leaves from our records; but what we have is suggestive enough. We have only to read the fascinating preface to Plummer's *Vitae Sanctorum Hiberniae* to realize what large lumps of pagan material the hagiographers utilized, in the construction of their new temples. If it be objected that these documents are late, and therefore worthless, the answer is ready to our hands. As records of history they are certainly worthless: as records of folk memory they are beyond price. The life of a saint, written in his own time and under his own censorship, would suppress the paganisms which it was his duty to supersede: they would be recognized as paganisms, and he would not permit his panegyrist to give them so dangerous a currency. But after a few centuries, when paganism as such was moribund or dead, these fragments of tradition would inevitably float to the surface. Their true nature would by now be forgotten, and they would readily find a place in an uncritical narrative, which its author was endeavouring to make as varied and as interesting as possible.

[1] *Revue Celtique*, vol. xix, p. 73.
[2] *L'enseignement des lettres classiques d'Ausone à Alcuin* (Paris, 1905), p. 204.
[3] *Nos origines, la Religion des Gaulois*, pp. 277 ff.

The modern science of Comparative Religion shews what these survivals mean. They correspond to standard pagan types, and most certainly they were not invented by the hagiographers who, in blissful ignorance, wrote them down.

The admission, through the gates of learning, of candidates other than students of druidry, completed the destruction of the 'druidic' language as a medium of discipline. We can compare what took place on a larger scale throughout Europe, when scholars began to express their learning, each in his own vernacular, instead of in the traditional Latin. Conceivably it would now be possible for a man to be the greatest biologist or mathematician in the world, if his special gifts lay in those directions, and yet be unable to write out the declension of *mensa*: and in like manner it was discovered that a larger learning than the druids could impart was available, outside the language to which these teachers had confined their attention. Ecclesiastical discipline introduced Latin into the schools: and Latin completely ousted the traditional tongue of pagan learning.

Dr M. Roger, in a book with which a trivial disagreement was expressed on the preceding page, has traced with fullness, accuracy, grace, and clarity the melancholy story of the decline and fall of Classical learning in Western Europe. He shews us, first, at the moment when paganism is about to feel the flowing tide of Christianity, how education in Gaul was still in the hands of pagan teachers, imparting their instruction on the lines laid down by Quintilian. Then he lets us see the perplexity of early Christianity, faced with a dilemma: should Churchmen continue to cultivate a literature, the atmosphere of which is altogether pagan, or should they discountenance it, thereby putting themselves into a position of educational and cultural inferiority to their still pagan neighbours? This last would be a serious matter, as they needed all the learning that they could muster for the endless controversies in which their circumstances involved them. Next, he shews us the curious 'half-way house' in which some of their leaders found a temporary refuge—that the Classics were to be cultivated for their educational value, and were then to be immediately forgotten. It is not surprising in such circumstances that the tradition of Classical learning should flicker, and all but suffer extinction, in Continental Gaul. Even Gregory of Tours writes Latin in a rustic uncivilized style: and if Venantius Fortunatus could write passable verse, it must be remembered that

he owed to Gaul neither his birth nor his upbringing. Pedantry
took the place of learning: appeals to authority took the place
of research. For the whole story we must refer the reader to the
works of Roger and of Laistner:[1] anything more than this slight
summary would here be out of place.

Among the British and Irish Christians, scholars lived and
worked in circumstances different from those of their Continental
brethren. On the Continent Latin was practically a universal
vernacular. It may not have been good Ciceronian Latin, but still
it was Latin, and the students were not under the obligation of
beginning its study at the first rudiments. The case was different,
however, in Great Britain, and even more so in Ireland. In both
countries the native Celtic vernaculars were the current speech:
Latin was practically unknown in Ireland, and even in Romanized
Britain was a sorry and ungrammatical veneer, if we may judge
from the inscriptions that have come down to us. Thus, students
entering a monastic school in either country had to pass through
a linguistic discipline, from which their Continental brethren were
exempt.

In another respect the insular conditions were different from
those of the Continent. The pagan associations of Classical literature were here less likely to be harmful. Jupiter and the rest of
the Roman divinities had never found a lodgement in the hearts
of the insular Celts. These had had their own paganisms, from
which it was necessary to safeguard converts and young students:
but they could read freely about gods whom they had never been
tempted to worship.

There is a third point of importance, which has a special
bearing upon our immediate subject. The druidic tradition, in
Ireland not as yet completely dead, had surrounded learning with
a certain supernatural halo. The druid, according to the most
probable etymology of the word, was the 'very knowing one': he
was the adept, the knowledgeable man in all matters in which
the life of this world came into contact with that of the other.
He presided over sacrifices, interpreted omens, and had skill in
the ways of the gods. Such a one would demand and would
receive respect: we have already seen how Irish literature corroborates the testimony of Caesar that the 'man with knowledge'
was set high above the common herd in the esteem of his people.

[1] M. L. W. Laistner, *Thought and Letters in Western Europe* A.D. 500 *to* 900
(London, Methuen, 1931).

A document of about the eighth century[1] enumerates the classes of learned men, two of which are named *ansruth* 'big river', and *sruth do aill* 'stream from a cliff' or 'mountain torrent'. The primary idea of the terminology is presumably relative size and importance: but the compiler, or a glossator, of the document explains the latter term as meaning one who drowns everyone small, light, or weak: that washes down loose rocks, and makes them like the sea-sand. In this manner does the mountain torrent act: in this manner does the man named after it act—he drowns bad scholars under the tide of his learning and crushes them under the rocks of evidence. Also he is tender to those of little learning, who would ebb away altogether in presence of a 'big river'. Whether this laboured explanation be or be not based on actuality, it betrays unequivocally the tradition of arrogance in learning: and we must envisage the possibility of this taint affecting the new teachers, as it had dominated the old.

Here once again we call to mind the so-called 'lives of the saints'. It cannot be said too plainly that anyone who wishes to retain his respect for the ancient saints of Ireland must approach these interesting and valuable, but essentially horrid, little tracts, in a spirit of uncompromising scepticism. They are a half-pagan smoke-screen, erected between us and the men with whom we should so heartily desire to become acquainted. Only here and there can we catch an occasional foggy glimpse of them; there are episodes, like the famous description of the death of St Ciarán of Clonmacnois, which must be true, because they are far too good for a hagiographer to invent. But for the rest, these 'lives' are at best mere dregs of the folk memory. We could pity, but could hardly respect, people whose conception of the beauty of holiness involved a total abstention from all ablutions except on Easter Sunday: or the keeping of a tame stag-beetle, and feeding it by allowing it to gnaw their own flesh: or sleeping with corpses: or cherishing the persons of lepers in ways which for loathsomeness could hardly be matched except, perhaps, in the slums of Arab or Indian literature—by no means benefiting the patients, with the self-sacrifice of a Father Damien, but rather insulting them by making their misfortune the means of displaying the 'pride

---

[1] Published in the Rolls Series of the *Ancient Laws of Ireland* (vol. iv, p. 344) under the title of 'Sequel to *Crith Gabhlach*': analysed by Professor MacNeill under the title *Miadlechta* ('Classes of Dignity') in *Proceedings, Royal Irish Academy*, vol. xxxvi, section C, p. 311.

that apes humility'. Such a 'saint' as Find-Chua son of Find-Lug
(the latter a theophorous compound, based on the name of a sun-
god), who is described by his panegyrist as 'a slaughterous
warrior'; who lives at 'the Smiths' Hill' (necessarily an uncanny
place), and who, when he is in a rage (apparently his normal
condition), emits flames of fire from his teeth, or burns by the
mere contact of his head the cowl of his instructor—such a
person can be restored by Christianity to the paganism where he
belongs, with unalloyed relief. Remembering that austerities as
revolting as those enumerated above are practised by Aghori,
Shamans, and other adepts of various Asiatic cults, it would be a
comfort to be able to feel that we could shift all these nasty stories
from the Christian saints on to the broad backs of the druids.

Especially suggestive in these documents is their constant
manifestation of this very attribute of arrogance. Let anyone
say anything rude, or refuse a request, or in any other way,
however trivial, offend the saint, and it is ten to one that the
holy man will snap out 'Be thou turned to stone' or 'Be thou
swallowed up in the earth' or 'May thine eyes burst in thy head'—
and forthwith the specified crime is accomplished, and the pious
homilist adds to his narrative the stock comment—and stu-
pendous blasphemy—'The names of God and of So-and-so [the
saint] were magnified by that miracle'! We take leave to dis-
credit all such crudities. It is not easy to believe that Christian
saints of old ramped over the country, shouting 'Off with his head'
at every turn, like the 'Queen of Hearts' in *Alice in Wonderland*.

But we must acknowledge that those who devoted themselves
to learning had more than a spice of the druidic Old Adam. In
privileges as well as in character the Irish saints enter into the
druidic heritage. Fruitfulness of crops is conditional upon obe-
dience to them: and they claim the druidic prerogative of exemp-
tion from taxes.[1] It is not improbable that the peculiar Celtic
tonsure, which was one of the subjects of dispute at the Synod
of Whitby, was ultimately of druidic origin.[2]

What lines of study did the learners pursue, in the Celtic
monastic schools? First and foremost, the reading of the biblical
texts, especially an intensive study of the Psalms. As a student
in the druidic school was called upon to learn a *corpus* of verses,
so a pupil in the monastic school began his studies by learning

[1] *Lives of Saints from the Book of Lismore*, ed. Stokes, line 2087.
[2] See Dom L. Gougaud, *Christianity in Celtic Lands*, pp. 201 ff.

the hundred and fifty psalms attributed to David. In some monasteries—Tallaght, for example—it is said, in the first-hand report of an inmate which a lucky chance has preserved for us, that each day the repetition of the entire psalter was a compulsory preliminary to dinner. This, however, we can hardly take literally. I have tested the unedifying exercise sufficiently to conclude that, gabbling as fast as the speech organs would move, and assuming them capable of keeping up at a uniform rate without any slackening, the task would occupy about two hours and a quarter: at the end of which time those who took part in it would be unfit for eating their dinner or for anything else. We must suppose that either the initial catchwords, or else the last three verses of each psalm, were repeated.[1]

Excursions into Vergil and other classical writers helped to lay a tolerably sound foundation of Latin scholarship: in this remote and extra-imperial island, Latin, a foreign language, took the place of the old 'Ogham' language as the *corpus vile* of grammatical study. The students read Priscian—with many groans, if we may judge from the *adversaria* scribbled on the margins of the St Gall copy. For general information they had the compilation of the dry-as-dust Isidore of Seville. For the philosophy of language they had Martianus Capella, and (it is to be hoped) earned merit by the success with which they resisted the seductions of that master-physician for insomnia.

While Latin was the principal language studied, some few scholars seem to have been led by their biblical and theological enquiries to adventure into Greek, and even to acquire a certain smattering of Hebrew. But that the latter language was not cultivated with excessive assiduity is amusingly suggested by one of the stanzas of a long poem upon the Creation and early History of Mankind, of which several copies are in existence. The writer is telling us an interesting bit of ecclesiastical folklore, referred to by other ancient authorities, to the effect that the first being to utter the name of God was Satan: and this is how he expresses it:

> Delb nathrach, corp aeoir sēim,
> Tuc leis diabul sin droich-rēim:
> Litri trias ro chan, nī as līach,
> Iae, Vau, Iae, ocus Īath.

[1] From several passages in the Irish *Liber Hymnorum* we learn that to gain the spiritual advantages earned by the repetition of unduly lengthy hymns, it was sufficient to repeat the last three stanzas.

A serpent's form, a body of thin air,
The Devil took with him upon the evil course.
The letters by which he made incantation, a thing that is evil,
Were He, Vav, He, and Yodh.

The poet knew what the Tetragrammaton looked like. He also knew the names of its component letters. But he did not know that, after the manner of the Hebrew language, it is written and intended to be read from right to left. He spells it out in the European way, the only way which he knows, from left to right; and thus he enumerates the letters backward. Obviously he at least knew nothing of Hebrew but the alphabet.

The easy toleration of pre-Christian tradition did not endure. When the position of the Church became more secure, there seems to have been a sort of 'tightening up'—a desire to hasten the end of paganism, in Ireland as in the other Celtic countries. Bertrand has collected a number of decrees of Church councils against well- and stone-worship, practices on which the earliest preachers had felt obliged to compromise[1]—just as Muḥammad had been obliged to compromise on the Ramaḍan fast and the Mecca pilgrimage, which heritages of paganism are even now the strongest elements in the system of Islâm. So in Wales there seems to have been an orgy of destruction of Oghams—what we have are only a few chance survivors. In Ireland such monuments were mutilated when they contained any hint of descent from a divine ancestor; and their essential paganism was exorcised by cutting a cross upon their sides. Here and there in the literature doubts are expressed as to the propriety of studying the ancient traditions. Patrick, in that valuable compilation of ancient folklore called *The Colloquy of the Ancients*, is represented as feeling qualms about it, till he is reassured by his guardian angel—a little hint which suggests that the compiler of the narrative would himself feel grateful for similar encouragement. 'Though I write about these people I do not adore them', says one. 'What we have here written is made for the amusement of fools', says another. 'Why is God said to regard a man who reads Gaelic as uncivilized?' asks a glossator of *The Scholar's Primer*, and he endeavours, without obvious success, to answer the searching question. This disconcerting principle was surely laid down by some stern instructor, who wished his students to understand that God would not love them unless they devoted them-

---

[1] A. Bertrand, *La Religion des Gaulois* (Paris, 1897), p. 400.

selves to the study of ecclesiastical Latin, and to the matters written therein; and left all worldly follies on one side.

Two causes may have led to this revolt against the old learning. The first was the crushing blow which Celtic Christianity had received at the Synod of Whitby. It is not pleasant for any community to be told that they have been all wrong, and that possibly in perfect innocence they have been imperilling their souls' salvation: a reform in such external matters as the Easter Computation and the Tonsure, which were the primary subjects decided at Whitby, may have led to a less spectacular reform in more spiritual matters as well. And the Scandinavian raids, which began not very long afterwards, may have been accepted as a further purging discipline. *Why are these dogs of Muslim infidels permitted to ravage the centres of Christendom?* asked the Byzantines: and when they found the answer in the exceeding sinfulness of images in the churches, they sought to turn away the divine wrath by the Iconoclastic upheaval. *Why are the pagan Saxons permitted to ravage the Christian Britons?* asked Gildas: and he found the answer in the sins which he denounced in the British rulers. *Why have these reivers from the East been permitted thus to afflict our holy house?* the heads of Clonmacnois might have asked, after burying their dead and deploring their depleted treasury: and they may have found the answer in the undue delight which they had taken in the vain tales of the world.

We may perhaps explain in this way the monastic failure in vernacular creative literature. The monks compiled, copied, translated: but on the whole, free composition was left to the hereditary bards attached to the heads of the important families, whose duty it was to provide panegyrics, laments, and other *pièces d'occasion*. As the monks were the successors of the druids on the religious side, these laureates were their heritors on the literary side. They likewise instructed pupils in their art, and classified their attainments by an elaborate system of graduation, not unlike the degrees of a university. In one respect their mode of teaching was closer to that of their druidic predecessors than was the monastic system: they depended on memory rather than on books. Their pupils carried their literary stock-in-trade in their heads: even new compositions were prepared without the use of writing, to be recited to their gratified patrons, as they feasted, in the form in which they had hammered them out in the recesses of their minds. The bards were not, primarily, bookmen. They left parchment and ink, speaking generally, to the monks; it is to the products of monastic scriptoria that we are indebted for most of what we know of early Gaelic literature.

Let us for a moment pause here to take stock of the situation. Let us suppose ourselves in Ireland at about the beginning of the sixth century.

(1) Druidism is still alive; druids were maintained by King Diarmait mac Cerbaill († A.D. 558) though he also was a beneficent patron of Christian monasteries. Oghams are still being written, so that the 'Ogham' language is not altogether forgotten. It is, however, no longer in practical use as a learned secret tongue.

(2) The monastic schools are revolutionizing learning, on a biblical basis. The Psalms (in Latin) are a standard textbook, and are repeated so often that they are known by heart. They practically take the place of the Druidic 'Vedas', and Latin is taking the place of the Druidic secret tongue.

(3) Vernacular poets, who are Christians, and often monastery trained, are feeling after new modes of expression.

(4) After the first impetus of Christianity and Christian learning, which introduced Latin with, perhaps, a little Greek and Hebrew to Ireland, there does not appear to have been much new influence from the outside. Learning therefore for a couple of centuries lived on its memories, and made no perceptible advance: the same is true of contemporary Christian art. It was therefore liable to fossilize.

(5) The men of learning, whatever their individual competence, are deeply conscious of the dignity of learning, and are arrogantly jealous for the respect due to its votaries. In this they carry on the druidic tradition.

We have said, in the last paragraph, 'whatever their individual competence'. This raises the interesting question, What was the average competence of the Irish preceptors? We are speaking at the moment of the sixth century: and Roger has given us a much needed warning against mixing up scholars of different generations together. Because the ninth century produced an Erigena, it does not follow that there were people of the same scholastic calibre in the sixth. Even if there were, it would prove nothing as to the *average* standard of scholarship. Because Germany has produced a Sebastian Bach and a Beethoven, whom it is not unreasonable to call the two greatest musicians that have ever lived, it does not follow that any music-teaching hack in a

German provincial town could compose a new B-minor Mass, or a new Choral Symphony. We must take warning from Roger's caustic comment on a certain popular book about 'Ireland's Ancient Schools and Scholars': *Nous laissons de côté toutes les écoles dont l'existence est signalée* [par cet auteur]. *Les moindres huttes où priaient des anachorètes deviennent à ses yeux des centres d'études considérables.*

To speak bluntly, there are certain outstanding names in the record of 'Ireland's Ancient Schools and Scholars' to whom all honour is due, and who are always brought into evidence when this question is under discussion. But what about the scholastic underworld, as we may call it, in the background of the picture? Let a personal experience provide the answer. Many years ago, in destroying an accumulation of old papers, I came across a note which I had taken down at school from the dictation of a preceptor, and at the time presumably believed, to the effect that the Greeks called the people of the outer world 'Barbarians' because they wore beards: and I well remember how the same simple soul, peace to his innocent ashes, once told me that the authority for some other unjustifiable dogma, which he had propounded, was to be discovered 'in a book in the British Museum'—a reference which I have never yet found time to verify. If a duck so very lame could be entrusted with the task of imparting instruction in a school of the last quarter of the nineteenth century, why should not similar portents have been possible in the sixth?

Such a one-eyed man is king among the blind, but only so long as they remain blind. When their eyes shew any signs of opening, and if he is unwilling to abdicate his sovereignty, he must imitate the octopus, and veil himself in an impenetrable sea of ink. And this is what actually happened. In an atmosphere of traditional scholastic prestige, but of a decline of genuine scholarship, charlatanism burgeoned and flourished. The Christian scholar, clerical or lay, sought to ape the druid. The vernacular Irish of the time was not enough: Latin was not enough: both, once more to quote Leland's knife-grinder, were 'gettin' to be too blown'. And so two portentous jargons were launched forth, based upon Irish and Latin respectively.

To these jargons we may give the names 'Hisperic Irish' and 'Hisperic Latin', adapted from their best-known literary product. Talking in riddles had been at all times a favourite amusement among the Celtic peoples. Diodorus (v, 31) tells us that the Gauls

north of the Alps spoke but little, and expressed themselves in
enigmas which they left it to their hearers to interpret: an exercise
which appears to have passed the wit of Strabo, for he says of
the same people that they were simple-minded and had no sense.
The kennings of the Icelandic bards shew us the kind of thing
that Diodorus or his informant was thinking of. When Cū Chulaind
was wooing Emer, he expressed himself in strings of allusions and
periphrases, which the lady was shrewd enough to interpret and
to reply to in the same spirit; so that although the courtship took
place in public, the bystanders were unaware of what was going
on—a fine example of what, in the preceding chapter, we called
Cryptolaly.[1] Words which convey no meaning to their hearer
are always impressive: a story used to be current of how Daniel
O'Connell put to silence an abusive fishwife by the use of a rigma-
role of long and in themselves innocent words, though except
that 'parallelepiped' was one of them, the details have slipped
my memory. A striking example in Middle Irish appears in the
extraordinary story called *The Ever-New Tongue*, an Apocryphon
probably of Syriac or some other Oriental origin, but preserved
in Irish only. The skeleton of the story is to the effect that the
apostle Philip's tongue was cut out nine times by the heathen,
and nine times restored; on which account his name in Heaven
is 'the Ever-New Tongue'. This Philip suddenly appeared, amid
all the impressive circumstances of a Theophany, to an assembly
of sages on Mount Zion, and told them everything, and a little
more, about cosmogony and eschatology—the whole forming a
composition that can challenge comparison even with the more
delirious chapters of *The Book of Enoch*.[2] Interspersed among the
revelations are tags of 'the speech of the angels', which it may
be interesting to collect together:

1. *Haeli habia felebe fae niteia temnibisse salis sal*—'Hear this tale,
ye sons of men, I have been sent of God to converse with you.'
2. *Nathire uimbae o lebiae ua un nimbisse tiron tibia am biase sau
fimblia febe ab le febia fuan*—'It was among the peoples of the earth,
in verity, that I was born, conceived of the union of a man and a
woman.'

---

[1] A translation of the text, by Kuno Meyer, will be found running through
the first volume of *The Archaeological Review* (London, 1888). The Irish
text is printed in *Zeitschrift für celtische Philologie*, vol. iii, pp. 229 ff.
[2] For references see Best's *Bibliography of Irish Philology and Literature*,
p. 232, to which add Stokes's edition (*Ériu*, vol. ii, p. 96) from which the
following passages are quoted.

3. *Lae uide fodea tabo abelia albe fab*—' In the beginning God made heaven and earth.'

4. *Ambile bane bea fabne fa libera salese inbila tibon ale siboma fuan*—' It would be tedious to tell in Hebrew everything that is related here.'

5. *Artibilon alma sea sabne e beloia flules elbiae limbae lasfania lire*—' God made also a firmament between the waters, and divided the waters which were above the firmament from those which were beneath the firmament.'

6. *Aibne fisen asbae fribae flanis lia sieth*—' God made in the third day lakes and all the seas and forms of water and of salt sea, and the circuit of the earth with its plains, mountains, forests, precious stones, and species of trees.'

7. *Abia feble abia alitrian afen alpula nistien erolmea leam*—' Patient is the gracious heart of the King of Heaven who does not pour the earth into the lowest depths of pains for its hourly manner, for the blasphemy and insult and unrighteousness with which every man's tongue affronts Him.' [1]

8. *Eui falia fasti; maria fablea nelise nam*—' I am a rod, crooked, irreligious; hard are the pains before me, awaiting me.'

9. *Na itho ad nacul lenisteia tibon talafi aia asfa bibo limbia flaune*—' Were all your kin, boys, girls, fathers, mothers put to the sword and cooked, for you to eat their flesh, it were sevenfold easier to forgive that crime than blasphemy against God and unbelief in His creation and miracles.'

10. *Alea fas uide nala nistien alme ama faus elobi reba*—' God made on the fourth day the seventy-two kinds of planets.'

11. *Alimbea fones arife aste boia fiten salmibia libe lib ebile nab lea fabe*—' On the fifth day God created seventy-two kinds of birds and seventy-two kinds of sea-beasts.'

12. *Et diresir alba sibe alea alib me lis*—' Were the seed of Adam to hear those birds, they would not be thankful if they were deprived of hearing them.'

13. *Efi lia lasien ferosa filera leus dissia nimbile nue bua faune intoria tebnae*—' Let us make man in our own image and likeness, and let him rule the fishes of the sea, and the birds of heaven, and the beasts of the whole earth.'

14. *Elestia tibon ituria tamne ito firbia fuan*—' I know not which is most, the sands under the seas or the sorts of beasts to mangle souls in hell.'

It is impossible to say whether all this nonsense was in the unknown original from which the story was translated, or was imported into the text by the Irish translator. There is a certain vague suggestion of method in the madness. *Temnibisse* in sentence 1,

---

[1] *Alice*'s remark 'That's a great deal to make one word mean' would not be inappropriate to this and some of the other sentences.

which seems to correspond to 'I have been sent', is similar in
form to *nimbisse* in sentence 2, which may be 'I have been born'.
Felebe fae in sentence 1, which may be supposed to mean 'sons
of men', has some similarity to *febe ab le febia fuan* 'of man and
woman' in sentence 2. *O lebiae* 'of the earth' in sentence 2 is
like *abelia* 'earth' in sentence 3, allowing for scribal blunders,
which in matter of this sort are only to be expected. But these
coincidences may be illusory, and in any case do not get us very
far: there is some similarity in the beginnings of sentences 5, 6,
10, 11, the 'translations' of which begin in the same way; but
sentences 4 and 7 are not widely diverse from the type established
by these four, although their translations are quite different. One
sentence would have been sufficient as a specimen of the incomprehensible 'speech of angels': that the writer took the trouble
to invent or to copy fourteen sentences shews a mental bias
toward such unprofitable mysteries. Which leads us back to the
Hisperic languages.

Of the compositions in 'Hisperic Irish' that have survived, the
best known, and most perfectly preserved, is Dallan Forgaill's
Elegy on St Columba, written, as Professor Zimmer has with
apparent success endeavoured to shew, soon after the saint's
death in the year 597. It is a typical example of its kind: in form
a sort of anticipation of the *vers libres* of modern affectation, with
no regular metre, unrhymed, and rendered difficult to us, probably
also to the contemporaries of the writer, by the use of peculiar
words, often artificially modified. The form in which the MSS.
present this poem to us is rendered obscure—it may not unfairly
be added, repulsive—by enormously long annotations interspersed through the text. All these impertinences, most of them
useless fatuities, have to be suppressed, in order to get some idea
of the composition itself. When we do this, and write out a translation of the text (or some approximation thereto) continuously,
the source of inspiration becomes obvious. Here is the preface
and the first strophe of the poem:

> God, God, I would make prayer to Him
>> Before I go into His presence, a chariot through battle.
> May the God of heaven leave me not,
>> Where there is lamentation for abundance of suffering.
> May the great God be my protection
>> from the abundance of fire and long tearfulness.
> God the righteous, who is ever near,
>> from the cloud-land of Heaven heareth my crying!

¶Not without tidings is the house of Niall,
    not from one plain only is great sorrow, great outcry.
The story cannot be borne, that Colum is not!
    That he hath no church!
Could a fool tell of him?
    Could even Nera?
The prophet of God hath set him down on the south of Zion;
    But now he lives not, none remaineth with us.
Our teacher is no profit for our souls, for he hath gone from us;
    He who protected life hath died.
For he who was for us prince of the poor hath died,
    He who was for us mediator with God hath died.
The man of knowledge who warded off our fears is not:
    The preacher of truth is not.
He who taught the peoples of the Tay is not.
The whole world was his, and is now a harp without soundboard,
    A church without abbot.

and we have only to read them to see that the Davidic Psalms
have supplied the model to the poet. There is, throughout, the
parallelism which is the essential element in Hebrew poetry, and
we observe the absence of regular metrical rhythm which is un-
avoidable in a 'prose' translation of the Psalms into Latin or any
other language. Even in phraseology there are Davidic reminiscences. The first words can hardly be dissociated from *Deus
Deus meus* at the beginning of Ps. xxii (=Vulgate xxi). Perhaps
it is not too far-fetched to see in the lines—

| Co india dui do | How should a fool tell of him? |
| sceo Nera | Even Nera? |

—a vague reminiscence of another Davidic fragment,

Nequaquam ut mori solent ignaui
Mortuus est Ab-ner

(II Sam. [=II Reg.] iii. 33). However that may be, we need say
no more about Hisperic Irish at the moment, except that even
in the short extract here printed there are many hard words, and
the whole composition is evidently the work of a man of learning,
who, in the words of the legal gloss already quoted, is engaged in
the congenial task of drowning everyone small, light, or weak.

We therefore turn to the sister jargon, 'Hisperic Latin' (or as
we may call it briefly, Hisperic), which for the purposes of our
present study is by far the more important of the two.

Our main source of information on this remarkable invention

is a document, or rather a group of documents, called *Hisperica Famina*: a title which, in humble emulation of its own style, we might render 'Occidental Talkitudes'. In its contents it unconsciously draws for us just such a picture as we have imagined —a group of impostors, clinging like grim death to their one-eyed kingship.

It is to be counted a heavy tragedy of scholarship that Henry Bradshaw's sudden death prevented those who came after him from enjoying the fruits of his colossal learning: a vast store of unrecorded knowledge was buried in his grave. Among the losses that must thus be deplored was the result of his labours upon *Hisperica Famina*, which had occupied his attention for several years; he was cut off just when he was about to begin to set down the discoveries which he had made, for the elucidation of these forbidding texts. We have to do what we can with it, unaided by the light which his work could have cast upon it.

The style of *Hisperica Famina* bears a certain resemblance to some of the parodies of *Euphues*: there is certainly more of Sir Piercie Shafton in it than of Lyly himself, who when all is said and done is a writer of considerable charm, if taken in judiciously small doses. A closer though a more modern analogy is, however, available. These days of ours have seen the rise of a school of writers, whom the reader can readily name for himself, for they have earned their full share of advertisement. I have no title to speak critically or otherwise of them: I have to read so many books on subjects that I can understand, that I have no time to spare over books that I cannot understand, especially as I have no consuming ambition to succeed in doing so. My knowledge of these works is therefore limited to the chance extracts from them which I have come across from time to time in the periodical press. If I may generalize from these fragmentary data, their language is fundamentally English: but the sense, if any, is placed beyond the reach of ordinary persons by anarchic neologisms of idiom, accidence, and vocabulary; by artificial deformations of words, and violent wrestings of their orthodox meanings; by an occasional admixture of French (sometimes of Stratford-atte-Bow, or of an unknown variety even more remote from the Parisian standard); and by interspersed combinations of letters, not always pronounceable, and to me, at least, unintelligible. I am quite ready to admit the possibility that these writers may have grounds for self-congratulation, hidden from my undiscerning eyes. Critics tell me so, and in matters so far outside my competence I must believe what I am told. But originality is not to be reckoned among these assets.[1] Every one of the vagaries above enumerated was anticipated twelve or thirteen hundred years ago by the authors of *Hisperica Famina*: the only novelty which has been introduced into the modern antitype is an occasional affectation of moral irresponsibility. The language of *Hisperica Famina* is fundamentally Latin: but the sense is often rendered at least elusive by anarchic neologisms of idiom, accidence, and vocabulary; by artificial deformations of words, and violent wrestings of their orthodox meanings; and by an occasional admixture of doubtful Greek, along with a faint suggestion of Hebrew, and a little unrecognizable gibberish. If those who contrived this jargon were able to speak it with any fluency, they would have puzzled any ordinary Latinist, at least as completely as the disputing judges puzzled king Conchobor. And this is precisely the effect at which they were aiming; in certain circles, by the practice of this accomplishment, they no doubt obtained a reputation for erudition far in advance of their deserts.

Only one complete manuscript of *Hisperica Famina*, now in the Vatican library, has come down to us. The text was first printed by Cardinal Mai,[2] with some inaccuracies: it was reprinted by Migne.[3] Henry Bradshaw worked long over it, but unfortunately the fruits of his researches were never fully recorded, and they are now lost beyond recovery. The few sheaves of the harvest which it was possible to garner were put forth in 1908 by F. J. H. Jenkinson, one of Bradshaw's successors as University Librarian at Cambridge. This publication contains a complete edition of the text and of some related documents, which is useful and on the whole very accurate.[4] But it gives the impression of being the work of a scholar saddled with an ungrateful task, which he carries through conscientiously, but is anxious to be rid of as soon as possible. In 1887, the year after Bradshaw's death, an earlier edition

[1] Even the ingenious mechanical device of enhancing literary effect by printing personal and geographical names with a lower-case initial instead of the orthodox capital is not original: I did it myself, in a dame-school, at the age of eight, and got 'kept in' in consequence; had I been born about fifty years later, I might have been rewarded with a whole holiday. Perhaps.

[2] *Auctores Classici*, vol. v, p. 479.

[3] *Patrologia*, vol. xc, col. 1185.

[4] I have checked it by a collation of the two poems *Rubisca* and *Adelphus Adelpha* with the Cambridge MS., and found very little to modify.

had appeared under the care of J. M. Stohwasser.[1] This seems to have been quite independent of any work that Bradshaw had done upon the text.

Mai, Migne, and Stohwasser printed the text as prose. Bradshaw came to the conclusion that it was quasi-metrical, and his arrangement of the text in this form, with a few trifling modifications, is set forth in Jenkinson's edition. There is no syllabic regularity: there may be as many as twenty-six syllables, or as few as seven, in one of Bradshaw's lines. The only formal device is a caesura dividing each line (at no definite place), and a rhyme between the caesura and the end of the line.

With all the reverence due to the memory of Henry Bradshaw, I cannot believe that these caesural rhymes are intentional. Without exception they are produced automatically, by the concord of substantive and adjective. One of the stock literary devices of the author (more properly the authors) is to replace a simple, normal substantive by an adjective (often a factitious adjective formed from the rejected substantive) coupled with some other, far-fetched or out-of-the-way substantive: as in the first line, where *pectoralis caverna* means nothing more than *pectus*. Such combinations in most cases rhyme automatically in their declensional terminations: and the frequency of the caesural rhyme is due to nothing more than the frequency with which the authors use these periphrases. That the rhymes are not intentional is, I think, proved by the following facts:

(1) Some of the rhymes are untrue, and would be rejected by an ear disciplined to Celtic assonances (as in line 1, *pectoral*EM *cauern*AM).

(2) Some of them are obtained by scarcely legitimate means, as when Jenkinson prints line 21 thus:

Cui: que adheretis rhetori

dividing *cuique* (the dative of *quisque*) in a way in any case improbable and, as the facsimile reproduced in his edition shews, not sanctioned by the MS.

(3) When a line does not happen to contain an adjective-substantive combination, the caesural rhyme is almost always absent.

---

[1] *Dreizehnte Jahresbericht über das k.-k. Franz-Josef Gymnasium* (Wien, 1887).

(4) There is sometimes ño caesural rhyme even when the adjective-substantive combination is present: as in *dexterali*... *iduma* in line 543.

In any case the suggestion made by Jenkinson that the Hisperic 'metre' had anything to do with the development of leonine hexameters is altogether beside the mark. However, though we reject the rhymes, we must retain the detached sentences, which are essential to the form of the composition. As in Dallan Forgaill's poem, already quoted, the text is in construction based upon, almost a parody of, the Psalter. It is curious that Roger, who has observed the characteristic parallelism, has missed its dependence upon biblical Hebrew poetic forms.

The text begins by shewing us a teacher glorying in his scholarship: vaunting himself in a way that would put Iagoo and all the other 'great boasters' of history and legend to the blush. Next he administers a snub to a countryman who has come to be taught learning: let him mind his own business and return to his sheep, says the master in effect, though expressing himself with bewildering circumlocutions—displaying a spirit of exclusivism truly druidic, and altogether antithetic to Christian universality.

A series of short essays follows: and though it is impossible to point to any definite indications, they leave the impression of being the work of different hands. Subtle differences in the choice and use of words may be detected. It seems most likely that we have to deal with something analogous to the 'golden book' of the Classical side of a school of to-day—a book for entering such compositions in prose or verse written by the students as are judged to be of outstanding merit. The essays are on just such subjects as a teacher would set: the adventures of a day: the four elements, fire, water, earth, air: the furniture of the schoolroom, a bookcase and a writing tablet: an oratory: and 'something that happened'—in other words, a story, to be narrated by the pupil in this jargon speech.

The true nature of these literary ineptitudes is revealed by the apologies for not making the essays longer, the exaggerated deference shewn to the teacher, the 'no time to finish' formula of examinees in every generation. We must infer that self-expression in this queer artificial language was actually made a subject of serious study: and that the students were required to set down

their inspirations within a space of time defined by the turn of
the hourglass, the shadow on the dial, or the dropping of the
clepsydra.

The sense of the essays is perfectly simple—so simple that it
hardly rewards the labour of digging it out. The syntax also is
of the simplest—not any more complex than in the detached
sentences about Balbus in the earlier exercises of *Henry's First
Latin Book*, and perhaps equally exhilarating. Subject-verb-
object is the model of almost all: there are only a few cases of
subordination of sentences, of interrogatives, or of other exceptional constructions. The *ordo uerborum* shews a certain balance:
the verb generally stands as a pivot in the middle of the sentence,
and the subject with its adjective, the object with its adjective,
range themselves about it, as in the first sentence:

Ampla pectoralem SUSCITAT vernia cauernam

But though sense and syntax may be simple, the vocabulary
is little short of diabolical. It is primarily Latin—a hotch-potch
of classical, colloquial, and ecclesiastical vocables, used either in
their orthodox form or distorted in one way or another, morpho-
logically or semantically. New derivatives are invented—as when
famen, plural *famina*, is constructed from *fari* on the analogy of
such a word as *flamen*. The enthusiasm of the author for periphrastic expressions of the form adjective+substantive leads, as
we have already said, to the invention of a large number of new
adjectival forms. Other words are inflated by the addition of
meaningless syllables. Greek, and a few Hebrew, words are pressed
into the service, as well as some unrecognizable forms. These may
be either factitious inventions, or may perhaps be corruptions
due to the scribes who have transmitted the text.

Now, it is of the essence of a secret language to confine itself
to a disguised *vocabulary*. There is seldom, if ever, any declensional or syntactic idiosyncrasy in slang, argot, or artificial speeches
generally. The speaker uses his mother tongue as the framework
of his utterances, and merely varies the verbal bricks with which
he constructs them. This is what we see in Hisperic. The accidence
and the syntax are ordinary Latin, but the words are different.
As to the place where it originated, the students in their rambles
are entertained by *Scottigeni*, that is by Irish, with whom they

may not converse in their vernacular, owing to the monastic rules which impose Latin (or Hisperic?) upon them. The most likely place for Irish-speaking Irish is Ireland, and we may therefore presume that it is an Irish invention. That some of the words are glossed in the MSS. in Breton, not Irish, does not count against this conclusion; rather does it favour it, as it is more common for foreigners to gloss a language than for its native speakers.

Hisperic words appear in the hymn *Altus Prosator*, which is very confidently attributed to Colum Cille († 597); and this indicates a sixth-century date, at latest, for the use and development of the jargon. Such a date is *a priori* the most probable. Christianity entered the British Islands and brought with itself, of necessity, an impulse to learning: Christianity is what Orientals call the religion of a book, and that book, in the form in which it was accessible, was written in languages foreign to the inhabitants of the islands—Latin or Greek. Some Latin and Greek must therefore have entered the islands with Christianity. The Briton (?) Pelagius and his Irish colleague Caelestius, in the fourth century, had very considerable learning at their command: we do not know where they acquired it, but the fact shews that in their time natives of Great Britain and Ireland were not debarred from scholarship if they desired to obtain it.

But after the first efflorescence, the church in the islands seems to have been left to itself. We hear nothing of new influences, except possibly the introduction of the Vulgate in the sixth century. Not till the Irish missionaries began their labours did Irish scholars come into contact with the remnants of Continental scholarship, such as they were. In the fossilizing of learning produced by such stagnation, the development of affectations like Hisperic is only to be expected—especially if there were a lingering trace of druidic occultism surviving to set the example. Scholarship, as distinguished from charlatanism, did not obtain a new lease of life till Gaulish scholars introduced Greek to the Anglo-Saxons, who had become established in Great Britain, and through whom Erigena appears to have acquired his profound learning.

Hisperic is removed from being a matter of mere local and transient interest by a curious literary episode, of which it now becomes necessary to speak, and which had far-reaching consequences.

At some time not later than the end of the seventh century—the date is fixed by quotations in Bede and in Aldhelm—and in some place which has been supposed, on grounds entirely unsatisfying, to have been Toulouse, there lived a scholar out of sympathy with the tendencies of his time. We may picture him, a clever, grimly humorous, and slightly eccentric recluse, lovingly fingering his manuscripts of the Classical age of Roman literature, and sadly contrasting them with the pribbles and prabbles of his contemporaries. At last he could no longer refrain, and his wrath poured forth in a Swift-like satire. Unfortunately for himself and, as it turned out, for the world, he gave his book the jocular name *The Epitomes of Publius Virgilius Maro*: it is as though the perpetrator of a dreary early Victorian jape called *The Comic English Grammar* had adorned his title page with the words 'by John Milton'. To the *Epitomes* was appended a series of *Epistles* in the same style.

The unknown writer, good easy man, did his best to make the absurd world realize that he was in jest. Like Socrates and his symposiasts in Plato's dialogues; like Mr Spectator with his Club; like Schumann with his portentous *Davidsbündler*; like Mrs Gamp with Mrs Harris and her family; like the excellent Sir Arthur Helps; he surrounded himself with an imaginary company of 'friends in council', whom we are to suppose working in harmony with him. To one of these airy fictions he gave the name 'Galbungus', which alone ought to have been enough to make the fortune of a humorist. These sages, it appears, had written marvellous books, the titles of which read like excerpts from the Academy Library Catalogue of Laputa: but not one of which has left the smallest trace behind, outside the casual references which our author makes to them. In the passage most frequently quoted, he shews us Galbungus and another colleague, Terrentianus, disputing day and night for a fortnight on the question whether the pronoun *ego* can have a vocative case. He affects a Latinity— or as he himself says, twelve different kinds of Latinity—never seen before on the earth, with all manner of spurious words and unheard-of grammatical forms. He discusses prosody, filling his illustrations with absurd false quantities. He teaches his readers how to make cryptograms which no human being could ever decipher, even though he knew the principle upon which they were constructed. He commends Cicero—another of his imaginary friends, not the orator—for inventing abbreviations equally impossible to comprehend. But to enumerate all his antics would involve a translation of the whole book.

It ought to have been obvious that the book is a parody, seasoned with bitterness. Galbungus and Co. are of one stuff with the Trissotins who haunt the salons of *Les Femmes Savantes*: indeed, the world lost much when Molière, who alone could have done it justice, passed from its ken without ever having had his attention drawn to the dispute upon the vocative of *ego*, and its dramatic possibilities. Like the schoolmen, 'Maro's' friends make their appeals to shaky 'authorities'. But, his joke missed fire: in vain did he call his fantastic phraseology 'pleasantries' (*leporia*): he shared the fate of Swift, to whom we have compared him. Swift wrote an appalling description of the travels of one Gulliver, whereby he sought to express his hatred of the world in which he found himself. The world took the book, tore out a few of the more lurid pages, and light-heartedly placed the incoherent remainder upon its nursery bookshelves, side by side with the whimsies of the blameless Lewis Carroll. The old scholar of the seventh century wrote a burlesque on the literary fads of his time. The world blinked owlishly over it—and solemnly accepted it as a serious textbook!

We do not look very hopefully for humour in mediaeval literature. There are a few more or less disreputable *farceurs*, like the MacConglinne of whom we shall hear on a later page. There is the brilliant but graceless Walter Map. And, of course, there is the gigantic and only too successful practical joke of Geoffrey of Monmouth. But otherwise humour seems to have been the special field of that dismalest of organ-grinders' anthropoids, the Court Jester. And so the joke of 'Publius Virgilius Maro' not only failed to come off in his own time, but has done so even to this day: for writers on mediaeval literature keep on taking the poor man seriously, and never resist the temptation of throwing stones at him. Perhaps, after all, he deserves his punishment. His jesting was untimely. Unconsciously he had much to do with the development of scholasticism and the substitution of authority for original research. In a word, he left the trail of Galbungus over the Middle Ages and all their works.[1]

[1] This is not a personal opinion of my own, else would I hardly venture to state it. I shelter myself behind the scholarship of Roger, who regards Maro as one of the developers of scholasticism and authoritativism. I disagree, however, with him for taking Maro seriously, as a Gallo-Roman or Barbarian who had acquired some rudimentary notions of grammar and of exotic words and who made up for his scholastic deficiency by his pretentious affectations. Rather is he to be compared to Archbishop Whately,

But now comes an interesting point. Kuno Meyer has examined philologically the names of Maro's fictitious companions: and he concludes that they have a strong Celtic element, if they are not actually Irish. Zimmer identifies Maro himself with an enigmatical Irish writer, who bears the name Fer Ceirtne. This identification is risky, to say the least: but there seems no reason to doubt that Maro had his eye on Ireland when he penned his satire. If we admit this, we must suppose that *Hisperica Famina* was the object of his attack. The sentence in *Hisperica Famina*, *Bis senos exploro vechros*, was once thought to refer to Maro's twelve kinds of Latinity. This has been shewn to be inadmissible: but we cannot overlook the possibility that Maro's twelve Latinities were suggested by the *bis senos vechros* of *Hisperica Famina*. In short, Galbungus and the rest are the first 'stage Irishmen' in literature: all the Micky Frees and Handy Andies are of their kin.

Maro's alleged connexion with Toulouse seems to have been inferred from a misunderstanding of his words 'Bigerro sermone clefabo'. The true meaning of this sentence is illustrated by the pleasing anecdote recorded by Prof. Jespersen in that delightful book *Language, its Development and Origin* (p. 148). The author's five-year-old son uttered some meaningless words, saying that they were 'English'. 'It is not English', said the father: 'I understand English, and I cannot understand that.' 'Do you know all languages, father?' 'No, there are many that I do not know.' 'Do you know Japanese?' 'No.' 'Good; then if I say anything you do not understand, you will know that it is Japanese.' In like manner an old native of Sligo, one of the rapidly diminishing company who have a knowledge of Irish as a birthright, said to a friend of mine: 'They do be teachin' what they call Irish in the schools now: but sure it isn't Irish at all: it's Welsh!' Of course he knew no Welsh, and of course Master Jespersen knew no Japanese: they simply meant what the old play calls 'a thing no fellow can understand'. And Maro's sentence, in like manner, means: 'This language isn't Latin at all: it's Basque'—probably the first reference in literature to the proverbial obscurity of that strange speech. But it is improbable that he knew a single word of Basque.

who, to parody the polemics of anti-religious writers, wrote an essay which professed to prove the non-existence of Napoleon. It is no more reasonable to take Maro's book as a serious index of its author's scholarship than it would be to take Whately's *jeu d'esprit* as a serious index of its author's sanity.

Roger sums up his severe criticism of Maro in these words: *Quand on songe qu'il est le seul théoricien gaulois du 6ᵉ ou 7ᵉ siècle qui ait été jugé digne d'être conservé, on touche forcément à la stérilité d'une époque aussi pauvrement représentée.* This sounds like a fair judgement, not on Maro but on his world. We must not, however, overlook the possibility that *some* of Maro's contemporaries and successors actually saw the joke! Human nature changes little during the centuries: and there can be no question that Maro's lively irresponsibilities provide more fun for scribes and students than the *pulvis et umbra* of those Dismal Jemmies, Priscian and Martianus Capella.

In one country Maro certainly was taken seriously; namely Ireland, the country which he parodied. To that one country seems to be due his preservation, for the MSS. of his work are apparently of Irish origin. Never did satirist earn a greater compliment: never was there a more humorous literary situation. Certain scholars in Ireland developed a vicious literary style. Maro wrote a parody of that literary style. And the scholars of Ireland adopted the parody as a grammatical explanation of their own style. It is like the Phoenician navigator who succeeded in voyaging to Scotland, according to a once popular lady novelist (if my memory does not err), by blowing the sails of his own ship with a pair of bellows.

The conditions which led to this extraordinary development were very simple. Hisperic Irish and Hisperic Latin were twins, starting in the same cradle. The peculiarities of one were the same as those of the other, differing only in the essential differences between the fundamental languages on which they were based. The artificial devices of the one were reproduced in the other. Maro made the Latin twin a butt: *mutatis mutandis* what he said was equally applicable to the Irish twin.

In a later generation, when the Hisperic craze was dying down, the compositions of Dallan Forgaill and his kind were sadly puzzling the learned. They could make little or nothing of them: and Maro came like a blaze of revelation. Poor souls, we can almost hear them contrast, like so many another self-deluded victim of bewilderment, their former blindness with their present sight. And so they took Maro to their hearts, and with his impish help they wrote their portentous commentaries on Dallan Forgaill, explaining his eccentricities by the mockery of those eccentricities: and, mixing Maro and Isidore into an incongruous and indigestible pie, they compiled the solemn monument of grammatical but mis-directed learning called *The Scholar's Primer*. And generations of scholars glossed it, and glossed it, and glossed it again, till it assumed a shape out of which it would pass the wit of an Aristotle to extract any coherent sense or meaning. The effect was disastrous. Pedantry and grandiloquence usurped the place of learning: and this sort of thing came into being, and is hardly dead yet:

'The Irish Antiquaries have preserved this Ogham in par-ticular as a pice (*sic*) of the greatest value in all their Antiquity and it was penal for any but those that were sworn Antquaries (*sic*) either to study or use the same Form [*read* From] those characters those sworn Antquaries (*sic*) wrote all the evil actions of their Kings and other vicious practions (*sic*) of their Monarchs and great personages both male and female that it should not be known to any but to themselves and their successors being sworn Antiquaries as aforesaid.'[1]

POSTSCRIPT. In *Studies in Early Irish Law*, a symposium recently published by the Royal Irish Academy, it is suggested that the Life of Find-Chua (p. 68 *ante*) is a goliardic parody of this type of literature. Quite possibly: but if so, it is one more joke which has missed fire, for it is preserved in a compilation certainly intended for edification. It must therefore be judged by its fruits rather than by its intentions.

The influence of an intensive study of the Psalms on some phases of Irish literature can be illustrated by a curious parallel. One Robert Walker, beadle of a Reformed Presbyterian Church in Glasgow (1813–1864), kept a record of the history of the con-gregation during his time. Apparently this good man never read anything but the Authorized version of the Bible, and he wrote in its idiom with a natural fluency far beyond the possibilities of mere parody.[2]

On the probable indebtedness of Erigena to Saxon teachers, see Roger *op. cit.* p. 206, also pp. 268 ff.

[1] From McCurtin's English-Irish Dictionary: I quote, not from the printed text, but from an eighteenth-century MS. transcript in my posses-sion, which no doubt brought much comfort and edification to its original owner.

[2] Extracts from this literary curiosity will be found in T. Binnie, *Sketch of the History of the First Reformed Presbyterian Congregation* (Paisley, Parlane, 1888), pp. 192 ff.

CHAPTER IV

BOG-LATIN

The volume class-marked H 2 15 in the library of Trinity College, Dublin, is, or rather was, an unwieldy collection of waifs and strays—fragments of books most of which Time had devoured— bound together in a *rudis indigestaque moles*. In February 1898 the collection was divided into two much more convenient parts.

One leaf in this miscellany, formerly pp. 116–17, now pp. 41–2 of the second part, is a sheet of paper with writing from the hand of the well-known Irish historian Dubhaltach mac Fir Bisigh (Duald mac Firbis, 1585–1670). Its contents consist of a vocabulary of factitious words, with a signification in Irish attached to each, arranged in four columns, two on each page. At the top of the first page is the heading, *Dūil*[1] *Laithne and so sios* ' A Book of Latin here below': at the bottom of the fourth column is the signature, in this form:

> *Finit. Dubaltach Fir Bisigh*
> *adomcomhnuic*
> *1643 5° maij*
> *Baile M^c[Aodhagāin]*
> *mo [locc]*

'It endeth. Dubhaltach Fir Bisigh am I: 1643, 5th May. Baile Mic Aodhagāin (=Ballymacegan, Co. Tipperary) is my place.'

The two words printed above in square brackets were apparently to be seen when Whitley Stokes made his transcript, over sixty years ago; but since then they have been torn from the leaf. Whitley Stokes published the text of the vocabulary, with an introduction and notes, and with a translation into Latin of the Irish explanations, in the second edition of his *Goidelica*.[2] Later, the pages were reproduced in facsimile, but on a scale rather too small for pleasant reading, in the *Journal* of the Gypsy Lore Society, Series II, vol. ii (1908–9), pp. 244–5. (The original leaf measures 11¾ by 7³⁄₁₀ inches.) I have collated Stokes's edition

---

[1] Throughout this book long vowels will be marked with a horizontal stroke, instead of the conventional but misleading 'acute accent'.

[2] Published in 1872: pp. 71–83.

with the MS., and have found it almost completely accurate: the
only serious error (*gath* for *gaoth*, no. 283) had already been
observed by Kuno Meyer.[1] But there are one or two trifling
misprints as well: and here and there Stokes has endeavoured to
remodel the MS. forms in accordance with Middle Irish spelling.
Thus for no. 15, *tionnor*, he prints *tinnor*, giving the MS. form in
a footnote. It is doubtful whether it is desirable thus to stan-
dardize an irresponsible jargon: in the present edition I have set
forth the words (as well as the Irish explanations, which are very
unsystematically spelt, and hardly ever shew the mark of vowel-
prolongation) exactly as they appear in the MS. An exception
is made in the case of the symbol 'vi', which Stokes prints in
that form: but as it clearly has everywhere the signification 'ui',
which it possesses universally in Irish MSS., it would seem misleading to retain the 'v'.

Dūil Laithne is the name of the 'book', not of the jargon to
which it introduces us. As a name for the latter, I have ventured
to adopt the expression 'Bog-Latin', a common derisive term
for 'gibberish' in Ireland, in order to distinguish it from ordinary
Latin.

When I examined the MS., I was surprised to find a number of
additional words, which both Stokes and Meyer had unaccount-
ably overlooked, beneath the signature. They are here printed
for the first time. As in Stokes's edition, the words are numbered
for convenience of reference. In the manuscript, the vocabulary
is expressed throughout by the formula 'Dairtinne .i. [=*id est*]
duine. Troicit .i. corp', and so forth. The words are not in 'list'
form, one beneath the other: and needless to say no reference
numbers are used.

Stokes identified some of the words as genuine old or obsolete
words, recorded by the ninth–tenth century glossator Cormac mac
Cuillennāin. Others he saw to be deformations of their Irish
equivalents. But in many of his attempts at explaining these, he
went astray, because he missed the clue detected and published
by Professor Thurneysen, fourteen years afterwards.[2] The principle is, that *for certain letters in the word, the name of the letter in
the Irish or Ogham alphabet is substituted*. [The names of the
letters are the tree-names, already referred to, *ante*, p. 41.] It is
as though a Greek, wishing for some reason to refer cryptically

---

[1] *Journal*, G.L.S. ii, ii, p. 245.
[2] 'Du langage secret dit Ogham', *Revue Celtique*, vol. vii (1886), p. 169.

to a person called Iasōn, should call him 'Iōt'alphasōn': it is the converse of our expression 'Figure-of-8' or of the schoolboy joke 'Qcumbers Wup'. This key unlocks many, perhaps most, of the riddles; but, as we shall see, it is not applicable to all of them.[1]

While there can be no doubt that Professor Thurneysen has found the principle of the construction of much of the Bog-Latin vocabulary, his identification thereof with the 'Ogham' of Morish O'Gibellan is open to question—though not, perhaps, to the severe rebuke which it received from the pen of Mr H. F. Berry.[2] The very sound conclusion of Professor Thurneysen's paper—*que la connaissance de ce jargon ait été jugée une qualité digne d'être mentionnée dans les annales, cela ne parle pas trop en faveur de la culture intellectuelle de l'Irelande au moyen âge*—is a good argument against the identification suggested. Bog-Latin is too naïve to have been taken seriously, even in the Middle Ages. A little consideration of the classes into which we can group the words chosen for deformation leads to the inference that this is no scholars' vocabulary; it is of the earth, earthy. Parts of the body, garments, utensils, human occupations, cooking vessels, food, music, animals, metals, a few natural geographical features, colours, points of the compass, some commonplace verbs, relationships, numerals—these are what interested those who contrived it. It resembles the freak of a pack of schoolboys more than anything else: and the same explanation is indicated by some touches of coarseness, such as the unpleasant rendering of 'flesh-meat' by a word which means 'maggot'. I regret to learn, from a schoolgirl relative, of a modern analogy even less agreeable, current among her associates—the term 'dead baby' applied to a suet dumpling!

Besides, if this were really 'the speech called Ogham', it would be so called in the MS., and not ridiculously labelled 'Latin'.

We can never expect to interpret all these words: nor can it be hoped that all the suggestions given below are successful 'hits'. Many of the words may have owed their origin to some combination of circumstances, now utterly irrecoverable. Here again an instructive modern analogy is at hand. Probably every family, even of moderate size, has a more or less extensive vocabulary of

[1] The cypher called *Ogam romesc Bres* (*ante*, p. 46) differs in degree: there apparently *every letter* of the concealed words is spelt out one by one. In Bog-Latin, only one or two letters of each word are called by their names.

[2] *Journal*, Royal Society of Antiquaries of Ireland, vol. xxxii (1902), pp. 158 ff.

current words and phrases, the sources of which may have been forgotten—may even never have been known to the junior members—but which are quite comprehensible in the household, though totally unintelligible outside. How could any non-initiate guess that 'to sing the hundredth psalm' meant 'to fetch a glass of water'—as it does in a family known to me? If he be admitted to the domestic arcana so far as to learn the phrase and its meaning, how could he guess the nexus between the two ideas—a chance remark made upon a midsummer day, that to allow the heated water to run off from the cold-water tap took about as long a time as it would take to perform the act of piety specified? For all we know, the links between some of these Bog-Latin words and their meanings may be just as fantastically casual.

Meaningless words, and proper names, are notoriously liable to corruption in the course of scribal transmission. This vocabulary has certainly suffered at the hands of its copyists. In a few cases it is possible to suggest emendations, more or less certain; but we cannot legitimately assume that a word is necessarily corrupt because we are unable to explain it. Corruption is probably indicated by the many forms in which some of the Ogham names appear: the copyists failed to recognize them, embedded in the different words, and transcribed them in a haphazard fashion.

The most probable date for the vocabulary is some time in the latter part of the fifteenth century. This is not rendered impossibly late by the presence of ancient words recorded by Cormac: a copy of his glossary may have been accessible to, and utilized by, the inventors of the jargon. We should wander in a sad maze of error, in criticizing undated English compositions, if we were invariably to accept the chronological indications of words like 'methinks', 'yclept', 'albeit' and so forth, at their face value!

In Stokes's edition of O'Donovan's translation of Cormac's *Glossary*, he made the tentative suggestion that some of these hard words may be of Pictish origin. This is possible, and would be extremely interesting if it could be proved. Every scrap of that lost language is welcome. But it is only a possibility at best, and in any case leads us nowhere. To try to explain anything on earth with the help of Pictish is as futile as to try to illuminate crepuscular shadows by means of the blackness of Tartarus.

Of special interest are the words which Bog-Latin and Shelta have in common: of equal interest are the abrupt contrasts between the two languages. Consideration of these points must necessarily be postponed till the Shelta material has been laid before the reader.[1]

What of the grammar of Bog-Latin, its accidence and its syntax? The chief indications are contained in the two sentences, nos. 194, 195:

loisiom ar collait 'let us eat our portion'.

edmam ar ndoib 'let us drink our draught'.

Here *ār* (as it should be written) is the ordinary Irish word for 'our'. It produces nasalization (or 'eclipsis') of the initial consonant of the following word: hence the spelling *ndoib*; *doib* means 'drink', according to no. 82. *Collait* should certainly be written *ccollait* or *gcollait* for the same reason: the unaffected form used here is doubtless a scribal error. The important point is, however, that if we were allowed to assume verbal stems *lois-*, *edm-*, meaning respectively 'to eat' and 'to drink', and a substantive *collait*, meaning 'a portion of food', then the above sentences would be straightforward Irish for the meanings alleged. This leads us to conclude that, so far as the evidence goes, speakers of Bog-Latin used a framework of ordinary Irish accidence, and did no more than substitute their jargon vocabulary for the orthodox Irish words. And that the Bog-Latin syntax was also essentially Irish is indicated by the presence of a number of equivalents for that very characteristic Irish formation, the preposition-pronoun compound; which exercises numerous syntactic functions in the Irish language. In this respect, therefore, Bog-Latin is exactly analogous to Hisperic (see *ante*, p. 82).

Professor Thurneysen has indicated the following rules of construction: others are added below as the result of the present analysis. [It may be said, once for all, that the Ogham names are henceforth printed in small CAPITALS, Bog-Latin words in heavy-faced **type**, Irish and Shelta words in *italics* (the latter *leaded*), English translations in 'inverted commas'.]

(1) One or more letters in each word are replaced by the name of the letter in the Ogham alphabet. Thus *dūn* becomes DAUR-**un**.

(2) These names are often turned into adjectives, by the use of the ordinary adjectival formative *-ch*, *-ach*, *-ech*: thus *tair* becomes TINNE-CH-**air**. The *ch* is frequently de-aspirated: thus *medg* becomes MUIN-C-**edg**.

(3) Vowels are sometimes omitted: thus *mac* becomes MUIN-COLL.

[1] In the Bog-Latin vocabulary, the few Shelta words quoted are distinguished by being *leaded*.

(4) Consonants also are omitted, especially when they exist in the name of the letter 'oghamized': thus *cuile* becomes COLL-ue, not COLL-*uile*. Sometimes they are omitted when this reason does not exist, as when *merdrech* becomes MUIN-drech, not MUIN-er-drech.

The following is a list of all the Ogham letter-names used; for convenience we call the substitution of the Ogham name 'oghamizing': with the adjective termination, 'oghamizing adjectivally'. In this list, the correct forms are printed first, in capital letters: varieties follow, in italics. Those in square brackets are not found in the vocabulary.

B	BEITH, *beth, bet, bed*	NG	[GETAL], *goithial, goith,*
L	LUIS, *lois, los, les, lus, losc,*		*geitheil*
	leisc, loisg, loisc	Z	[STRAIF]
F	FERN	R	RUIS, *rois, ros, rus, roisc, rosc*
S	SAIL	A	AILM, *eilm*
N	NÍN, *niam* (?), *nann* (?), *nion*	O	ONN, *oind, ond, an, oinc*
H	[HUATH], *cuith, caith*	U	UIR, *ur*
D	DAIR, *daur, der, dur*	E	EDAD, *eo*
T	TINNE, *tionn, thini*	I	[IDAD] *iodad-m > iodamm*[1]
C	COLL, *cuill, cul, caill*	EA	[EBAD]
Q	[QUEIRT], *cert, cirt*	OI	[OIR]
M	MUIN, *man, mun, main,*	UI	[UILLENN]
	muinc, minc	IA	[IPHIN]
G	GORT, *gart*	AE	[EMHANCOLL] *amloic*

DŬIL LAITHNE AND SO SIOS

1. **Dairtinne** *duine* 'person', DAIR-TINNE = 'D.T.' This is one of a number of words having what we may call 'elemental' meanings, which are represented by their initial letters, oghamized. Thus 17 LUIS = *l(āmh)* 'hand': 60 FERN = *f(er)* 'man': 66*c* DAUR = *D(ia)* 'God': 136 UR = *u(lc)*, properly *olc* 'bad': 140*b* TINNE = *t(alamh)* 'earth'. In this particular case the simple initial could not be used, as that was already pre-empted by DAUR ('God'). The inventors therefore added their word TINNE 'earth' for defining purposes, so that the significance of the word is 'the god of earth'.

2. **Troicit** *corp* 'body'. This seems to be a genuine old word. Cormac offers one of his guesswork etymologies of the word *fothrucud* 'washing' as *trochit* 'a body', *fo* 'under' [water]. Quoted by Stokes: the word is by him connected with Latin *truncus*.

---

[1] See no. 92 for the explanation of this.

3. **Muinbuid** *menma* 'mind'. MUIN is the oghamized initial: the word is formed in the same way as 37 *a* DUR-**buid**=*dealg* 'pin', and more doubtfully 155 TIN-**buid**=*erges* 'which ariseth'. The termination is arbitrary, so far as I can see.

4. **Cud** *ceann* 'head'. A genuine word: see Kuno Meyer, *Contributions to Irish Lexicography*, under *Caut, Cod, Cud*.

5. **Fualasg** *folt* 'hair'. Stokes prints **fualasc**, and compares a word *fualascach*, glossing '*arbusta*' in the St John's College Psalter (*Goidelica*,[2] p. 60). But there can be little doubt that it is a jargon word, cognate with the Shelta *balast*.

6 *a*. **Eochaille** *einech* 'face'. Conceivably this difficult word was evolved thus. EDAD is the oghamized initial: this word means 'yew'. Another word for 'yew' is *eō*: but as this also means 'salmon', a defining word *chaille*, meaning 'of a forest', is added.

6 *b*. **Aga** (same meaning). An apocopated form of the common word *agaid* 'face'.

7. **Sabar** *suil* 'eye'. One of several words formed by substituting the syllable **bar**, or something like it, for the termination. Such are 8 **sro-pur**=*srōn* 'nose': 16 **cu-far**=*cos* 'foot, leg': 131 **ar-bar**=*argad* 'silver': 135 *b* **ma-bar**=*mōr* 'great': 147 *b* **li-ber**=*ler* 'sea'. Compare the modern public-school or university slang *brekker, bedder, footer*, for 'breakfast', 'bed-maker', 'football', *et multa similia*: these are absolutely analogous.

8. **Sropur** *sron* 'nose'. See foregoing article.

9. **Beilflesg** *bel* 'mouth'. This is a kind of kenning, the literal meaning of which is 'mouth-switch'. Conceivably there is a reference to the *flesg* or rod which is the stem-line upon which Ogham letters are formed.

10. **Feirchinn** *fiacail* 'tooth'. Originally another kenning, *fer cinn* 'man of a head', clearly a sort of punning corruption of the Irish word; but corrupted by scribes after the meaning had been forgotten.

11. **Ligair** *tenga* 'tongue'. This is another of Cormac's words; he gives it in the form *ligur*.

12. **Groithial** 'g̅íni'. This abbreviation is expanded, by Stokes, *grēini*, and translated, with a query, 'whiskers': apparently thinking of Cormac's *grend*, O'Clery's *grenn* 'beard'. From the neighbouring words we may judge that it denotes some part of the head, but the expansion and the translation are alike doubtful. As for the word itself, the *r* is to be elided: it will then be possible to explain it as a form of GETAL, the name appropriated for the sign of NG; compare 51 GOITHIALL-**ad**=*gad* 'a withe': 64 GEITHIL-**le**=*giolla* 'a boy'.

13. **Baicead** *braige* 'neck'. As Stokes observes, O'Clery's *Glossary* gives *bacad* = 'neck'.

14. **Drogmall** *druim* 'back'. The consonantal skeleton of the Irish word, farced with nonsense syllables, = *dr*-og-*m*-all: compare 85 *sc*-eg-*lan* = *salann*. This is one of the commonest of all devices in forming an artificial speech.

15. **Tionnor** *tōn* 'podex'. This is the Shelta *tūr*, with the initial oghamized: TIONN-or.

16. **Cufar** *cos* 'foot, leg'. See no. 7 above.

17. **Luis** *lamh* 'hand, arm'. The initial oghamized.

18. **Bisi** *mēr* 'finger'. The same word reappears at no. 46 in the sense *deimis* 'shears'. It is apparently the Welsh *bys* 'finger'. A similar word appears in orthodox Irish, but only in the expression *bisi ega* 'an icicle'.

19. **Aicris** *inghin* [finger]-'nail'. Obscure: query, Greek ἐν ἄκροις.

20. **Bethul** *biach* 'penis' ⎱ These words may be taken together.
21. **Losuill** *caull* 'testicle' ⎰ The first word is the oghamized initial (the *first* letter of the Ogham alphabet) + the arbitrary syllable -ul: the second is formed by analogy with the *second* letter of the Ogham alphabet: BETH-ul, LOS-uill. The variations in spelling of the added syllable are due to the scribes. For the formative compare 142 **usguile** [which perhaps should be **usguill**] = *uisge* 'water', and possibly 200 **caill** = *cler* 'cleric'. And for more or less similar doublets of words see nos. 121, 122 and 279, 280.

22. **Goll** *caoch* 'blind'. A perversion of the Irish word *dall* 'blind'.

23. **Coich** *cnaimh* 'bone'. This is perhaps a genuine word, but so far as I am aware it occurs only once, in the tale called *Tāin Bō Cūalnge* (ed. Windisch, p. 371), where we read *for cōich a muineōil*, which would thus appear to mean 'on the bone of his neck'.

24. **Muincedan** *medhōn* 'middle'. Oghamized initial with adjective termination, de-aspirated: MUIN-C-edan.

25. **Slacc** *claideabh* 'sword'. Stokes quotes from O'Reilly's *Irish Dictionary* a word *slacān* 'club', which appears to be a diminutive of this.

26. **Cuitheilm** *cluas* 'ear'. In the MS. we find 'cuitheilm o .i. cluas': but the 'o' is an insertion by a different hand, in different ink. It should be on the other side of the sign .i., for it is really an alternative explanation: *ō* is another word for 'ear' in Irish. It helps to unravel this rather recondite word. **Cuith-eilm** is for HUATH-AILM, which spells *ha*. This is meant for *hō*: an unnecessary *h* prefixed to an initial vowel is a commonplace in Middle Irish; and we shall find several cases of oscillation between *a* and *o* in this vocabulary.

27. **Caithen** *cac* 'excrement'. Here again **caith**=HUATH, and the word spelt is thus *hen*. *En* is an old word for water, made use of by Cormac in his etymology of *mūn* 'urine'. The association of ideas need not be emphasized.

28. **Dercuill** *derc* 'eye'. This may be formed with the -uill suffix which we have already seen in nos. 20, 21: but on the whole it is more probably a corruption of DUR-COLL (oghamized *d–c*, the initial and final).

29. **Coimhgeall** *cochall* 'hood'. Apparently nothing more than a facetious mispronunciation of the Irish word, on the level of the Cockney's *picture-skew* for 'picturesque'.

30. **Brael** *brat* 'mantle'. This looks wrong, and may be corrupt. It is possibly for br-AIL(M), equivalent to the first three letters of the Irish word; but no weight can be attached to this suggestion, and the word must be left doubtful.

31. **Crosar** *ionar* 'tunic'. This perversion seems to be suggested by a common MS. contraction, whereby the cross-like symbol ł represents *in*. For *ion* is thus substituted *crois* 'a cross'.

32. **Luisnech niamnach** *lēne* 'shirt'. **Niamnach** is probably for *nionnach*, the two *n*'s having become differentiated by a natural and frequent process. We should then have LUIS-nech-NION-nech, corresponding to the spelling *L-e-N-e*, the consonants being oghamized. How then does **nech** correspond to *e*? Perhaps arbitrarily: but perhaps because *nech* in Irish means 'person', and *an t-ē* also means 'the person, he who'. By this means a kenning was produced, meaning something like 'shining, sparkling', which would be suitable enough to describe a white linen garment.

33. **Carosar** *corrt(h)ar* 'fringe'. The Irish word is shortened (by a loss of *th*, frequent in the vocabulary) to *corar* and the middle letter is oghamized: ca-ROS-ar.

34a. **Ailmsi** *asan* 'shoe'. Word shortened and initial oghamized: AILM-si = *asi*.

34b. **Oindsi** (same meaning). Same process, with a vowel-shift = ON-si = *osi*.

35. **Deilenn corb** *maolasa* 'sandals'. This seems to be an obscure kenning, literally meaning 'spear of chariots', suggested by some now unknown circumstance.

36. **Crionna** *cris* 'girdle'. An arbitrary substitution, having some analogy with 'rhyming slang'—we may call it 'alliterative slang'—and suggested by *crinna* 'wise'.

37a. **Durbuid** *dealg* 'pin'. See the analogous 3 **muinbuid**.

37b. **Delesg** (same meaning). *De*-LES-g, the *l* oghamized (LES miswritten for LUIS).

38. **Cotan** *laoch* 'hero, warrior'. (1) De-aspirate [**laoc**]: (2) reverse **co-la**: (3) substitute for *lā* ('day') the word which, whatever its origin, reappears in the Shelta *tån*, with the same meaning. The word could have been produced in this way, but that is a different thing from saying that it was so produced! No other suggestion occurs to me, and on the whole it is better to admit that its etymology is obscure.

39 *a*. **Crisgeo** *gaoi* 'javelin'. If we take **geo** as a perversion of *gaoi*, this word would mean 'girdle-javelin': but that is not very intelligible. Another obscurity.

39 *b*. **Goithni** (same meaning). A contraction of GOITHIAL-ni: see no. 12. The termination -ni is also found in 78 **creithne** = *criathar* 'sieve'; 117 *a* **cetaimni** = *cairigh* 'sheep'; 132 **onduenne** = *uma* 'copper'. But see alternative explanations of the two last in their own articles.

40. **Sgillenn** *sgian* 'knife'. Apparently *sgi-n* with the arbitrary **llen** inserted. Compare 108 **pip-len-nan** = *tiompanān* 'tambourine'. Uncertain.

41. **Lethten** *altan* 'razor'. Apparently an arbitrary modification of the Irish word.

42. **Loarn** *loman* 'rope'. Perhaps another modification based upon MS. conventions (like 31 **crosar**, above). *Loman* would be written 'lŏan', and if badly written this would resemble 'lŏan', which would mean **loaran**. It may be that this was an actual mistake in reading committed by some student, and perpetuated in semi-mockery by his fellows: compare 284 **bellit**.

43. **Berrech** *brothrach* 'a bed-cover' (or, 'a rich garment'). This is a contraction of the word, analogous to that in no. 33, where *corrthar* becomes **corar**; but in the present case none of the letters are oghamized. The sound of *th* is very apt to disappear in Bog-Latin.

44. **Gortlomnach** *gemin* 'a fetter'. An adjectival form derived from *loman* 'a rope' (see no. 42, above) with GORT (=*g*) prefixed. This is therefore a case of initial oghamization with a defining adjective added—'the ropey G'.

45. **Betbec** *blath* 'flower'. This should doubtless be BETH-*becc* 'the little B'. Compare 113 **beth-an** 'the noble B' (=*bo* 'cow') and 128 **bed-ban** 'the white B' (=*bradan* 'salmon').

46. **Bisi** *deimis* 'shears'. Doubtless from the finger-like appearance of the tool: see no. 18.

47. **Cremad** *crann* 'tree' (or 'wood', or 'pole'). Apparently another wilful MS. misreading, 'crād' (=*crand*) being read as though 'crad' (=*cr(e)mad*).

48. **Collann** *calg* 'sword'. Clearly like no. 44, an oghamized initial with a defining word added: COLL-(l)ann 'the C of blades'.

49. **Giusalath** *guin* 'wound', or *giuchnad* (a word of uncertain meaning). Obscure. Conceivably a kenning, 'javelin-shield' (compare the modern phrase 'you will stop a bullet'=be shot). For **giu** might=*gaoi* (compare 39a, **cris-geo**) and **salath** may be the same word as is rendered **sebath** in no. 50. But this is mere guesswork, *faute de mieux*.

50. **Sebath** *sgiath* 'shield'. This word looks wrong: it should surely be SAIL(=s)-ath.[1] See preceding article.

51. **Goithiallad** *gad* 'withe'. GOITHIALL (=GETAL)+*ad*.

52a. **Clitach** *cleirech* 'cleric'⎫ Though the Bog-Latin words have
52b. **Cliath** (same meaning)⎭ a general resemblance to their Irish equivalents, their actual formation is obscure; but we may compare 62 **cetech**=*ceallach* 'ecclesiastic' and 200 **caill**=*cler* 'cleric'.

53. **Bethlosach** *bathach* (a rare word, glossing *moribundus* in the Saint-Gall copy of Priscian: see Meyer's *Contributions*, s.v. Thurneysen would emend it to *blathach* 'buttermilk'. There is, however, another word for *blathach* below, no. 100). The word seems to be formed analogously to no. 45, and the other words there quoted—BETH *līach* 'the wretched B', the initial of the adjective being also oghamized (LOS=LUIS=*l*).

54. **Aeile** '*leach*' (query, *leacht* 'a grave', or *leac* 'a stone'). Apparently a sort of anagram; but obscure.

55. **Muindrech** *meirdreach* 'harlot'. Oghamized initial+last syllable: MUIN (=*m*)+*drech*.

56. **Ondach** *aithech* 'tenant'. The first syllable is OND, the oghamized *o*. For the vowel-shift, *o* for *a*, compare 34b, **oindsi**=*asan*.

57. **Eorosnach** *abb* 'abbot'. Apparently a word formed like no. 53: **Eo rosnach**. *Eo* may be meant for the letter *e*, as in no. 6, above: or it may have the meaning 'salmon', used in the figurative sense (as sometimes in poetry) of 'chief, lord'. **Rosnach** will then be an adjective beginning with *r* (ROS=RUIS=*r*): probably *ruithneach* 'brilliant, splendid'.

58. **Roiscith** *ri* 'king'. This is the initial adjectivally oghamized ROIS-C, as in no. 24, plus -ith, a lengthening of the final vowel: **th** is a mere breathing.

[1] It might even conceivably be a blundered version of the Hebrew שֶׁלֶט (šelet) 'a shield'.

59. **Oirthine** *oigthigern*, a word for which the German 'Junker' is perhaps the best available translation. Etymologically it means 'young' (*ōg*), 'lord' (*tigherna*), and is represented by the oghamized initials OIR (=*oi*) TINNE (=*t*).

60. **Fern** *fer* 'man'. See no. 1: initial oghamized.

61. **Biairt** *ben* 'woman'. Compare the Shelta *b'ōr'*.

62. **Cetech** *ceallach* 'hermit, ecclesiastic'. See no. 52, above.

63. **Eongort** *ingen* 'girl, daughter'. Apocopated to *ing*, and the *g* oghamized (GORT). For the vowel-shift *eo* > *i*, compare 69 eonann=*ian*.

64. **Geitheille** *giolla* 'boy, attendant'. GEITHEIL (=GETAL)+*le*. The vowel-shift appears to be arbitrary, or may be the work of copyists. Here and elsewhere GETAL is used instead of GORT, merely for the sake of added complication.

65. **Muincoll** *mac* 'son, boy'. Consonants oghamized, vowel omitted: MUIN-COLL.

66a. **Teo** ⎱ *Dia* 'God'. The *-mudh* in the second of these
66b. **Tiamudh** ⎰ words is presumably *muadh* 'great', so that the two words are practically the same: Teo=Tia. This seems to be merely a wilful mispronunciation of *Dia*.

66c. **Daur** (same meaning). The initial oghamized; see no. 1.

67a. **Tinim** *t(e)ine* 'fire'. The first syllable with *-im* added—an arbitrary suffix. Compare 169 fer-im=*fir* 'true'.

67b. **Fuilgen** (same meaning). An etymology—Latin *fulgens*—which Stokes considers (and rejects) is on the whole the most probable.

68. **Baisi** *dabhach* 'tub'. Obscure, unless from O'Reilly's *baise* 'round'.

69. **Eonann** *ian* 'cup'. Compare 63 eon-gort=*in-g(en)*. The nann is possibly a corruption of NION=*n*.

70. **Coiclenn** *ciolurn* 'pitcher'. It is just conceivable that *ciolurn* was analysed into *c-iolur-n*, the *iolur* equated to *iolar* 'an eagle': that translated into Latin, *aquila*, and c-aquila-n became corrupted in pronunciation or writing to c-oicle-nn. It is the sort of thing these silly boys would do!

71. **Collscoin** *cuirm* 'ale'. COLL (=*c*)+scoi (cf. Shelta *skai* 'water')+arbitrary *n*. But perhaps the -scon is itself an arbitrary suffix: compare 198 sailscon.

72. **Muadailm** *oilldearb* 'large bucket'. *Muadh*-AILM 'large A'. The connexion between this and the signification is, however, obscure, unless the *A* be the initial of *aighen* 'pan, vat' (see no. 79 below).

73. **Coillsge** *cuad* 'wooden cup'. The -sge termination is something like -sgith in 217*a* muin-sgith = *mag* 'plain': but the word is obscure. COILL is presumably COLL = *c*.

74. **Bruinioch** *mias* 'platter'. Perhaps we may equate to *bruinech* 'a ship' (Meyer, *Contributions*).

75. **Boige** *caire* 'pot'. According to Cormac, *bôge* or *boige* was the name of a magical 'cauldron of covetousness'.

76*a*. **Cluipit** *cloch* 'stone'. Perhaps it should be **cluipist**: 122 luipist = *luch* 'a mouse', and so cluipist would be *cluch*. Even so have I heard the children of an Arab gentleman named Barakât facetiously referred to as 'the Barakittens'.

76*b*. **Coparn** (same meaning): c + par (see no. 7) + n (see no. 71).

77. **Scartlann** *scaball* 'kettle'. Obscure. Sca-rt-l seems to correspond to *sca-ba-l*, but the actual connexion cannot be traced.

78. **Creithne** *criathar* 'sieve'. Analogous to the **sabar**-group (no. 7 *ante*): the first part of the Irish word with an arbitrary termination. See 39*b* **goithni**.

79. **Artoichenn** *aighen* 'pan'. Oichenn looks like a perversion of the Irish word, with the favourite *a-o* vowel-shift. The prefixed **art** may be the word *art*, which *inter alia* means 'noble' or 'a chief'. For references see Meyer, *Contributions*.

80. **Loisgestar** *lestar* 'vessel'. Initial oghamized in adjective form = LOISG (= LUISC)-**es**tar.

81. **Anrad** *biad* 'food'. I cannot suggest an explanation, unless it be a wilful mispronunciation of *annlann* 'sauce'.

82. **Doib** *deogh* 'drink'. Apparently a quasi-childish mispronunciation, possibly helped into shape by the verb *do ib* 'he drank'.

83. **Muincir** *mir* 'mouthful'. Initial oghamized in adjective form, MUIN-C-*ir*.

84. **Betroisgenn** *bairgen* 'cake'. BET (= BEITH = *b*) + ROIS (= RUIS = *r*) + *gen*, with the final *n* doubled, perhaps intentionally, or perhaps by a copyist's error.

85. **Sceglan** *salann* 'salt'. For sc- corresponding to an initial s- compare 235 scillber = *siorlaige*. For the formation of the rest of the word, compare no. 14 above, **drogmall** = *druim*.

86. **Anros** *arbar* 'fruit'. Apparently AN (= ONN = *o* = *a*) + ROS (= RUIS = *r*): the first and last letters oghamized, and the form further modified by the *a–o* vowel-shift.

87. **Bloa** *ubla* 'apple'. An anagram; a rare device in this jargon.

88. **Gortran** *cainenn* 'leek'. The same word is used at no. 107 for *cuislinn* 'a flute'. GORT is *g*; but the connexion of the jargon word with either of its Irish equivalents is obscure.

89. **Roinn** *coirm* 'ale'. *Roinn* means 'a portion, share'; and it may be that ale was doled out to the students in the refectory in measured quantities. Drink is not infrequently referred to by its consumers in quantitative terms ('give me half-a-pint', and so forth); the actual name of the substance being understood.

90. **Ailmis** *as* 'milk'. AILM ($=a$)$+i$ (to help pronunciation)$+s$.

91. **Mincill** *mil* 'honey'. Formed as in no. 83: M(U)IN$+$C($=m$) $+il$. Final l doubled like n in no. 84.

92. **Iodamm** *im* 'butter'. This is apparently for IDAD ($=i$)$+m$: the final D of the letter-name has been assimilated to the m.

93. **Collruim** *feoil* 'flesh-meat'. This is COLL ($=c$)$+ruim$, i.e. *cruim* 'a worm, maggot': a kenning, would-be-humorously depreciatory, like the millionaire's 'my old 'bus' for his latest extravagance in motor-cars or aeroplanes.

94. **Gech** *saillte* 'salted provision'. Quite obscure.

95. **Sailailm** *saill* 'fat'. SAIL ($=s$)$+$AILM ($=a$): the first two letters oghamized, with the additional suggestion of a parody of the word itself.

96. **Gortgruth** *gruth* 'curds'. In the MS. the first t is expuncted: but the deleting-point should be under the following g, for the word is obviously GORT ($=g$)$+ruth$.

97. **Gortrus** *grus* 'cheese'. A similar formation: GORT ($=g$)$+rus$.

98. **Muincedhg** *medhg* 'whey'. Identical in construction to no. 83: MUIN-C ($=m$)$+edhg$.

99. **Muinchidh** *miodh* 'mead'. Similar to the last, except that the adjectival formation is here allowed to keep its aspirate: MUIN-CH ($=m$)$+idh$.

100. **Brasach** *blathach* 'buttermilk'. A wilful perversion of the word, formed by interchanging the related sounds r–l and s–th.

101. **Lemocen** *lemhnacht* 'new milk'. A rather complex formation: apocope of final t, de-aspiration of the mh and the ch, and reversal of the second syllable. This is much more like a Shelta than a Bog-Latin process.

102. **Muadhgalan** *muillenn* (so written, with the second l expuncted) 'a mill'. *Muadh*='great'$+gal\bar{a}n$='a puff of wind' (??): if so, presumably suggesting a windmill, not known to have been in use in Ireland in mediaeval times. The etymology is admittedly *longe petitum*, but so, I venture to think, is Stokes's endeavour to connect the word with the root *grî*, meaning 'grinding'. We must class it among the 'obscurities'.

103. **Amloicit** *aith* 'oven'. AMLOIC seems to be a perversion of EMANCOLL = (*ae* or *ai*), and the **it** represents the *ith* of the Irish word.

104. **Culorn** *corn* 'horn'. CUL (= COLL = *c*) + *orn*.

105. **Culaire** *cornaire* 'horner'. An abbreviation of what would be in full **culornaire**.

106. **Ninan** *tiompan* 'drum'. This is a sort of rhyming slang, the letter-name NION being used, not because there is an N in the beginning of the word, but because it is suggested by the sound of the first syllable. Compare 205 **nionta** = *cainte* 'satirist'.

107. **Gortran** *cuislinn* 'flute'. See no. 88.

108. **Piplennan** *tiompanān* 'tambourine'. This seems to be an artificial perversion: **piplennān** < tiplennān < timplennān < *tiompanān*. For the intrusion of **lenn** see no. 40, above.

109. **Daurrusus** *druth* 'jester, fool'. DAUR (= DAIR = *d*) + RUS (= RUIS = *r*) + **us**, a perversion of *uth*. For s < *th*, compare no. 100, above.

110. **Eabadcoll** *ech* 'horse'. EBAD (= *ea*) + COLL (= *c*). The word de-aspirated and spelt oghamically.

111. **Ebandan** *ech* 'horse'⎫ Stokes translates *ech* under no. 110
112. **Ebathan** *lair* 'mare'⎭ as *grex equorum*, and under no. 111 as *equus*; his reason for doing so is not clear. This pair of words is interesting, for it seems to contain a stray tag of Hebrew—*ben* 'son' and *bath* 'daughter' being inserted into the masculine and feminine words respectively. The initial **E** doubtless stands for *ech*: the final **an** is like the otiose **n** in 71 **collscoin**.

113. **Bethan** *bo* 'cow'. See no. 45 above.

114. **Daurailm** *damh* 'ox'. DAUR (= *d*) + AILM (= *a*): the first two letters.

115. **Duraibind** *dartaid* 'yearling calf'. 'The *aibind* ("pleasant") DUR (*d*).' An oghamized initial with qualifying adjective. Compare 45 **betbec**, and others enumerated in the same article. Compare also 240 **a daurutan** 'my little D', corresponding to the Irish *a laegoucan* 'my little calf'—a term of endearment.

116. **Buiglen** *laogh* 'calf'. Stokes has probably hit the nail on the head by comparing Latin *bucula*.

117 *a*. **Cetaimni** *cairigh, caora* (written *cairidh*) 'sheep'. **Aimni** is most likely a corruption, in speech or writing, of *ainmide* 'animal' (compare **pist** = *piast* 'beast', 'reptile', in nos. 121, 122). The word would thus mean 'first animal' but it is probably mere alliterative slang. Compare no. 118 *a*, below.

117*b*. **Rosca** (same meaning). A reversal of the syllables of the word: **ra-cao**, simplified, and the *r* of the new first syllable óghamized; ROS (= RUIS = *r*).

118*a*. **Glaedmuine** *gabar* 'goat'. There can be little doubt that this is a corrupt form, and that it was originally similar in shape to cetaimni, no. 117*a* above, and in the form **glet-** (or perhaps even **get-**) **aimni**. A metathesis of the **ai** and the **m** has somehow taken place. These two words formed a couplet like nos. 121, 122 and 279, 280.

118*b*. **Gairmnech** (same meaning). This is a development of no. 118*a*. **Glaed-** has suggested *glaod* 'a call, cry', for which is substituted *gairm* (same meaning), and the termination has been shortened and made adjectival.

119. **Muinscuill** *muc* 'pig'. MUIN (= *m*) + COLL (= *c*); compare the same combination for *mac* 'son' (no. 65, above). The *s* has probably been interjected artificially, owing to the necessity of differentiating these two words.

120. **Collar** *cu* 'hound'. For COLL-UR.

121. **Caipist** *cat* 'cat' ⎱ These two analogous words are the
122. **Luipist** *luch* 'mouse' ⎰ beginning of the Irish words, with *pi(a)st* 'beast', 'reptile' substituted for the terminations.

123. **Luathan** *en* 'bird'. A diminutive from *luath* 'swift', used as a kenning.

124. **Sceman** *sionnach* 'fox'. May be an example of initial sc = *s* (see no. 85, above): but possibly derived from *sceamh* 'a bark, a howl'. Obscure.

125. **Lornan** *patu* 'hare'. Formed similarly to the two preceding, but the origin is quite obscure.

126. **Orail** *eilit* 'deer'. Professor Thurneysen, no doubt rightly, emends this word to **osail**, i.e. *o* + SAIL (= *s*), *ōs*, another word for deer.

127. **Roscon** *rōn* 'seal'. Initial adjectivally oghamized: ROS-C + *on*.

128. **Bedban** *bradan* 'salmon'. See no. 45.

129. **Snuad** *cech lus* 'any sort of plant'. Perhaps a kenning: *snuad* = 'hair', according to Cormac.

130. **Bibe** *bech* 'bee'. A case of reduplication—a rare device. Compare 165 cicinel = *cinel*.

131. **Arbar** *argad* 'silver'. One of the **-bar** group of words: see no. 7, above.

132. **Onduenne** *uma* 'copper'. The simplest explanation of this strange-looking word is that it is miswritten for OND-*umae*. For an otiose letter, oghamized, and prefixed to the Irish word, compare 211 DAUR-*lar* = *lar* 'floor'.

133. **Ergrand** *iarann* 'iron'. This word suggests another touch of Shelta formation: in that language *gr* is constantly used for disguising words, so that **ergrand** might represent *iar-gr-ann*. This is probably the way in which the word is formed, but the Shelta analogy may be a mere coincidence: it must not be overlooked that in Shelta *gr* is used as an initial sound only.

134. **Betenghort** *bech* 'bee'. We have already had a word for 'bee' at no. 130. *Bech* is written quite clearly and unmistakably in the MS.: but Stokes is probably right in emending it to *becc* 'small', especially as the word which follows immediately is equated to *mōr* 'great'. Assuming this, the word must be analysed BET-en-GORT, where **en** is a name for *e* formed on the analogy of ON for *o*. This implies the late spelling *beg*: before about 1500, the word would usually be spelt *bec* or *becc*. If we are to retain the sense 'bee', the word would apparently mean BETH *i ngort* 'a B in a field'.

135*a*. **Muinrois** *mor* 'great'. MUIN-ROIS: the consonants oghamized, as in no. 65.

135*b*. **Mabar** (same meaning). One of the -**bar** words: see no. 7.

136. **Ur** *olc* 'bad'. This word is recorded in Cormac.

137. **Manaith** *maith* 'good'. MAN-*aith*: initial oghamized.

138. **Fairc** *forguth*. As obscure as its alleged meaning.

139. **Nionon** *nimh* 'heaven'. Evidently one of the 'elemental' words noticed under no. 1, represented by their oghamized initial: NION = *n*. It is reduplicated (see no. 130); but I suspect that in the original MS. the entry read *nīon ōn .i. nimh* 'Nīon that is, which is *nimh*'.

140*a*. **Tamor** *talamh* 'earth'. Apparently one of the -**bar** words, though there is no other case of this nasal form of the suffix.

140*b*. **Tinne** (same meaning). The initial oghamized. See no. 1.

141. **Bar** *muir* 'sea'. In Cormac.

142. **Usguile** *uisge* 'water' (the word is misprinted **Vsgulie** in Stokes's edition). Evidently the first syllable with an arbitrary suffix **uile** (or perhaps **uill**: see nos. 20, 21).

143. **Ged** *fidh* 'wood'. Origin doubtful. It looks like a piece of common rhyming slang, the Irish word being de-aspirated.

144. **Bliadh** *sliab* 'mountain'. A similar rhyming slang effect.

145. **Ruodmarg** *moin* 'bog'. Quite obscure. **Ruod** may conceivably come from *ruad* 'red', but this cannot be stressed.

146. **Certlus** *cealbh*. Whatever this word may mean, it is denoted by oghamizing the first two consonants: CERT = *q*, LUS = *l*.

147*a*. **Loircis** *ler* 'sea'. We may compare 153 **hais-cis** in its formation, but neither word is very intelligible. Possibly this word should be emended to LOIS-C-is.

147*b*. **Liber** (same meaning). A -**bar** word; see no. 7.

148. **Daurun** *dun* 'fort'. Initial oghamized: DAUR + *un*.

149. **Fedseng** *nad* 'rump'. A coarse schoolboyish kenning, meaning literally 'narrow pipe'.

150. **Oinciu** *Ere* 'Ireland'. An initial vowel-shift oghamized in adjectival form: OIN-C (= *o*) + *iu*, the old form of the nominative termination of the word (*Ēriu*).

151. **Ondlosbu** *Albu* 'Britain'. A similar initial vowel-shift, the first two letters oghamized: OND (= *o*) + LOS (= *l*) + *bu*.

152. **Loscan** *lan* 'full'. Initial oghamized in adjective form: LOS-C-*an*.

153. **Haiscis** *bru* 'belly'. No satisfactory solution presents itself, and even comparison with no. 147*a* gives no help.

154. **Fīac** *dece* 'see, behold'. The Irish *feuch* with the same meaning, de-aspirated.

155. **Tinbuid** *erges* 'which arises'. The formation is identical with that of 3 **muinbuid**: but what is the meaning here of the oghamized initial T?

156. **Gortinne** *facaib no beir no tug no tabair* 'leave, or bring, or give, or donate'. An interesting word, apparently the Shelta *get*, which has a similar range of meaning: the consonants oghamized: GOR(T) (= *g*) + TINNE (= *t*).

157. **Bruicnet** *cen i͞peter 7 buain*. This obscure entry is a clear proof that we must look for occasional scribal corruptions introduced into the vocabulary in the form in which Mac Fir Bisigh received it. For 7 (= 'and') we must read .i. (= *id est*). The whole is to be read: bruicnet *cen iphin etir* .i. *buain* 'Bruicnet without an *iphin* at all, that is, reaping'. IPHIN means *ia* or, indeed, any diphthong beginning with *i*. Apparently the purpose of the proviso is to guard against confusion with 74 **bruinioch**. This suggests that the c is a spurious intrusion: the word seems to be *buain*, farced with arbitrary letters.

158. **Feimen** *aratar* 'plough'. Doubtful.

159. **Bedhb** *dub* 'black'. Doubtful: a sort of half-anagram, half-rhyming slang.

160*a*. **Luan** *fionn* 'white'. Stokes's reference to the Irish *luan* 'moon' is hardly convincing. No other explanation suggests itself.

160*b*. **Socon** (same meaning). Still more obscure. The word looks wrong.

161. **Brech** *derg* 'red' ⎱ Quite obscure. In form, the second
162. **Breiche** *glas* 'green' ⎰ word is the comparative degree of the
first—which certainly does not make matters any clearer.

163. **Loiscia** *liath* 'grey'. The initial is oghamized in the adjectival form. The omission of the *th* (as well as its intrusion in
58 **rois-c-i-th**=*Ri*) tends to shew that its sound had already
become a mere breathing, as in Modern Irish. Compare the
equation between -sge and -sgith, suggested above under
no. 73.

164. **Cert** *cidh* 'what?' This is QUERT($=q$), the initial of the
corresponding Latin interrogative.

165. **Cicinel** *cinel* 'race, tribe'. A case of reduplication.

166*a*. **Meinichedh** *mennot* 'house' ⎱ *Mennot* is an old word re-
166*b*. **Mennrad** (same meaning) ⎰ corded by Cormac. The two
jargon words appear to be arbitrary modifications. **Meinichedh** is perhaps formed by making the first syllable of the
Irish word adjectival, as is sometimes done with the Ogham
letter-names.

167. **Coilliuch** *crioch* 'end'. Initial oghamized. The *r* suppressed
or assimilated to the preceding *l*: compare no. 100.

168. **Gin** *go* 'false' ⎱ These words are evidently formed in the
169. **Ferim** *fir* 'true' ⎰ same way—the initial or the opening
syllable with an arbitrary suffix. Probably both were either
-in or -im: 67*a* **tinim**=*teine* 'fire' suggests that -im is the
correct form of the suffix.

170–173. **Dairet, Dairi, Dairib, Daurub,** respectively *teit* (correct
this to *duit* 'to thee'), *do* 'to him', *doib* 'to them', *duibh* 'to
you': also 234 **duruit,** likewise rendered *teit,* for *duit* 'to thee'.
All these are DAIR, DAUR($=d$) + the appropriate pronominal
suffixes. The vowel harmony is interesting: **dairi** instead of
dairo,* **daurub instead of **dairub.*

174. **Eptem** *arbur* 'a troop' (?). Obscure.

175. **Atroibethe** *adrubuirt* 'he said'. The beginnings of the
words are the same: in the Bog-Latin word the Ogham name
for the *b* occupies the place of the last syllable.

176. **Onncaill** *adhlaic* 'bury'. Another case of the *a–o* vowel-
shift. It is simply ONN-COLL, *o–c*; the vowel of the last
syllable has been assimilated to the corresponding sound in
the Irish.

177. **Beitid** *ata* 'it is'. The word ought clearly to be rendered
by *bid* 'let it be': BEIT-*id.*

178. **Achobar** *acobar* 'will'. An unusual case of modification by
aspiration.

179–182. **Lorum** (for which read **Losum**), **Losob, Losca, Loisi,** respectively *liom, lib, leo, lais* 'with me', 'with you', 'with them', 'with him' (meaning, according to the context, 'in my possession', 'in my opinion', etc. etc.). Like the series at no. 170 above, formed with the oghamized initial LOS (=LUIS) used adjectively in one case, and the appropriate pronominal suffix. To these add 232 **leicet**, which ought most likely to be **leiscet**=*let* 'with thee'.

183. **Roimincailg** *ro-mairg* 'great sorrow'. *Ro*+MUIN+C+*airg*, with the *r* turned to *l*: compare 167 **coilliuch** < *crioch*.

184. **Bruipill** *trochmail* 'pitiful'. The Bog-Latin word has a certain resemblance in outline to the Irish word, which suggests that it is a puerility resembling the 'tummy' of contemporary pseudo-refinement.

185–190. **Tinneachair, Tinnices, Tinnichiar, Tinnechuaidh, Tinnichis, Tinnechuas,** respectively *tair, tes, tiar, tuaidh, tis, tuas* 'in the east', 'south', 'west', 'north'; 'below', 'above'. All formed with the adjectively oghamized initial, TINNE-CH, + the appropriate suffix of the Irish word.

191, 192. **Aninches, Aninoibiar** (which must surely be emended to **Aninchiar**), *andes, aniar* 'from the south', 'from the west'; these are secondary formations, from the Bog-Latin words under no. 185 above; made on the model of the corresponding Irish words.

193. **Toiriadai, Toraitne** *dodheachaidh* 'he has come'. These two words are one and the same, with different spellings. We easily recognize the Shelta *tōri* 'to come'.

194. **Loisiom ar collait** *etham ar gccuit* 'let us eat our portion'. **Loisiom** would be the ordinary 1st person plural imperative of **Loisim** (pronounced lus'im) if there were such a word. It exists, not in Irish, but in Shelta (*luš*). *Ār* is the ordinary Irish first plural possessive pronoun. It causes initial nasalization ['eclipsis'], changing as here a *c* to a *g*. **Collait,** for **colluit,** is the Irish *cuit* 'a share, portion', with the initial oghamized, and no doubt helped into its present form by the influence of the Latin *collatio*.

195. **Edmam ar ndoib** *eabam ar ndeogh* 'let us drink our draught'. The source of this factitious verb **edm-** 'to drink' is obscure. The rest of the sentence is easy. We have seen **doib** at no. 82: under the influence of the preceding *ār*, the d becomes an n.[1]

196. **Sgeng** *iomda* 'bed'. An old word, recorded by Cormac.

---

[1] It may possibly be a further indication of the manner of persons who invented this vocabulary, that the only recorded sentences refer to the pleasures of the table!

197. **Collterniud** *codlud* 'sleep'. Most likely a corruption for COLL-DAIR-*iud*. In Irish script, carelessly written DAIR, might with little difficulty be misread TERN.

198. **Sailscon** *snadud* 'needle' (?). This looks like a word similar to 73 **coill-sge** = *cuad*, which has become modified under the influence of such words as 127 **roscon** and 152 **loscan**. SAIL is, of course, the oghamized initial.

199. **Comroisge** *comairce* 'safety'. One of the less numerous groups in which a medial letter is oghamized: *com*-ROIS-*ce*.

200. **Caill** *cler* 'cleric'. See no. 52.

201. **Gem** *gaib* 'take'. Appears to be like 168 **gin** (read **gim**) = *go* 'false', 169 **ferim** = *fir* 'true'; and corroborates the inference there indicated that the suffix is im, not in.

202. **Bailir** *urcetal* 'a poem'. Quite obscure.

203. **Colliusuid** (so it seems to be in the MS., but Stokes prints **Colluisuid**, which in any case is a very likely emendation) *coblaigid* 'lie together' (or the corresponding noun, 'copulation'). The two most prominent consonants oghamized: COLL-(L)UIS-*uid*.

204. **Cerbele** *fer cerda* 'artisan'. The opening syllable suggests the *cer* of *cerda*, but I can venture no further.

205. **Nionta** *cainte* 'satirist'. See no. 106.

206. **Brainionta** *ban-chainte* 'female satirist'. A compound of 61 **biairt** 'woman' with the preceding word.

207. **Certrann** *cetum*. Meaning and formation doubtful.

208. **Aneolsin** *andisin*. Ditto.

209. **Idluisne** *itarmna*. Ditto. Stokes emends the Irish word to *itharna* 'a rushlight'. But this does not help in explaining the Bog-Latin word, which appears to have an oghamized L in the middle.

210. **Gortrailbe** *caoin* (read *cain*) *dealbh* 'a fair form'. GORT = *g* corresponds to an initial *c* in nos. 88, 107; there **gortran** represents *cainenn* and *cuislinn*: the former offers further a parallel of -r- corresponding to -*n*-, so that **gortr**- corresponds to *cain*- in both words. The remainder -ailbe is mere rhyming slang for *dealbh*.

211. **Daurlar** *lar* 'floor'. The oghamized D is prefixed merely to make the word incomprehensible to outsiders.

212. **Ardoballaib** *ar belaib* 'in front of'. Here also a *d*, this time not oghamized, is inserted for disguise, and the word is otherwise arbitrarily modified.

213. **Anrosar** *pater* ⎫
214. **Manrosar** *mater* ⎬ A Latin translation is given of these three words in the MS. They are curious
215. **Bertrosa[r]** *frater* ⎭ formations: the basal words are evidently the Irish *athair, māthair, brāthair*; but the termination -rosar, which ought to represent -*rar* (= ROS-*ar*), is not here appropriate. It belongs properly to a word like 247 **certrosar** = *cethrar*; but it evidently took the fancy of the inventors of the jargon, so that they extended its use to words like these, and 288 **muinrosar** = *muinter*.

216. **Salur** *siur* 'sister'. Initial oghamized: SAL (= SUIL) + *ur*.

217 a. **Muinsgith** *mag* 'plain'. Apparently formed on the analogy of **roiscith** = *ri* or *rig* 'king'.

217 b. **Muingort** (same meaning). This is simply MUIN + GORT, *m–g*.

218. **Garta** *guth* 'voice'. The evanescent *th* dropped, the initial oghamized (GORT-*u*), and the vowels modified.

219. **Gorm** *gort* 'garden'. This is a case of what we have called 'alliterative slang' at no. 36 above.

220. **Munchaol** *maol* 'bald'. Initial oghamized adjectivally: MUN-CH + *aol*.

221. **Eoindir** *innsi* 'there'. For the vowel-shift compare 69 **eonann** = *ian*. The **nd** of the Bog-Latin word corresponds to the Irish **nn**. The word reappears at no. 276, where it is equated to *ann* 'in it, there'. This possibly may help to explain the termination -**ir**. We learn from nos. 244, 254 that **aoinder** means 'one' (Irish *aon*), based on *aonar* 'one man'. The vague similarity of sound between *ann* and *aon* suggests that there should be a like similarity between their Bog-Latin equivalents.

222. **Ornuit** *tret* 'herd, cattle'. Obscure.

223. **Onnbealascan** *obele* 'open'. The initial *o* and the *l* oghamized, the latter adjectivally: ONN + *bea* + LAS-C + arbitrary suffix **an**.

224. **Derclīthe** *dūinnte* 'shut'. The initial is oghamized, but the rest is obscure.

225. **Mainiciall** *mall* 'slow'. Initial adjectivally oghamized: MAIN-IC-(*i*)*all*.

226. **Maincir** *cir* 'comb'. If this is right, it is another case of an arbitrary oghamized letter prefixed, as in 211 DAUR-*lar*. But see no. 83, where the word appears again, with a more probable meaning.

227. **Maincil** *mil* 'honey'. Compare no. 91.

228 *a*. **Maincirt** *mītig* 'a fitting time' (for doing anything) } These

228 *b*. **Munghort** (same meaning: but see no. 217 *b*) } two
words are examples of initial and final oghamization. The
second is MUIN-GORT, *m-g*: in the first the *g* has been changed
to *q*, MUIN-QUEIRT.

229. **Sailbledhach** *saithech* 'sated'. SAIL = *s*, and the ach corresponds to the final -*ech* of the Irish. The word is constructed
in a manner similar to 261 **dobethagres** = *dogres*. Perhaps
the word before us is to be corrected by the analogy of the
latter.

230. **Cestne** *cena* 'nevertheless'. Correct to CERT-ne, and compare no. 233, below.

231. **Henir** *edir* 'altogether, at all'. This seems to be a case of
arbitrary nasalization, but I do not find any analogous
example in the vocabulary, unless we count no. 255.

232. **Leicet** *let* 'with thee'. This should no doubt be **leiscet** or
loiscet, and associated with nos. 179 ff.

233. **Foicert** *focen* 'welcome!' QUERT = *q*, as initial of the second
syllable.

234. **Duruit** *teit* (read *duit*) 'to thee'. See no. 170.

235. **Scillber** *sior-laige* 'lasting weakness'. The **sc**- corresponds
to **s**- as in no. 85 and perhaps no. 124. The *r* is assimilated to
the following *l*: and the syllable **ber** substituted for the end,
as in no. 7 and examples quoted there. Why there should be
a special word for this expression is not clear: does it perhaps
adumbrate the possibility that our schoolboys were sometimes guilty of capturing a holiday by malingering?

236. **Bercon** *briathair* 'word'. Obscure. For the termination
compare 198 **sailscon**. The word would be more intelligible
if it were **bescon**, that is BEITH-scon; this is perhaps the
correct form.

237. **Loscog** *log* 'a place, a hollow'. Initial oghamized adjectivally: LUIS-C-*og*.

238. **Ailmin** *alainn* 'beautiful'. Initial oghamized: AILM-*in*.

239. **Durlus** *dal* 'division'. Initial and final oghamized: DUR-LUS.

240. **Adaurutan** *a laegoucan* 'my little calf!' (term of endearment). Probably **A Daurucan** (the letters *t* and *c* are very
liable to be confused in Irish script, especially in copying
unfamiliar words). *A* is the ordinary Irish sign of the vocative case. For the initial DAUR, compare no. 115.

241. **Cunculut** *cutut* (read *cucut*) 'to thee'. With this must be associated 267 **cuncullum**=*cugum* 'to me'. This is a combination of the preposition *cum* with the pronominal suffixes. For the middle *c* (written in the later spelling *g* in no. 267) the ogham COLL is substituted: and the nasal is restored to the preposition. **Cun-COLL-ut, cun-COLL-um** would be more exact spellings.

242. **Rothinnicht bas** *dac(h)uaidh bas* 'who died'. More correctly, perhaps, *ro thicht bās* 'death arrived' (TINNE=*t*). *Bās* is the ordinary Irish word for 'death' and *ro* is the preverbal particle prefixed to the preterite tense.

243. **Muncorbad** *marbad* 'slaughter'. Initial oghamized adjectivally, MUN-C-*orbad*. Another illustration of the *a-o* vowelshift.

244. **Aoinndir** *aonar* 'one man'. Apparently a mere arbitrary mispronunciation, perhaps suggested by the next word.

245. **Anduiris** *andis* 'two men'. The *an* is the Irish article: the word is *dīs*, the initial being oghamized.

246. **Atreisiur** *a triur* 'three men'. The Latin *tres* 'three' substituted for the Irish *trī*.

247. **Certrosar** *cet(h)rar* 'four men'. QUEIRT+RUIS+*ar*=*q*+*r*+*ar*. For the termination -*rosar* see no. 213 above.

248. **Collcur** *cuigiur* 'five men'. COLL (=*c*)+cur, a modification of -*giur*.

249. **Sealsor** *seisior* 'six men'. The SEAL should probably be SAIL=*s*: the formation would then be similar to the last.

250. **Sechtrosar** *secht* 'seven' (but it ought to be *mōrseisior* 'seven men'). A formation suggested by no. 247, being simply the termination -*rosar* (here meaningless) added to the Irish *secht*=seven.

251. **Ochtrosar** *ocht* 'eight'⎫ Formations similar to no. 250. The
252. **Naerosar** *naoi* 'nine'⎭ real meanings, however, seem to be *ochtar, naonbar* 'eight, nine men'.

253. **Leited nietrosar** *leth-fichit* 'half-score, ten'. This is a curious formation. **Leited** is a reduplicated form of *leth* 'half'. The genitive *fichet* 'twenty' is generally written in MSS. 'xx^et', and in certain forms of handwriting the 'xx' approximate in appearance to 'ni' sufficiently to be read as such, with a certain amount of good-will. The abbreviation thus becomes niet, and the -*rosar* termination is then added.

254. **Aoinder ciach** *a haondeg* 'eleven'. We have seen **aoinder**, with a different spelling, at no. 244. and if these are to be equated **ciach** must somehow mean 'ten': a kind of rhyming slang for *deach*. But there is a possible alternative explanation which seems to me to be preferable: that the word should be *aoin*+DER-C-*iach*, a slight modification in pronunciation of *ōendēg* with the *d* oghamized adjectivally. This is confirmed by the analysis of the next word.

255. **Daernoerciach** *a dhodeg* 'twelve'. This is DAER-DOER-C-*iach*, the two *d*'s being oghamized (the second adjectivally), and the initial of the second DAER nasalized.

256. **Anduiriu** *andiu* 'to-day'. Similar in essential details to no. 254, the central *d* being oghamized.

257. **Anduire** *andee* 'yesterday'. Of identical formation to the last.

258. **Imbethrar** *imarach* 'to-morrow'. The Bog-Latin word presupposes a different and more accurate spelling of the Irish *i mbārach*. The *b* is oghamized, and the final apocopated. The **r** has probably crept in between the BETH and the *ar* through the influence, on a copyist of the vocabulary, of some of the words immediately preceding. The word should be **imbethar**.

259. **Inionghort** *innocht* 'to-night'. An obscure formation; it spells *i*-N-G.

260. **Etaingi** *bes* 'custom'. I can make nothing of this.

261. **Dobethagres** *dogres* 'always'. See no. 229 above. The interpolation of BETH-*a* (=the syllable *ba*) is meaningless.

262*a*. **Niec** *neach* 'anyone'. A case of de-aspiration.

262*b*. **Nionac** (same meaning). The same word with the initial oghamized. By an error (already detected by Professor Thurneysen) this word is given in the vocabulary as an alternative for the following, not for the preceding, item.

263. **Roisciut** *riut* 'with thee'⎱ Words formed similarly to 127
264. **Roisciam** *riam* 'ever' ⎰ roscon=*rōn*. Initial oghamized adjectivally.

265. **Collue** *cuile* 'kitchen'. An example of the rule laid down by Professor Thurneysen, that a consonant in an Ogham name may absorb a similar consonant in the word which is modified. **Collue** is for COLL-*ui*(*l*)*e*, the *l* being absorbed by the *l*'s in COLL.

266. **Colluicenn** *coicenn* (read *coitchenn*) 'common'. Oghamized initial: the *t* suppressed: the *ch* de-aspirated.

267. **Cuncullum** *cugum* 'to me'. See above, no. 241.

268. **Betlim** *deabaid* 'a contest'. Obscure.

269. **Motuillsi** *misi* 'myself'. This is incorrectly written 'motn̄llsi' in the MS. It is analogous to the Shelta *mo d'il-ša* or *mwilša*.

270. **Foratmillsi** *ol misi* 'said I'—a frequent interpolation in reported speech in Irish. *For* is an old form of *ol*: **atmillsi** is almost certainly a copyist's blunder for **matillsi**, the same word as the last.

271. **Goirtnide** *tabair* 'give'. This is the same word as no. 156.

272. **Domthmilsi** *damsa* 'to me'. This is misprinted 'donith-' in Stokes's edition; the word is the same as no. 269, with prefixed *do* 'to'. It should be corrected to **dom'thuillsi**.

273. **Uncullut** *ocut* 'with thee' ⎱ ON + COLL + the appropriate
274. **Uncullum** *ocum* 'with me'⎰ pronominal suffix.

275. **Iomcollamar** *imcomair* 'very short'. The *c* oghamized.

276. **Eoindir** *ann* 'there'. A duplicate of no. 221.

277. **Blaistiud** *seinm* 'a sound'. Obscure.

278. **Collumac** *cumac* (*sic*) 'power'. Initial oghamized.

279. **Betc(h)ennacht** *bennacht* 'blessing'. Initial oghamized adjectivally: BET-CH-*ennacht*.

280. **Metchennacht** *mallacht* 'a curse'. Adapted from the last word by the appropriate change of initial.

281. **Muincesg** *mesg* 'drunken'. Initial oghamized adjectivally.

282. **Firial** *fleacad* 'moisture'. Obscure.

283. **Bue** *gaoth* 'wind'. Obscure.

284. **Bellit** *bliadhain* 'year'. This word is commonly abbreviated bl◦ in MSS., and 'bellit' may be a quasi-facetious pronunciation of the contraction, read as b-l-t.

285. **Sceb** *sgel* 'story'. Another wilful misinterpretation of MS. reading. The Irish *b* and *l* are sometimes almost indistinguishable, in careless writing.

286. **Cloinntinne** *cluinnte* 'heard'. The *t* oghamized.

287. **Almaig** *adaig* 'night'. For AILM (=*a*)+*aig*: initial and final of the word, the middle suppressed.

288. **Muinrosar** *muinter* 'people'. An arbitrary adaptation of the favourite -**rosar** termination, which we have already met with several times.

289. **Srolan** *slugad* 'swallowing'. Obscure.

290. **Durunad** *dunad* 'closing'. Initial oghamized.

291. **Machain** *matain* 'morning'. Arbitrary change of central consonant. Perhaps arising from a MS. misreading, as the letters *t* and *c* are very similar.

The following are the additional words which have been inserted below the signature. They are for the greater part extremely obscure, and are partly quoted from the document called *Coire Erma*, attributed to the mythical poet Amorgen.

292. **Adhbha** *dath* 'colour'.
293. **Eataim** *tuitim* 'I fall'.
294. **Urrthuastair** *eister* 'an art, trade'.
295. **Tomadh** *bagar* 'threat'.
296. **Goiriath** *gar dhamh in gach iath* 'near to me (?) in every country'. This is a gloss from *Coire Erma*.
297. **Erma** *uasal iompa no iariompa*. This is a corrupt form of an obscure gloss, also in *Coire Erma*.
298. **Dliocht** *slonnadh .i. cendfhocras fil ann*. Also from *Coire Erma*.
299. **Sionnadh** *aoir* 'satire'. This word is in O'Davoren's *Glossary*.
300. **Bara** *deabuid* 'dispute, skirmish'.
301. **Leithe** *slinnen* 'shoulder'.
302. **Sabh** *tren* 'strong'. This is a well-known word.

It is evident that in this small vocabulary we strike an entirely different stratum, and that it has no real connexion with what has gone before.

The conclusion indicated in our introductory remarks, that this is not a vocabulary of 'the speech called Ogham', appears to be contradicted by Francis O'Molloy, in a passage which must not be neglected. O'Molloy published at Rome, in the year 1677, a small and now very scarce book, entitled *Grammatica Latino-Hibernica*. Chapter XIII of this work, which occupies pp. 128–42, is headed *De Contracto scribendi modo*, and describes the commonest scribal abbreviations and other conventions to be found in Irish MSS. About half-way through the chapter, however, the author suddenly shifts his attention to cryptography, giving the Ogham alphabet and some simple cyphers founded upon it; prefacing his remarks with these words: *Praeter obscurum loquendi modum, vulgo* ogham *antiquariis Hiberniae satis notum, quo nimirum loquebantur syllabizando uoculas appellationibus litterarum, diphthongorum et triphthongorum, ipsis dumtaxat notis*. This certainly describes a jargon similar to, if not identical with, the vocabulary which we have been considering. Here also the words are pronounced by making syllables with the names of letters and diphthongs—not, however, of triphthongs. But the passage means no more than that O'Molloy knew of the existence of a language called 'Ogham': that he had access to a vocabulary similar to that in *Dūil Laithne*: and that he anticipated Professor Thurneysen in recognizing the Ogham names embedded in most of the words. Mac Fir Bisigh knew as much antiquarian lore as any other Irish scholar of his time: and had he known or believed that the *Dūil Laithne* vocabulary was 'Ogham' he would have said so. That it is called 'Latin' is merely part of the freak: we can compare the use of the names of 'Japanese', 'Welsh' and 'Basque' in incidents referred to in the preceding chapter.

It has been suggested above that the vocabulary has suffered some dislocation. It begins in an orderly way: with a few irregularities, the words are regularly classed, thus:

1–28	Parts of the body,
29–37	Garments,
38–51	Warfare, woodcraft, etc.,
52–65	Groups of humanity,
66, 67	God: fire,
68–80	Vessels,
81–103	Food,
104–109	Music, amusement,
110–130	Animals,
131–137	Metals; adjectives,
138–151	Elemental and geographical names.

But after this point, the selection becomes haphazard, though we can recognize a few groups here and there: such as

159–163	Colours,
185–192	Points of compass, etc.,
213–216	Relationships,
244–255	Numerals.

The groups of preposition-pronoun compounds are also kept together, but the separation of 241 **cunculut** from 267 **cuncullum** calls for explanation. There are two ways in which a list like this can become disjointed. A scribe may copy horizontally across a number of columns which are meant to be taken vertically: or he may reverse the position of a loose leaf, copying the *verso* before the *recto*. I have not been successful in finding evidence of the former kind of disturbance; but the latter kind is probably responsible for the divorce just noticed. I take it that one of the leaves of the exemplar ended with 241 cunculut.

The next leaf contained the words

267 cuncullum to ⎫
291 machain   ⎬ on the *recto*, and

242 rothinnicht bas to ⎫
266 colluicenn   ⎬ on the *verso*.

The leaf was loose, and our scribe turned it the wrong way. Of another reversal I do not feel quite so sure, but if the original last leaf contained

168 gin to   ⎫
192 aninoibiar (*sic*) ⎬ on the *recto*, and

143 ged to   ⎫
167 coilliuch   ⎬ on the *verso*,

it would appropriately close the vocabulary with a word said to mean 'end'. This assumes an average of twenty-five words on each page of the exemplar.

It has been said already that no claim can be made that all the shots in the foregoing commentary have 'hit the bull's eye'. But it is encouraging to note that practically all the explanations can be classified into a limited number of types, which we may here enumerate.[1]

1. *Old Irish Words*: troicit, cud, ligair, baicead, coich, slacc, ur, bar, sgeng, for.

2. *Irish words modified in form or meaning*: aga, goll, coimhgeall, sgillenn (?), berrech, Teo, Tiamudh, bruinioch, boige, artoichenn, doib, roinn, brasach, lemocen, piplennan, caipist, luipist, onduenne (*read* ondumae), fiac, meinichedh, mennrad, bruipill, daurlar, ardoballaib, aoinndir, niec, machain.

3. *Kennings*: beilflesg, feirchinn, deilenn corb, giusalath (?), collruim, luathan, snuad, fedseng.

4. *Beginnings of Irish words with arbitrary termination*:
   -*bar*: sabar, sropur, cufar, coparn, arbar, mabar, tamor, liber, scillber.
   -*im*: tinim, gin (*read* gim), ferim, gem.
   -*rosar*: see below, under no. 8.

---

[1] The words are given in the order in which they occur in the vocabulary.

5. *Initials of words oghamized*: g(r)oithial, luis, fern, daur, tinne, cert.

6. *Initials of words oghamized, and some or all of the rest of the word preserved*: muincedan, caithen, ailmsi, oindsi, muindrech, ondach, roiscith, geitheille, loisgestar, muincir, ailmis, mincill, iodamm, collruim, gortgruth, gortrus, muincedhg, muinchidh, amloicit, culorn, culaire, roscon, daurun, oinciu, loscan, loiscia, coilliuch, dairet, dairi, dairib, daurub, beitid, lorum (*read* losum), losob, losca, loisi, tinneachair (*and associated words*, 185–190), collait, salur, garta, munchaol, mainiciall, cestne (*read* certne), lei(s)cet, loscog, ailmin, daurutan, thinnicht, muncorbad, collcur, sealsor, nionac, roisciut, roisciam, collue, colluicenn, collumac, betchennacht, muincesg, almaig, durunad.

7. *Initials of words oghamized with a qualificatory word added*: dairtinne, eochaille (?), gortlomnach, betbec, collann, bethlosach, eorosnach, collscoin, bethan, duraibind, collar, bedban.

8. *Initials of words oghamized with an arbitrary termination*:
   -*buid*: muinbuid, durbuid, tinbuid.
   -*ul*: bethul, dercuill, usguile.
   -*rosar*:[1] carosar, anrosar, manrosar, bertrosar, certrosar, sechtrosar, ochtrosar, naerosar, nietrosar, muinrosar.
   -*n, -ni*: goithni, collscoin, creithne, sailscon, coparn, onnbealascan.

9. *A middle or final letter oghamized*: delesg, eongort, eonann (?), orail (*read* osail), atroibethe, romincailg, comroisge, cunculut, anduiris, aoinder ciach, anduiriu, anduire, imbethrar, cuncullum, iomcollamar, cloinntinne.

10. *Two letters oghamized*: cuitheilm, dercuill (?), oirthine, muincoll, betroisgenn, anros, sailailm, daurrusus, eabadcoll, daurailm, muinscuill, collar (=collur), betenghort, muinrois, certlus, ondlosbu, gortinne, onncaill, collterniud (*read* colldairiud), colluisuid, muingort, onnbealascan, maincirt, munghort, durlus, certrosar, daernoerciach, uncullut, uncullum.

11. *Intentional or accidental misreadings of manuscript conventions*: crosar, loarn, cremad, nietrosar, bellit, sceb.

12. *'Alliterative' slang*: crionna, cetaimni, glaedmuine, gorm.

[1] Sometimes meaning -*rar*, but more often not. Also sometimes attached to the opening syllable without oghamization.

13. *'Rhyming' slang*: ninan, ged (?), bliadh, nionta, gortrailbe.

14. *Farcings with nonsense syllables*: drogmall, luisnech niamnach, sceglann, ergrand, bruicnet, sailbledhach, dobethagres.

15. *Reversal, complete or syllabic*: cotan (?), lemocen, amloicit, rosca.

16. *Anagrams*: aeile (?), bloa.

17. *Reduplication*: bibe, nionon, cicinel, leited.

18. *Words formed by analogy with other words*: losuill, cluipit (?), gairmnech, aninches, aninoibiar (*read* aninchiar), muinsgith, eoindir (?), sechtrosar, ochtrosar, naerosar, metchennacht.

19. *Influence of foreign languages:*
    Welsh: bisi (?).
    Greek: aicris (?).
    Latin: fuilgen, coiclenn (?), buiglen, collait, atreisiur.
    Hebrew: sebath (?), ebandan, ebathan.

20. *Words also found in Shelta:*[1] fualasg, tionnor, cotan (?), biairt, collscoin, gortinne, toiriadai, loisiom, motuillsi.

The following are the chief phonetic modifications which have been noticed:

Oscillation of *a* and *o*: nos. 22, 26, 34*b*, 56, 86, 151, 176, 243. Of *e* and *o*: 150.

Evanescence of *th*: 33, 43, 163, 218.

Oscillation of *eo* and *ia*: 63, 69, 221.

Oscillation of *r* and *l*: 100, 167, 183, 235.

Oscillation of *s* and *th*: 100, 109.

De-aspiration: 101, 110, 154, 262*a, b*, 266, 278.

Aspiration: 178.

Nasalization: 231, 255.

Of the following words it has proved impossible to find any thoroughly satisfactory explanation, though some tentative suggestions have been made in the foregoing pages: brael, cotan, crisgeo, lethten, sebath, clitach, cliath, cetech, baisi, muadailm, coillsge, scartlann, anrad, gortran, gech, muadhgalan, sceman, lornan, fairc, ruodmarg, loircis, haiscis, feimen, bedhb, luan, socon, brech, breiche, eptem, edmam, caill, bailir, cerbele, certrann, aneolsin, idluisne, ornuit, derclithe, bercon, inionghort, etaingi, betlim, blaistiud, firial, bue, srolan.

[1] Not necessarily in the same form.

Index Verborum

CHAPTER V

THE VAGRANTS OF IRELAND

It is alleged that some rustic *laudator temporis acti* in an Irish country public-house was once heard to lament the contrast between the toilsome days in which his lot was cast, and the happy time long ago when, as he expressed it, 'the laste of us was kings'. He laboured under a misapprehension, presumably induced by Moore's *Irish Melodies* and similar writings, patriotic, but imperfectly successful as approximations to historical actuality.

In fact, the underworld of life in ancient Ireland, like Sam Weller's knowledge of London, was extensive and peculiar. This was a natural consequence of the social organization. From top to bottom the community was divided into a series of castes, almost as rigid and as complex as the Indian system. Kings, nobles, non-noble freemen played the part of the big fleas and the little fleas in the epigram—only that the rôles of biter and bitten were reversed. Beneath the last-named was a sort of border-line group of people who might rise into freedom or drop into servitude according to circumstances; whose position must always have been anxious and precarious. And beneath these again were the unfree: slaves, who were their master's property no less than his cattle were, and homeless vagabonds, whose mode of life is summed up in one of the contemptuous names bestowed on them—'crumb-foxes'; ever sniffing around for something, however small, to put into their mouths, and not restrained by any undue feelings of delicacy or daintiness in their choice of victual. They had no civil rights whatsoever. They were not entitled to the protection of an 'honour-price'—a pecuniary sum, varying with the rank of its owner (so that it formed a convenient way of stating mathematically his position in society), and paid over to him as compensation for any injury or assault accounted as an infringement of dignity. They were not allowed to enter assemblies: their presence there would bring pollution. 'Freedom' and 'holiness' were synonymous terms in ancient Irish Law: the same word, *nemeth*, is used for both conceptions, in the law tracts that have come down to us. A freeman was a man who possessed

an innate right to take part in, or at least to be present at, religious
and other ceremonies. The unfree man must keep himself at a
distance: his presence at such ceremonies was *nefas*. His position
might be compared with that of the 'Untouchables' of India,
who, as these words are written, are calling for the notice of the
world with an insistency never known before in the long history
of that ancient land.

These miserable creatures appear to have moved about in
wandering bands, and they must have been a nuisance, if not an
actual menace, to ordered society. They picked up a living in any
way that presented itself: they had no regular trade, like the
tinkers, their much less disreputable successors in later times;
for a trade, if skilfully practised, conferred 'freedom' as much
as did property and learning, the two chief safeguards of this legal
brand of 'holiness'. They seem to have specialized in acrobatic
and clownish performances, sometimes of a very gross description.
On the outskirts of an assembly—for they could not enter the
sacred ground—they pitched their booths, like gypsy fortune-
tellers at a modern horserace. The author of an ancient poem on
the Assembly of Carman devotes a stanza to them:

> But what noisy rabble's there,
> On the border of the Fair?
> Vagabonds with drums and bones,
> Shrieking to their bagpipe drones.

And we learn from the life of St Findian[1] that if such a 'troublesome' or 'greedy' party should encounter the procurator of a
monastery—the official who in business affairs was the inter-
mediary between the Church and the world—he would not 'lose
his honour' if he repeated a Pater Noster at a certain holy well
dedicated by the saint. The *Northern Farmer* who observed that

> the poor in a loomp is bad

would have been quite at home in Ancient Ireland. So no doubt
would the person who contributed to the *Gentleman's Magazine*
a letter (published in the issue of January 1752, p. 30) discussing
whether it was a right policy to deny all amusements to the lower
ranks of people, in order to prevent robbery. And we now can
understand better the author of the prologue to *Hisperica Famina*,
who doubtless was an ecclesiastic, and whom we saw snubbing
an aspiring rustic and sending him about his business.

---

[1] *Lives of Saints from the Book of Lismore*, line 2711.

That these vagabonds protected themselves by some sort of thieves' jargon is quite probable, but no one thought it worth his while to write it down. At the moment, indeed, we are not concerned with these social dregs, beyond making ourselves aware of their existence: they come into the picture later on.

More to our immediate purpose is the wandering scholar, a class which seems, in Ireland, to have come into existence with the change of religion. All such changes are bound to upset somebody's arrangements. Pliny's famous letter to Trajan, consulting him as to what he should do with the Christians in Bithynia (of which province he was at the time Administrator), mentions that his attention had been called to these people on a complaint that the spread of this new cult was having a serious effect upon the temple revenues. In like manner those whose living depended upon their association, in whatsoever capacity, with the older creeds of Ireland were thrown out of work by the arrival and dissemination of Christianity. They had devoted their lives to the peculiar scholarship which their duties had prescribed: now their occupation was gone; they could not dig; and even if they did not share the qualms about begging felt by the man in the parable, they would find that their patrons would expect some return for their money, if they sought to follow that short cut to a livelihood. The patrons paid the piper, and expected to enjoy the privilege of calling the tune.

In this way, on the wreckage of the druidic schools, there grew up a guild of poets, some of whom became attached to the heads of the great native families, and acted as their domestic laureates, producing wedding-songs, laments, and other occasional pieces when required. Others wandered from house to house, and, in days when there were few organized amusements, they were usually sure of hospitality in return for their professional services as poets, harpers, or a combination of the two. In the beginning, when the prestige of druidry still clung to their garments, uncanny supernatural powers were attributed to them: their satires were still feared, still believed capable of producing even physical evils. It may quite well be that fear actually induced some of the dreaded consequences, so subtle are the incomprehensible links between the mind and the material body; and thus a fresh lease of life may have been given to the awe in which they were held. But gradually people began to realize that whatever may have been their powers in the days of paganism, when (as was only to be expected) the demons were at their beck and call, in Christian times, when the powers of the demons had been curbed, their supernatural gifts were greatly curtailed. Still, the traditional respect for those who practised the poetic art remained steadfast, even in the adverse circumstances of the eighteenth century; as can be seen from a perusal of that most fascinating book, Corkery's *The Hidden Ireland*.

With these later developments we have here nothing to do. But we must notice that as belief in the efficacy of the poet's curse waned, there were found wits so wanting in reverence as to turn the tables, and satirize the poets. We possess two entertaining compositions of this kind, which give us some insight into the life of these wanderers and of their contemporaries.

The first of these relates how a bard of the seventh century, Senchan Torpēist by name, with his suite, billeted himself upon Guaire, king of Connacht: it tells of the outrageous demands which the party made of him: and of the way in which Guaire rid himself of the incubus. The tale was published with a translation by the Irish 'Ossianic Society' in the year 1860, under the bombastic title 'Proceedings of the Great Bardic Association', which does not prepare us for its farcical absurdities: a better edition, but without translation, has been published in a series of texts under the authority of the Government of the Irish Free State. Guaire, distracted by the impossible desires of his guests—which included such things as a lapful of blackberries (unobtainable, the month being January), and a repast of the flesh of 'a cow having a lump of tallow instead of a liver', is fortunate in possessing a knowledgeable brother, who shews him how to provide them. In the course of the story Senchan, wishing to eat an egg, has found that he has been forestalled by some mice. He satirizes them, and they drop dead. Then he remembers that the cats should have kept the mice under control, so he satirizes the King of the Cats. That fearsome monster comes in revenge, to carry off Senchan and to eat him; and this leads the story into further preposterous situations, whither the reader can follow it at his pleasure.

Jocular though this story may be, it comes from a time when the efficacy of the poet's curse was still remembered, if not actually credited. Our other satire shews the poet with most of this supernatural aura dispelled. It is the tale of a gleeman by name Aniēr mac Conglinne, to be found in the great fifteenth-century MS., now in the Royal Irish Academy's Library, and called *Leabhar Breac*, 'the Speckled Book'—where it stands in startling contrast with the solemn theology which occupies the rest of the volume. Aniēr was a student of Armagh, and had acquired some reputation for learning. But he wearied of the drudgery of scholastico-ecclesiastical life, and one day he forsook it all, sold his little store, bought provisions and made him shoes for the road, and set out 'to follow poetry and to abandon his reading'. Such things happened sometimes. In 742 there died one Cū-Cuimne, who had so far fallen from grace as to leave his books and to take him a wife: which provoked this epigram, alleged to be the work of Adamnān—in any case, we suspect, of some misogynist:

> Cū-Cuimne read half the pages
> Ever written by the sages.
> At the rest he never fags:
> He has left it all—for hags.

We are glad to learn that this reproof taught Cū-Cuimne the error of his ways. He meekly endured the unkind and apparently baseless insinuation of polygamy, and the ungracious epithet applied to his wife; expiated his fault by composing a hymn to the Virgin Mary; and made a promise of amendment in these terms:

> Cū-Cuimne read half the pages
> Ever written by the sages:
> Now the rest with care he'll read
> Till he is a sage indeed.

But no kindly mentor intervened to check Aniēr mac Conglinne on the downward path. He turned his back on Armagh and walked to Cork; there he was housed in the unspeakable guest-chamber of the monastery, in which, among other inconveniences, the fleas were 'as numerous as the sand of the sea,˙ or sparks of fire, or dew on a May morning, or the stars of the sky'. No one came to visit him, or to do reverence to him: the breakfast served to him on the morrow's morn was a paltry cup of whey-water. He sought, poor wretch, to wield the ancient weapons of the order which he had entered with such precipitation; and he satirized the Abbot and his hospitality. But he had fallen upon days when Abbots were dangerous game for the satirist, and the indignant ecclesiastic gave orders that he should be stripped, flogged, soused in the river, and, on the following day, hanged. To make a long story short, he saved himself from the tragical consummation of the sentence by relating a dream of a land in which everything was made of food. It was suggested that he should be conveyed to Cathal, king of Munster, who was suffering from the unpleasant malady then described as 'a demon of gluttony', but in these less unsophisticated days known as bulimia: in the hope that the demon might be induced to crawl out of his victim when he overheard the appetizing narrative. The suggestion was carried out, the demon was exorcized, and the poet was rewarded. For these details we may refer the reader to the original text, in the erudite edition of Kuno Meyer.

It is obvious that this story is a satire on the Church and its officials quite as much as on the poet. Renegade and rascal though the latter may be, it is for him, rather than for the other actors in the drama, that the reader's sympathy is claimed. We are inclined to suspect that the author was one who had himself taken the step which he imputes to his hero. Quite possibly it was not an infrequent case: students did not take to learning as ducks to water in Ireland any more than elsewhere. The margins of MSS. record many grumbles—*difficilis est haec pagina* and the like: or (as in a fifteenth-century MS. which I was working over only a few days ago), 'This is a very long poem to have to copy out'; a plaint in which my ancient predecessor had my whole-hearted sympathy. Every now and again one of these rebellious spirits must have 'cut the painter': and what happened then? He was a lost soul: he was a wanderer—and if in the case of some, like Mac Conglinne in the story, strokes of luck came in their way, others must have sunk down very low. And finally the dissolution of the monasteries must have thrown whole schools-full of persons, unprepared for any ordinary way of making a living, out on the roads. Some of these found their niches: but what of the rest?

We picture them gradually dropping to the level of the vagrants spoken of at the beginning of this chapter: living their out-caste life, and acquiring their criminal cunning in its many manifestations; and to this superadding their own equipment of scholarship, such as it might be. The broken-down scholar, the unfrocked and dilapidated Clerk once in Holy Orders, can be dangerous allies of the criminal classes. Among other gifts which they can bestow must be counted effective means of secret communication, by cipher or otherwise; such as would be far beyond the inventive powers of their uneducated associates.

Here we find a reasonable solution for what would otherwise be a very real perplexity. How did the tinkers and other adepts in secret languages command the grammatical and analytical skill necessary to contrive them? We shall see that these cannot be taken as being modern dialects of the ancient secret languages which have till now been occupying our attention. Though there are some reminiscences—such as a degraded scholar might incorporate in his inventions—they are virtually a new creation. This requires at least a certain degree of scholarship; and the present chapter is inserted in order to shew how that scholarship could have become available.

From the solemn druids, teaching to their students lessons in natural philosophy, theology, language, and poetry, down to the three vagrant desperadoes, figuring in the following chapter, from whom John Sampson learnt Shelta in a disreputable slum tavern in Liverpool, the traditional succession is thus complete.

CHAPTER VI

SHELTA

I. A History of the Discovery of Shelta

It appears that there are occasional references in literature, published during the last three centuries, to the fact that itinerant tinkers have a secret jargon of their own. But in any case these references do not take us very far: and they must not be made to bear a greater weight than they can carry. For example, the frequently quoted boast of prince Henry, that he 'can drink with any tinker in his own language',[1] does not appear, on a critical examination of the context, to mean much more than a recent acquisition of a few words of ephemeral cant or slang.

It was not until 1876 that any very definite facts came to light. In that year Charles Godfrey Leland chanced to encounter an itinerant knife-grinder on a road near Bath.[2] He knew a little Romani, but said that his fraternity were giving up Romani because, as he expressed it, it was getting 'to be too blown'. He further stigmatized back-slang, canting, and rhyming as 'vulgar', and Italian as 'the lowest of the lot'. Indeed, in a passage suppressed on republication, he is reported as expressing surprise, on learning that Leland could speak Italian, that he should have come to such degradation. But, he added, there is another tongue that is *not* 'blown'—mostly Old Irish, 'and they call it *Shelter*'.

At this point it must be remarked that the use of the expression 'Old Irish' by Leland and his tramp informants is misleading. 'Old Irish' has the specific philological meaning of a language spoken and written in Ireland down to about A.D. 900: but in Leland's pages it does not appear to have any more significance than the language of the stage Irishman's 'Ould Oireland', irrespective of its historical development. Further, it may be suspected that the expression was not used by the tramps themselves, but has been put into their mouths by their reporter.

[1] Shakespeare, *First Part of King Henry IV*, Act II, Sc. iv.
[2] C. G. Leland, *The Gypsies* (London: Trübner, N.D. [1882]), p. 354: reprinted *Journal*, G.L.S. II, i (1907–8), p. 168. Also *New Quarterly Magazine*, New Series, vol. III, p. 136 (London, 1880).

The Bath tramp led Leland no further than this: and Leland admits that he was not greatly impressed, assuming 'that the man merely meant Old Irish', that is, presumably, Modern Irish. But, a year later, Leland was on the coast at Aberystwyth, in the company of that extraordinary and ill-fated linguist, E. H. Palmer: and there they fell in with a wretched outcast, shewing withal some evidence of having had a fair amount of education. Finding that this vagrant possessed some knowledge of Romani, he was invited by the two enthusiasts to join them. In answer to a question as to what he did for a living, he puzzled the experts by replying, *Shelkin' gallopas*; and when pressed for an explanation, he told them that in 'Minklas' Thari'—as Leland writes the words—otherwise 'Shelter' or 'Shelta', the expression meant, 'Selling ferns'. From this man Leland obtained the first vocabulary of the newly discovered language. In the list of words below, those from this vocabulary are marked L'.

Some time later, Leland had the good fortune to discover a polyglot Irish tramp in the neighbourhood of Philadelphia. He prints his name as Owen Macdonald, but as this form of the surname is essentially Scots, we may suggest that it was more probably MacDonnell. This tramp claimed to speak 'Old Irish' (*sic*), Welsh, a little Gaelic (presumably Scots Highland), Romani, and also Shelta, to a knowledge of which he confessed after some pressure: and he consented to impart to Leland a second and much longer list of words, the items of which are marked L (without accent) in the vocabulary below. It must be mentioned that Leland appends to this list the following discouraging admission (expunged on republication): 'Of Celtic origin it [Shelta] surely is, for Owen gave me every syllable so garnished with gutturals that I, being even less of one of the Celtes (*sic*) than a Chinaman, have not succeeded in writing a single word according to his pronunciation of it.'

From both these vocabularies (L', L) a number of words have to be excluded as being Romani, Cant, or Slang, and not true Shelta.

In 1886 Leland read a paper before the Oriental Congress in Vienna on 'The Original Gypsies and their Language', in which he returned to the subject of Shelta. A long extract from this paper was published in *The Academy*,[1] from which it appears that he went over the same ground as in his previous publication;

[1] 20 November 1886, p. 346.

adding, however, the following as an indication of the widespread knowledge of the language—a point which he was fond of emphasizing: 'I doubt if I ever took a walk in London, especially in the slums, without meeting men and women who spoke "Shelta"; and I know at this instant of two...little boys who sell groundsel at the Marlborough Road Station, who chatter in it fluently.' We hear of these little boys again, in a paper published after Leland's death.[1] They are there transferred to 'Euston Road or Saint John's Wood Road Station'—a curious alternative —and their 'fluent chatter' has dwindled to a comprehension of some of the words and phrases which Leland had picked up from MacDonnell.

The publication of Leland's communication in *The Academy* led to a letter from Mr H. T. Crofton, giving a short vocabulary, which he had acquired from two wanderers,[2] and pointing out, apparently for the first time, that Shelta was formed by the application of 'back slang' to Irish or, as he regrettably calls it, 'Erse'. Thus *od* 'two' is the Irish *dō*, reversed. He also observed some ordinary rhyming slang derived from English words, such as *grascot* 'waistcoat', *grawder* 'solder', *grupper* 'supper'. Words from this list are marked C' in the vocabulary.

Among the MSS. placed in my hands was a notebook in Crofton's handwriting, containing what at first sight appears to be an extensive Shelta-English and English-Shelta vocabulary. This is, however, disappointing; its contents consist almost exclusively of an uncritical collection of every word in the published vocabularies enumerated in this survey of the material, without any attempt to weed out even the most obvious non-Shelta elements.[3] The few words from this source which I have included, and which I have found it impossible to trace to any other authority, are marked C (without accent) in the vocabulary.

Shortly afterwards another collector, Mr T. W. Norwood, supplemented Crofton's list with further words, which he had acquired more than thirty years previously,[4] twenty years before Leland first heard the name of Shelta. Most of the words in Norwood's list are very strange, unlike anything recorded by other collectors.

[1] *Journal*, G.L.S. II, i (1907–8), pp. 73–82.
[2] *Academy*, 18 December 1886, p. 412.
[3] Many of these are derived from the vocabularies in Andrew McCormick's *Tinkler Gypsies*—a canting thieves' jargon that has little or nothing in common with Shelta.
[4] *Academy*, 1 January 1887, p. 12.

The true Shelta element among them seems to be very small. Words in the vocabulary adopted from this list are marked N.

In 1891 Mr G. Alick Wilson published a short list of words, taken down from a child belonging to a tinker family in the island of Tiree.[1] They were originally noted by a lady on the island, and the child's mother afterwards endeavoured to persuade her that the child herself had invented them. That this, however, was a falsehood, prompted by the desire to keep the language secret, is shewn by the similarity of the words to those in other lists. The name of the lady collector not being recorded, words from this list are denoted with W.

In publishing this list of words, Mr Wilson indicates certain faults in Leland's arbitrary orthography: he also notices that the numerals, as given by him, are nothing but mis-spellings of the numerals of ordinary Gaelic. This obvious fact had already been detected by at least one of the reviewers of Leland's *Gypsies*, and had even aroused the suspicion that Leland had been the victim of a 'mystification' on the part of his tinker friends.

In the same issue of the *Journal* of the Gypsy Lore Society there appeared another short vocabulary, taken down by 'Mr Ffrench of Clonegal': otherwise the rector of that parish in County Wexford, the Rev. Canon J. F. M. ffrench—for in this awkward manner he habitually spelt his name. In strange contrast to Leland's difficulty with MacDonnell's gutturals, the Canon confesses that *he* found it hard to note down the words 'as the pronunciation is very soft and liquid': so that he was not certain that he had recorded them all quite correctly. Such as they are, however, they are given below marked F.

Two other vocabularies, both from Scotland, belong to about this time. The first of these is in manuscript, found among Dr Sampson's papers: the words were taken down from tinkers named MacDonald in the island of Barra. The second is a long list of words derived from tinkers in the island of Arran, and appended to a paper by Mr David MacRitchie.[2] This latter list is, however, overloaded with Romani and cant, and it has to be drastically weeded with the help of Mr Alexander Russell's most valuable vocabulary of *Scoto-Romani and Tinker's Cant*.[3] Both these collections are due to Mr Alexander Carmichael, and

[1] *Journal*, G.L.S. I, ii (1891), p. 121.
[2] *Transactions* of the Gaelic Society of Inverness, vol. XXIV (1899–1901), pp. 429 ff.
[3] *Journal*, G.L.S. II, viii (1914–15), p. 11 ff.

as the initial C has already been pre-empted, their contributions to the vocabulary are marked K' and K respectively.

In 1890, Mr John Sampson, as he then was styled, came upon the scene, and immediately put the enquiry upon a scientific basis. He had the advantage of an extensive experience in the noting of Romani, and he possessed in consequence a skill in practical phonetics not at the command of any of his predecessors. Moreover, his unique knowledge of Romani, and his wide acquaintance with cant jargons, enabled him to distinguish between true Shelta and borrowings from these other sources.

In an unfinished MS. found among his papers, he tells how he had come to take up the study. Leland's chapter in *The Gypsies* had been his first introduction to it, but he had regarded it with the same scepticism as the reviewer mentioned above. Mr David MacRitchie, at the time president of the Gypsy Lore Society, had, in Sampson's words, 'a more robust faith' in Leland's discovery, and he wrote to Sampson, urging him to take the matter up. 'Probably', says Sampson, plaintively, 'he selected me as the least squeamish of his members. But even to me it sometimes occurred that Shelta was a language which no gentleman should be asked to collect.'

The quest took him into vile and even dangerous slums in Liverpool, and involved him in some very unpleasant adventures. 'My first collections', he writes, 'were made from a knife-grinder named Brennan,[1] who, as he afterwards confided to me, took me for "an old lag as was making himself a bit wide". From this man I collected a moderate vocabulary, of which a large proportion were obviously mere flash or cant words.' Brennan, as the other MS. referred to in the footnote tells us, 'disclaimed any deep acquaintance with Shelta, which he stated was gradually passing into disuse.... While making use of a few Romani and cant words, he discriminated pretty accurately between the indigenous and foreign elements of his vocabulary.

'Later, in a low quarter of the city, I met two knife-grinders leaving their model lodging-house to start out on a day's work, and an umbrella-mender working in partnership. These men were not encumbered by any prejudices in favour of personal decency or cleanliness, and the language used by them was, in every sense, corrupt. Etymologically it might be described as a Babylonish,

---

[1] In another MS. this man is called *Mahmon*, which can hardly be correct.

model-lodging-house jargon, compounded of Shelta, "flying cant", rhyming slang, and Romani. This they spoke with astonishing fluency, and apparent profit to themselves.

'I worked for some time with these men, until I had collected all their words. Three more uncleanly and evil-looking men I never saw. One, an Irish tinker, passed under the name of "Manni" Connor: another was known as the *Re-Meather* or "Double Devil":[1] and the third was a tall cadaverous man called "The Shah".

'My collections from these men were made in tinkers' taverns: and on the last occasion I was in their company we were seated in an inner room with wooden table and sanded floor. For obvious reasons I had placed them on the bench against the wall, occupying, myself, the other side of the table. Something, I forget what, aroused suspicion in their minds, and there was an air of immense trouble which I hoped at any rate would not be mine. I saw Manni rise to get between me and the door, while the Re-Meather was surreptitiously unbuckling his belt. Grasping the table with both hands, I turned it on its side, jamming them to the seat, the three blue and white pots of beer sliding down on them. Glancing back as I left the room, I saw those three worthies framed in a kind of triptych against the wall, and as I passed through the door I wished that I had more time to admire their astonished faces.'

He was now obliged to seek another instructor: and he had the good fortune to make the acquaintance and to win the confidence of one John Barlow, a tinker aged seventy-nine years, whom he found 'in the Irishries of Liverpool, in a street which at the time was safe only for... the dispensary doctor and the Catholic priest'. Barlow 'possessed a large stock of words, and his Shelta was unmixed with Irish, Romani, or Cant'. Sampson acquired from him an extensive vocabulary, as well as other materials for the study of the language.

Leland says of the Bath tramp from whom he first heard the name of Shelta that 'of course he knew a little Romani: was there ever an old traveller who did not?' But Sampson says definitely that none of these Liverpool vagrants spoke or understood Romani, although they had adopted some Romani words.

According to Barlow, the speakers of Shelta 'constitute a caste rather than a mere class: their common bond is one of heredity

[1] Or perhaps 'king-devil'. See **ri-mider** in the vocabulary.

as well as of craft. They intermarry, are not recruited from other classes of society, and do not turn to other forms of livelihood.' Barlow professed to be able to recognize a tinker woman by her face, as though this exclusiveness had affected the physical type. They 'travel from place to place, in small bands or families, plying their craft, frequenting fairs, and trading in calves and asses; while their women gain money by hoaxing, telling fortunes, cutting cards, and tossing cups [divination by tea-leaves]'. On the other hand, incredible though it may appear, we have been told that tinkers in America 'consider fortune-telling wicked'.[1] Barlow gave to Dr Sampson a long list of the surnames usual among the Irish tinkers; a similar list for American tinkers is given by Mr Arnold in the paper just quoted; and these lists are amplified in a paper by Mr Patrick Greene, Ballinalee, Co. Longford, the latest recruit, and one of the most valuable, to the study of the tinkers and their language.[2]

There is no doubt that Shelta is a hereditary possession of the Irish tinkers, handed down from father to son. From the tinkers it naturally filters in a greater or less degree to other classes of vagabonds, but these do not speak it in its purity. The story $\gamma 3$, below, shews that a knowledge of Shelta might be expected from sieve-makers, pipers, and beggars; presumably from other vagrants as well. Barlow himself learnt Shelta in infancy from his mother, who spoke it habitually; and Brennan had an uncle, Ezekiel Brennan, who never spoke anything else unless he was actually obliged to do so. Indeed, 'an old Connaught tradesman', whom Sampson came across, told him that the tinkers made such a habit of conversing in their own tongue that they could speak neither English nor Irish correctly. (Clearly a jargon which is essentially a perversion of these languages would predispose the speakers to unconscious solecisms when they endeavoured to converse in them.)

Barlow frequently dwelt upon his father's threats and warnings against divulging the language to outsiders. We have seen something of the same kind in the episode of the child in Tiree. He

[1] Frederick S. Arnold, 'Our old Poets and the Tinkers', *Journal of American Folklore*, vol. XI (1898), p. 210.

[2] See his papers in *Béaloideas*, the journal of the Folklore of Ireland Society, vol. III (1931–2), pp. 170, 290, vol. IV (1933–4), p. 259. These papers are indispensable to the student. Besides materials for the study of the language second in bulk only to Sampson's, they give by far the fullest available account of the mode of life of the speakers of Shelta. There are a few folk-tales printed in translation only. I have drawn on the vocabularies, with the Society's kind permission.

further related how upon two occasions he pretended not to understand a conversation between a farmer and a herd-boy, who had somehow contrived to acquire a knowledge of Shelta. Barlow had a very exaggerated idea of the antiquity of the language: according to a note found among Dr Sampson's MSS., he seems to have told him 'to my knowledge (!) it has been spoken generation after generation for the last 800 years'. In the West of Ireland, he went on to say, the talk was different: 'they can't pronounce the word[s]: they put too much of a drone and [blank in MS.] about it'. Apparently he also made the statement that [the speakers were] the old original travellers [who had] no connexion with [the] Irish, good, bad or indifferent; [adding that] 'there's only one on them (*sic*) living now, and she kilt her husband, poor man—hit him on the head with a razor'. The bracketed words are my conjectural linkages of these disconnected sentences; the latter are no more than rough jottings of which Dr Sampson made no further use, and to which he probably attached little importance.

Following Leland, who first popularized the name, the language is usually called 'Shelta'. This, however, is not quite accurate. The right name is 'Sheldru' or 'Shelŏru', 'Shelta' being a corruption due to imperfect speech or hearing. Other variants are 'Shelter' or 'Shelteroχ'—all being perversions of the Irish *bēlra* or *bērla*, in modern spelling *bēarla*, meaning 'speech, language, jargon', and now most commonly, though not exclusively, used in the sense of 'English'. It may also be heard of under the names *Mink'ers' tāri* or *Mink'er-tāral*, ('tinker-speech') or in Gaelic *Cainnt cheard* ('craftsmen's speech') or *Laidionn nan ceard* ('craftsmen's Latin').[1] It is also called *Gam* (or *Gamoχ*) *cant*, which would seem to mean 'Bad Talk'. Dr Sampson makes the interesting suggestion that this may be a corruption of *Ogam-cant*, which is, however, inadmissible, as the *g* is probably palatalized (*g'am*). Other names are 'Bog Latin', 'Tinkers' Cant', and 'The Ould Thing'.

Dr Sampson published a paper upon this collection,[2] which attracted the attention of Professor Kuno Meyer, then resident in Liverpool. Through Dr Sampson, the latter got into touch with Barlow; and his study of the old man's speech enabled him to publish an analysis of Shelta word-formation which advanced the

---

[1] In the Gaelic Dictionary of the Highland Society (1828), vol. I, p. 113, under the word *Beurl'eagair*.
[2] 'Tinkers and their Talk', *Journal*, G.L.S. I, ii, p. 204.

subject beyond the stage reached by Sampson himself, handicapped as the latter admittedly was by the want of a practical knowledge of Irish. In his essay on the subject,[1] Professor Meyer supported Sampson's contention that Shelta was a secret language of great antiquity, formed on a basis of Irish at an early stage of its development. He further claimed for it a close connexion, if not an identity, with the secret tongues referred to here and there in Irish literature. These claims must be considered later.

The remaining contributions to the study of Shelta may be enumerated more briefly. Mr D. Fearon Ranking narrates an interview of twenty minutes with a family of tinkers speaking Romani and Shelta at Crinan Harbour in Argyllshire:[2] but he records only one of their words (*yergan* 'tin'). In Mr Frederick Arnold's paper, already quoted, he gives some words derived from one Costello, with whom he had established friendly relations at Poughkeepsie, N.Y.—a friendship much strengthened 'when he found that I knew a little Old Irish'—once more, that troublesome ambiguity! Costello, we cannot but feel, must have been easily satisfied: for we find on referring to Mr Arnold's vocabulary that he was unable to recognize the Irish words underlying *chi'ni*[3] 'fire', or *grau'mach hrī hū* (which he translates 'I'm very fond of you in my heart'), or to resolve the doubts of his tinker friends as to whether *krūk mor* means 'a river' or 'a big hill'.

After the above publications, and one or two popular magazine articles of no special importance, the subject seems to have disappeared from literature, till revived by Mr Greene.

II. CONTINUOUS SPECIMENS OF THE SHELTA LANGUAGE

The following materials are available for the study of the construction of Shelta:

(α) A translation of the Lord's Prayer, dictated to Dr Sampson by John Barlow, and published in his article on *Shelta*, in Chambers's *Encyclopaedia*. (Here printed from Sampson's MS., with interlined phonetic transcript and literal translation.)

(β) A collection of one hundred sentences in Shelta, published by Dr Sampson in *Journal*, G.L.S. II, i (1907–8), p. 272.

---

[1] 'The Irish Origin and the Age of Shelta', *Journal*, G.L.S. I, ii (1891), p. 257.

[2] *Journal*, G.L.S. I, ii, p. 319.

[3] In words quoted here and elsewhere from Arnold, the accent-mark is always accentual, not, as here used, a symbol of palatalization.

(γ) Two short stories in Shelta, published by Dr Sampson in *Journal*, G.L.S. I, iii (1892), p. 23. Referred to below as γ1, γ2. A third story, found among Dr Sampson's MSS.: γ3, below.

(δ) A number of sentences printed in Mr Greene's papers in *Bēaloideas*: also a few sentences in MS., from the same collector, found among Dr Sampson's papers.

The matter in β, γ is here reprinted, with some corrections. In addition I have given a phonetic transcript and literal translation of the first seventy-eight sentences in β. The words in Mr Greene's communications are incorporated in the vocabulary.

There is a reference among Dr Sampson's MSS. to a fourth story called *Tharsp malya* (tarsp mἀl′a), but this appears to be lost.[1] Nor have I been able to discover the 'specimens of the dialect of the south', of which a promise (unfulfilled) of publication appears in a footnote to γ in *Journal*, G.L.S.

(α) THE LORD'S PRAYER

[The first line is the form as given by Dr Sampson in his MS. copy; the second is the phonetic rendering; the third is a word-for-word literal rendering.]

Mūilsha's gather, swŭrth a mŭnniath, mŭnni-graūa-kradyi
Mwīlša('s) gāter swurt a mun′iaθ | mun′i-grἀ [a] krad′i
I's father up in goodness | good-luck at stand[ing]

dhūilsha's mŭnnik. Gra be grēdhi'd shedhi ladhu, as aswŭrth
dīlša('s) munik | grἀ (be)[2] grēdi(d) šedi ladu (as) a-swúrt
thou's name | love be made upon earth as up

in mŭnniath. Bŭg mūilsha thalosk-minŭrth goshta dhurra.
(in) mun′iaθ | bug mwīlša talósk- min′úrt gošta dura |
in goodness | give I day- now enough bread |

Gretul[3] our shakū, araík mūilsha getyas nīdyas grēdhi
get′al (our) šako arék mwīlša get′a(s) nīd′a(s) grēdi
forgiveness our sin like I forgives persons to do

gamiath mūilsha. Nijesh solk mwī-īl stŭrth gamiath, but bug
g′amiaθ mwīlša | nīd′eš salk mwi'l sturt g′amiaθ (but) bog
badness I | not take I into badness but take

---

[1] I suspect that sentences 28, 45, 49, 58, 63, 76, 78, under β (below), are fragments of this tale.

[2] Words and inflections in round brackets are borrowed from English, those in square brackets from Irish.

[3] A slip in pronunciation or writing for *get′al*.

mŭĭlsha achim gamiath. Dhī-īl the srīdug, thardyūrath, and
mwīlša aχím g'amiaθ | dī'l (the) srīdug tăd'iraθ (and)
I out-of badness | thou the kingdom strength and

mŭnniath, gradhum a gradhum.
mun'iaθ gradum a gradum.
goodness life and life.

(β) SENTENCES[1]

1. *Mwĭlsha bog'd Sheldrū swŭrth nadherum's miskon* (mwīlša bog(d) Šeldrū swurt nad'ram('s) m'iskon—I got S. on mother's breast). 'I learned Shelta on (my) mother's breast.'

2. *A thārī shīrth gather to kam* ((a) tări šīrt gāter (to) kam— A talk down-from father to son). 'A speech, come down from father to son.'

3. *Mŭĭlsha's kam granhēs od luba* (mwīlša('s) kam grani(s) od luba—I's son knows two word). 'My son knows (only) two words.'

4. *Stēsh gloχ ār-gwilyō* (stěš gloχ [ar] gwil'o—Yes-is man after lying). 'The man has lain down.'

5. *Thŭm thol gyuksta* (tom tul g'ūksta—big price monkey). 'A big price, old man!'

6. *Nĭjesh kradyī a simaja* (nĭd'eš krad'i (a) sumad'—Not stop a moment). 'Don't stay a minute.'

7. *Bĭðer a kyena krish blanōg* (b'ŏr' [a'] k'ena kriš blānōg— Woman of-the house old cow). 'The woman of the house is an old cow.'

8. *'Nyŭrth lesk mīlsha thwŭrl', thārīs bĭðer* (n'urt l'esk mwīlša tul, tāri(s) b'ŏr'—Now tell I value says woman). '"Now tell me the price", says the woman.'

9. *Thōrī nolsk and thāri to the lakin* (tōri nolsk (and) tări (to the) lakīn—Come near and speak to the girl). 'Come here and talk to the girl.'

10. *Get nōberī Sheldhrū* (gēt nŏb'ri Šeldrū—Stop bog Shelta). 'Leave off your Bog-Latin."[2]

11. *Mŭĭlsha's karb thōrī'd aχĭm ken-goþ* (mwīlša('s) karb tōri(d) aχím k'en-gop—I's hag come-d out house-poor). 'My old woman came out of the workhouse.'

---

[1] In these sentences the form as given by Sampson is printed first: then follow the rendering into the phonetic system here adopted, an absolutely literal translation, and a free rendering—the latter normally that given by Sampson.

[2] Or preferably 'your bad [attempt at talking] Shelta'.

12. *Nījesh, swiblī, getŭrl* (nĭd'eš sŭbl'i getul—Not boy to-fear). 'Don't be afraid, boy.'

13. *Skŭldrŭm kadyog nap* (skuldrum kad'og nap—To-burn stone white). 'Burning lime.'

14. *Mŭénya grādnī, nījesh grādnī thōrī·in* (mwĕn'a grādni nĭd'eš grādni tōri(in)—Last Saturday not Saturday coming). 'Last Saturday, not next Saturday.'

15. *Mŭĭlsha sunīd gloχ rilhū inoχin kadyogs asthŭrth the skruχ and jŭmikin* (mwīlša sūni(d) gloχ rilū inoχ(in) kad'ōg(s) astúrt (the) skraχo (and) d'umik(in)—I see-d man mad, 'thing'-ing stones in the bush and cursing). 'I saw the [*read*, a] madman throwing stones into the bush and cursing.'

16. *Nūs a Dhalyōn, mislī* (nūs a' Dāl'on misli—Blessing of-the God go). 'By the help of God, I'll go.'

17. *Thom graχū, nījesh mŭĭlsha kradyī* (tom graχu nĭd'eš mwīlša krad'i—Big hurry not I to-wait). 'Great hurry, I can't wait.'

18. *Get swiblī, gami gloχ gruχ dhī-īl* (get sŭbl'i, g'ami gloχ gruχ dī'l—Stop boy bad man shoot thou). 'Stop, boy, the bad man will shoot you.'

19. *Nījesh mislī gruχasha dhī-īl* (nīdeš misli gruχa [s'ē] dī'l—Not to-go will shoot he thou). 'Don't go, he'll shoot you.'

20. **Bog sik granlum.** 'Get some condiment.'

21. *Stēsh thâp minŭrth* (stĕš tâp min'úrt—Yes-is alive now). 'Faith, he's alive now.'

22. *Gloχ, lask gwīsh* (lăsk gwĭš). 'Man, light the straw.'

23. *Gloχ srenthū a thāsp* (gloχ srentu [a] tarsp—Man raving in death). 'Old[1] man raving in death.'

24. *Krish karb roidyō gāt lakin* (krĭš karb rud'u gât lakĭn—Old hag sweethearting young girl). 'The old woman courting like a young girl.' Probably the English *like a*, or the Shelta **arĕk**, has accidentally dropped out before **gât**.

25. *Dhalyōn awárth stēsh shīka nīdyas* (Dāl'on awá'rt stĕš šīkr nĭd'a(s)—God one yes-is three persons). 'Three Persons and one God.'

26. *Binī sharog lakin mŭnī spŭrkera* (b'in'i šarog lakĭn mun'i spurk'ra—Little red girl good *meretrix*). 'The little red[-haired] girl is a fine flirt.'

27. *Sharū olsk âd* (šaru olsk ăd—Quarter after two). 'A quarter past two.'

---

[1] This is as printed: but *gloχ* here should be **g'ŭk**, as one of the notebooks shews. Otherwise there is no justification for 'old'.

28. *Korī in the mamerum, sik nīdya grāfsha* (kŏri (in the) mam'rum, sik nīd'a grāfša—Foot in the room some person ghost). 'A foot in the room, some person haunting the place.'

29. *Nŭrth, Nyēthus, gloχ granhēs thōman* (n'urt, N'ētas, gloχ grani(s) tōmān—Now, James, man knows too-much). 'Now, Jimmy, the man knows too much.'

30. *Nījesh grabaltha thrīpus in gloχ* (nīd'eš grȧbalta trīpus [in] gloχ—Not enabled to fight the man). 'I'm not able to fight the man.'

31. *Thōman guredh, thōman kīénthis, thōman grāg grē swŭrth* (tōmān gored, tōmān k'enti(s), tōmān grāg' grē swurt—Too-much money too-much houses too-much streets to-rise up). 'Too much wealth, too many houses, too many streets sprung up.'

32. *Mŭīlsha shkimashk, mīdril a milk gamier the gloχ* (mwīlša škimišk, mīdril (a) milk g'ami(er) (the) gloχ—I drunk devil a bit worse the man). 'I am drunk, but devil a bit the worse man for that.'

33. *Get grimsha thōrīin, guŏp grimsha mislīin* (get' grimšer tōri(in) gwŏp grimšer misli(in)—Hot time coming, cold time going). 'Hot weather [summer] is coming, cold weather [winter] is going.'

34. *Stēsh charp minkur bīŏer, granhē her grēdhurn* (stēš d'arp mink'er-b'ōr', grani (her) grēdan—Yes-is real tinker-woman know her face). 'That's a true tinker woman, I know by her face.'

35. *Mŭgathon nījesh granīs mŭīlsha* (mugatȧn nīd'eš grani(s) mwīlša—Fool not knows I). 'The fool does not understand me.'

36. *Gorī stŭrt dhī-īl myiskon* (gori sturt dī'l m'iskon). 'Cover up your breast.'

37. *Aχ! Gison, bŭga dhū guredh gyē Sibbi guvéuχ grostār* (Aχ G'ison buga [tū] gored g'e Sibi [go bhēadh] grȧsta—Oh John will-give thee money with S. till you-are satisfied). 'Ah John, I will give you money with Sibbie until you are pleased.' [A rare example of Irish auxiliaries being preferred to English.]

38. *Nījesh mŭīlsha medherī, medherī dŭīlsha* (nīd'eš mwīlša med'ri, med'ri dīlša—Not I carry carry thou). 'I won't carry it, carry it you.'

39. *Thōrīin mŭénya mŭīlsha* (tōri(in) mwēn'a mwīlša—Coming after me). 'Following me.'

40. *Gothena gēeg'd mŭīlsha aχim to myausō* (gȧt'na g'ēg(d) mwīlša aχi'm (to) m'aūso—Youth asked I out to dance). 'The young one asked me out to dance.'

41. *Stēsh ȧd gloχhē thāral* (stēš ȧd gloχi tāral—Yes-is two men talking). 'There are two men talking.'

42. *Dūĭlsha thāri gāmi labŭrth?* (dīlša tāri g'ami laburt—You say bad swear). 'Did you say a bad curse?'

43. *Krish gyukera have mŭni Sheldrū* (kriš g'ūk'ra (have) mun'i Šeldru—Old beggar have good Shelta). 'Old beggars have good Shelta.'

44. *Glōrhī bĭŏr-skēv* (Glōr'i b'ōr'-skev—Hear woman-fish). 'Listen to the fishwife.'

45. *Grē and mislī, stēsh nedhas a mīdril* (grē (and) misli, stēš n'edas-[a']-mīdril—Rise and go yes-is place-of-the-devil). 'Rise and be off, this is a devil's place' [rather '*the* devil's place, hell'].

46. *Mwīlsha's bĭŏr thāsp'd aχẽr* (mwīlša'(s) b'ōr' tarsp(d) aχér— I's woman died last-night). 'My wife died last night.'

47. *Nījesh stamara* (nīd'eš stam'ra). 'Don't spit.'

48. *Nījesh thwurl your grŭber* (nīd'eš tul (your) gruber—Not worth your work). 'Not worth your notice.'

49. *Mūĭlsha lī nedhas a dhalōn* (mwīlša lī n'edas-[a']-Dāl'on— I bed place-of-the-God). 'My bed and lodging in heaven.' [For *mūĭlsha* we should read *mūĭlsha's*: *lī*=bed, but there is no word for 'lodging', which should be expunged from the translation. N'edas-a'-Dāl'on means 'Heaven' (compare n'edas-a'-mīdril in 45, above), and the sentence means 'Heaven is, or may Heaven be, my bed.']

50. *Gushin nedhas a shīrk* (guš(in)-n'edas [a] šīrk—Sitting-place in field). 'Sitting on the grass.'

51. *Chinoχ awarths lorsp'd, the gâthena's rīpuχin' and grŭberin'* (t'inoχ awárt('s) lōsp(d the) gât'na('s) rīpuχ(in and) gruber(in)— Thing one's married the youth's playing-the-*meretrix* and working). 'One's married, the young one's carrying on and working.'

52. *Nedhas aχím in the shkiblin* (n'edas aχím (in the) škiblin— Place outside in the barn). 'A lodging out in the barn.'

53. *Nurth get in gather* (nurt get [in] gāter). 'Now, leave the beer.'

54. *Solt, skait, and surt* (salk(t) skāī(t) surk(t)). 'Arrested, transported (lit. "watered") and hanged.'

55. *Get mūĭlsha sunī* (get mwīlša sūni—Stay I see). 'Wait till I see.'

56. *Mūĭlsha's mŭni grau* (mwīlša's mun'i grå—I's good love). 'My best love.'

57. *Grīchas asthŭrt, nījesh mislī asthŭrt the kĭéna* (Grīt'aθ astúrt, nīd'eš misli astúrt (the) k'ēna—Sickness inside, not to-go inside the house). 'Sickness inside, don't go into the house.'

58. *Klisp'n thalósk, soon be ludhus thōrī-in stŭrt the grenōg* (klisp(in) **talosk** (soon be) **ludus tōri**(in) **sturt** (the) **grin'óg**— Breaking day, soon be light coming into the window). 'Day is breaking, light will soon be coming through the window.'

59. *Mŭtlsha's grostār to sunī dhī-īlsha râgli* (mwīlša('s) **grâsta** (to) **sūni dī'lša râgli**—I's satisfied to see thee to laugh). 'I am pleased to see you laugh.'

60. *Lesk mŭtlsha and mŭtlsha lesk dhī-īlsha* (l'esk mwīlša (and) mwīlša l'esk dī'lša—Tell me and I tell you). 'Tell me, and I'll tell you.' Probably what the speaker said was **mwīlša('ll) l'esk**, the three l's having fallen together.

61. *Stēsh bīōr yīlsha* (stēš b'ōr' (dh)'īlša—Yes-is woman you). 'There's your woman.' [This is an unusual case of the Irish lenition following a feminine noun—the only case of a recognition of grammatical gender to be found in the recorded specimens of the language.]

62. *Rinshkal nīdēsh minŭrth* (**Rinškal nīd'eš min'úrt**—A-sieve-maker not now). Translated 'Sieve-makers are nothing nowadays', but more probably meaning 'There is no such thing as a sieve-maker now'.

63. *Mŭtlsha grēdhi mi lī nedhas in this lŭrk* (**Mwīlša grēdi** (my) **lī-n'edas** (in this) **luk**—I make my bed-place in this corner). 'I'll make my bed in this corner.'

64. *Gamiest od gamī lakin thribli mŭtlsha ever suni'd* (**G'ami**(est) **od g'ami lakīn tribli mwīlša** (ever) **sūni**(d)—Worst two bad girl family I ever see-d). 'The worst family of two daughters I ever saw.'

65. *I suni'd the gothena spŭrkin axĭm axĕr* ((I) **sūni'd** (the) **gât'na spurk**(in) **axim axér**—I see-d the youth playing-the-*meretrix* outside last-night). 'I saw the younger one carrying on outside yesterday.' [The translations of this and the preceding sentence are slightly euphemistic.]

66. *Nĭjesh stafa bŭga dhī-īlsha* (nīd'eš **stafa buga dī'lša**—I not ever will-give thee). 'I'll never give it you.'

67. *Rabin's nŭp surxa medherin lampa* (**Rābīn**('s) **nup surxa med'r**(in) **lampa**—Mary's back tired carrying bag). 'Mary's back's tired carrying (the) bag.' Probably the speaker said **nup('s) surxa**, the two s's having run together.

68. *Mŭnkerī nīdyas sheb gamī guredh 'Donovan'* (**munk'ri-nīd'a**(s) **šeb g'ami gored** D.—Country-persons call bad money D.). 'The country people call a bad coin "a Donovan".'

69. *Gorī mūilsha sik* (gori mwĭlša sik). 'Give me some.'

70. *Thom kamera shŭral gamī grīchath* (tom kam'ra-šural g'ami grĭt'aθ—Big dog running bad sickness). 'The big racing dog [=greyhound] (has some) bad sickness.'

71. *Geth in gloχ* (get [in] gloχ—Leave the man). 'Let the old man be.' [For gloχ read g'ŭk, as in no. 23 above.]

72. *Mūilsha gamī in grīt shīkr grathon, my krish karb gamī minyárth, mūilsha's kam and the bīōr nījesh thōri'd to sunī my dyīl* (Mwĭlša ga'mi (in) grĭt' šĭkr graχton, (my) krĭš karb g'ami min'úrt, mwĭlša('s) kam (and the) b'ōr' nĭd'eš tōri(d to) sūni (my) d'ĭl—I bad in sick[ness] three week my old hag bad now I's son and the woman not come-d to see my self). 'I've been very ill these three weeks, my old woman is ill now, my son and his wife never come [misprint for *came*] to see me.' [Probably we are to read grĭt'aθ; the θ, if pronounced in a slightly sibilant way, might be lost before the following š.]

73. *Lŭsh goštya of the stīma* (luš gošt'a (of the) st'īma—Drink plenty of the pipe). 'Have a good suck at the pipe.'

74. *Aχ, Hibbī, ke nyīpa thū, Hibbī? O gather, gwilyin násdĕsh—A chĕrpa thū mwog's nyuk?—Mūilsha sunīd nījesh mwog's nyuk, gather.* (Aχ Hibi, ke n'īpa tū, Hibi—O gāter, gwil'i(in) nasd'ĕš—A t'ĕrpa tū mwog('s) n'uk? Mwĭlša sūni(d) nĭd'eš mwog('s) n'uk, gāter—O Sibbie, where are you, Sibbie?—O father, lying here.—Have you cooked [or, will you cook] (the) pig's head?—I saw no pig's head, father). 'Ah! Sibbie, where are you, Sibbie? O father, lying down. Have you cooked the pig's head? I never saw the pig's head, father.' [Hibi is vocative of Sibi, no. 37.]

75. *Nŭlsk you sunī mūilsha? Aχáram?* (Nulsk (you) sūni mwĭlša? Aχáram?). 'When [will] you see me? To-morrow?'

76. *Gop gradhum shedhīs getŭl and nījesh a nark, sŭnal od sharker mŭniāth or gamiāth thōrīs shīrth* (Gop gradum šedī(s) getul (and) nĭd'eš (a) nāk', sūnal od šark(er), mun'iaθ (or) g'amiaθ tōri(s) šĭrt—Poor soul stands frightened and not a stitch, seeing two-cutter, goodness or badness goes down). 'The poor soul stands naked and afraid, watching the scales to see whether the good or evil weighs the heavier.'

77. *Sunī got lakin, od miskōn aχím, nīdēsh gotherin, nīdēsh inoχin miskōn* (Sūni gåt lakĭn, od m'iskon aχím, nĭd'eš gåt'rin, nĭd'eš inoχ(in) m'iskon—See young girl, two breast outside not a-child, not 'thing'ing breast). 'Look at the young girl with her two breasts out; she has no child, so she's not been giving it the breast.'

78. '*Lŭgil aχĭm dhī-īl grēdhī* about *mŭīlsha's gulimas*', *thāri''d*
the *gloχ thăsp*, '*athómier* than *gulimas* a *gloχ ērpa?*'—and he *bŭg'd*
a *milk* of his *dīl* by the *kōrīs*, and *klisp'd* his *nyuk swŭrth* the *klaithon*
a *nedhas ladhū* (Lugil aχĭm dī'l grĕdi (about) mwĭlša('s) gulima(s),
tări(d the) gloχ tarsp atóm(ier than) gulima(s a) gloχ ĕrpa? (and
he) bog(d a) milk (of his) d'īl (by the) kōri(s and) klisp(d his) n'uk
swurt (the) klaiton [a'] n'edas ladu—Shout out you make about
I's boots said the man dead, more than boots [of] a man other:
and he took a bit of his self by the legs and broke his head upon
the wall of-the-place-[of]-earth). '"What alarm do you make
about my boots", said the corpse, "more than about another
man's boots?"' and he caught him by the legs and dashed his
brains out against the wall of the graveyard.'

It is hardly necessary to duplicate in this way the remainder
of the sentences in this collection; the above will suffice to illustrate the formulae of phonetic representation here adopted, and
to indicate the method by which the speakers of the language
convey the sense which they intend. The following are given as
written and translated by Dr Sampson: borrowings from English
are printed, as he prints them, in ordinary type, Shelta words
in italics. The translation is free in one or two cases, the phrases
being rather too free (in another sense) for literal rendering.

PROVERBS

79. *Stīmera dhī-ĭlsha, stīmera*[1]
aga dhī-ĭlsha.
If you're a piper, have your
own pipe.

80. *Gloχ nīdēsh* a *gloχ rāks
abŭrth*[2] *od grifin.*
A man's no man at all without two coats.

81. *Thōman thāral* and *nījesh
mŭnīāth.*
Much talk and no good.

82. *Kŭldrŭm nījesh spŭrkŭ.*
Recumbere non est coïre.

83. *Bĭôer medheris gĭôer.*
The woman wears the breeks.

84. *Sŭnal chima* in *tharpōn, binī
mŭnīāth, binī gamīāth.*
Like a chip in porridge, small
good and small ill.

85. *Nap grĕdhŭrn χurī nījesh
munī.*
A white-faced horse is never
any good.

86. *Mwik bĭôrs nījesh nyĕfn.*
Connaught women have no
shame.

87. *Sŭgū thôris, mŭīlsha mislī
glīét thom* to *loban.*
War is coming, I'll be off to
my cabin in the mountains.

[1] Probably a slip for *st'īma*.
[2] Probably we should read *abŭrt rāks* ('at-all without').

88. *Mislō granhēs thâber.*	The traveller knows the road.
89. *Thom Blōrnē nījesh Nīp glox.*	Every[1] Protestant isn't an Orangeman.

WISHES GOOD AND EVIL

90. By the holy *Dhalyōn, sōblī,* I'll *solk your gradhum!*	By the holy God, fellow, I'll have your life!
91. *Gamī grau* to that *glox.*	Bad luck to that man!
92. *Dâlyon mislī* with you, *swiblī.*	God go with you, boy.
93. *Dhuīlsha kurog* for *glox.*	[Insult.]
94. *Nūs a Dhâlyon dhuīlsha.*	The blessing of God on you.
95. *Mislī, gamī grā dhī-īl!*	Be off, and bad luck to you!
96. *Lŭsh* my *kunya lyē smolkera.*	[Insult.]
97. *Gâp* my *thūr.*	[Insult.]
98. *Nūs-a-Dhalyōn mwīlsha hāvarī.*	God bless our home.
99. *Spŭrk dhī-īlsha!*	[Insult.]
100. *Labŭrth shelthū a Dhalyōn dhī-īl!*	The seven curses of God on you.

(γ) SHELTA STORIES

1. *Glox sharog na Srōinya*	The Red Man of the Boyne
(a) *Dŭilsha axiver glōrhi Glox Sharog na skai Srōinya? Grēs swŭrth chal* the *skai* when a *glox's mislïin'* to *sahu* his *dīl. Gyetas a gyetas* and *thribli grīnthala sūni* his *dīl, gramal glox sharog, rīlthug sūlya nyuk.*	Did you ever hear of the Red Man of the river Boyne? He rises half out of the water when a man's going to drown himself. Scores and scores and families of friends have seen him, like a red man, with a sheet around his head.
(b) *Thalosk awárth, larkr sheb'd* Sharkey *mislïin' swŭrth lim a Srōinya, sūni'd sharog glox, chal swŭrth skai. Sūni'd* and *thari'd nīdesh. Larkr sūni'd od-lim* to *sūni* some *nīdya skai* his *dīl. Nīdesh nīdya. Nŭrth grē'd swŭrth od thwŭrk, thari'd 'Nījesh thōri!'* and *misli'd shīrth* the *skai yīrth. Grē'd swŭrth shīka thwŭrk, gorri'd swŭrth mālya warth,* and *thari's 'Simaj swŭrth; glox nijesh thōrïin'!' Nŭrth larkr sūni'd glox shurral thom, nap'd*	One day a tailor named Sharkey, walking by the bank of the Boyne, saw the Red Man, half out of the water. He [the Red Man] looked and said nothing. The tailor looked each way to see some person drown himself. There was nobody. Now he [the Red Man] rose up a second time, and said, 'Not come yet!' and sank down again into the water. He rose a third time, put up one hand and says, 'Time's up, and the

---

[1] Better, 'Many a'.

a *grifin*, and *goihe*'d on the *thōber. Larkr misli*'d *swŭrth, granhēin*' the *gloχ*, and *bug*'d a *milk* of his *dīl*.

(c) '*Car dhī-īlsha mislüin*'*?*' '*Get mī-īlsha! nījesh sŭmaj* to *kraji.*' '*Kradyi*, my *mŭni gloχ*.' '*Nijesh thari dhī-īl!*' *Larkr bug*'d a *milk* of the *gloχ ayīrth, stēsh thom thrīpus lim a skai. Larkr lōber*'d *gloχ shīrth od thwŭrk*, and *shīka thwŭrk gloχ gwili*'d on *thōber.* 'What's to *grēdhi* with *dhī-īl?* Do you *granhē mīdhril thōri*'d for *dhī-il?' larkr thari*'d. *Gloχ gop gorri*'d *swŭrth od mālya, thariin*' *stafaris.* '*Nūs a Dhalyon! Bug mŭīlsha gather skai!*' '*Thōri swŭrth ken gather' larkr thari*'d *gloχ.* '*Bug dhī-īl slunya skaihōp.' Sroidyan aχárram, gloχ bug*'d *larkr od nŭmpa.*

(d) *Thalosk ērpa, gushin' lim slarskr skai, mū-īlsha* and *gloχ slarskr thariin*' of *thrīpusin' gloχis. Nŭrth gloχ slarskr sūni*'d *gloχ sharog stŭrth skai.* '*Stēsh minŭrth a sahū!*' and he *sūni*'d *gloχ swŭdhal rilhu—stēsh gloχ radhum—shurral thom shīrth skai.* '*Get swibli, get! Sūni* in *gloχ-swŭdhal sahu* his *jīl!' Gloχ misli*'d *shurral, thariin' gami lŭbas a mīdhril,* and *misli*'d *shlīm stŭrth skai. Mū- īlsha nap*'d my *grifin* and *gulimas. Gloχ slarskr bŭg*'d a *milk* of my *dīl.* '*Kradyi!*' he *thari*'d, '*Kradyi mŭilsha. Sūni mŭilsha grēthi.*' '*Gloχ* be *sathŭ.*'

man's not coming!' Now the tailor saw a man in a great hurry, who took off his coat and threw it on the road. The tailor went up, knowing the man, and caught hold of him.

'Where are you going?' 'Let me go! I haven't a minute to wait.' 'Hold on, my good man.' 'I have nothing to say to you!' The tailor caught hold of the man again, and there was a great fight on the bank of the river. The tailor floored the man three times, and three times the man lay on the ground. 'What's the matter with you? Do you know that the devil came for you?' said the tailor. The poor man put up both hands, saying his prayers. 'For God's sake, give me a drink of water.' 'Come down to the inn', said the tailor to the man, 'and I'll give you a glass of whisky.' Next morning the man gave the tailor two pounds.

Another day, sitting by the river lock, I and the lock gate-man were talking of [famous] fighting men. Now the gate-man saw the Red Man in the water. 'Now for a drowning!' [he said]: and he saw a mad gentleman (he was a soldier) hurrying into the water. 'Hold on boy, hold on! Watch this gentleman drown himself!' The man came rushing on, saying bad words of the devil, and went with a leap into the water. I took off my coat and boots, but the gate-man caught hold of me. 'Wait!' he said, 'wait for me. See what I'll do!'

'*Nīdesh! Get! Nījesh misli stŭrth* till *mūilsha lesk* you. *Nurth bŭg sŭrhū; stēsh thardyur mīdhril!*' *Gloχ swŭdhal misli*'d *shīrth od thwŭrk thūur an skai, jŭmmik*in' *gami lŭbas, thari*in' *a mīdhril. Nŭrth* the *gloχ slarskr shlīm*'d *asthŭrt* and *bŭg*'d a *milk* of his *dīl, solk*'d *mālya, lōber*'d *gloχ swŭdhal, gorri*'d him on his *nŭp*, and *solk*'d his *dīl lim a skai. Mūilsha solk*'d *gloχ swudhal* on *ladhu. Shika gloχi misli*'d *shurri*in', *cholli*in' *gloχ-swudhal rilhu.* '*Goihe* his *dīl*' *gloχ slarskr thari*s *mīlsha.*'*Thōri mīlsha*, and *suni thōman gurredh* we *bŭg.*' *Misli*'d *shīrth ken thom.* '*Nŭrth* this *gloχ* and *mūilsha solk*'d him *aχim skai*' *gloχ slarskr thari*s, '*Bug mūilsha shŭka nŭmpa*', '*Nīdesh* a *skurrig!*' *yēdug thari*s, '*Mūilsha bŭg dhī-īl od thwŭrk* or *shika thwŭrk* if *dhī-ilsha bŭg* him to *tharsp.*' *Bīuer-swŭdhal shērku na slī, getūl a gather rilhū.*

(e) *Stēsh gloχ bog*'d *ar-mislo thwŭrk mŭénya ayirth* and *skai*'d his *dīl. Od thwŭrk sahu*'d; *gloχ slarskr nyēsh naper*'d his *dyīl.*

(f) *Lim a Srōinya thoman nīdyas misli rilhū. Goshta rilhū nīdyas, gāt lakins* and *gāt swiblis, stēsh* and *krish gloχi* and *krish karbs mukinya lim a Srōinya. Lashul*est *nedhas* you could *misli, skai* and *slūfa* and *ken thoms—stēsh grēdhi*s *nīdyas rilhū.*

'But the man will be drowned.' 'No! wait! don't go into the water till I tell you. Now he's getting tired. Sure he's a strong devil!' The gentleman sank twice to the bottom of the river, cursing out bad words, talk of the devil. Then the gate-man jumped in and caught hold of him, took his hand, and struck the gentleman [insensible], carried him on his back, and took him to the river-bank. I lifted the gentleman on land. Three men came running, following the mad gentleman. 'Leave him there', the gate-man says to me. 'Come with me, and let's see how much money we get.' We went down to the great house. 'Now this man and myself got him out of the water', says the gate-man; 'give us five pounds.' 'Not a farthing!' the lady says, 'but I'd have given it to you two or three times over if you had let him drown.' The lady was his daughter-in-law, and she lived in dread of her mad father.

The same man escaped again on a later occasion and threw himself into the water, and on the second time he was drowned: the lock gate-man never interfered with him.

By the bank of the Boyne many people go mad. Numbers of mad people, young girls and boys, yes and old men and women too, dwell near the Boyne. It's the loveliest place where you could walk, with water and wood and houses of great folks; but it drives people mad.

2. Od Minkur Kunyas

The Two Tinker Priests

(a) *Od minkur, münni thari*ers *of staffri, misli'd* through the *münkera,* where they were *nijesh granhē'd, tharal* they were *od klisp kunya*s. *Stēsh od nyark minkur. Od bŭg'd gashta grīnlesk, stēsh glŭtug, stēsh* and *bug'd goshta lŭog. Kunya-a-rabbister glōrhe'd* the *od nyark, shēb'd* them *chŭrpera*s, *tharal* '*Mwī-īl thori asthurt* their *nedhers* to *sŭnni* their *dīls.*' The *swiblis* and *gloχis thari'd gami* of the *kunya* for *nappin'* with their *dīls, lesk'd od klisp kunya*s *kunya-a-rabbister thōri olomi ahŭnshk. Minkur thari'd* '*Mwīlsha grostar* to *sŭnni* the *kunya.*' *Stē-esh gredhe'd nīd'ha*s *munnier grostar.* (*Nŭrth* the *od nyark minkur*s *grostar* to be *gyeta līman ar-mislo, getterl kunya* and *stēsh nīd'ha*s.)

(b) *Nŭrth* they *misli'd tharain' staffari*s. *Grag* was *thâon nid'ha*s, *kiéna bwikadh nīdesh thomier. Chinnoχ-awárth minkur thari'd kunya*'s *tharal:* '*Oχ! gettūl ar mo thŭr-sâ. Oχ! gettūl ar mo thŭr-sâ.*' *Sharkar kunya thari'd, lōber'n'* his *grīsh, athómier gredhiin' aχím* he was *sraiχa:* '*Mŭilsha arárk! mŭilsha arárk!*' *grassiin' nīd'ha*s *lyē charp staffri*s.

Two tinkers, good sayers of prayers, travelled through the country, where they were not known, giving out that they were two suspended (lit. broken) priests. They were, however, two rogues of tinkers. The pair got plenty of flax and wool, and also plenty of meal. The parish priest heard of the two rogues, and called them impostors, saying: 'I am coming to their lodgings to see them.' The boys and men spoke ill of the priest for meddling with them, and told the two suspended priests that the parish priest was coming next night. The tinkers said, 'We shall be pleased to see the priest', and this made the people still more delighted. (Now the two tinker rogues would have been glad to have been twenty miles away for fear of the priest and the people too.)

Now they went on saying their prayers. The road was full of people and the houses could hold no more. One tinker would say, pretending to talk Latin (lit. priest's language), *Oχ! gettūl* [1] *ar mo thŭr-sa.* His brother priest would say, beating his breast and making out that he was the clerk, *Muilsha arark!* ['I'm the same!'] charming the people with their fine prayers.

---

[1] *Ar mo* is Irish. The point of the story lies in the superstitious fear formerly inspired by an unfrocked priest, who, having by his profession acquired the secrets of Heaven, and by his misdemeanours sold himself to the devil, had at his disposal the supernatural powers of both departments of the unseen world. The bogus priest's "prayer" means, in essence, "I'm afraid for my"—[appropriate place for being kicked].

(c) *Sroijan misli'*d and *lyesk'*d the *nīd'has*, '*Mūilsha thori agrésh ōlomi axárrm*', *goixe'*d *grīnlesk, klūtya, lūog, shūkr numpa thwūrl, mūéna, nīdēsh thori'*d *axíver*.

3. *Karb a Thriblī*

(a) *Thōrīin agrēsh* the *grīnthus thalosk awárth, thōrīin axim Skaithwūrd, mūilsha sunī'*d a *krish karb skimashk*, a *bini lakin swūrth karb's nup—sheb'*d her *Rab—od kōrī shīrth* her *miskon*.

(b) *Stēsh od thārī in Sheldrū. Mūilsha kradyi'*d a *milk, glorhīin karb* and *bini lakin thāral. Gothena thārī'*d as *mūni Sheldrū* as *krish karb: grē'*d *swūrth arárk*.

(c) *Mūilsha mislī'*d *shlug* to *glorhī sik* of their *swūrth-a-munkeri Sheldrū. Stēsh* same *rark a thāral. Mislī'*d *shlug, glōrhīin* their *thāral*.

(d) *Krish* and *gāt mislī'*d *asthúrt ken-gather. Karb thōrī'*d at my *kōris. Thōrīin asthúrt, bini lakin malya*s *nyakerlt karb's grēdhūrn, lober't goixera's nyuk a rudhus, shlug'*d her *axim shlōhya, goixin'* her *dīl* that *nedhers chal karrib'*d, and *gush'*d *shīrth* the *mamerum gather. Sunī'*d her *malya. Thanyuk*.

(e) '*Mărro thanik ūggum, buggama[3] slunya*.' Then, in *Palanthus*: '*O glox thom, bug* the *krish karb thanyuk, nūs-a-Dhalyōn!*'

In the morning they went away, and told the people they would return the next night, left flax, wool, and meal, five pounds' worth, behind them, and returned no more.

The Grandmother of the Family

Coming back from the fair one day, coming from Waterford, I saw an old woman drunk, a little girl across the old woman's back—she called her Mary—her two feet across her breast.

Those two were talking Shelta. I stopped a little, listening to the old woman and the little girl talking. The child spoke as good Shelta as the old woman: grew up that way.

I went slowly to listen to some of their up-country[1] Shelta. Just the same sort of talk.[2] I went slowly, listening to their talk.

Old and young went into a public house, the old woman coming at my heels [lit. feet, or legs]. Going in, the little girl's hands clasping the old woman's neck, she struck the child's head on the door and threw her out [on the] ash-heap, leaving her half-killed there, and sat down in the tap-room. She looked at her hand: a halfpenny [was there].

'If I had [another] halfpenny, I should get a glass.' Then, in English: 'O big man, give the poor old woman a halfpenny, for the love of God.'

---

[1] I.e. Munster. [2] *Scil.* 'as I was accustomed to'.
[3] Properly *boga mē*, 'I shall get'. [*Mē* = Irish first personal pronoun.]

(f) '*Nījesh.' 'Aχ! Minkur hū?' 'Nījesh minkur.' 'In stīmera hū?' 'Nījesh stīmera.' 'Rinshkal hū?' 'Nījesh rinshkal.' 'Nījesh gyukera hū?' 'Nījesh a gyukera.*'

(g) *Karb lŭggd aχĭm: 'Ke nyĭpa hū, Rabin, O!' 'Aχĭm ara χarnan snēli: klĭspa hu* my *nyuk, natherum thom, thōrīin' asthŭrt* the *rudus.*'

(h) '*Dhalyon swuther, noχ mīdher mŭĭlsha!'—'Stesh, rī-mīdher!*'

(i) '*Thōrī asthŭrt, Rabin, O!' Karb lyag* her *thāral. 'Aχ, Minkur hū?*' [etc.]. *Dhalyon swŭrth! Rī-mīdher's karb!*

(j) *Thom munkera-gloχ lushin'* a *slunya gather, thōrīin' grēsh na grinthus: 'Lush swŭrth, swŭbli! Karb's kam's thōrīin' minurth, skimashk. Gami thriblī: thripus karb karribin'* and *lushin'* the *olomy. Grē swŭrth dhī-īlsha! Mislī!*'

(k) *Mŭĭlsha salkt gloχ's lubha,* and *stēsh mislī'd. 'Gāt gloχ, stēsh* a *gransha* in the *munkera: granī dhī-īl's thāral* a *luthera. Stēsh gamī McDonaghs', gloχ lyesk'd: 'stēsh krish karb natherum thom* a *thribli,* and the *gamiest krish karb grē* the *karribin* of the *thribli,' gloχ lyesk'd. 'Aχĭm* o' the *mīdher, gamiest.* They'll be *thōrīin'* from the *grintha skimashk. Dhī-īlsha* the

'No!' [I answered, in Shelta]. 'What, are you a tinker?' 'I am no tinker.' 'Are you a piper?' 'I am no piper.' 'Are you a sievemaker?' 'I am no sievemaker.' 'You are not a beggar?' 'I am not a beggar.'

The old woman called out: 'Where are you, Mary?' 'Out on the heap of rushes: you broke my head, grandmother, coming inside the door.'

'God Almighty, am I not a devil!' 'You are—a king-devil!'

'Come in, Mary, O!' The old woman forgot her talk. [She again asked for a half-penny in English, and I refused in Shelta.][1] 'What, are you a tinker?' [and so forth]. Almighty God! The king-devil's old woman!

A big countryman drinking a glass of ale, coming back from the fair. [He said] 'Drink quickly, lad! The old woman's son is coming [back] now, drunk. A bad lot—fighting, killing, stealing, and drinking the night. You get up! Be off!'

I took the man's word [advice], and went off. 'Young man, you're a stranger in the country: I know your northern speech. Those are the bad McDonaghs', the man said, 'and the old woman is the grandmother of the family, and the worst old woman of the lot to raise the fighting', the man said. 'Except the devil, the worst. They'll be coming from

---

[1] Interpolation in English in the Shelta text.

SHELTA 153

mĭdher with their *dŭl*s and *lober*
their *gloχ-thribli*, if you *kradĭ*,
you'll *bŭg* the *ladher thwurk*.
Grē, swŭbli, mislĭ mŭĭlsha!'

(1) *Stĕsh solk'*d *gloχ*'s *lŭbba,*
grēd and *mislĭd od lyĭmon.*
*Thārĭ*s: ' *Na havara mŭĭlsha bŭg*
your *lĭ* and your *gripa srag-*
*āster'. I bŭg*d *karb od nyuk* and
mislĭd, stĕsh the *karb'*s *staffarĭ*s.
I'd as lief have the *mĭdher'*s
*staffarĭ*s as the *karb'*s *staffarĭ*s.

the fair, drunk. If you [play]
the devil with them, and light
upon their men-folk, [and] if
you stay, you'll get the dirty
time. Up, lad! I'm going myself.'

I took the man's advice,
rose, and went two miles. He
says: 'At home I'll give you
your bed, and your supper
[and] breakfast.' I gave the
old woman twopence and went
with the old woman's blessings.
I'd as lief have the devil's
blessings as the old woman's
blessings.

III. CONSTRUCTION OF THE LANGUAGE

In the first enthusiasm of the discovery of Shelta, it was claimed,
by no less a scholar than Kuno Meyer, to be a relic of high
antiquity, identical with the secret languages, of which we hear
from time to time, in Irish literature, and, though now degraded
to the jargon of itinerant tinkers and other vagrants, to have
once been the freemasonry sign of the scholars and craftsmen of
ancient Ireland. The disreputable vagabonds from whom Sampson
acquired his knowledge of the tongue were the heirs of a state of
society when masters of science and of art ranked by virtue of their
attainments with nobles, and even with kings: and when those
wonderful works of art were executed, which have come down
to us out of the early Christian antiquity of Ireland.

Leland, writing to Sampson in 1899, said: 'It is one of the
awfully mysterious arcana of human stupidity that there should
have existed for a thousand years in Great Britain a cryptic
language—the lost language of the bards—which no scholar ever
heard of, and of which Borrow was totally ignorant: that I should
have discovered it and hunted it up: that you should, with
K. Meyer, have made such marvellous further discoveries, and
shewed what it was: *et pour combler* and for a crowning sheaf of
stupidity, that neither you nor I have ever published a book on
the most curious linguistic discovery of the century. For even
yet there is hardly a scholar who knows of its existence—of the
fifth British Celtic tongue!'

That there is some material of great antiquity in Shelta is

unquestionable: but the following analysis will probably make it clear to the reader that, at least in its present form, it cannot as a whole be considered as a heritage from a remote past, and that in any case to describe it as 'a Celtic tongue' is hardly admissible.

PHONETICS

The present writer is partly a compiler and editor from the work of others, and has not acquired a first-hand knowledge of the Shelta language as it is spoken by those to whom it belongs. It is, however, possible to form a fair idea of how the words are pronounced, by taking the average of all the varied spellings used by different observers. In the following vocabulary, an attempt has been made to present every form in which the words appear in different collections, in addition to the phonetic spelling which those forms suggest. Those from Dr Sampson's collections, published and unpublished, are left unmarked: the others are assigned to their authors by initials (for particulars and references see the opening section of this chapter). These are as follows:

A = Arnold	K' = Carmichael [MS.]
C = Crofton [MS. book]	L = Leland [Pennsylvania list]
C' = Crofton [in *Academy*]	L' = Leland [Aberystwyth list]
F = ffrench	N = Norwood
G = Greene [in *Béaloideas*]	R = Russell
G' = Greene [MS.]	W = Wilson
K = Carmichael [pub. by MacRitchie]	

The usually obvious etymology of the words helps to determine their phonetic form; but this is not invariably trustworthy. It has been found impossible to determine the true vowels in many cases: they are given by different collectors almost at haphazard.

In the consonants, there are two outstanding difficulties. The palatalized consonants have proved a serious stumbling-block to collectors, and evidence for this Gaelic characteristic, which is taken over into Shelta, has to be carefully looked for. Thus, the word for 'bad' is usually spelt *gami*: but it sometimes appears as *gyami*, which indicates that the g is palatalized. A study of etymologies makes it clear that what collectors write as *ch* (=č as in 'church') or *j* are really palatalized *t* and *d* respectively. For example, the word given as *jumik* 'to swear' must be derived from the Irish *mõidighim* 'I swear'. The *-im* is the personal ending:

the -*igh*- is represented by the Shelta -*ik*: the Shelta *jum* is a
reversal of the Irish *mōid* [mōd'], and the *j* is therefore not *dž*,
but d' [=dy].

The second difficulty which faces the editor of these collections
is that singular phonetic freelance the English *r*, which intrudes
unbecomingly where it should be absent ('my idea*r* is'), and
absents itself disconcertingly when it should be present ('that's
ɥaðə [=rather] fine'). In many cases I suspect that collectors
have inserted it merely to lengthen a preceding vowel—just as
those who write the 'answers to correspondents' in popular
periodicals shock us with such statements as, 'The word should
be pronounced *sonartar*'. This letter behaves with perfect propriety in Irish, in Irish-English, and presumably also in Shelta:
but it seems to deviate from the paths of rectitude when Shelta
is written down by non-Irish collectors. Thus, we are told that
grimsha [grimša] means 'time'. Obviously this comes from Irish
aimser [ams'er]; from which it follows that the word must surely
have been pronounced, and ought to have been written, *grimšer*.
On the other hand, *grostar* 'satisfied' clearly comes from Irish
sāsta, and should therefore be written *grāsta* or *grâsta*. Leland
seems to have been very deaf to this letter, and he often drops
it where it *must* have been present on the lips of his informants.
The word 'Shelta', which owes its current form to him, is a case
in point: it ought to be *Sheldrū*.

The following are the phonetic symbols used in the Vocabulary.
[In the 'Connected Specimens' of the language, printed above,
it has been considered advisable to reproduce the spelling followed by Dr Sampson.]

VOWELS

a Short a, as in *pan*.
ā Long a, as in *father*.
å A more closed long a, as in *awe*.
e Short e, as in *pen*.
ē Long e, as in *pain*.
i Short i, as in *pin*.
ī Long i, as in *machine*.
o Short o, as in *pod*.
ō Long o, as in *mode*
u Short u, as in *pun*.
ū Long u, as in *moon*.
ə The neutral vowel-sound.

The diphthongs are

ai or ei	i in *pine*.
oi	oy in *boy*.
au	ow in *cow*.

In the phonetic representations of Irish (not Shelta) words, nasalization is indicated by the symbol ∼.

A dot is used to discriminate syllables where necessary, especially when two consecutive vowels do not form a diphthong as in *tāri·in*. A diphthong is implied by the absence of the dot between vowels.

CONSONANTS

b, p, k, as in English.

g, always hard.

d, t, *always* as in Irish, the tip of the tongue being pressed against the roots of the teeth. These are the characteristic dentals of the so-called 'Irish brogue' [Irish-English phonesis]: to write them *dh*, *th* is quite misleading. The ordinary English *d, t* are absent, both from Irish and from Shelta.

All consonants have a second set of sounds (palatalized). This may be described as being, as it were, the normal sound *plus* a 'y', as in the provincial English *cyow, cyard* for *cow, card*. Palatalized consonants are here indicated by a mark resembling an acute accent (*c'ow, c'ard*). The sounds of **g', d'**, approximate sufficiently to one another to cause confusion; thus *giliχon* (=g'iliχon) 'a book' is sometimes written *jiliχon* (=d'iliχon), which seems at first sight to contradict the statement that *g* is always hard.

The sound č (*ch* as in 'church') is here represented by c, which is not otherwise required. But in any case it is not really a Shelta sound, appearing only in some borrowed words: the sound written *ch* by collectors should really be regarded as t'. In some cases, however, it seems to mean χ—by which character Dr Sampson is here followed in representing, conveniently but not quite accurately, the guttural sound ḥ (*ch* in 'loch').

The symbols θ, ð are used whenever necessary to represent the sounds of English *th* (in *think* and *this* respectively). The Irish *th*, which is an *h* rather more fully breathed than in English, is denoted phonetically by ḥ.

Liquid consonants (*l, n, r*), when immediately following a long vowel, tend to become vocalic (*ḷ, ṇ, ṛ*), as in the Dublin street child's pronunciation of 'aeroplane' in five distinct syllables (*ē·ṛ·ō·plē·ṇ*) or 'It's going to rain' (*əts gōn to rē·ṇ*). This is why collectors so constantly write *dī-īl*, or *dhī-īl*, and similar cumbrous forms. In the phonetic transcript here this tendency is indicated by an apostrophe (dī'l). An apostrophe is also used to denote a swabharakti vowel, which if written in full tends sometimes to obscure the etymology. Thus **munk'ri** is written instead of *monkery* 'country'.

The 'broad' (unpalatalized) liquids are pronounced in Irish rather further back in the throat than in English. This has induced collectors to insert an *h* after them in some cases (*glōrhi* 'to hear'; *rīlhu* 'mad'). It is here omitted, as being unnecessary and misleading: the liquids, like other consonants, when not distinguished with the mark of palatalization, must be pronounced in the way indicated.

The symbol *š* is used for palatalized *s*. Properly speaking it should be s' (=sy), but even in Irish this difficult sound has become practically indistinguishable from *š* (sh).

The accentuation of syllables is denoted (with an acute accent on the vowel) only when it falls otherwise than on the first syllable.

For the sake of simplicity the semi-vowels **w**, **y** are used in preference to *u̯*, *i̯*.

ACCIDENCE

THE ARTICLE

There is no article native to Shelta, either definite or indefinite. In Irish, the absence of an article or of any other defining word is equivalent to the indefinite article. This idiom is common in Shelta: but the English indefinite article *a* is sometimes borrowed, as in the common phrase **he bog'd a milk of his d'ï'l** 'he took hold of him'. Both usages are illustrated by β 80, **glox nīd'eš a glox** 'a man is not a man' [unless, etc.].

The definite article is often omitted where both English and Irish usage would require its presence. Thus β 8, **n'urt l'esk mwilša tul, tāris b'ōr'**, means 'now tell me [the] price, says [the] woman'. Otherwise the Irish article *an*, usually shortened or carelessly pronounced *in*,[1] or the English *the*, are borrowed indefinitely. An example is **trīpus in glox** 'fight the man'. The Irish article appears more frequently in the genitive case. This is *an*

---

[1] This cannot be regarded as a survival of the Old Irish form *in*, *ind*: rather is it a reversion thereto.

masculine, *na* feminine: but grammatical gender is evanescent in Shelta, and both forms are represented by *a*, as in **b'ōr' a k'ena** 'the woman of the house'.

This expression illustrates the Shelta recognition of the Irish idiom which forbids two words to be provided with the definite article when one is in genitive relationship to the other ('woman of the house' not 'the woman of the house'). But when English particles are used, English idiom is followed, as in Leland's sentence: *The nidias of the kiena don't granni what we're a tharyin'* (The **nīd'as of the k'ena** don't **grani** what we're **a-tāri·in**) 'The people of the house don't know what we're saying'.

The Substantive

There is nothing in Shelta comparable with the elaborate declensions of the substantive in Irish. Practically the only inflexion is **s**, borrowed from English to form the possessive case and the plural number: **Nad'ram's m'iskon** (β 1) 'mother's breast'; **inoχin kad'ōgs** (β 15) 'flinging stones'.[1]

There are, however, some traces of a native plural. Thus, in β 41, **ād gloχi** 'two men' gives us a plural of **gloχ** 'man'. Incidentally, this is not idiomatic Irish: here the *dual* number should be used, which is identical in form with the dative singular. **Kriš gloχi** (γ 1f) 'old men' is another illustration. In γ 2 a we find a double plural, Shelta and English, **gloχ-i-s**.

The other oblique cases are formed periphrastically as in English, and usually with English prepositions. Thus, **tāri to the lākīn** (β 9) 'talk to the girl'.

The Irish vocative prefix *a* never appears in any of the extracts or specimens. But we may trace its influence if, as seems probable, the person referred to as *Sibi* in β 37 be the same as the person addressed as *Hibi* in β 74. The Irish particle produces the initial consonant-change called lenition (or, less accurately, aspiration) in the word to which it is prefixed: and under its influence initial *s* becomes *h*.

---

[1] There is probably something wrong with Leland's *strepuck lusk* ('meretricis filius'); *lusk* is not found elsewhere, and this form of expressing genitive relationship has no parallel in recorded Shelta.

THE ADJECTIVE

Adjectives are incapable of inflexion, except in the expression of degrees of comparison, which they form with English suffixes (as g'ami 'bad', g'amier, g'amiest). These forms are used even when, as in the word quoted, both the Irish and English corresponding adjectives form their degrees of comparison irregularly.

K'en toms (γ 1 f) is not an exception to or disproof of the above statement. This does not mean 'big houses', as it was translated when the story was first published, but (on the analogy of k'en gop 'poor house' and k'en gruber 'workhouse') 'houses of great [folk]s'.

In Irish, adjectives all but invariably follow the substantive which they qualify. In Shelta, under English influence, the order has become indifferent: thus we find g'ami lākīn 'a bad girl', side by side with grēt'in gūt 'a black bird'. This freedom extends even to numeral adjectives, which precede the noun both in Irish and in English: laburt šeltū 'seven curses', but šūka numpa 'five pounds'.

The numerals, so far as they have been recovered, are as follows:

n'uk (='head'), wart, awárt	one
od, ȧd (also d'asag)	two
šīka or šīkr	three
šāka or šākr	four
šūka or šūkr	five
šē (Irish)	six
šeltū	seven
probably oχt (Irish)	eight
„ nī (Irish)	nine
t'al g'et'a (='half score')	ten
g'et'a	twenty
ȧd g'et'a	forty
šūka g'et'a	a hundred

These numerals can also be used as ordinals.

Adjectives may do duty as adverbs, and can also be adapted on occasion as verbal roots, without any change.

The Pronoun

Except the personal pronouns, all pronominal forms used in Shelta are derived from English.

The personal pronouns are formed with the help of a word **d'i'l, d'il**, which apparently means something like 'self', but, so far as the available specimens of the language go, appears never to be used in any other connexion. The appropriate possessive pronoun of the person is prefixed. In the first and second persons singular the Irish possessives *mo, do* are used; in the remaining persons, singular and plural, the English possessives are preferred. This is probably for the sake of distinction, for, in Irish, 'his', 'her', 'their' are alike represented by *a*, distinguished only by their influence (lenition or nasalization) on the initial letter of the following word. As these initial modifications are hardly traceable in Shelta, the Irish possessives would lose their individuality.

The Irish possessives *mo, do* produce lenition of the following consonant, and in this exceptional case the effect persists in Shelta. Initial *d'* becomes y, so that **mo d'il** becomes **mo yil**, which coalesces into **mwil**, the regular word for the first personal singular pronoun. **Do yil** coalesces into **dil** (with unpalatalized *d*), which is the second personal singular pronoun. As a rule the Irish emphatic suffix *-ša* is appended, making **mwilša, dilša**. The first of these is sometimes, as in the translation of the Lord's Prayer (α), rather loosely used for the first person plural: but as a rule the other persons are *his* or *her* **d'il**, *our, your, their* **d'ils**. All three persons are constructed with the third person of the verb ('My self is' for 'I am').

The genitive of **mwilša, dilša** is formed in the usual English way—**mwilša's, dilša's**. Even for these two pronouns, as well as for the others, the ordinary English personal pronouns are frequently used.

The Verb

For the greater part, the verbal inflexions are English. They are (1) Present tense, third singular *-s*: **taris b'ōr'** 'says [the] woman'. (2) Past tense, all persons *-d*: **mwilša sūnid** 'I saw'. (3) Present participle *-in(g)*: **tōri·in, mislī·in** 'coming, going'.

With verbal stems ending in *i*, the two *i*'s are usually kept distinct, as in these examples. But their occasional coalescence may be indicated in some collections by such spellings as *tōryin*.

There are traces of a few native inflexions, which seem to be evanescent. These are:

1. A future in -a: **gruχa šĕ** (β19) 'he will shoot': **nĭd'eš buga** (β66) 'I will not give'. It seems to be used only when there is a possibility of misunderstanding: thus, in β60 **l'esk** is used both for the second person imperative or the first person future. In β74 **a t'ĕrpa** was rendered by Dr Sampson 'have you cooked?' More probably it should be 'Are you going to cook?' [The *a* in this case is the usual Irish interrogative prefix *an*, *a'*.]

2. A participial form in -o, -u: as **ar gwil'o** (β4) 'after lying down, having lain down': **grat' gušu** 'place [of] sitting' (= a saddle).

3. A verbal-noun formative in -al: **sūnal** (β76) 'seeing, sight'; **tāral a lut'ra** (γ3k) 'speech of the north'. [This is not identical with the Irish -*āl* (with long *a*), which has a different function, at least in the modern speech: that of forming a verb out of a substantive (most commonly a non-Irish substantive), as in *sketch-āl*, a monstrosity which I have heard on the Aran Islands, meaning 'to photograph'. Compare the German -*iren*.]

The English -*er* is frequent to form the noun agent, as in **tāri·er** 'a speaker'. The participial -*in* is also used to form a verbal noun. **Tāri·in a mīdril** (γ1d) was translated, on the first publication of the text, 'talking to the devil'. It should have been 'talking [i.e. mode of talk] of the devil, blasphemy'.

Verbal stems and their substantive cognates are almost always identical. **Labúrt** means 'to swear' and also 'an oath, a curse': **gruber** means 'to work', 'work' in general, or, specifically, 'a piece of work, a job'.

There is very little direct connexion between the Shelta and the Irish verb, either in accidence or in idiom. Perhaps the most obvious is the periphrastic perfect and pluperfect forms with *ar*, *īar* 'after', as in **ar gwil'o**, cited above. But as this is a very common construction in Irish-English ('I am after going' = 'I have gone': 'I was after going' = 'I had gone') it was not necessarily adopted in Shelta directly from Irish.

In general, it must be said that in the verbal construction of Shelta we can see the same helplessness as in the Broken-English of Negroes or Polynesians. Roots are strung together with few or no connecting inflexions or particles, and only the context, or the tone of voice, can indicate the exact meaning intended by the speaker. Thus β42, **Dīlša tāri g'ami labúrt**, is translated by

Dr Sampson, no doubt correctly, 'Did you say a bad curse?' The literal meaning is 'Thou. Speak. Bad. Swear', and there is nothing in the words themselves to indicate whether the speaker is asking a question, making a statement, or issuing a command; all three are possible: nor is there any clue as to whether the action indicated is in the past, the present, or the future. Again, β70, **Tom kam'ra šural g'ami grīt'aθ**, translated 'The big racing dog has some bad sickness', rendered literally is a mere string of unconnected ideas—'Big. Dog. To-run. Bad. Sickness'.

SYNTAX

In idiom and in construction Shelta is far more English than Irish. It has been fashioned into its present form by persons whose major language was English, pronounced according to Irish-English phonesis, though they admittedly possessed an extensive vocabulary of words in common use in Irish. Not infrequently, however, these Irish words are used in collocations which no native speaker of the Irish language in its purity would think of. Now and then we come across phrases made of Irish words, with or without artificial deformation, which are as un-Irish as, let us say, *das will nicht tun* for 'that will not do' would be un-German. For example, to translate 'daughter-in-law' literally, word for word, into Irish, would make unmeaning nonsense for one not acquainted with English; but Shelta speakers have no difficulty with the analogous rendering **šērkū-na-slī**, which we find in γ1d. We have already seen that the idiom of **Stēš gloχ ar gwil'o** 'the man is after lying down' is ultimately based on an Irish linguistic formula: but against this may be set the uncompromisingly English **he g'ēg'd mwīlša aχím** (β40) 'he asked me out' (=invited me).

The following considerations will justify the above conclusion regarding the authors of Shelta:

(1) The normal syntactic order of the Celtic sentence is verb, subject, object. The verb cannot be degraded from its initial position except for special purposes of emphasis, and by special grammatical devices. It is as natural to an Irish speaker to begin his sentence with a verb, as it is unnatural to an English speaker. In Shelta, the sentences *never by any chance* follow the Irish order, except when (as in imperative sentences) the verb would naturally come first even in English.

(2) In Irish, the adjective regularly follows its substantive. This, as we have seen, is not uncommon in Shelta, but on the whole the English order (adjective preceding) seems to be more frequent. In the analogous case of a substantive in the genitive case qualifying another, again the English order (genitive preceding) is preserved, as in **gloχ's n'uk** 'the man's head'—except in a few more or less formal phrases such as **b'ōr' a k'ena** 'the woman of the house'.

(3) A leading characteristic of the Celtic language is the elaborate system of initial mutations (lenition and nasalization) induced in various syntactic combinations. It is practically impossible to construct a naturally phrased sentence of ordinary length without introducing one or two of these. In Shelta they are not wholly unknown, but are very rare: so much so, that when they occur they look rather more like Irish influence on an English basis than an Irish idiom almost completely swamped by intrusive English.

(4) There is no more trace of grammatical gender in Shelta than in modern English, though this linguistic nuisance is of great importance in the modern Celtic languages, which possess no neuter gender.

(5) The very few inflexions used are, as we have seen, for the greater part English; and even the non-English inflexions are not obviously Irish. Some peculiar Irish idiomatic formulae, such as the construction of the two verbs that express *being*, and the very remarkable verbal formation of the superlative degree of adjectives, are totally absent from Shelta. There are some native prepositions, clearly based on Irish ones; but the majority of the particles of speech are English.

(6) When words are borrowed to make up the deficiencies of the language, English is almost invariably preferred to Irish. In β37 some Irish words are introduced, but are not used with perfect grammatical accuracy. Some even of the Irish words adopted are primarily loan-words from English. Thus, **grábalta** comes from Irish *ābalta*, which is merely a modification of the English 'able' or '(en)abled'.

In short, the Shelta language, in its accidence and syntactic construction, contains next to nothing ancient and exclusively Celtic. In its vocabulary, some of the marks of antiquity that had been most confidently indicated prove on closer examination to be illusory. But there remains a small heritage of early material, enough to shew that for all its spuriousness it has some few links with the older secret languages of Ireland. This will appear in the sequel.

FORMATION OF WORDS

The methods of word-formation, or rather deformation, followed by the inventors of Shelta have been so fully studied by Dr Sampson[1] and Prof. Meyer[2] that there is little left for their successors to do, except to amplify their observations in some details and, perhaps, to suggest here and there a few slight corrections and modifications in the conclusions suggested by them.

Shelta is a language concocted for purposes of secrecy, by a community living parasitically in the midst of Irish speakers. When these people began to fashion Shelta, they may possibly have been, primarily, Irish speakers: but they gradually adopted English from other wanderers with whom they joined forces. A sufficient number of the Irish-speaking hosts knew enough English to make English alone insufficient as a disguise. But they were not well enough acquainted with it to enable them to follow a conversation in English when it was freely interspersed with jargon words. These being adapted from Irish had to be sufficiently modified to prevent eavesdroppers from analysing them, in the instantaneous moments of time to which rapid conversation would limit them. This is the reason for the anomaly that except for a few cases of rhyming cant (like **grascoat** for 'waistcoat'[3]) English words are used without modification, while all but a microscopic proportion of the Irish words suffer alteration of one kind or another.

The methods of word-formation now to be enumerated apply almost exclusively to the consonants. The vowels of Shelta words have been so imperfectly and ambiguously recorded that it is impossible to determine if there is any systematic process of vowel-shift followed in the construction of the jargon. On the whole the evidence, such as it is, is negative. In some cases the

---

[1] 'Tinkers and their talk', *Journal*, G.L.S. I, ii, pp. 204 ff., especially pp. 207–15.

[2] 'On the Irish Origin and Age of Shelta', *ibid.* pp. 257 ff.

[3] This is not strictly rhyming cant, the essential of which is that the rhyming word is an actual word, though making nonsense in the context in which it is used—as though one should say 'coach-and-four' instead of 'store', or 'door', or 'shore'. The example quoted above is a case of initial substitution. True rhyming cant does not appear to exist in Shelta.

vowel is lengthened, as in kūt'i < [1]*cuid*: in others it is shortened, as is the second vowel of lāk(ĕ)r < *tāilliūr*. This is evidently in most cases a result of accent-shift, as the accent in Shelta appears to be thrown almost universally on to the first syllable of the word, irrespective of the accentuation of the corresponding Irish word. This is another indication of a predominating English influence.

The modifications may affect (A) single letters or consonant-groups, (B) syllables, or (C) entire words, and they may be classified under the following heads:

1. De-aspiration of aspirated or lenited consonants, and (more rarely) the reverse process.
2. De-nasalization of nasal consonants, and, again more rarely, the reverse process.
3. Arbitrary substitution of one consonant or consonant-group for another.
4. Apocope, initial or final.
5. The addition of arbitrary prefixes or suffixes.
6. Metathesis, which may sometimes amount to a complete ana-gram of the letters of a word.
7. Reversal of syllables.
8. Reversal of entire words.

Any number of these methods of deformation may be combined together in the treatment of a single word.

I. DE-ASPIRATION

This is a process which it is very important to understand clearly, because more than anything else it has been responsible for a misapprehension of the date and origin of Shelta.

In the Irish language the consonants have, in addition to their fundamental sound, an 'aspirated' or lenited sound, usually denoted, in modern Irish print, by a dot over the letter, or by the letter *h*. Thus *b* dotted, or *bh*, is pronounced as *w*, or, when palatalized, as a bilabial *v*: the sounds of the other consonants in like circumstances can be ascertained from any Irish grammar.

All the lenited consonants[2] are marked uniformly in modern script: but in early Irish manuscripts the sonant consonants *d, g, b*, when lenited, are not usually marked as such. On the contrary, there is a convention of expressing them by the symbols

---

[1] The symbol < is to be read 'derived from'. In this section Shelta words are printed in ordinary type, to avoid typographical unsightliness: Irish words in italics. For their meanings, see the vocabulary.

[2] Except *l, n, r*, which are left unmarked.

t, c, p, when they are *not* to be lenited. The surd consonants *t, c, p,* when lenited, are marked as such by a simplified form of the letter *h* written above them, from which the modern dot is derived. An eliminating dot was used for *f* and *s* from the first, as these letters are more or less silenced by the syntactic processes which produce lenition in the other consonants.

But it does not follow that because the word for 'I arise' is spelt *ērgim* in an ancient manuscript it was so pronounced. The lenition of the *g* in this and similar words (expressed in the modern spelling *ēirghim*) is far older than the oldest MS. in which it is indicated. Thus if (as was assumed by the first students of Shelta) the word grē 'to arise' was derived from *ērg-im* when *g* was pronounced hard, the language would not be a mere relic of the eighth or tenth century A.D.: it would be prehistoric.

This being incredible, we must find some simpler explanation: and the explanation surely is that the inventors of the language worked it out from *written* forms of Irish: they disregarded the dots of lenition, and so pronounced the words with the consonants hardened. The following examples illustrate de-aspiration of nearly every consonant, including those of which the lenition is marked in the earliest MSS.:[1]

B < *BH*: bog or bug < *gabh*; brauen < *arbhar.* In d'arp < *dearbh* and t'erp < *beirbh* the final position of the de-aspirated letter has sharpened it to p.

C < *CH*: d'umnik < *domnach*; srēk < *crīoch.* A further change **G** < *C* is shown by grin'šeg < *ōinseach.*

D < *DH*: lud'ra < *tuaidh.* This is a rare modification; as a rule we have **D** < *TH* as in glader < *leathar,* nad'ram < *mathair,* grūt < *nuadh*; or **G** < *DH* as in gl'åg < *sneadh,* g'ēg < *guidhe,* šarig < *cradh.* The sounds of Irish *dh* and *gh* are practically indistinguishable, and the symbols are frequently interchanged in writing.

F < *FH*: no example. (*Fh* is silent in Irish.)

G < *GH*: grē < *ēirigh*; gwil'i < *luighe*; srīgo < *rīgh.* Besides **G** < *DH,* noted above, we sometimes have **D** < *GH,* as srīdug < *rīoghacht*; **K** < *GH* in d'umnik < *mōidigh.*

M < *MH*: mark < *cnāmh*; mål'a < *lāmh.*

P < *PH(F)*: skōp < *fosgail.*

S < *SH*: no example. (*Sh* is reduced to a mere breathing in Irish.)

---

[1] Some of the examples shew other modifications, such as letter-substitution or reversal, which for the moment may be disregarded.

T < *TH*: aburt < *ar bith*, datair < *athair*; gåt'a < *dath*; get'a < *maith*; talósk < *láithe*; t'al < *leath*. A tendency is to be seen in some of these and in other examples to palatalize a de-aspirated *TH*, and (less certainly) *DH*.

The reverse process, the aspiration or lenition of a letter which is not lenited in Irish, is rare: I have noted five examples: l'ivin < *muilleann* (mh < *m*, but de-nasalized), rōī̄χa < *carta* (ch < *c*), grēχol < *fiacail* (ditto), gifan < *capall*, gafa < *bacach* (f < *p* or *b*).

2. De-nasalization

This also is an important process, illustrated by the following:

B < *M*: bīn < *mīn*; b'in'i < *min*; labērt < *malairt*; laburt < *mal lacht*; l'ibis < *milis*; nōb'ri < *mōn*. In nup < *muin* we have P < B < M. Rubōg < *mealbhōg* is ambiguous, as the b may be either a de-nasalized *m* or a de-aspirated *bh*.

D < *N*: dura < *arān*; gradum < *anam*.

De-nasalization of vowel preceding *mh*: graura < *samhradh*.

De-nasalization of *mh* (BH < *MH*): l'ivin < *muilleann* above quoted; gov'li < *gamhnach*.

The contrary process is found, but it is much less common:

M < *B*: elum < *baile*; l'īman < *bliadhain*; mantri < *anbruth*; med'ri < *breith*. In mīder < *diabhail* we have the composite change M < B < BH.

N < *D*: enaχ < *ēadach*.

In some cases this change may have been induced by the syntactic nasalization of the initial in Irish. Thus *bliadhain* (pron. bl'i·an') after *sa'* (='in the') becomes *mbliadhain* (pron. ml'i·an'), and thus easily paves the way for the formation of līman.

3. Substitution

Arbitrary substitution of one consonant for another may take place at the beginning (by far the most common), in the middle, or at the end of the word. In the following table, only one example of each substitution is given; but the number of cases that I have noted is added, which will show what are the most favoured formulae:

B for *G* (1)	karbu < *margadh*	**D** for *R* (1)	kaihed < *cathaoir*
B for *GH* (1)	tribli < *teaghlach*	**D** for *S* (1)	ludus < *solas*
D for *G* (5)	dolsk < *gall*	**G** for *B* (2)	grīt' < *breōite*
D for *K* (1)	kraudug < *cearc*	**G** for *D* (4)	gåt'a < *dath*

G for K (10)	gafa < *bacach*	L for B (1)	losport <
G for χ (1)	g'et'a < (*fi*)*chet*		'bastard'
G for χT (1)	gop < *bocht*	L for D (3)	lūrk < *dearc*
G for L (1)	g'e < *le*	L for K (1)	lur'ān < *cuarān*
G for M (1)	get'a < *maith*	L for χ (1)	lutram < *meird-*
G for S (2)	grāg' < *srāid'*		*reach*
G for SN (1)	gut < *snāth*	L for N (1)	skudal < *scadan*
G for T (3)	garo < *tarbh*	L for R (4)	slang < *sreang*
G for TH (1)	grug'im < *gruth*	L for T (1)	lud'ra < *tuaidh*
GL for SN (1)	gl'åg < *sneadh*	L for TH (1)	lobān < *bothān*
GL for ST (1)	glogē < *stoca*	M for D (3)	m'aunes < *deagh-*
GR for B (1)	gruska < *bosca*		*nōs*
GR for D (4)	grat < *deatach*	M for DR (1)	mišūr' < *drosur*
GR for F (11)	granko < *francach*	M for K (1)	mašur < *casur*
GR for G (5)	grala < *guala*	M for N (1)	mūskōg < *spunōg*
GR for H (1)	grata < *hata*	M for P (1)	st'īma < *pīopa*
GR for K (1)	grupån < *cupān*	M for R (1)	m'aur < *reamhar*
GR for KL (1)	grūd' < *clumh*	M for S (2)	mam'rum <
GR for L (2)	gruχ < *lamhach*		*seomra*
GR for M (2)	grašano < 'mason'	M for ST (1)	mēri < *staighre*
GR for N (1)	grūt < *nuadh*	M for T (2)	mink'er < *tinncēir*
GR for P (3)	grārk' < *pāirc*	N for L (2)	gifan < *capall*
GR for R (1)	agrḗš < *ar ais*	N for NG (1)	gran'a < *tairnge*
GR for S (22)	graχton <	N for R (1)	Sranī < 'Mary'
	seachtmhain	N for S (1)	n'ētas < *Sēamas*
GR for SN (2)	graisk < *snath*	N for T (1)	nongas < 'tongs'
GR for ST (2)	grānša <	P for B (2)	gop < *bocht*
	strōinsear	P for T (2)	klīspis < *brīste*
GR for T (6)	gran'a < *tairnge*	R for B (3)	ruket < 'bucket'
K for D (2)	burik < *bord*	R for L (1)	mīder < *diabhal*
K for M (2)	karib < *marbh*	R for N (6)	t'era < *teine*
K for NG (1)	kart < *tarraing*	R for S (1)	glōrōg < *cluas*
K for P (1)	mūskōg < *spūnōg*	R for T (1)	skrubol < *tobar*
K for T (6)	lākr < *tāilliūr*	RK for S (1)	tūrk < *sūas*
K for TH (4)	kamair < *mathair*	RT for χ (1)	asturt < *isteach*
χ for F (2)	goχ' < *fag*	RT for N (1)	awárt < *amhāin*
χ for R (2)	aχér < *aréir*	RT for $\check{S}$ (2)	arīrt < *arīs*
χ for $R\check{S}$ (1)	d'aχag < *tuirseach*	S for B (4)	sugūn < *bagūn*
KL for BR (2)	klisp < *bris*	S for D (4)	subōl < *buidēal*
KR for N (2)	kriš < *sean*	S for DH (1)	sakel < *leagadh*
KR for ST (1)	krad'i < *stad*	S for G (3)	sorm < *gorm*

S for *K* (5)	sugu < *cogadh*	Š for *G* (1)	šark < *gearr*
S for *M* (2)	Sartin < 'Martin'	Š for *K* (4)	šlug < *clog*
S for *N* (1)	sumad' < *nōimid*	Š for *P* (1)	šant < 'pint'
S for *P* (3)	sārk' < *pāirc*	Š for *T* (1)	šoru < *torramh*
S for *R* (1)	sumōl < *robāl*	ŠK for *T* (1)	aχónšk < *anocht*
S for *T* (1)	sori < *torramh*	ŠR for *D* (1)	šriš < 'dish'
SK for *TH* (2)	gresko < *guth*	ŠR for 'J' (1)	šrug < 'jug'
SP for *BH* (1)	tarsp < *marbh*	ŠR for *K* (1)	šrittle < 'kettle'
SR for *B* (2)	Srōn'e < *Bōinne*	ŠR for *M* (2)	Šrorten <
SR for *G* (1)	srat < *geata*		'Martin'
SR for 'J' (1)	srug < 'jug'	T for *B* (1)	t'ērp < *beirbh*
SR for *K* (1)	Srat'rin <	T for *BH* (2)	gūt < *dubh*
	'Catherine'	T for *G* (1)	talop < *bolg*
SR for *M* (4)	srōīd'an < *maidin*	T for *K* (2)	tirpa < *ceart*
SR for *N* (1)	srōmēd' < *nōimid*	T for χ (2)	tul < *luach*
SR for *P* (1)	srunta < 'pint'	T for χ*T* (1)	grata < *tacht*
SR for *R* (3)	srīgo < *rīgh*	T for *L* (2)	tād'ir < *lāidir*
ST for *B* (1)	strod < *brōg*	T for *M* (3)	tarsp < *marbh*
ST for *D* (2)	awást < *i bhfad*	T for *N* (1)	grit'ūn < *inniūn*
ST for *P* (1)	st'īma < *pīopa*	T for *R* (1)	tom < *mōr*
Š for *B* (2)	šeldrū < *bēlra'*	T for *S* (1)	tūrk < *sūas*
Š for *D* (1)	šurog < *dearg*	TR for *T* (1)	tribli < *teaghlach*
Š for *F* (2)	šl'uχ < *fliuch*		

The above list will shew with tolerable clearness that the substitutions are essentially of a random nature, not governed by any phonetic principle. As has been noticed from the first, *gr* is by far the most favoured substitution, and next to it is *g*. S comes next, and then, *t, k, l, m*.

4. APOCOPE

(1) Initial apocope: examples are

d'ūχ < (*ea*)*dach*   rīpuχ < (*st*)*riopach*
g'et'a < (*fi*)*chet*   skai < *uisge*
gloχ < (*o*)*glach*

In munik < *ainm* there is initial apocope, reversal, and an added suffix (munik = mun + ik < *n*(*u*)*m* < (*ai*)*nm*): in nāk' < *snaithe* there is apocope and final substitution (nāk' < (*s*)*nāk* < *snath-*): in riltōg < *braitleōg* there is apocope with metathesis (rīltōg < (*b*)*rīltōg* < *braitleōg*).

(2) Final apocope:

      clima < *lem(naχt)*   fē < *fe(oil)*
      gesti < *giuisti(s)*   krimašt < *minist(eir)*

In the last there is reversal of the first syllable and substitution of **KR** for *N*. Especially common is apocope of final *χ*:

      granko < *franc(ach)*   graro < *searr(ach)*
      grasano < *Sasan(ach)*   g'ūk < *geōc(ach)*

In scop < *fosgail* there is apocope, de-aspiration, and metathesis.

(3) Double apocope, initial and final:

      ligi < *(ea)gl(ais)*   miš < *(ai)ms(igh)*

Under this head may also be noted a few cases of medial deletion, as of 1 in rubōg < *mealbhōg* and of *χ* in sud'ata < *cuideachta*, grē·ed < *droichead*.

5. PREFIXES AND SUFFIXES

The following arbitrary prefixes, in addition to (not as under (3), in substitution for) the true initial of the Irish word, have been noted:

A, Ā: āvali < *baile*, anált < *nighe*.

B: bl'antaχ < *leinteacha*, bwikad < *coimhead*.

D or G: datair, gāter < *athair*, gasal < *asal*, get' < *tē*, glader < *leathair*.

GR: a large number (about 20), including gradum < *anam*, gramail < *amhail*, granta < ' aunt ', gruber < *obair*.

L: lōsp < *pōs*, lugil < *glaodh*.

M: mwēn'a < *i ndiaidh*, m'ēna < *indē*.

N: nad'ram < *mathair*.

S: sloχa < *lobhtha*, slūn < *lūain*.

SG: sgrubul < *earball*.

Š: šlīar < *leathar*, šlōh'a < *luaith*, šl'an < *leann*.

ŠR: šroχar < *eochair*.

T: tūrk < *ūair*.

Suffixes are either letters or letter groups, or else syllables. Some of the latter are merely used for disguise, but others have a formative purpose, making abstract or verbal nouns.

    Letter suffixes:

T: gåt < *ōg*.

Š: grīš < *croidhe*, gwīš < *tuighe*.

P: klisp < *bris*.

SK: talósk < *lāithe*, Libisk < 'Philip' (with initial apocope), horsk < *thar*, dolsk < *gall*, grisk < *tuighe*, linska < *sloinne*, nolsk < *i ndāil*, olsk < *ōl*.

Syllable suffixes:

AST: balast < *bal* (very doubtful).

ER: lōber < *buail*, lud'ra < *tuaid*.

IM, UM: grug'im < *gruth*, g'ēt'um < *gate*, mam'rum < *seomra*.

IN: grōkin < *stōcach*.

LESK: granlesk < *green*, grīnlesk < *līn*, Grunles(k) < 'Annie', krōlušk < *ocras*.

LI: rågli < *gāire*.

MUG: grōmug < *ubh*.

OG, ŌG [an Irish diminutive suffix, but apparently not always possessing this force in Shelta]: gaverog < *gabhar*, glōrōg < *cluas*, grārnog < *dearnad*, kad'ōg < *caid* (itself a jargon word), karbug = karb, kraudug < *cearc*, lūrkōg < *lūrk*, tirpōg < *ceart*, tōrog < *tori*.

RUM: kuldrum < *codlad*.

SAG: bilsag < *bēl*.

Formative suffixes are as under:

AL(T), making verbal nouns: anált, getul (?), mīderal, tāral.

AN, making abstracts (as English '-ness'): b'in'ian, grolan, kasin (?), tōmān.

AΘ, also making abstracts: b'in'iaθ, grīt'aθ, grolsin'aθ, g'amiaθ, mugataθ, mun'iaθ, rud'uaθ, tād'iraθ, tomiaθ.

AχT, Irish suffix for abstract nouns: only in buriaχt.

ER, ERA, indicating an agent: g'ēgera, g'ūk'ra, k'erpera, mislier, nob'ri, slāsker.

HAN, only in skaihan 'a sailor' (skai = 'water').

IK, probably borrowed from Irish verbal formative -*uigh*-: munik.

O, making participles or verbal nouns: l'esko, lōspo, l'īrko.

6. Metathesis

Metathesis may be operated upon an otherwise unmodified Irish word, or else upon a word which has already undergone one or more of the deformations above described.

Examples of simple metathesis are (the transposed letters are printed in capitals) aBúRt < *aR Bith*, GoRed < *aiRGead*, lūrP < *Plūr*, L'īM < *iMeaL*, L'išGaï < *skiLLet*.

Consonant groups may be treated as units, as in NūSPŏg <
SPŭNŏg, or they may be dismembered, as in LasP < BLas,
RĭSPūn < PRioSŭn.

Examples of metathesis after de-aspiration are: BRauen <
aRBHar, G'iSon < SeaGHan, TŏBer < BoTHair.

Examples of metathesis after substitution: LoSK < SToL,
LuSKån < SCaDan [L < D], L'oGaχ < BuaCHaiLL (a complete
anagram, in which G < B). In šaragi < saighdiur we have a complicated deformation, in which Š < S, the gh is de-aspirated, and
the d elided. [But this word may also be explained, more simply,
as a derivative of šurog 'red'.]

Example of added prefix after metathesis: LŏSP < PŏS.

Example of metathesis after de-nasalization: Man-TRi < anB-
RuTH, in which there is metathesis in both syllables, de-nasalization of B, and de-aspiration of T.

A few special cases may be noted. Koldni < coinnle may possibly
be a heritage from a pre-Shelta jargon, as it seems to presuppose
the older spelling coindle.[1] Kon < (a)nocht is also interesting. Irish
*nocht 'night' has been killed by nocht = 'naked', and survives
only in the adverb. The Shelta is formed by reversal after de-
aspiration and final apocope. In l'ivin < muilleann we have a rare
case of aspiration (with de-nasalization) after metathesis. In
riltŏg < braitleŏg we have metathesis after initial apocope: in
rabl'ĭn < braitlĭn we have metathesis after deletion of an inner
letter (t). On the other hand skurlum < loisg gives us metathesis +
insertion of r + addition of a suffix; and šarpŏg < gasūr is a case
of metathesis + insertion of p.

Metathesis of syllables—after the fashion of a foreigner little
skilled in English, whom I heard speaking of a 'spring-main'
when he meant 'main-spring'—is rare: in fact I can find only
one case, and that is uncertain, as the etymology is insecure. If
mun·k'ri be derived from tearmann (K < T) we have an example:
but I can find no other.

7. REVERSAL OF SYLLABLES

Some of the examples of metathesis quoted in the preceding paragraphs. might have been equally well mentioned in the present
section. This kind of deformation consists of reversing the letters
of one or more syllables of a word, but not the whole word; with

---

[1] Compare kuldrum < codladh, which, however spelt, is now pronounced
colla.

or without one or more of the other forms of modification already discussed.

Simple examples are: d'um-ik < *moid-ighim*, lāk-īn < *cail-īn*, nuga < *gunn-a*, n'āk-a < *cann-a*, n'ugi < 'guin-ea' (or Irish *ginī*), rab-ista < *par-ōiste* (with B < P), lūbīn < *buil-īn*, nīd'-a < *duin-e*, rusp-ān < *spar-ān*, rod-us < *dorus*.

A more elaborate example, with two syllables reversed, is a-χáram < *amarach*. This is very unusual.

It is usually the first syllable which is reversed. The example just quoted is an exception; another is aχím < *amach*, aχónšk < *anocht*: in the latter case is a substitution, ŠK < T.

In bagail < *gabhāil*, there is reversal of the first syllable after de-aspiration. Another instance is muk-in'e < *comh-naidhe*. Reversal of the first syllable after de-aspiration and de-nasalisation is shewn by bwik-ad < *coimh-ēad*.

Reversal of the first syllable after various substitutions is illustrated by gōpa < *pōca* (G < C), gopa < *pota* (G < T), kamāīr < *mathair* (K < TH), kam'ra < *madra* (K < D), krimašt < *min-ist-[ēir]* (KR < N). Reversal after de-nasalization is shewn in labērt < *malairt*; reversion with insertion of additional letters in lam-p-a < *māla*, las-k-on < *salann*.

8. COMPLETE REVERSAL

In this form the whole word is presented backward, with or without other modifications.

Simple examples are: åd < *dō*, gåp < *pōg*, kam < *mac*, lud < *dall*, lūk < *cūl*, rīk < *cīar*, n'ērp < *brēan*. Such elementary cases seem to be confined to monosyllables.

Reversal after de-aspiration is shewn by: bog or bug < *gabh*, gafa < *bac-ach*, grē < *ēirigh*, gwil'i < *luighe*, liba < *fuil*.

In some interesting cases, when one of the consonants in a monosyllable is palatalized, the palatalization remains in its place to affect the new consonant. Thus we have: n'uk < *ceann* (k'an), t'al < *leath* (l'at, after de-aspiration). The rule is not, however, regularly observed: in d'ima < *maide* (mad'ə), the palatalization is preserved with the d to which it belongs. In l'esk < *sgēal* we have the rule observed, and the letter group sg treated as a single unit.

Reversal after de-nasalization is shewn by: dura < *arān*, elum < *baile*, nup < *muin*.

Prefixes or suffixes added after reversal are shewn by: g-et' < *tē*, gōt-i < *tug*, lōb-er < *buail*, råg-li < *gāire*. In tal-ósk < *lāithe* there is reversal after de-aspiration, with an added suffix. Compare t'irp-ōg < *ceart* (P < K).

Reversal after various substitutions is illustrated by: goχ' < *fag* (χ < F); gop < *bocht* (G < χT); kriš < *sean* (KR < N); ladu < *talamh* (D < T, *amh* de-nasalized); lutram < *meirdreach*, in which so much substitution has taken place that the word is hardly recognizable; naper < *rāmhan* (P < MH); sakel < *leagadh* (K < G, S < DH).

In nīp < *buidhe* we have a rare case of nasalization following de-aspiration preceding reversal (N < D < DH).

IV. Vocabulary

The following is the arrangement of the vocabulary. The alphabetical order is **a ā ȧ b b' c d d' e ē f g g' h i ī k k' χ l l' m m' n n' o ō p p' r r' s š t t' θ u ū v w y**. The references, α, β, γ, are to the specimens of the language printed above. The word is spelt on the phonetic principles already laid down. After the standardized spelling comes the meaning, followed by the renderings of different collectors, examples of the use of the word, and the etymology, when that can be identified (B-L = Bog-Latin, Chap. IV).

A

1 **a, an** The English indefinite article. An inoc li (G) 'another one' = *An inoχ* [*e*]*la*.

2 **a** The English preposition o' = 'of'. *Trīp a gāter* 'a sup of drink'.

3 **a** The Irish definite article in the genitive case, a' = an = 'of the'. *Kam a k'ena* 'son of the house'.

4 **a** The Irish interrogative prefix, a' = an n-: no English equivalent. Latin nonne, -ne. *A t'ērpa hū* 'will you cook?'

5 **a** The Irish preposition i, a = 'in'. Also i. *Swurt a mun'iaθ* 'up in heaven' (α); *aχim a Skai-grūt* 'out in America'.

6 **a** The conjunction 'and'. *G'et'as a g'et'as* 'scores and scores' (γ 1a).

7 **a** The Irish possessive 'his', 'her'. *A grifin* 'his coat' (γ 1b).

8 **a** The Irish preposition a' = ag = 'at'. Prefixed to participles to denote continuous action in the present. *A krad'i* (α) 'standing'.

9 **a-** The English prefix, as in 'a-float', 'a-dying'. Frequent in Shelta.

abúrt (abůrth) 'at all'. See β 80. Irish ar bith [ər bíḥ].

addis See *n'edas*.

aga (β 79): *aga dī'lša* = 'at thee', i.e. 'in thy hands' or 'possession'. Irish ag-a-t, the pronominal t being removed, the Shelta pronoun substituted, and the prepositional portion of the compound retained.

agétul 'afraid'. See **getul**.

agratīs 'afraid', 'fear' (G). See **getul**.

agréš 'backward': *tōri·in agréš* 'coming back', 'returning' (γ 3a). Irish ar ais [ərás'].

aid 'butter'. See **oid**.

ain 'one'. See **ĕn**.

ainoχ 'a thing'. See **inoχ**.

aχ 'Oh!' 'alas!' 'indeed!' etc. Interjectional sound common to many languages, Irish, Romani, Russian, German, etc.

aχáram 'to-morrow'. *Sroid'an aχáram* 'to-morrow morning'; *olomi aχáram* 'to-morrow night'. Irish amáireach [əmā́r'aχ].

aχér 'last night' (β 65). Irish arēir [ər'ér'].

aχím 'out', 'outside' (awhim G). Of rest: *aχím a Skai-grūt* 'out in America'. Of motion: *aχím k'en-gop* 'out of the poorhouse'.

1 **aχíver** 'before'. Irish roimh [rēv].

2 **aχíver** 'ever'. *Nīd'eš aχíver* 'never more'; *dī'lša aχíver glōri*, 'did you ever hear?' (γ 1a). Irish riamh [rīv].

aχónšk 'to-night' (ahunshk; achunsk G). *Olomi aχónšk* (γ 2a) means 'to-night', i.e. the night following the day of the speaker's statement. Irish anocht.

ala 'another'. Irish eile [el'ə]. See **ela**.

alamaχ 'milk'. See **elima**.

an 'of the'. Usually abbreviated to a' (see 3 a, above). Rarely in full, but *tūr an skai*, 'bottom of the river', occurs (γ 1d).

anált 'to wash' (L gives anālt 'to sweep', anālken (=anālk-in') 'washing'). Irish nighe [n'ī] 'washing' + participial suffix *al*.

and English conjunction, freely used.

1 **ar** 'on', 'upon'. Irish preposition ar, freely used: *ar a'* 'on the'.

2 **ar** 'after'. Irish preposition īar, freely used, especially as in Irish to express perfective (cf. Anglo-Irish 'after going' = gone). *Ar mislō* 'gone': adverbially in *g'et'a líman ar-mislō* 'twenty miles away' (γ 2a); *ar gwil'o* 'having lain down', 'lying down' (β 4).

a-rárk 'similarly', 'in the same way' (arék(α), araik A). See **rāk**.

aráš 'back', 'backward'. Irish. The Shelta form is **agréš**, q.v.

arék See **arárk**.

arírt 'again' (ariart G). Irish arís [ərīs'].

aspra 'a sixpence' (G). Origin obscure: the Irish word is raol [rēl].

astúrt 'in', 'into' (astŭrth, asthŭrt, asthŭrth). Used both of
motion and of rest: the two senses will be found in β 57.
See sturt. Irish isteach [is't'áχ].

aswúrt 'on', 'upon'. See swurt.

ašírt 'down'. See šírt.

atǎ'p 'alive'. See tǎp.

atómier 'all the more', 'moreover' 'further' (γ 2b): used in the
sense 'any more' (β 78). Comparative of tom 'great' (q.v.)
with prefixed a.

awárt 'one'. See wart. Irish amhāin.

awǎst 'away' (C). Irish a bhfad [awád].

ayen 'nine' (L). Irish naoi [nī].

ayírt 'again' (ayírth, ayirt C). See arírt. Irish arís [ərīs']. Laisk
my dheel and my dheel will laisk your gilhairt (G) is L'esk my
d'ī'l and my d'ī'l will l'esk your d'ī'l ayírt 'Tell me, and I will tell
you again' [=in my turn].

Ā

ǎvali, ǎvari 'a town' (oura L, aavali, aavari C, veil N, owera G).
Compare elum: both forms probably from Irish baile [bal'ə].
Āvari tom 'a big town' (=Dublin). Dublin is also called
Āvari l'írk, which does not mean (as might appear) 'witty
town', but is a corruption of the Irish name Baile A'tha
Cliath [b'lǎkl'ī].

Å

ǎd 'two' (awd). See od.

ǎdi A gives ǎ'di nyuk 'on the head'. Not corroborated.

B

bagail 'taking', 'catching'. S'guidh a bagail ar mo ghil 'it is
raining' (W), properly skai a' bagail ar mo d'īl 'Water
a-catching of myself'. Perversion of Irish gabhāil [gawǎl']
'taking'.

balast 'hair' (ballast K). Romani bal+arbitrary syllable ast(??).
But compare fualasg [B-L, no. 5].

bani 'meal' (K). Doubtful if true Shelta.

batoma 'a policeman' (bathoma K). Probably miswritten for
gūtena, q.v.

bilsag 'lips', 'mouth' (K'). Irish bēal [b'ēl] 'mouth'+meaningless syllable (?). Compare beilflesg [B-L, no. 9].

binsi 'wings' (K). *Binsi bēro* (K) 'a sailing ship' [bēro='ship' in Romani].

bĭn 'great', 'good', 'grand' (bin K, been C). *Bĭn-chit* 'a brooch' (bĭn+cant word); *bin-l'ŭr'* (bin-liuer K), also said to mean 'brooch', but l'ŭr'='money'; *bĭn-lightie* 'daylight'; *bĭn-lightment* 'Sunday' (both from K: bĭn+cant words). Irish mĭn [m'ĭn'] 'fine'.

blaci 'coal' (blatchi C, blatchy N). Probably cant, from English 'black'.

bladunk 'prison' (bladhunk L). Irish braighdeānach [brēīd'å'naχ] 'a captive', 'a prisoner' seems analogous.

blaiki 'a pot' (bláiky 'a tin vessel' N, blaikie 'a pot' K, blawkie 'a kettle' C). English 'blackie' (R).

blānōg 'a cow' (blan, blanag, blanig K, blànag W, blainteag K', blánóg brāingōg G). Irish blēaghnach [bl'ēnaχ] 'act of milking'. Used abusively of a woman, β 7. *Blānōg-kar'ber* 'a cow-killer', 'butcher'; *b'in'i blānōg* (G) 'a calf'.

blå 'meal', 'oatmeal' (blaa, blaw C). Probably not true Shelta.

bleater 'a sheep' (G). English.

blinkam 'a candle'; **blinkie** 'a window'; **blinklum** 'light'. Factitious words from English 'blink' (K).

blōrna 'a Protestant' (blōrne: pornuc G), β 89.

blyhunka 'a horse' (L). Doubtful: not corroborated.

bl'antaχ 'a shirt' (bliantach K'). Irish lēine, plur. lēinteacha [l'ēnə, l'ēnt'aχa].

bl'ŭr 'a young woman' (blewr, bloor C).

bog 'to get', 'find', in a large variety of senses: bogh (L). 'To learn' in β 1. *Bog ar-mislō* 'to escape', 'make off' (γ 1e); *to bog a milk of his d'ĭ'l* 'to get hold of him'; *bog mwǐlša aχĭm g'amiaθ* 'take me out of, deliver me from, evil' (α): 'that bhogd [in first publication bhoghd] out yer mailya' 'you let that fall from your hand' (so in L) should be *that bogd out a' yer mål'a* 'that got out of your hand'. *Bag siort a leagauch mhin* 'go down, boy' (K') should be *bog šĭrt a l'agaχ m'in'* 'go down, little boy'. *Boga mē* 'I shall get' (written buggama, γ 3e). *Bog astúrt*, lit. 'to take in'='to assume'. *What munika did you bog astúrt?* 'What name did you assume?' L's *bog'hin brass* 'cooking food' needs corroboration. In the English sense of an auxiliary verb, *bogin surχa* 'getting tired' (γ 1d). Often confused with **bug**, Irish gabh- [gaw-], which has a similar range of meanings.

bonar 'good' (C'). Probably cant, from French *bon*: not corroborated.

bord 'table' (L). Irish.

borer 'gimlet' (L). English or cant (Sampson).

bovi 'a bull' (K). Not corroborated.

brahan Mo bhrathan gan bhras air a chom, gun ghrad a bhagos e 'Me without food to-night, and I without money to buy it' (K') should be *mo bhrahan* ['myself'?] *gan* [Gaelic, 'without'] *brās* ['food'] *ar aχón* ['on to-night'] *gan gored* ['without money'] *a baga sē* ['that will get it']. The word brathan [**brahan**] is not elsewhere recorded.

brauen 'corn', 'grain' (bravan G). Also used to translate the tinker surname 'Oates'. Irish arbhar [arwar] 'corn'.

brās 'food' (braas, brass L, pras W, brás G). O'Reilly's dictionary of Irish gives bras 'bread, means of living' from an 'Old Glossary' unspecified.

brāsi 'to feed' 'dine' (braasi).

brikler 'a bowl', 'cup' (brickler C, briagalair K', brickcler 'a cup and saucer' C). English: see R, no. 110.

brod 'a house' (C).

brogies 'breeches' (C'). Probably English.

bruskler 'a bowl' (K). Compare **brikler**.

bug 'to give'; in a variety of senses. *Can you bug Shelta?* (L') 'Can you talk Shelta?' *Bug me a gåp* 'Give me a kiss'; *buga* 'I will give' (β 37, 66). Irish gabh.

bul 'a crown', 'five shillings' (bool, bûl N, bull C). Cant, not Shelta.

bulla 'a letter', 'note' (L). Not Shelta.

bulscur 'wire' (G).

bura, buri 'great', 'fine', 'beautiful' (bori K, baro, bare, bawrie C, burry, buri G). Perhaps Romani båro, but the first syllable is always written as with a short vowel.

buriaχt 'goodness', 'good'. *A gloχ is no buriaχt except he granis a buri gloχ* (G) 'a man is no good unless he knows a good man' [=has a good companion].

burik 'a table' (burrik). Irish bord.

bwikad 'to hold', 'contain', but with various meanings: bwikadh (γ 2b). *B'ōr' a k'ena bwikads the rīšpa* (G) 'the woman of the house wears the breeches'; *any inoχ you bwikad* (G) 'anything you like'. Irish coimhēad [kiw͠ēd] 'keep', 'hold'.

bwikads 'a pair of pincers'.

B′

b′anag 'a coif' (beannag K').

b′ĕg 'to steal' (bīog, byŭg, biyēg, biyêgh, biyêg L, begg G). Irish gabhaim 'to take'.

b′in′i 'little', 'small' (binni, binya: binny L, bini AG). *B′in′i tobar* 'a footpath'; *b′in′i sŭbli* 'a boy'. Also b′in; *l′agaχ b′in* 'small boy' (W). Irish min 'small'.

b′in′ian 'a little'.

b′in′iaθ 'smallness'.

b′ŏr′ 'a woman' (bīor, bīŏer, būīer: biuoer, beör C, bewr, bewer LL', biorr K', beor KW, bioer, biuoer F, beóir G). *B′ŏr′ a′ k′ena* 'woman of the house'; *b. lugil* 'wailing woman', 'banshee'; *b. ar-mislŏ* 'wandering woman', 'female tramp'; *b. skĕv* 'fishwife'; *b. srīgo* 'queen'; *b. swuder* or *b. swudal* 'a high woman', 'lady'; *b. šĕkr* 'a nun'; *b. mwīlša* 'my wife'; *b. yīlša* 'thy wife' (β 61). Irish bean [b′an]. The Scots Gaelic piuthair is a less likely source.

C

Except for the few loan-words given below, for words beginning with c see under **k**: for words beginning with ch see under **d′**, **t′**, or **χ**.

cackler 'a duck' (G), 'an egg' (C). Also **cattler**. *Šelkin g′ami cattlers* 'selling bad eggs'. English.

cȧlra (c = č) 'a knife' (chali, chālra, cholra: cealrach, čarloc, čadlach G, chaldroch L). *Chȧlra gruber* 'knife-grinding' ('knife-grinder' in a MS. note, but **gruber** means 'work', not 'worker'). *Chȧlra šarku* 'cutting knife', 'a saw'. From Romani čuri.

cid (c = č) 'a lamb' (K). By R connected with English 'kid'.

cuk (c = č) 'credit'. Doubtless the English slang 'tick'.

D

dȧd′e 'bread' (dha′de A). Not corroborated.

dȧl′on 'God' (dalon, dalyon, dālyon, dhalyōn, galyōn: dhāluin G). *D. swudr* 'God above!' 'God Almighty!'. *D. awȧrt stĕš šĭkr nīd′as* 'One God who is three persons'. *N′edas a Dāl′on* 'God's Place', 'Heaven'. *Dȧl′on a ladū* 'Lord of the earth'. No satisfactory etymology has been suggested: hardly connected with Irish Día [d′īa] 'God', as the d is not palatalized.

dȧtair 'father' (datir, dataír K). See **gȧter**.

dĕnoχ 'to lose' (dainoch L). Uncorroborated. Misli dainoch, said in L to mean 'to write a letter', 'send' or 'go', means properly *misli d'inoχ* 'to go to something' (*d'* = Irish preposition do 'to').

dīl, dī'l, dīlša, dī'lša (duīlsha, dūilsha, dhī-īlsha). A combination of do [Irish possessive 'thy']+d'īl, q.v. The hard d replaces the palatalized d in the compound, which is the regular word for the second personal pronoun singular, 'thou', 'thee'. Genitive formed as in English; *dīlša's munik* 'thy name' (α). Dative as nominative, *buga dīlša* 'I will give you' (β66). Rarely used without the emphatic suffix -ša; apparently this is more frequent in the oblique cases: *dī'l* appears in α, and in β 36 in the sense 'thy', in β 18 in the sense 'thee'.

do 'two' (L). This and some other numeral forms given by L are Irish, and need not be inserted in this vocabulary.

dolimi 'dark of the night' (dholimi G). Probably th' [English 'the']+olomi, q.v.

dolsk 'a Protestant' (G). Irish gall 'foreigner', 'protestant'+ arbitrary sk.

dorahōg' 'dusk', 'evening' (dorahoig G). *Bura d.* 'good evening!' A perversion of Irish trāthnōna [trånōna] 'evening' (?).

drīper 'a bottle' (dreeper G).

dunik 'a cow' (dunnick, dunny C', dun'nuχ N).

dura 'bread' (dŏra, dŭra, dorra, durra, dhurra: derra L', d'erri L, dora G). *Dura gloχ* 'a baker'; *šark a' dura* 'a slice of bread'. Irish arán [ərå'n] reversed and de-nasalized.

D'

d'anadair 'a hammerer' (deannadair K'). Irish geannaire 'a hammer'.

d'aχag 'tired' (W). Perversion of Irish tuirseach [tur's'aχ] 'tired'.

d'arelallan 'an eye' (dearelallan K').

d'arp 'true', 'real', 'excellent': 'truth' (charp). *D'arp sl'ūχter* 'a good scholar'; *nīd'eš d'arp* 'that is not true'; *d'arp staf'ris* 'fine prayers'; *d'arp m'inker-b'ōr'* 'a true tinker woman'. Irish dearbh [d'arw] 'right', 'true', 'real'.

1 **d'asag** 'a person' (deasag W). *D. šean* 'a ragged person'; *d. tom* 'a great person'. Uncorroborated: probably by-form or perversion of nid'a, q.v.

2 **d'asag** 'two' (deasag K).

d'iger 'a door' (jigger G).

d'ima 'a stick' (chima, cima K, ch'immel L, chimmes (*plur.*) L, chimma G, chimi A). *D'ima t'ira* 'a match'; *d'ima de t'ira* 'a tongs' [de = Irish preposition, 'of', 'from']. Signifies 'a chip' in β 84. Irish maide [mad'ə] 'stick', 'rod'.

d'il, d'i'l A word apparently meaning 'self' or something analogous, exclusively used to form the personal pronouns (dyīl, dīl, deal L, jeel G). It is used either with the two Irish possessive pronouns mo ('my') and do ('thy'), or with any of the English possessive pronouns. Thus *mo d'īl* [shortened into *mwīl*] or *my d'īl*; *do d'īl*(> *dīl*) or *your d'īl*: but only '*his d'īl*', '*her d'īl*', '*their d'īls*'. *My d'īl* is rarely used in the nominative; an example is *my d'īl is misli·in* 'I am going' (L). Thōri my jeel (= *tōri my d'īl*), translated 'Follow me' (G), is anomalous, as it makes tōri ('come') transitive.

d'oχ In L we find dioch man krädyin in this nadas, translated 'I am staying here'. It is probably incorrect. Dioch may be *d'oč* miswritten for *d'eš* (see nīd'eš), but this is doubtful: it may also be a misheard *gloχ*, if ch = χ and not č. 'Man' is unintelligible.

d'onâdu 'to go' (jonâdu).

d'orker 'tin' (diorcar K'). See **yergan**.

d'umik 'to swear' (jŭmik, jŭmnik; jummik [γ I d]). Irish mōidighim [mōd'īm].

d'umnik 'Sunday' (jumnik). Irish domhnach [dŏnaχ]. D palatalized by influence of preceding word.

d'ūka 'a ragged beggar' (dyūka, jūka). According to L, 'a Gentile', in the Gypsy sense. See **g'ūk'ra**.

d'ūχ 'clothes' (chīuχ). *D'ūχ kuldrum* 'bedclothes'. Irish ēadach [ēdaχ].

E

ela 'another'. Also **ola**. Irish eile [el'ə].

elima, elimloχ 'milk' (alemnoch L, alamuk A, alamach G). *Grūt elima* 'new milk'; *g'ami e.* 'bad milk', 'buttermilk'. [But G gives *alamach grut* 'buttermilk'; *a. ly* 'fresh milk'.] Irish leamhnacht [l'aŭnaχt] 'milk'.

elum 'a town' (ellum: helm G). See **āvali**. Both seem to be formed from Irish baile.

enaχ K' gives *eannach* 'a cap', 'bonnet'. *E. tobhair* [= tōr'] or *e. touin* [= tōn'] 'trousers'. Probably from ēadach: see **d'ūχ**.

enok, enoχ 'a thing'. See **inoχ**.

Ė

ėn 'one' (ain L). Irish aon [ēn]. On other Irish numerals given by L, see do.

ėrpa 'another'. *A gloχ ėrpa* 'another man'. Etymology obscure.

F

feadar 'a gull' (K). Irish faoilltheān [fwĭl'ḥ'ăn].

fĕ 'meat' ('fay, vulgarly[1] fee' L', faihé, feyé L, fĕ'he A, féha G). *Fĕ gāt* 'veal'; *fĕ klĭtug* 'mutton' (but G gives *bleater's fĕ* for 'mutton'); *blanog's fĕ* 'beef'; *mwōg's fĕ* 'bacon'. Irish feoil [f'ōl'].

fĕ-t'ėrp 'a pan'.

finnif 'a five-pound note' (N). Cant of Yiddish origin.

fĭk'ir 'a sweep' (fĭcir G).

fĭn 'a man' (feen G). Irish fian.

fleece 'hair' (G). English.

fōki 'people' (N). Romani.

fōrgarl 'tobacco' (G).

fōros 'a fair' (N). Not corroborated as Shelta: a Romani word from modern Greek φόρος.

G

gafa 'lame' (gaffa). Irish bacach [bakaχ].

galapa 'fern' (gallopa L'). Cant, not Shelta (Sampson).

garo 'bull' (garro, gorro, gurro). Irish tarbh [taru].

gasal 'donkey' (gassel F). Irish asal.

1 **gāter** 'a drink', specifically 'beer'; but F gives gath = 'whisky': gatter (N) 'rain', gaθ (G) 'intoxicating drink' (gather, gatter). *K'en-gāter* 'public-house'; *mam'rum-gāter*, 'tap-room'; *trĭp a gāter* 'a sup of drink'; *gāter skai* 'a drink of water'. Etymology obscure: Irish deoch [d'oχ] 'drink' (?).

2 **gāter** 'father' (gather, gatter: gâ'thera A, gátera G). *G. tom* 'grandfather'; *kriš-gāθer*, ditto; *mo dhatair* 'my father' (W). Irish athair [ahir].

gaverog 'a goat'. Irish gabhar [gawar].

gåp 'a kiss', 'to kiss' (gāp, gâp). Irish pōg.

gåt 'young' (gāt, gâth, got, goth). Irish ōg.

---

1 It is interesting to learn that even in Shelta there are degrees of vulgarity!

gåt'na 'a young person' (gothena, gâthena), β 51.

gåt'rin 'a child' (gatherin, goiχera, goχera, goχerē, gotherin: gothlin, gocht'thlin (!), goch'thlin, goch'lin L', gothni, gāchlin L, gâ'hedi A, goyan F, gorya, goya, gohera G, gochlin K). K gives gochlim 'a ninny'.

gåt'a 'colour' (gatyu, gocha). Irish dath [daḥ].

ged 'a bog' (K). Doubtful if Shelta.

gesti 'a magistrate' (ghesti, ghesterman L'). Irish giūistīs [g'ūs't'īs'] from English 'justice': or perhaps maighistir [māīs't'ir'] 'master' de-aspirated and anagrammed.

get 'to leave', 'cease', 'wait' (get, geth). *Get in g'ūk* 'leave the old man alone'; *get till mwīlša sūni* 'wait till I see'; *get your tari·in* (A) 'stop your talking'. Perhaps Irish stad 'stop'.

getūl 'to shake', 'tremble', 'to fear', 'a trembling', 'fear', 'afraid'. (Also spelt geturl, getterl [γ 2a], gettūl [γ 2b].) *A-getul* (agratīs G) 'afraid'; *getuls in the mål'a* 'tremblings in the hand'; *getul'd* (spelt geturlt) 'frightened'. *Getchell* (G) 'fear', as though get'ul. Irish eagla [agla] 'fear' (?).

get' 'hot'. Irish tē [t'ē] 'hot'.

get'a 'to forgive' (get, getyū). *Mwīlša get'as nīd'as* 'I forgive people' (α). Irish maith [mwaḥ] 'to forgive'.

get'al get'a+suffix al 'forgiveness' (α), miswritten *gretul*.

gifan 'a horse' (W, K). In K' giofan, as though g'ifan, g'ofan. Irish capall 'horse'.

gilhairt See ayírt.

gilifon 'a waistcoat'. G. *swurt* 'an inner waistcoat'; French gilet (?).

giligopa 'a teapot'.

gin 'brooch' (ginn K). Doubtful if Shelta.

gisteramån See gesti (géstimer N, gistremán G).

gita 'fear' (G). See getul.

glader 'to swindle' (gladher, gledher, gladdher, glad'herin, glant-'herin, glantherin L'). According to Leland's Aberystwyth tramp it signifies any form of swindling, such as 'ringing the changes'; but this explanation is not accepted by Sampson. In *Journal*, G.L.S. I, ii, p. 218 he says that the word means nothing but 'skin' (Irish leathar [l'aḥar]): and that a *gladeri* is a half-naked beggar who dresses in rags to attract charity; *gladerin'* he explains as shewing one's *glader*. May it not simply mean 'to skin', in the common colloquial sense of to 'chisel out of money'? *Gladar-box* (G) 'a [coiner's] mould'.

glask 'grass'. Either Irish glas 'green', or English 'grass'.

Gliderox 'Munster'.

glodax 'dirt', 'dirty'. *That the mīdril may tarsp you, you glodach
kriš b'ōr* 'That the devil may kill you, you dirty old woman'
(G); *glodach of the t'era* 'dirt [i.e. ashes] of the fire'. Irish
cladach 'dirty'. See **ladu**.

glogē 'stocking' (glogaidh, plur. glogaidhean K'). Irish stoca.

glox 'a man' (glox, glōx, glok: glomhach, tr. 'old man' W;
glom, glomhach K; gleoich, gleoch (as though gl'ox) G).
A plural form, *gloxi* (spelt gloxhē, β 41), γ 1 d, is preserved:
the English plural suffix is added to it in *glox-i-s* (γ 1 d), but
it is not invariably used. *Glox gūt* 'black man', 'policeman';
g. a k'ena 'man of the house'; *g. krū* 'smith'; *g. ar-mislō*
'tramp'; *g. rilū* 'madman'; *g. šl'ī·ux* 'schoolmaster'; *g. srugad'*
'doctor'; *g. sūnal* 'showman'; *g. surdu* 'tradesman'; *g. swuder*
(*g. sūdil* G) 'gentleman'; *g. tom* 'rich man'; *g. turpog* 'a
ragged [beggar] man'; *g. radam* 'soldier'; *g. tarsp* 'dead man',
'corpse'. Perhaps Irish ōglāch [ōglåx] 'a hero', 'champion',
but the word, as the above examples shew, has no such
specific meaning in Shelta.

glōkot 'police' (glócote G).

glōral 'listening'.

glōri 'to hear', 'listen to'; 'to hear a report of' (γ 2 a) (glōrhī:
chlorhin L). Irish cluinim [klun'im] 'I hear'.

glōrōg 'an ear' (glōrhōg: glorhoch L). *Glōrōg* (G) 'an ear', also
'a pot'. Irish cluas 'ear'.

glūtug 'wool' (γ 2 a). Irish olann (?).

gl'åg 'a nit'. Irish sneadh [s'n'å].

gl'īt 'a mountain' (glēt, glīe't). Irish slīabh [s'l'īw].

gl'ōnsk 'a man' (gleoinsc G, gleoinshe [*sic*] G').

goixera 'child'. For this and a variety of similar words see
gåt'rin.

goixil 'all', 'every'. *Goixil tūrk*, 'every time'. Irish gach uile
[goxíl'ə] 'each and every'.

goithean 'dog' (K').

gox', gox'i 'to leave', 'put', 'place' (gox, goixi, goixe, goxhi,
goihe: ghoi, goih'ed L). *Gox' it to the Dāl'on* 'leave it to the
Lord'; *gox'i his d'ī'l* 'leave him alone' (γ 1 d); *gox'id* [goihe'd]
"he put it" (on the ground, γ 1 b). Irish fag [fåg] 'leave'.

gop 'poor' (gup G). *K'en-gop* 'a poorhouse'. Irish bocht.

gopa 'a pot' (goppa: guppa G). Irish pota. But L gives *goppa*, and translates it 'furnace', 'a smith', as though Irish gabha [ḡaūa] 'smith'.

gored 'money', 'a coin' (garedh, gorred, gurredh, gureddh: gorhead, godhed, gorheid L, gáredh A, gáiread G). *G'ami gored* 'a bad [counterfeit] coin'; *g. nap* 'silver money'; *g. grât* 'gold coins'; *b'in'i gored* 'little money'; *gošta gored* 'plenty of money'. Irish airgead [ar'g'ad] 'silver', 'money'.

gori 'to give', in a variety of senses (gorri, ghoi 'to put' L, guri G). *Gori'd swurt mâl'a wart* 'he put up one hand' (γ 1b); *gori sturt* 'cover up' (β 36). 'To put', 'place', as in *gori'd him on his nup* 'he put him on his back'. The Irish root gabh- [gav, gau] has a similar range of meanings.

goro 'a bull' (gorro, gurro). Irish tarbh [tarū]. Also **garo**.

gošta 'plenty', both adj. and subst.: 'many'. *Gošta gored* (or *gošta a gored*) 'plenty of money'; *gošta dura* 'bread enough'. In β 73 spelt goštya, as though *gošt'a*. Perhaps Irish sásta [såsta] 'satisfied', for which cf. **grâsta**: but compare Romani kušto 'good'.

got 'young'. For this word and its derivatives see **gât**.

got'a 'colour' (gocha). Irish dath [daḥ] 'colour'.

gov'li 'a cow' (göveli C'). Irish gamhnach [gaw̃naχ] 'a stripper'.

gōpa 'a pocket'. Irish pōca.

gōpan 'an umbrella'. Perhaps Irish pōcān 'a little bag'.

gōti 'to give' (gothi, grothi, gōti G). *Gōti mwīša a milk of dura* 'give me a bit of bread'. Irish tug 'gave'. Compare **gori**.

gradum[1] 'life', 'soul' (gradum, gradhum). *Gradim* 'life' (G); *I solk'd his gradum* 'I took his life'; *gradum a gradum* 'for ever and ever' (α). Apparently Irish anam 'soul'.

graisk 'thread' (G). Irish snath.

graχt 'to quench'. *Graχt ludus* 'quench the light'. Irish tacht. Compare **grata**.

graχton 'a week' (graton, grathon, groχthon, groχton, graχthon, graχtern: gratchūil, grastōg G). Irish seachtmhain [s'aχt'ãn'] 'week'.

graχu 'hurry'. Etymology doubtful.

graχul 'towards'. *Gloχ graχul mwīša* 'the man on my side'. Etymology doubtful.

[1] It is probable that some of the many words beginning with gr should be spelt with gr', but there is not sufficient material available to differentiate them.

grala 'a shoulder'. Irish guala.

gramail 'like'. Irish amhail [aẁal'] 'like', 'as'.

granĕl 'knowledge' (granhĕl).

1 **grani** 'to know' (granhē, grani: grāni, granni, granny L); in β 35 'to understand'. *Grannis to my deal* (L) explained as 'it belongs to me'; *nīd'eš grani* 'I don't know'. Irish aithnim [aḥn'im] 'I know'.

2 **grani** 'to want'. *Do you grani gored?* 'Do you want money?' (G).

granko 'a turkey'. Irish francach.

granlesk 'green' (gronlesk). English 'green' + nonsense suffix lesk.

1 **granlum** 'brass'. *Šarog granlum* ['red brass'] 'copper'. Etymology obscure.

2 **granlum** 'a neighbour'. Etymology obscure.

3 **granlum** 'sauce, condiment'. Irish annlann.

granta 'an aunt'. English, or perhaps Irish loan-word aintīn.

gran'a 'a nail' (granya L, omitted on republication; grä'ni A). Irish tairnge [tarŋ'e].

gran'en 'pregnant' (grannien L). Uncorroborated.

graro 'a foal' (grarro). *Grifi tom a graro* 'a mare with foal'. Irish searrach [s'arraχ] or possibly Romani k'uro.

grasal 'an ass' (grasol). Irish asal.

Grasano 'Scotland', 'England', 'Scottish'. Irish Sasanach 'Saxon'.

graskal 'to open' (graskal, gruskal). Irish foscail. Also, as adj. 'open': *pī graskal* 'an open mouth'.

graskot 'a waistcoat'. From English.

grašano 'a mason'. Probably from English.

grat 'smoke' (grat, grath). Irish deatach [d'ataχ].

1 **grata** 'a hat' (grata, gh'rata, gh'ratha L, grū'thi A). Irish loan-word hata, from English.

2 **grata** 'to choke' (gratha). Apparently Irish tachtaim 'I choke'.

1 **grat'** 'a place' (grach, grat). *Grat' gušu* ['a sitting place', i.e.] 'a saddle'. Irish āit [āt'] 'place'.

2 **grat'** 'to watch'.

1 **grat'i** 'to make', 'to do'. Presumably by-form or mistake for grĕdi, q.v.

2 **grat'i** (grachi). Meaning uncertain: *grat'i grifin* or *grat'i gruna* is translated 'petticoat' [a modification of petti- (?)].

graura 'summer'. Irish samhradh [saŭra].

grādna 'a nail'. Compare **gran'a**.

grădni 'Saturday'. *Grădni olomi* 'Saturday night'. Irish Sathairn [Saḥarn'].

grăfša 'cursed' 'haunted' (graafsha, grāfsha): in β 28, 'haunting'. Irish taidbhse [taivs'e] 'a ghost'.

grāg' 'a street' (graag, graog). *Mislí·in to the grāg'* is translated by G 'going to town'. Irish sráid [srād'] 'a street'.

grālt'a 'welcome'. Irish fáilte [fălt'e].

grănša 'a stranger' (γ 3k). Irish strōinsear [strōn's'ēr], a loan-word from English.

grăn'e 'a ring' (grānya, graanya: graini, graineol K, grainne G). G. *t'evpin* 'a finger-ring'; *g. grăt* 'a gold ring'; *g. šelker* 'a seller of rings'. Irish fáinne [făn'e].

grārk' 'a field' (graak, grark). *Grārk' a naps* 'a field of turnips'. Irish pāirc [părk'].

grārnog 'a flea' (graarnog). Irish dearnad [d'arnad].

1 **grå** 'love' (α), grau (β 56). Irish grādh [grå].

2 **grå** 'luck'. *G'amī grå* 'bad luck'; *mun'i-grå* 'good luck', apparently the only available equivalent for 'sanctification' in (α). Irish ādh [å].

grăbalta 'able' (grabaltha). Irish ābalta, loan-word from English.

grăd 'a sod'. Irish fōd.

grăder 'solder' (grádher G, grawder L, groder K). English.

grăkin 'a boy', 'lad' (grākin, grāχin, grōkin). See **grōkin**.

grăser 'a saucer' (grāser G). English.

grăsi 'to please' (grassi·in in γ 2b). Irish sāsamh [såså] 'satisfaction'.

grăsta 'satisfied' (graster, groster, grostar). Irish sāsta [såsta].

grăt 'gold', 'golden' (grâth, grāth). *Grăt guris* 'a gold watch'. Irish ōr (?).

gredicoat 'a petticoat'. English: not used in true Shelta (Sampson in *Journal*, G.L.S. I, ii, p. 213). See under **grat'i**.

grent'a 'quick' (grencha). Etymology doubtful.

gresko 'a voice'. *Glōri gloχ's gresko* 'hear the man's voice'. Irish guth.

grespan 'to shew', 'exhibit'. Irish taisbeān [tas'b'ån].

1 **grē** 'tea'. Irish tae [tē], loan-word from English.

2 **grē** 'to arise', 'to rise', 'to raise' (grī K). *Grē swurt* 'risen up, sprung up' (β 31); *grē'd swurt arárk* [the child] 'grew up in that fashion', 'with that peculiarity'; *grē karib* 'to raise a fight'; *grēs* (γ 1a) 'he rises'. Irish ēirighim [ēirīm].

grēdan 'a face' (grēdhan, grēdhŭrn, grēthern: grēdin G). *Nap grēdan χuri* 'a white-faced horse' (β 85); *g'ami g.* (lit. 'an ugly face') 'a scoundrel'; *dd-grēdan mugatŏn* 'a two-faced fool'—a name for a hammer with two round faces. Irish ēadan [ēdan].

grēdi 'to make', 'to do' (grēdhi, grēthi [γ 1d]; grachi [as though *grēd'i*]). *Grēdis nīd'as rīlū* 'it makes people mad'; *what's to grēdi with dī'l?* 'what's the matter with you?' (γ 1c); *nīd'as grēdi g'amiaθ mwīlša* (α) 'people who do me evil'. *Grēdi aχím* ['to make out' =] 'to pretend' (γ 2b); *grēdi grīson* 'to tell the news'; *grēdi sūgu* 'to make fun'. *Grēti my fleece* 'cut my hair' (G); *grēti a buri t'era* (G) 'make a good fire'; *to bog the kuri's kōris grēdid* (G) 'to get the ass's hoofs done' [=shod]. Irish etymology doubtful: perhaps déan ('make', 'do'), reversed, with gr substituted for n after reversal.

grēd' 'hair' (grēid G). Irish gruaig.

grē·ed 'a bridge' (grē-edh, greath). Irish droichead [droχ'ad].

grē·er 'hay' (A). Irish fēar [f'ēr] 'grass'.

grēχol 'a tooth' (grēχol, grīχol). Irish fiacal.

grēpul 'a chapel' (grēpēil G). Irish sēipēal (s'ēp'ēl): loan-word from English.

grēsol 'a beard'. See **grisōg**.

grēsub 'a pan'.

Grētis 'James' (G). Irish Sēamas [S'ēmas].

grēt'īn 'a bird', 'chicken'. *T'al grēt'īn* ['a half-bird' =] a 'linnet' or 'canary'; *swurkal g.* 'a singing bird'; *tāral g.* ['a talking bird' =] 'a parrot'; *grēt'īn gūt* 'a blackbird'. Apparently Irish sicīn [s'ik'īn], from English 'chicken'.

1 **grifi** 'a mare', 'female' of any animal. *G. kam'ra* 'bitch'; *g. klītug* 'ewe'.

2 **grifi** See 1 **grifin**.

1 **grifin** 'a coat', 'a skirt' (G) (grifi, griffin: griffin, gruffin L, griffin F, gruffan G, grivin K). *Grat'i grifin* 'a petticoat' (also *g. b'in'i* (G)); *dd g.* 'two coats' (β 80).

2 **grifin** 'a groat', 'fourpence'. *Ǎd g.* 'eightpence'. K' gives *grosan* [<groat]. [These two words seem to be formed from 'coat' and 'groat' respectively, on an analogy from brauen or bravan = 'oat'.]

griml'ōr 'a chimney'. Also **grinl'ōr**. Irish simlēir.

grimšer 'a month', 'year', 'time', 'weather' (grimsha, grimshar). *Get' g.* ['hot time' =] 'summer'; *gwōp g.* ['cold time' =] 'winter' (β 33). Irish aimsir [əm's'ir] 'time', 'weather'.

grin'ŏg 'a window' (grenŏg: grīnŏg G, grainyog L). G also gives a word 'glazier' for window, presumably from English. Irish fuinneŏg [fwin'ŏg].

grin'šeg 'a she-fool' (griniseag K). Irish óinseach [ōns'aχ].

grip 'money' (grop, goup K). Probably not Shelta.

griper 'supper' (gripa L, gruppa K). From English.

1 **gris** 'fortune', 'charm'. *Gris b'ōr', gris gloχ*, 'a fortune [-telling, i.e. Gypsy] woman', 'man'; *l'esk gris* 'to tell fortunes'. *The swibli a' k'en-gāter had bogd his gris l'eskd* 'the boy of the public-house had got his fortune told'. Irish fios, 'knowledge'.

2 **gris** 'a watch': also **guris**, or **grisūl**. Compare **grat'** 'to watch'.

3 **gris** 'soul' (G).

griso 'to tell fortunes'.

Grisod 'Brigid' (grisödh).

grisōg 'a beard'. Also **grēsol**. Irish feasōg [f'asōg].

grisūl 'a watch'. See **gris**.

grit'ēr 'dinner' (grichēir G).

grit'ūn 'an onion' (grutan G). Irish inniún.

grī·ed 'silk', 'silken'. *Gūna grī·ed* 'a silken gown'. Irish síoda [s'īda].

grīlt'ūr 'a miller'. Irish muillteóir [mwilt'ōr].

grīnlesk 'flax'. G. *mun'i* translated 'flax [of the] good [people]', i.e. fairies' flax, 'ferns'. Irish lín [l'īn].

grīnta, grīntus 'fair', 'market'. *Grēš the grīntus* 'back from the fair' (γ 3a); *grīnta-talósk* 'fair-day'. Irish aonach, plur. aontaighe [ēntī].

grīntala (γ 1a), where it is translated 'friends'. See **menthroḥ**.

grīnt'ūr 'dinner' (grīntyūr, gritche L). Irish dinēar [d'in'ēr], from English.

grīrse 'hair' (griorse G).

grīsk 'straw' (G). Irish tuighe [tī].

grīson 'news'.

grīš 'heart' (grish). *G'ami grīš* 'ill-will'; *mwīlša's grīš* or *mwīlša's mun'i grīš* 'my good heart'—a Shelta toast. *Lōberin his grīš* 'beating his breast'. Irish croidhe [krī] 'heart'.

grīto 'wind' (grītho). *Turpōg grīto* ['wind-rag'=] 'a sail'. Irish gaoth [gēḥ] 'wind'.

Grītus 'Peter'. Also **Yītus**. Irish Peadar.

grīt' 'sick'. *G'ami in grīt'* (β 72) 'very ill' (we should probably read *grīt'aθ*). *Gritch* (G) 'illness'. Irish breðite [br'ŏt'ə].

grīt'aθ 'sickness' (grīchas [β 57], grichath [β 70]).

grīt'i 'dinner'. See **grīnt'ur**; but perhaps L's *gritche* may be derived from Irish cuid [kud'] 'a portion, share'.

grīwa 'to sweep', 'a sweep'. Perhaps Irish sguabaim 'to sweep'(?).

grīwog 'a fairy'; also 'a witch' (grīwog, grüvog). *G'ami grīwog* 'bad fairy'—a term of endearment (!). Irish sīdheŏg [s'īyŏg] 'fairy'.

groχta 'snow' (graχta). *Groχta-nap* 'snow-white'. Irish sneachta [s'n'åχta].

grolan 'noise'. *Grē grolan* 'to raise a noise'; *get grolan* 'stop the noise!'; *tŏmān g.* 'too much noise'. Irish glōr.

grolsa 'lazy' (gralsa). Irish fallsa.

grolsin'aθ 'laziness' (grolsinyath).

gropa 'a shop' (gruppa G).

grŏda 'soda' (G). English.

grŏkin 'a lad' (grŏken, grãχen). Irish stŏcach [stŏkaχ], a contemptuous word for 'lad': 'lubber'.

grŏmug 'egg'. Also **rūmŏg**. Irish ūbh or ugh [ū] 'egg'.

grŏpa 'soap'. Irish sŏpa, loan-word from English.

gruber 'work', 'a job': 'to work'. *Nid'eš tul your gruber* (β 48) translated 'not worth your notice' [perhaps better, 'not worth your trouble']. *Gruberin* 'working'; *grubin* (K) 'digging'; *grubin-ciar* (K) 'workhouse' [ciar = Romani kēr, 'house']. Grubacht (G). Irish obair [ubar'].

grug'im 'curds' (gruigim K'). Irish gruth.

1 **gruχ** 'frost', 'ice'. Also **gruk**. Irish sioc [s'uk].

2 **gruχ** 'to shoot'. Future gruχa (β 19). Irish lamhach [lãaχ]; or conceivably an anagram of urchar 'a cast', 'a shot'.

grunim 'oat-meal' (G).

grunkel 'uncle'. English: or Irish loan-word oncal.

Grunles 'Annie'.

grunsa 'a [barrel-]hoop' (G). Irish fonnsa.

grup *grup rēib* (see **rēb'**) (G) 'a wisp of hay'. Irish sop.

grupån 'a cup' (grupān G). Irish cupān, from English.

gruska 'a tinsmith's box' (grusca G). Irish bosca 'box'.

gruti 'a hat' (grüthi A, gruta G). See also 1 **grata**.

gruvog 'a fair'.

1 **grūd'** 'a feather'. *Grūd'-lī* 'a feather-bed'. Also **klūd'**. Irish cleite [kl'et'e], or perhaps *clūmh* [klū] 'feather'.

2 **grūd'** 'tea' (grūj G).

grūker 'sugar' (grucera G). Irish loan-word siūcar [s'ū'kṛ] from English.

grūla 'apple'. *Skaihop grūla* 'cider'. Irish ubhall [ūl].

grūna 'a gown', 'dress'. Irish gūna, loan-word from English.

grūskal 'to awaken'. Irish mūsgail.

grūskil 'a punch'. *Grūskil šarka* ['a cutting-punch'=] 'chisel'. Irish loan-word sīsēal [s'īs'ēl] 'chisel' (?).

grūsku 'whilst'. Probably Irish sīost [s'īst] 'a while'.

grūt 'new' (gruth). *Grūt elima* 'new milk'. Irish nuadh [nūa].

grūti 'to shut' (G).

Grūtīn 'Winifred' (G).

gulima 'a boot' (gulimug, gullima: gullemnock, gullemnoch L, gillamese F, gaileamuck, guilimīn G, guilbneach, guilbeannach K'). Etymology doubtful.

guris 'a watch'. See 2 gris.

guš, gūš 'to sit'. *Guš šīrt* 'sit down' (also *guši išīrt* G); *grat' gušu* 'a saddle' ['sitting place']; also *gušu* alone. *Od gloχ gušin in the mam'rum gāter* 'There are two men sitting in the tap-room'. Irish suidh [sī].

1 **gušu** 'a kettle' (gushū, gushūχ, gushuk: gūshūk L; guiseach 'a porringer' G). Irish soitheach [soḥ'aχ] 'a vessel'.

2 **gušu** 'a saddle'. See **guš**.

gušul 'a porringer' (guiseal G). See 1 gušu.

gut 'wire' (G). Irish snāth [snaḥ].

gūt 'black' (gūt, gūth). *Gūt-gloχ* 'a policeman'. Irish dubh [duw].

gūtena 'a smith', 'blacksmith' (gūtherna). Also *gloχ gūtena*. *Gotherma, guttema* (L) 'a policeman'; *guthanna* (G) 'a smith'.

gwil'i 'to lie', 'lie down' (gwilyi). *Gwil'i·in nasdēš* 'lying (down) here' (β 74); *gwil'id on tōber* '[he] lay down on the road'; *Ar gwil'o* 'lying down' (β 4). Irish luighim [lwīm].

gwīš 'hay', 'straw' (gūīsh). Irish tuighe [twī]. Grīsk (G).

gwŏp 'cold' (gūop; goo-ope, gūop L). Apparently Irish bog, literally 'soft', but often applied, with euphemistic optimism, to a cold, wet day.

G'

g'al 'yellow', 'red' (gial L). But cf. Irish geal [g'al] 'white'.

g'ami 'bad' (gami, gyami, gamoχ: gyami L, gammy G). *G'. griš* 'ill-will'; *g'. elima* 'buttermilk'; *g'. lākīn* 'prostitute'; *g'. sūner b'ōr* ['a bad-looker woman'=] 'a woman with the evil eye'; *g'. grēdan* ['bad-face'=] 'a scoundrel'; *g'. tăn* 'a bad-[weathered] day'; *g'. gured* 'a false coin'; *g'. grå* 'bad luck' (β 91); *g'. in grīt'* ['bad in sickness'=] 'very ill' (β 72); *g'. ned'as* 'an unlucky place' (G). Comparative *g'amier* (β 32); superlative *g'amiest* (β 64). Etymology uncertain. 'Gammy' is a common cant word for bad, but whether it is derived from Shelta or vice versa is uncertain. Pace Barrère and Leland (s.v.) there is no Gaelic word gam 'lame', 'crooked', 'bad': presumably they were thinking of *cam*.

g'amiaθ 'badness', 'evil'.

g'amoχ 'bad': by-form of g'ami.

g'e 'with' (gyē), β 37. Irish le [l'e] 'with'.

g'et'a 'twenty', 'a score' (getya, geta, gyeta). *T'al g'et'a* 'a half score', 'ten'; *ăd g'et'a* 'two score', 'forty'; *šūkr g'et'a* 'five score', 'a hundred'. Etymology doubtful: perhaps from the genitive of fiche [fiχ'et] 'twenty'.

g'et'um 'a gate'. Irish geata [g'ata] 'gate'.

g'ēg 'to ask', 'beg' (gēeg, gēg, gīēg; gayg G). *G'ēgin g'ŭk* 'a beggar-man'; *He g'ēgd mwīlša aχim* 'He asked me out'. Irish guidhe [gī] 'pray'.

g'ēg'ra 'a beggar' (gīégera, géger G). Compare d'ūka, g'ūk'ra, yūk'ra.

g'iliχon 'a book', 'a bible'. (Also spelt jilihon.)

G'ison 'John' (Gisān G). Irish Seaghan [S'ån].

g'ofag 'a sow' (giofag K').

g'ofan 'a horse' (giofan K').

g'ōr' 'penis' (gioer, gyor). *G'ōr' šed'in t'era* 'a poker'. Irish bod(?).

g'ŭk 'an old man', especially 'a beggar', 'vagrant' (gyuk, dyuk, juk, yuk, yook: gyuch or gyŭrch A, 'a man'). *G'ŭk a k'ena* 'old man of the house': *moryenni yook* (L) should be *muni g'ŭk* 'a good man'. Irish geōcach [g'ōkaχ] 'a vagrant'.

g'ŭk'ra 'a beggar' (jūka, gyukera, yukera), γ 3f; in β 43 used as a plural. *Grag' g'ŭk'ra* 'a street beggar'; *g. lampa* 'a bag-beggar' [a tramp who travels the country with a bag]. Irish geōcaire [g'ōkərə] 'a vagabond'.

g'ŭksta 'a monkey': also (contemptuously) 'an old man' (β 5). *Karb g'ŭksta*, female of the same. A superlative formation from g'ŭk (?).

H

hal 'across' (G). *Hal skai* ['across water'=] 'across the sea'. Irish thar [har].

hawrum 'morning' (G). Otherwise sroid'an, q.v.

hălor 'a cap' (G).

hăvari 'home'. In Shelta *na-havari* is used for 'homeward' or 'at home': na=in (q.v.). *Are you misli·in na-havari to gruber?* 'Are you going home to work?' *Nus a Dāl'on mwīlša's havari* 'God bless my [or our] home'. Also **āvari, havalo, havara**. Probably from Irish a-bhaile [awa'l'e] 'at home', 'homeward'.

helm 'a town' (G). See elum.

Hibi Vocative of Sibi, n. pr. fem.

horer 'a clock' (yewr: both forms given by N). Probably cant (from Yiddish?) or Romani hora 'watch, clock'.

horsk 'across', 'over'. *Misli·in horsk the skai* 'crossing over the water'. Irish thar+nonsense addition sk. See **hal**.

hū 'thou', 'you'. *In st'īm'ra hū* (γ 3f) 'Are you a piper?' Irish thū [hū].

I

i 'in' (also **a**).

1 in 'the'. *Sūni in gloχ-swudal* 'Look at the gentleman'. Irish an.

2 in Irish interrogative particle (=Latin *nonne, -ne*). See quotation under hū above.

inoχ 'a thing' (inok: ainoch L, eenik L', innock G). Often used, like 'thingamy' and such nonsense words, to fill the vacancy, when a name for something does not exist, is forgotten, or is undesirable to mention. G gives *šark my inoχ* for 'cut my hair', and *gopa-inoχ* (an essentially English construction) for 'a pot-hook'. *Sūni the inoχ* 'look at that!' *eanach meilg* (K'=*inoχ mal'a*) 'a finger-ring'. *Inoχ-n'ab, Inoχ-nīp* (G) 'turnip' (but *innocniap of gairéad*='a sovereign', '£1'). The word is also used in the same general way for a non-existent or forgotten verb. *Inoχin roiχas* 'playing cards'; *inoχin m'iskon* 'giving the breast' [to a child, β 77]; *inoχin kad'ogs* 'throwing stones' (β 15); *inoχin the stama* 'writing the letter'. *Can I inoχ my st'īmera* [recte st'īma] *at the t'era?* (G) 'Can I light my pipe at the fire?' *Inoχ libis* ['the sweet thing'=] 'sugar' (G). *Inoχ you škimašk* 'make you drunk'; *inoχ the ludus aχim* 'put the light out'; *Nad'ram of the Dal'ōn inoχ you* 'the Virgin Mary bless you'. (These three sentences from G.) Also **t'inoχ, ainoχ, enoχ**.

K

kad'ōg 'a stone' (kadog, kadyog, kajog, kajic: khädyog L, caideóg G). *Kad'og a t'era* 'hearthstone'; *k. muni* ['good stone'=] 'diamond'; *k. šarko* ['sharpening stone'=] 'grind-stone'; *k. nap* ['white stone'=] 'lime'; *k. ladu* ['stone of earth'=] 'gravel'. *Kadog-grāšano* 'a stone-mason'. Caid (Bearlagair word, see following chapter) + ōg.

kaihed 'a chair' (L). Irish cathaoir [kaḥīr].

kaine 'ears' (kyni L'). Perhaps Romani kanya, 'ears'.

kam 'son' (com, cam G). *Kam a k'ena* 'son of the house'. Irish mac.

kamag 'a hen' (camag, caimeag K').

kamair 'mother' (camir K, mo chàmair W). Irish māthair.

kam'ra 'dog' (kamera, kameri: kā'mbre A, comera G, cāmbra C). *K. šural* 'racing dog', 'greyhound'; *k. n'āk* (or *m'āk*) 'a fox'. Irish madra.

kamrailid' 'a quarrel', 'fight' (camrailid, camarailid K').

kant 'a gill'. Also chant.

kar 'whither?' (car, γ 1c). *Kar dī'lša misli·in?* 'Where are you going?' Apparently an abbreviation of kē ar 'what on?'

kara 'a boat' (cara K'). Irish curach 'a canoe'.

karb 'an old woman', 'grandmother' (krab, karbug [a diminutive form, with Irish dim. suffix ōg]). *Karb lugil* 'a banshee' [wailing woman]; *k. g'ūksta* 'a female monkey'; *kriš karb* 'an old hag' (β 24). Used sometimes contemptuously, but not always. Connected by Kuno Meyer with an obscure and obsolete word fracc, recorded in O'Davoren's *Glossary*.

karbu 'market' (kắribu, kŭribu, kŭrbug). *Karbug talósk* 'market-day'. Irish margadh [marga].

kari 'to buy', 'to pay' (karri). Irish ceannuigh [k'ani].

1 **karib** 'to kill' (karb [γ 3j], kurob L', carob 'to cut' L, koreb A, koriben 'fighting' A, corrib G; carab 'to hit', carob 'to cut' C). *Stēš karibin od grit'in kad'og awárt* 'that's killing two birds [with] one stone'; *Mwīlša's karibd with the gwop* 'I'm killed with the cold' (G). In English Shelta always used instead of **lober** 'to strike': *By the Holy Dal'ōn, sūbli, I'll karib you in the pī* 'By the Holy God, mate, I'll hit you in the mouth' (Sampson). Irish marbh [marw] 'to kill', 'dead'.

2 **karib** 'to steal' (carab C, corrib G, karrib [γ 3j]). *Do you karib the t'imas in the šark?* 'Do you steal the sticks in the field?' (G).

karmuš 'a shirt'.

karnag 'drawers' (carnag K').

karnān 'a dungheap', 'rubbish-heap'. In γ 3g with lenition of initial, χarnān. *K. snēli* 'a heap of rushes'. Irish carnān.

karniš 'meat' (G).

kart 'a trail' (cart, chart C). Irish tarraing.

kartson 'a needle' (carthson K). Doubtful if Shelta: but conceivably an anagram of Irish snāthad.

kasin 'cheese'. (Also **kesum**.) Irish cāis [kās'].

kauvi 'testicle'.

kåb 'cabbage' (cab L', cāb G).

kåmpa 'a camp' (kā'mpa A). English. According to A the tinkers in America speak of *kāmpan klúgen e mukya [kåmpa 'n klugen a' mwog'a]* as 'a famous camp in Wales'. This would mean 'the camp of the pig's head': in seeking to identify it we may neglect the actual meaning of the name, or even its apparent meaning to Welsh ears, and think only of the meaning which itinerant tinkers with a smattering of Welsh might extract from it. *Penmachno* has occurred to me as a possible identification, but some Welsh friends whom I have consulted are doubtful of this. Klugen = Irish cloigionn 'skull'.

Kerribad 'Margaret' (Kerribadh).

kesig 'a mare' (kessig N).

kē 'where?' *Kē nyīpa hū?* 'Where have you gone?' 'Where are you?' See **kar**.

klaiton 'a ditch', 'wall' (klaithon: claidhán G 'a fence', 'bank'). *Ladu klaiton* 'a clay bank'. Irish claidhe [klī] with diminutive suffix ān.

klisp 'to break' (clisp, chlispen, clispen L, cheisp G) 'to break by letting fall' (L). *Klispa hū* 'thou didst break'; *klisp kun'a* 'a suspended priest'; *klispin talósk* 'day (is) breaking'. Irish bris.

klīspis 'trousers' (also klīšis). Variant of **rīšpis**, q.v. Irish brīste, with English plural ending s.

klītug 'a sheep'. *Fē klītug* 'mutton'. Etymology doubtful.

kluš 'easy' (clush C). Doubtful if Shelta: possibly from Irish furas.

klūd' 'a feather'. *Klūd'-lī* 'a feather-bed'. Compare **grūd'**.

klūt'a 'wool' (klūtya). Compare **glūtug**.

kogi 'turnips' (koggies C). Probably not Shelta.

koi 'pincers' (khoi L).

koldni 'a bud' (coldni, coldi K). Irish coinnle, coindle.

kolum 'a sheep' (colum K').

kom, kombat 'a clergyman' (com, combat C).

kon 'night' (conn K'). Irish (a)-nocht [ənoχt] 'to-night'.

kon'īn 'a child' (K). Perhaps the slang kindšin (from German
   or Yiddish: cf. 'the kinchen lay' in *Oliver Twist*). Or possibly
   a hypocoristic adaptation of the Irish coinīn [kon'īn'] 'a
   rabbit'.

korib 'to warm' (corrib G). *Korib your mǎl'as at the t'era* 'warm
   your hands at the fire' (G). Etymology doubtful.

kŏri 'foot', 'leg' (kora 'leg' L'; kori 'foot' L; cŏra G). *T'ēvpins
   a kŏli* ['fingers of the foot'=] 'toes'. Also kŏli. Etymology
   doubtful. Hardly from Irish cos.

kŏrig 'vulva' (kurrog). *Lub a kŏrig* 'vagina'; *kŏrig a gloχ* 'a
   despicable man'. Etymology doubtful.

krad'i 'to stop', 'stay', 'wait', 'to be, or to lie in a place' (kradyi,
   kraji [γ ɪc], krädyin L, hatchi N 'to remain'). *Krǎd'hyī*
   'slow' (L); *krad'al* 'stopping', 'remaining'. See quotation
   under d'oχ. *Krad'i your pī* 'stop [shut] your mouth'. Irish
   stad.

kran 'a farm' (cran(k)). Doubtful if Shelta.

kranko 'a turkey'. See granko.

krauder 'string' (crowder L).

kraudug 'a hen' (kaldthog L, crowdhel, croudóg, crŏd'ŏg G,
   kraudug, kraudog). Craodag 'an egg' (K'). Irish cearc
   [k'ark].

kretum 'sand' (cretum K). Doubtful.

krimašt 'a clergyman' Also kummašt. Irish ministēir, loan-
   word from English.

kriš 'old'. *Kriš karb* 'an old hag'; *kriš nad'ram* 'grandmother';
   kriš tobar ['an old road'=] 'a lane'. Irish sean [s'an].

krišena 'the old one', 'the elder', 'the eldest'.

krīmūm 'a sheep' (crīmūm L, but omitted on republication).

krīpa, krīpuχ 'a cat' (krépoch L, crīpach G). *K. šural* ['a running
   cat'=] 'a hare'.

krīp'īn 'a stool' (crípín G).

krīs 'a saddle' (krees N). See grat'.

krop 'money' (crop F). Uncorroborated.

krŏker 'a doctor' (N).

krōlušk 'hungry' (A: clōrus, crolusc 'hunger' G). Irish ocras [ukras] 'hunger'. More properly the word should be rendered 'hunger'. A gives the sentence tha królushk amílth [*Tā krōlušk a' mwīlša*], a literal rendering of the Irish tā ocras orm 'there is hunger on me', 'I am hungry'.

krū in *gloχ krū* 'a smith'. Meaning uncertain.

kuldrum 'asleep', 'to sleep'. *T'ūχ kuldrum* 'bed-clothes'. Irish codladh 'sleep'.

kuler 'a shilling' (kuller, kalor N). Not corroborated.

kun'a 'excreta'. *Kun'a k'ena* 'a latrine'.

kun'el 'a potato' (cunnel kunyel L, cullen, cullīon G). Cant, not Shelta.

kun'i 'cacare'.

kuri 'a horse, donkey' (kŭri, χuri, curry 'an ass' G, curragh 'a horse' F, kūri A). *T'al kuri* 'a mule', or 'jennet'; *kuri b'in'i* 'a donkey'; *kuri tom* 'a horse'; *kuri šural* 'a horse-race' (*sic* in a MS. note, but more probably 'race-horse'); *kuris' k'ena* (crois-kaona G) 'a stable'. Irish gearrān 'a horse'.

kurlim 'to close' (G). *Kurlim a lūrk* 'to close an eye'.

kut'er 'a cat' (cutcher G).

kūn'a 'a priest' (kūna, kūnya: okonneh L, cuinne G). *Kūn'a a abista* 'parish priest'; *klisp kūn'a* 'a suspended priest'.

kūt'i 'a piece', 'bit'. N gives hatchi kootschi [*kad'i kūt'i*] for 'stop a little longer'. Irish cuid [kud'] 'a piece, share'.

K'

k'en, k'ena 'a house' (kīéna, kyena, kena, ken; kiéna, kîéna LL', kin C', keen F, cian K', ciam, cian, ciar C, ce'na G). *B'or' a k'ena* 'woman of the house'. *A šéd's-k'en* (shades-cane G) 'police-barrack'; *cian toim* (W) ['big house'=] 'a cottage'; *cian b'in'* (W), ceampain (K'), *b'in'i k'ena* (G) ['little house'=] 'a tent'; *k'en-gāter* 'a public house'; *k'en gropa* 'a shop'; *k'en ned'as* 'a lodging house'; *k'en spurko* 'a brothel'; *k'en-gop* 'a poorhouse'; *kiēnthis* [k'entis] 'houses' (β 31). Sometimes interchanges with Romani kēr.

k'erp 'to lie', 'to peach', 'give information' (chirps L 'lies'). *Lyeskin chirps*, or *k'erpin'* 'telling fortunes'. *Cherpin* (L), said to mean 'a book'. Also chirp, churp. Probably from breag [br'eg] 'a lie', which suggests the spelling here adopted, with k' rather than with t'.

k'erp'ra 'a liar', 'impostor' (churpera, γ 2a).

k'ēdi 'a cap' (céidi G). Probably cant.

k'ĕrk 'a garment' (cheirk, pron. chair-k (G) but here spelt with k' rather than with t' on account of apparent connexion with Irish ceart [k'art] 'a rag'). *G'ĕg an old k'ĕrk from the gloχ* 'ask the man for an old garment'.

k'ima 'a stick'. Properly **t'ima** or **d'ima**, from Irish maide [mwad'ə].

χ

χaran 'S'deis sium a meartsacha air aicharan' (W) = *stĕš-im a* '*march*'-*aχa ara χaran* 'we are "marching" [=going] on the sea'. χaran, not otherwise recorded, must be a perversion of Irish fairrge [far'g'e or war'g'e] 'sea'.

χurīn 'a can' (khurrhīn). Said to be a Munster word.

L

labĕrt 'to exchange' (laberth). Irish malairt.

laburt 'to curse', 'a curse' (labŭrth). Irish mallacht.

lad'ram 'soap' (latherum). English 'lather'.

ladu 'earth'; 'dirt', 'dirty' (ladhū, ladher [γ 3k]). Loda (G) 'a [clay] floor'; lodach (G) 'dirt'. *Ned'as ladu* 'a graveyard'; *on ladu* (γ 1d) 'on land'. Irish talamh [talã].

lad'n'aχ 'daughter' (laidneach G).

lag 'to conduct'. *He'll lag you home* 'he'll see you home'.

lagprat 'a fish' (N). Not corroborated, but compare laprōg.

lagūn 'a porringer' (G). Possibly from Irish noigīn.

lampa 'a bag' (lampē). *Lampa munt'es* 'tobacco-pouch'; *l. gored* 'a purse'. Irish māla.

lampĕid' 'a blanket' (G). Irish blaincéad, from English.

lampōg 'a tinker's budget' of tools, etc. (G). Diminutive of **lampa**.

lanach 'a highway' (W).

laprōg 'a duck', 'goose' (G): laprogh 'a bird' (L).

laskon 'salt' (laskern: lascon G, lóskum A). Irish salann.

lasp 'taste' (larsp, lesp). Irish blās.

lašūl 'nice', 'pretty', 'a flower' (lashool L, loshul, loshūn 'sweet' L, łáshuwul A). Superlative lašūlest (γ 1f). *Lasūir dora* 'nice bread' (G); láshúil thálosk (*lašūl talósk*) 'fine day', 'good morrow' (G'). Irish deiseamhail [d'ēs'ūl].

lat'rum 'butter' (latherum).

lābi 'to hide'. Irish foluigh [folī] (?).

lākīn 'a girl' (larkin L', leicheen L, lâk'ĭn, lârkīn A, lackeen F, lackan C', lakīn G). *G'ami lākīn* 'a prostitute'. Irish cailīn.

lākr 'a tailor' (larkr [γ 1b]). Irish tāilliūr [tâl'ūr], from English.

lākūn 'a stool' (G).

1 **lāsk** 'to light' (larsk). Irish las.

2 **lāsk** 'a stool' (lesk G). Also **losk**. Irish stol.

lāsūn In the expressions *lāsūn gāter, l. nad'ram* 'grandfather', 'grandmother' (G). Irish sean-athair, sean-mhathair, but the prefixed la- is obscure.

lēdōg 'a lady' (G). From English. The by-form **yēdug** (q.v.) suggests that this should be spelt **l'ēdōg**.

liba 'blood'. Irish fuil.

Libisk 'Philip'.

ligi 'a church'. Irish eaglais [aglis'].

linska 'a name'. Irish sloinne. See **munik**.

lī 'a bed'. *Lī-ned'as* 'a bed-place', 'lying-down-place'. Irish luighe (lī) 'lying down'.

līspa 'a dish' (G): līspog (G) 'a basin'. *Od mid'ōg līspa* 'a two-shilling piece' (G). Etymology doubtful.

lobān 'a cabin: a tent' (G). Irish bothán [boḥån].

lod 'white' (G). *Gored lod* 'silver money'.

lodaχ 'mud', 'dirt', 'soot' (G). Also **glodaχ**. Irish lathach [laḥaχ].

lork 'a car', 'cart' (lorch 'a two-wheeled vehicle' L, lorc G). Etymology uncertain.

losk 'a stool' (lorsk: losc G). Irish stol. See **lāsk**.

losport 'a bastard' (G). Perversion of the English word.

lōber 'to hit', 'strike', 'beat'; γ 1d (lubrān, lūber 'to hit' 'strike' L). Lō'be dhīl är'e pī (A), translated 'hit him on the mouth', but properly *lōb(r)a (mē) dī'l ar a' pī* 'I'll hit you on the mouth'. A also gives 'lóbrâme dhīe'l', which is the same expression. Irish buail.

lōsp 'to marry' (lorsp). Irish pōs.

lōspo 'married' (lorspo: lospi G). *L. b'ōr'* 'a married woman'.

lub 'a hole' (lub G 'a chimney'). *Lub gūt* 'prison'; *lub a kōrig* 'vagina'; *lub a tūr* 'anus'. Irish poll 'a hole'.

luba 'a word' (lubba: lob, loba G; in γ 3k 'advice'). Perhaps Irish labhradh [laura] 'talk', but doubtful.

lubān 'a tent' (G). See **lobān**.

lud 'blind'. Irish dall.

ludni 'haste' (K). Doubtful.

lud'ra 'north'. *L. munk'ri* 'north-country', 'Ulster'; *tāral a lud'ra* 'north-country accent' (γ 3k). Irish tuaidh.

ludus 'light' (ludhus, ludhers). Irish solas.

lugil 'to cry out', 'to cry aloud'. Also lugil aχím. In γ 3g karb luggd aχím should be *lugild aχím*. *B'ōr'-lugil* 'a crying woman', 'banshee'. *Lūgīn* (G) 'crying'. Irish glaodh (gle).

lumī 'a tent-cover' (lomī G).

lur'an 'shoes' (luirean W). Irish cuarán.

lusk Only found in the expression *strépuck lusk* (L'), 'son of a harlot', uncorroborated and doubtful.

luskan 'hoop' of a tin can (luscan G).

luskân 'a herring' (luscán G). Irish scadán.

1 **luš** 'to eat', 'drink', 'bite', 'smoke'. *Luš brās* 'to eat food'; *luš gāter* 'to drink'; *luš št'īma* 'to smoke a pipe'. *Lušin-k'ena* 'an eating-house'. Etymology uncertain. Lush is a common cant word, but as in the case of g'ami (q.v.) it is not certain which language has the priority.

2 **luš** 'porter' (the drink): F, G.

lutram 'a prostitute': in the expression *luthrum's goiχera* (L'). Irish meirdreach.

lūbīn 'a loaf' (G). Irish builín.

lūk 'a corner' (lurk). Diminutive *lūrcān* (G). Irish cūl.

lū·ōg 'meal' (G). *Lū·ōg nap* 'flour'; *l. bravan* 'oatmeal'.

lūrk 'an eye' (lurrk, lūrk: lurk, lūrk L, lū'rki A, lúrc G). Irish dearc.

lūrkōg 'belonging to the eye'. *Lūrkōg slun'a* 'spectacles'.

lūrp 'flour' (G). Irish plūr.

lūt 'porridge' (G).

1 **ly** 'fresh' (W). See **elima**.

2 **ly** 'another' (G). *A nīd'a ly* 'another person'. See 1 **a**.

3 **ly** 'queer' (G). *K'ena ly* 'a queer house'; *gloχ ly* 'a queer man'.

L'

l'ag 'to lose', 'to forget' (γ 3i), 'to pawn' (lug, lyag: l'yogh L).
L'ag k'ena 'a pawnshop'. Irish caill.

l'agun 'a loss' (lyagurn). Irish cailleamhain [kal'ā·an'].

l'art 'mind' (liart G).

l'e 'white'. Irish geal.

l'esk 'to tell' (laisk G'). *L'esk d'arp* 'to tell truth'. Irish sgēal
'a story'.

l'esko 'a story'. Irish sgēal.

l'ibis 'sweet' (G). Irish milis.

l'im 'a side', 'edge': 'beside'. *Od l'im* 'both ways', 'both sides'
(γ 1b); *l'im a Srōn'ə* 'beside the Boyne'. Irish imeal [im'al]
'border'.

l'išgad 'a skillet' (lishgadh).

l'it'en 'people' (lychyen L). Not corroborated.

l'ivin 'a mill'. Irish muilleann. The initial m has suffered lenition
after being taken over into Shelta.

l'īma 'a louse'. Irish mīol. Also lyūma.

1 l'īman 'a mile' (γ 2 a).

2 l'īman 'a year' (laiīmon, lyīmon: līmina G). *L'īman wart* 'one
year'; *od šīkr l'īman* 'two or three years'. From the dative
of bliadhain: 'sa' mbliadhain [sa ml'īan'] 'in the year'.

l'īrk 'wit', 'sense': also yīrk. So spelt, but most probably *lī·ak*.
Irish ciall.

l'īrko 'witty'.

l'ogaχ 'a small boy' (liogach bin W). Irish buachall.

l'ūr' 'money'.

M

madel 'a tail' (L). Irish earball, but the connexion is doubtful.

maksti 'a cat'. Prob. Romani mačka.

maχal 'a church'. Also maχer. Perhaps Irish caipeal 'chapel'.
Compare grēpul.

maχon 'a cup'. *Klispu maχon* 'a broken cup'. Irish cupān, from
English.

mam'rum 'a room' (nomroom, nomera G). *Mam'rum gāter* 'tap-
room'. Irish seōmra, from English 'chamber'.

mang 'talking' (manging C').

mankers, mankerso 'handkerchief'. English Shelta only. *Tom mankerso* 'a shawl'; *mankers grī·ed* 'a silk handkerchief'.

mantri 'soup, broth'. Irish anbruth.

mark 'a bone'. *Mark-nid'as* ['bone-place'=] 'Marylebone': an interesting example of folk-etymology. Irish cnámh [knåẅ: in North Ireland and Scotland pronounced kråẅ]. See the note under **kåmpa**, above.

marro In γ 3e is a corruption of incorrect Irish mā raibh 'if there were'.

mašīn 'a goose' (masheen L, maisīn G). Doubtful etymology. Also translated 'cat', in which case it will come from puisīn 'pussy'.

mašūr 'a hammer' (mosūir G). Irish casūr.

mål'a 'hand', 'arm'; 'a handle', 'to handle' (mailya, mālya: máile G, mâ'lyl A). *Māl'a nap* 'a white handle'. *Mailyas, moillhas* 'fingers' (L); *mailyen* 'feeling', 'taking', 'handling' (L). *Māl'a'd* (G) 'arrested'. Irish lamh [laẅ] 'hand', but compare the English cant 'mawleys'.

medel 'black' (medthel L).

med'ri 'to carry' (medhri, medheri). *B'or' med'rin* (G) 'a pregnant woman'. Irish breith 'to carry'.

megit 'a sheep' (K). Not Shelta.

meilor 'an ass' (N). Not Shelta.

menthroḥ A gives a sentence I'm méslīen [=*mislī·in*] to sūni nī [read *my*] nídhe [*nīd'a*] 'menthroḥ', translated 'I'm going to see my friend'. Compare **grīntala**. Both words are probably corruptions of the Irish muinntear, a person's 'people' (i.e. family, friends, followers, etc.).

mer'gin 'a tinker's box' (merigin G).

mēri 'stairs' (merhi, merra). *Sturt the mam'rum, swurt the mēri* 'Into the room, up the stairs'. Irish staighre [stāīr'e], from English.

mērko, mērkōg 'nose' (mearig G, merrih L, menoch (misprint for merroch) L, smär'agh A). Etymology doubtful.

mid'og 'a shilling' (midyog, mijog, mijik: midgic L, mideōg G, mídyok A). *Od mid'og* 'a florin'. Etymology doubtful.

mileš. *Tush é* [=Gaelic tā sē 'he is'] *milesh* (L), translated 'he is staying there'.

milk 'a bit', 'a piece'. *Mwīlša krād'i'd a milk* (γ 3b) 'I waited a bit'; *he bug'd a milk of his d'īl* 'he took hold of him'. Doubtful etymology.

mink'er 'a tinker' (minkr, minkūr, minkyer: minkler L', mínkier A, nacer G). *Mink'er tāral* 'tinker's talk', 'Shelta'. Irish, from English, tinncéir [tink'ēr].

min'úrt 'now', 'to-day' (minárt, minyárth, minŭrth, minyŭrth, mŭnyŭrth). See **n'urt**. *Talósk min'úrt* 'to-day'. Irish indiū 'to-day', or perhaps anois [anís'] 'now'.

misla·in 'raining' (mislain L). Probably English 'mizzling'.

misler 'a doctor' (missler G).

1 **misli** 'to go', 'walk', 'depart': in L incorrectly rendered 'come', 'coming', 'to send'. *Misli aχím* 'go out'. *Ar-mislo* 'gone': adverbially in *g'et'a l'īman ar-mislo* (γ 2a) '[twenty miles] away'. Needi-mizzler (L') 'a tramp', should be *nīd'a ar-mislo* 'a person "on the go"'. *Bog ar-mislo* 'to escape', 'get away'. As in English periphrastic future, 'going' to do anything: *misli·in to sahu his d'īl* 'going to drown himself' (γ 1a). Miesli, misli (L); miseli (L) translated 'quick'. *Misli gl'ēt tom* (β 87) means 'to walk [to a] big mountain'; *a'maslachadh* (W) 'walking'. Sometimes in a causative or transitive sense: *misli gošta lū·ōg on the lūt* (G) 'put enough meal on the porridge'; *misli the lodus aχím* 'put the light out'. Perhaps Irish siubhal (s'ūwal) 'to walk', but rather remote.

2 **misli** 'to want' (G). *Do you misli gored?* 'Do you want money?' Possibly Irish teastuighim [t'astim] 'to want', but again, rather remote.

misli·er 'a walker', 'tramp', 'vagrant' (misleór G).

miš 'to hit'. *Mish it thom* (L), translated 'hit it hard'. Irish aimsighim [aims'īm] 'to hit (a mark)'.

mišūr' 'a dresser' [cupboard for holding china, etc.] (misúir G). Irish drosūr.

mit'ni 'a policeman' (mithani, mithni L').

mīder, mīdril 'devil' (mīderr, mīdher, mīdhurl, mīdhril: medhil, mīdil G). *Rī-mīder*, translated 'double devil' (but see **rī**, below). *Ned'as a mīder* 'Hell'. Irish diabhal.

mīderal 'devilment'.

mīltōg 'a shirt', 'shift', 'sheet' (milthug, mīltug: mīltōg G, melthog L', milltog N, millthogue F).

mīrsrūn 'shawl' (G).

mīšōg 'tongue' (mīlšog).

mīšur 'scissors'. *M. b'in'i* 'a scissors'; *m. tom* 'a shears'. Irish siosūr.

mo 'my' (Irish). Sometimes rendered emphatic by addition of -sa to the following noun (Irish).

molem 'cold bruised potatoes' (mollem).

molson 'an ass' (N).

mong 'a fool' (G). Probably back-slang from Anglo-Irish 'gom'.

mongas 'tongs' (G). From English.

morghen 'a rabbit' (N).

mošona 'a goose'. See **mašĭn**.

Mōtas 'Thomas' (Mothas: Mūtās G).

mugataθ 'folly' (mugadhath).

mugatån 'a fool' (mugadh, mugadhon: mongadān G). Irish amadān, with influence from **mong**, q.v.

mugel 'an apple' (mugel A, muggle G). *Mugel-ned'as, mugel-rãgli* 'an orchard'. Irish ubhall [ūl] 'an apple'; mogall in Irish means 'apple of the eye'.

mukin'e 'dwelling', 'living' (mukin, mukinya [γ 1f]). Irish comh-naidhe [kōnī] 'inhabiting', 'habitation'.

mul 'a woman' (mull G).

mund'ari 'lunch' (munjari). Probably cant from French *manger*.

mungin See **mut'i**.

1 **muni** (K) 'a dyke', 'wall'.

2 **muni** In the sentence *muni t'era* 'light the fire'. Perhaps from Irish adhnadh [eina] to 'kindle' a fire.

munik, munika, munska 'a name'. Perhaps Irish ainm 'name'; but cf. common cant word moniker.

munk'ri 'country' (munkera, munkeri, mackrey=monkery L'). *Munk'ri-nĭd'a* 'a country fellow'; *gŭt munk'ri* ['black country'=] 'an ill-omened place', 'place of witchcraft'; *Grŭt Munk'ri* ['New Country'=] 'America'; *Lut'ra munk'ri* 'Ulster'; *Swurt-a-Munk'ri* ['Up-country'=] 'Munster'. Possibly from Irish tearmann 'a church glebe', but being a common cant expression may not be true Shelta.

munt'es 'tobacco' (munches, munshi K, mŭ'ncias A). *Lampa munt'es* 'tobacco-pouch'; *såpa munt'es* 'twist tobacco', *šark munt'es* 'cut tobacco'.

mun'i 'good', 'well' (muni: mōīnni, moryeni L, mŭ'ni A, muɲe G). Comparative *mun'ier*; *mun'ier gråsta* 'still more pleased'. Doubtful etymology.

mun'iaθ 'goodness', 'blessing' (muniath, muniarth). In (α) 'Heaven'. *Mun'iaθ a Dal'ōn dĭ'l* 'The blessing of God upon you'.

muskro 'a policeman' (N). Romani moskerō.

mut′i 'a rabbit' (muiti, mungin, mungen K).

mūrīn 'a cow' (mooreen G).

mŭskŏg 'a spoon' (mūstŏg G). See **nŭspŏg**. Irish spūnŏg, from English.

mūti, mūtŏg 'a stocking' (G). Also **mūtana**. From Irish miotŏg or mitīn 'a mitten'.

mwēn′a 'last', 'behind', 'yesterday' (mūénya, mūréna, myēna). *Stĕš a gloχ tāri·in mwēn′a mwīlša* 'There's a man talking behind me'. *Mwēn′a Grādni* 'Last Saturday'. Irish i ndiaidh [in′īay] 'behind'.

mwik 'West'. *Mwik gloχ* 'a Connacht man'.

Mwikamo 'Connacht'.

mwi′l, mwīlša 'I', 'me' (amīlth A). See **d′īl**. Sometimes used for the plural, as in α, γ 2a. Genitive, mwīlša's.

mwog 'a pig' (mūog, mūogh L, moo-og G, mouge F, mough K). Irish muc.

M′

m′ali 'sweet' (mealaidh W, meali K). Perhaps Irish meala 'honey'.

m′aunes 'decent'. Irish deagh-nōs [d′ai-nōs] 'decency'.

m′aur 'fat'. *M′aur sugūn* 'fat bacon'; *skai m′aura* 'oil'. Irish reamhar [r′aŭar] 'fat'.

m′auso 'a dance', 'a dancer', 'to dance' (β 40). *Mwīlša's a mun′i m′auso* 'I'm a good dancer'. Irish damhsa [daŭsa] 'to dance'.

m′ena 'yesterday'. Irish indē. But see **mwēn′a**.

m′iskon 'a woman's breast' (miskon, myiskon). Etymology doubtful.

N

1 **na** 'of the' (γ 1a). Genitive of Irish article.

2 **na** 'in'. *Na-havari* 'at home'; *šerku na slī* 'daughter-in-law'.

nad′ram 'mother' (nadherum: naderum G, nâ′dhrum A). *Nad′ram tom* 'grandmother' (γ 3g); *Nad′ram a Dal′ōn* ['Mother of God'=] 'The Virgin Mary'. Irish māthair [māḥer].

nagat 'a donkey' (naggat).

naker 'a tinker' (nacer G). See **mink′er**.

nalk 'to clean', 'to wash'. *Nalki* 'clean'. See **anált**.

nanti 'a turnip' (K).

1 **nap** 'white'. *Nap gored* ['white'=] 'silver money'. Irish bān.

2 **nap** 'to take off' [clothes]. *Napd a grifin* 'he took off his coat' (γ 1b). Irish bain.

3 **nap** 'to milk'. *Goiχera napin nad'ram's m'iskon* 'a sucking child'. Irish bainne 'milk'.

4 **nap** (n'ap) 'a turnip'. *Inoχ niap* (G).

1 **naper** 'to meddle with'. *Naperd his d'īl* 'meddled with him' (γ 1e). In γ 2a, nappin should apparently be *naperin*. Etymology uncertain: Irish bain (?).

2 **naper** 'a spade' (napr, nepr). Irish rāmhan.

nark 'a stitch'. See **nāk'**. G gives *a nork of inoc libis* 'a pinch of sugar'.

nasd'ĕš 'here', 'with' (násdésh, násjésh). *Tōri nasd'ĕš* 'come here!'

nāk' 'a stitch', in the sense of 'a small rag of clothing'. *Nid'ĕš a nāk'* (β 76) '[He has] not a stitch [upon him]'. Irish snāithe [snāh'e], which is used in the same way. Irish faic [fwăk] is also used in the same sense and might be the origin of the word: but the r inserted in the spelling *nark* suggests that the a is long.

nåp 'to give' (naup G). Irish gabh.

nglū 'a nail' (nglou L).

ng'aka 'a tin can' (ngeacca G). Also n'āka.

niba 'a pin, pen'. *Niba lūrk* 'a needle'; *n. šl'uχ* 'a pen'. English 'nib' or 'pin'.

nimpa 'a pint'. Corruption of English.

nimpīn 'a pin' (G). Perhaps Irish cipīn [k'ip'īn] 'a small [wooden] pin'.

nīd'a 'a person', 'a fellow' (nīdha, nīdya: noid W, noig K; nīja G, nīdia L, needi-mizzlers L' [=*nīd'a ar-mislo*]). *Nīd'ĕš nīd'a* 'There is no one'; *nīd'a mun'i* 'an angel'; *nīd'ĕš nīd'a but mwīlša* ['no one but I'=] 'I am alone'. Irish duine [dun'e].

nīd'eš 'no', 'not', 'nothing', 'do not', 'is or are not', and, generally, an expression of negation in assertion or command (nīdash, nīdēsh, nīdyēsh, nyēsh, nijésh, nījish, nījes). *Nīd'ĕš kari* 'do not buy'. *Nejish* (C'), translated 'stand back! look out!' Irish nī h-eadh [nī ha] 'it is not'. Compare **stĕš**.

nīp 'yellow'. *Nīp gloχ* 'an Orangeman'. Irish buidhe [bwī].

noχ Interrogative prefix=Latin *nonne*. Irish nach [noχ].

nolk 'clean'. See **nalk**, and **anált**.

nolsk 'near'. *Tōri nolsk* 'come near'. Irish i ndáil [i nål'] 'near'.

nongas 'tongs' (G). Also **mongas**. From English.

nōb'ri 'turf', 'peat', 'a bog' (nōberi: nobera G). *Nōb'ri Šeldrū* ['Bog-Shelta'=] 'Shelta'.¹ Compare the common phrase 'Bog-Latin'. Irish mōn.

nuga 'a gun' (nugga: nuggus, nuggle G). *Nuga b'in'i* 'a pistol'. Irish gunna, from English.

nulsk 'when?' *Nulsk you sūni mwīlša?* 'When [will] you [come to] see me?' Perhaps Irish nuair 'when', but this is not interrogative.

numpa 'a pound '(sterling or avoirdupois); (nump, numpa G), 'half sovereign'. *Šūkr numpa tul* 'five pounds' worth'; *numpa oid* 'a pound of butter'; *tom numpa* 'a bank note'. Irish pūnt.

nup 'back', 'at the back of'. *Sūnid the gloχ spurku the b'ōr' nup of the grē·ed* '[I] saw the man (misbehaving) behind the bridge'. Irish muin.

nuta 'a hat' (nutha F).

nūp 'to micturate'. *Nūp k'ena* 'a urinal'. Irish mūn 'urine'.

nūs Apparently used only in the expression *nūs a Dal'ōn* 'Blessing of God', 'for God's sake', 'with the help of God', and similar meanings. Irish son, used exclusively in the expression ar son 'for the sake of'.

nūspōg 'a spoon' (G). Irish spūnōg.

N'

n'akul 'to tie', 'a binding' (nyakŭrl). *N. a mūti* 'a garter'; *n'akult* [nyakerlt γ 3d] 'tied', 'clasped'. Irish ceangal.

1 **n'āk** 'to lack'. Doubtful etymology.

2 **n'āk** 'a rogue' (nyāk, nyark). *Od nyāk mink'er* (γ 2a) 'Two rascals of tinkers'. Contraction of Irish bitheamhnach [b'ihūnaχ (?)], 'a thief'.

n'āka 'a bucket', 'can' (nāga). Irish canna, from English.

n'ākiš 'roguish'. 2 n'āk, with English formative suffix -ish. *N'ākiš rēglum* ['roguish iron'=] 'brass'.

¹ It is not clear whether this means 'Shelta' in general, or 'bad Shelta', i.e. a learner's halting effort at speaking Shelta. More likely the latter.

n'edas 'a place': 'to lodge' (nedas, nedhers, nyedhers: naddis, nadas G, nethrus='bed' C'). *K'en n'edas* [nedhers kena, nêdaskan (L')] 'a lodging-house'; *n. gāter* 'a drinking place', 'public-house', 'drinking booth'; *n. a Dal'ōn* 'Heaven'; *n. a mīder* 'Hell'; *n. a t'era* 'grate'; *n. ladu* 'a graveyard'; *n. rēlti* 'a camping place'; *n. šural* 'a racecourse'; *mugel-n'edas* 'an orchard'. Nyadas (L), translated 'table'. Irish ionad 'place'.

n'ēfin 'shame' (nyēfn). An eifish 'a shame' (G): read *a nēf'iš*. Doubtful etymology.

n'ērp 'to smell', 'a smell'. Irish brēan 'fetid'.

N'ētas 'James' (Nyethus). Irish Sēamas [S'ēmas].

N'ikair 'Barlow', a Tinker surname.

n'īpa Used only in the phrase *kē n'īpa thū?* 'Where are you?' [Prof. Ō'Māille, University College, Galway, suggests to me that this may be a perversion of cé ndeachaidh tū? 'where have you gone?' Pronounced in the west of Ireland cē ndeaghaidh tū [ke n'īa tū], the p being inserted for disguise.]

n'ok 'to wish', 'to want'. *L'esk the b'ōr', n'ok to sūni her d'īl* 'Tell the woman I want to see her'. Possibly Irish cion 'affection'.

n'ok'lur 'a chain' (nyokalŭr). See n'akul.

n'okul 'a candle' (nyokurl: nuckle G). *N'okul sorš* 'a resin-candle'; *n'ukl'ōr* (nucleōir G) 'a match'. Irish coineall.

n'ugi 'a guinea' (nyuggi: nyō(d)gee 'a pound' L'). From English 'guinea'.

n'uk 'a head', 'top', 'penny': 'one' (numeral) (niuc G, nyock, nyok L' L, nyuk A). Plural *n'uki* as in *mwīlša's and dīlša's n'uki* 'our heads'. *Šēkr n'uk* 'threepence'; *n'uk a k'ena* 'roof of the house'. Irish ceann (k'an) 'head'. A gives nyŭk= 'one', ōn nyŭk='two', on the authority of one of his tinker informants, but admits that other tinkers laughed at these expressions.

n'urt 'now' (nurth, nyurth). Irish anois [anīs'].

n'ūkal 'a bridle'.

O

1 od 'two' (od, ăd: odd L'). *Od grifin* 'eight-pence'; *od t'alson* ['two half-crowns'=] 'five shillings'. *Ōd-lim* [he looked 'two sides'=] 'both ways' (γ 1b). In ordinal sense *od tŭrk sahu'd* 'the second time, he was drowned' (γ 1e). Irish dō.

2 od 'to' (preposition). *Od lim* 'beside'. Also 'too': *Stēš, and mun'i od* 'Yes, and well too'. Irish do.

oid 'butter' (oidh, oiith: aidh L, ide G). *Oid t'erpu* ['cooked butter'=] 'cheese'. Etymology doubtful: Irish im is rather remote.

ola See ela.

olomi 'night' (dholimi (G) [=*th'* *olomī*].) *Olomi ahúnšk* 'to-night, this coming night'; *olomi aχáram* 'to-morrow night'. Etymology doubtful.

olsk 'over', 'past'. *Šarū olsk od* 'a quarter past two'. Irish i n-ōl 'after'.

opagrō 'a shop' (G). See gropa.

oura 'a town' (G). See āvali.

P

Palantus 'England', 'English' (palanthus, parantus).

1 pāni 'water' (pāni G, pawnie K). Borrowed from Romani: the usual Shelta word is skai.

2 pāni 'a hare' (pānie G).

pek 'bread' (peck G).

pī 'mouth' (pee L, pī G). Apparently Hebrew pī, perhaps borrowed from Yiddish, perhaps a scholastic reminiscence.

pokkonus 'a magistrate' (N). Not Shelta: Anglo-Romani pokonyus, 'justice of the peace'.

pornuc 'a Protestant' (G). See blōrna.

pras 'food'. See brās.

prask 'to break wind'.

R

rabēd' 'a cap' (rabēid G). Irish bareud.

rabista 'a parish' (rabbister). *Kūn'a a rabista* 'the parish priest'. Irish parōiste.

rabl'īn 'a sheet' (raiblīn G). *Nalki rabl'īn* 'a clean sheet'. Irish braitlīn.

radam 'war' (?). *Gloχ radam* 'a soldier' (γ 1d).

rā A gives *Nad'ram kē rā* [kerâ'] *thu mo gāθera?* 'Mother, where did you leave my father?' Nothing like rā seems to occur elsewhere.

Rāb, Rābīn 'Mary'. Irish Māirīn [Mår'īn].

rāg 'a car' (rawg L' 'waggon'; roglan L 'a four-wheeled vehicle'; rawg F). *Rāg-t'era* [a 'fire-car'=] 'a train'. English car.

rågli 'a garden'. Possibly Irish garrdha, but doubtful.

råk, rark 'a way', 'manner'. *Arårk* 'in the same manner'; *that rark* 'then', 'in that case'. Possibly, but doubtfully, adaptation of do rēir 'according to'.

råks 'without'. Etymology doubtful.

rågli 'to laugh' (raglīn G 'laughing'; r'ghoglin, gogh'leen L). Irish gāire.

rån'al 'beer' (rauniel, runniel L). The word was never heard by Sampson (*Journal*, G.L.S. I, ii, p. 219) and he supposed it to be another form of sinål. But R gives it in his vocabulary, from M'Cormick's *Tinkler Gypsies*. Etymology doubtful.

Relantus See **Rilantus**.

relti See **riltōg**.

rengan 'a kettle', 'pot' (K). Etymology doubtful.

rēb' 'hay' (rēib G). *Grup rēb'* 'a wisp of hay'.

rēglum 'iron' (räglan, rēglan L 'a hammer'; riaglon L 'iron'. Perhaps reagain W 'kettle' should come here. Rīglum G 'a soldering-iron'). *N'akiš rēglum* 'brass'; *gūtena's rēglum tom* ['a smith's big iron' =] 'an anvil'; *māl'e rīglum* G 'a tinker's hand-stake'. Etymology doubtful.

ribad 'a hat' (ribadh). See **rabēd'**.

rid'u 'enceinte' (ridū, ridyū).

Rilantu 'Irish'. *Tār·in Rilantu* 'talking Irish'. Perversion of the word 'Ireland'.

Rilantus 'Ireland', 'Roman Catholic'. Compare **Palantus**.

riltōg 'a quilt', 'a sheet' (rilthug). *Ned'as riltōg* 'a camp'; *riltōg-rēglum* 'sheet-iron'. Also **relti**. Irish braitleōg.

rilū 'mad' (rilhu: rīlye G). *Gloχ rilū* 'a lunatic'; *b'ōr' rilū* 'a mad woman'; *t'al rilū* 'half mad'. Irish buile. Perhaps to be spelt **rīl'u**.

rinškal 'a sievemaker' (γ 3f).

risp 'to christen'. *Rispu* 'christening': *talósk rispa* 'Christmas Day'; *olomi risp* 'birthday' [or name-day?]. Either from baisteadh ('baptism') or the name Crīost (Christ). In a rough note of Dr Sampson's rīsp is translated 'born'.

rī **Rī-mīder**, translated 'double devil'. There seems no other evidence for rī='double': possibly it is Irish rī 'king' and denotes a pre-eminence of diabolism in the person to whom the word is applied. [In γ 3h, however, it is applied to a woman.[1]]

[1] But this is ambiguous: comparison with the following paragraph (γ 3i) suggests that the full expression should be rī-mīder's karb 'the king-devil's [=Satan's] old woman'.

Rībĭn 'Bridget'.

rĭk, rĭrk 'a comb'. Irish cīar.

rīl'e 'intoxicating'. Perhaps identical with rilū, which see.

rĭpuχ 'a prostitute' (rīpu, rīpuk: rīpoch G, reepuck L'). In β 51, as a verb, 'to play the prostitute'. Irish striopach.

rĭsbat 'a basket' (rīspog: rīsbaith, rásbeth A, raspéid G). *Rīspog lākĭn* 'a basket-girl'. Irish bascaod [baskēd], from English.

rĭsk 'a razor'. Irish sgian.

rĭspūn 'a prison', 'gaol' (reesbin L', réspun L, rispen, reespoon G; réspun 'to steal' L). Irish prīosūn, from English.

rīšpa 'a pair' (rispes: réspes L, rishpah F 'a pair of trousers'). *Rīšpa gulĭmas* 'a pair of boots'. Query, from Irish briste 'breeches'.

robikin 'rain' (robicin, robbiniuc G).

rodus 'a door' (rudhus: rodus G). Leland's impossible th'm'ddusk seems to be a misreading of th'ruddusk in a badly written note (th'=English 'the'). Leland's handwriting was not of the most legible. Irish doras.

roiχa 'a card' (playing-card). Probably from Irish cārta 'a card'.

rubōg 'a box', 'a bag'. Irish mealbhōg [m'alwōg] 'a bag'.

rud'u 'a sweetheart': 'to woo'. Etymology doubtful.

rud'uaθ 'courtship' (rujūiath).

ruket 'a bucket'. English.

ruspān 'a purse'. Irish sparān.

rūmōg 'an egg' (rumug: rumogh L', rumug L, rúmōgh, plur. rúmōghe A). See **grōmug**.

rūski 'a basket'. See **rĭsbat**.

S

-sa, -ša Irish emphatic suffix, especially after pronouns, as in *mo d'īl-ša, mwīl-ša.*

sacānta 'quiet' (sucánti G). Irish macānta.

sahu, satu 'to drown', 'drowning'. *To be sahud* 'to be drowned' (γ 1d). Irish bāthadh [bāha] 'drowning'.

saiher 'a chair'. Irish cathaoir (kahír).

sakel 'to demolish'. *Saklin inšīrt* (G) 'pulling down'. Irish leagadh.

sak'rente (sakerente). *Gloχ s.* 'a respectable man'. Query, from Irish galānta (=English 'gallant').

salk, solk 'to take', 'to arrest'. *Salt* (properly salk't L) 'arrested'. L also gives salkaneoch 'to taste or take': this is *salk inoχ*. 'To take' (advice) (γ 3k). 'To shut', 'close', 'steal' (G). *Salk the t'imas and grēdi a buri t'era* (G) 'Get the sticks and make a good fire'. Perhaps Irish glac, but this means rather 'to accept' than actively 'to take'.

salta 'a belt' (saltha). *Šlīa salta* 'a leather belt'. Irish beilt, from English.

Sartin 'Martin' (G).

satu See **sahu**.

Sat'lĭn 'Kathleen', 'Kate'. Irish Cāitilīn [Kåt'il'īn].

Sāhon 'Kane', a surname. Irish Cathāin [Kaḥān].

sārk' 'a field'. Irish pāirc [pārk']. Compare **grårk'**.

sgrubul 'a tail' (sgrŭbŭrl). Irish earball [ér'bal].

sg'ibŏl 'a barn'. Irish sgiobōl. Diminutive *sgiobōlīn* (G). See also **šk'ibl'ĭn**.

Sibi n. prop. fem. (='Sabina' or the like), β 37. Vocative **Hibi**, β 74.

siblĭn 'a boy' (G). Diminutive of **sŭbl'i**, q.v.

sik 'some'. Irish cuid 'a portion, share'. [Probably to be written **sik'**.]

sikdūr' 'a doctor' (sicdūir G). Irish doctūir [doktūr'].

simi 'broth' (simmy N). Anglo-Romani zimin.

sinål 'beer' (sinaul, sunōl). Compare **rån'al**. Doubtful etymology.

sinta 'a pint'. *Sinta luš* (G) 'a pint of porter'. From English.

siskår 'a sister' (G). Also **šišer**. From English.

sīk In the expletive *Dalōn sīk sudil* (G), translated 'Good God Almighty'. Etymology doubtful.

skai 'water', 'sea': 'to sail' (skoichen L 'rain'; shoich L 'water', 'blood', 'liquid'; scoi G). *He skaid his d'īl* 'he threw himself into the water' (γ 1e). *Skai-grūt* 'America'. *Skai m'aura* 'oil'. *Skai šural* 'a river'. *Hal skai* 'over the sea'; *skait* 'transported'. Irish uisge [is'g'e].

skaihan 'a sailor'. *Skaihan havari* 'a sailor's home'.

skaihōp 'whisky' (skaihōpa: skoihopa L). *Skaihōp grūla* ['apple whisky'=] 'cider'. Irish uisge beatha [is'g'e b'aḥa] 'water of life'.

skai-t'elpi lit. 'cooked water' (scoitchelpi (G) 'tea with milk and sugar').

Skaitwurd 'Waterford'. (*Skai*='water', *twurd* a perversion of ford.)

skåfer 'silver' (skawfer, skawper L) [sic: but perhaps a mistake for 'solder'].

skēv 'a fish'. *B'ōr' skēv* 'a fishwife'; *skēv šrugu* ['a speckled fish'=] 'a trout'. K gives selvings='fish', which is probably not true Shelta. Irish iasg.

skipsy 'a basket' (N). Anglo-Romani kipsi.

sklátaχ' 'tea' (sclataich W).

skoi 'a button' (skoich L).

skok 'water' (scoc G). See skai.

skol'a 'to know' (skolaia L). Perhaps Irish eolas 'knowledge'; or connected with sgol 'a school'.

skol'ami 'a good scholar' (L).

skōbug 'a ship'.

skōp 'open' (scōp G). Irish fosgail 'open'.

skraχo 'a tree, bush'. Also šk'aχo, škráχ. Irish sgeach.

skrál 'decent' (skraul). Etymology doubtful.

skrīn 'to counterfeit money' (G).

skrīv 'a cart' (K). Probably not Shelta.

skrubol 'a well'. Skai skrubol 'a water well'. Irish tobar.

skudal 'a herring'. Irish scadan.

skukar 'five'. See šūkr.

skurik 'a farthing' (skurrik, skurrig [γ ɪd]).

skurlum 'to burn' (skuldrum, skürdhem). Irish loisg.

slang 'a chain'. Irish sreang 'a rope'; but 'slang' is also a well-known cant word for a chain.

slāhog 'a rat'. B'in'i slāhog 'a mouse'; tom slāhog 'a rat'. Irish luchōg [luχōg] 'a rat', 'mouse'.

slāsk 'a lock' (slarsk). Slāsk a skai 'a water-lock' (of a canal) (γ ɪd). Irish glas.

slāska 'a belt'. Query, from Irish crios 'a girdle'.

slāsker 'a locksmith'.

slāta 'a plate, dish' (slatha). Irish plāta.

slesker Tom slesker is interpreted as meaning 'a farmer'.

slim Slim your d'īl (A) 'to beat you'. Query Irish lēasaim 'to lash'.

slī 'law'. Šērku nā slī (γ ɪd) 'daughter-in-law'. Irish dlīghe [dlī].

sloχa 'rotten'. Irish lobhtha (lōfa).

slosk 'kitchen'.

slug 'to fall'. Etymology doubtful.

slum 'good' (K).

slun'a 'glass' (sluna, slunya). T'al slun'a 'a half-glass' (of drink); bug me a slun'a 'give me a glass'. Irish gloinne [glin'e].

sluχul, sruχul 'a wood'.

slūfa 'wood'.

slūn 'Monday'. Irish Dīa Lūain (d'ī'lūan').

slūpen 'a watch' (sloopen N).

slūya 'soot'. Irish suithche [suḥχ'e].

smaχ 'to spit'.

smarag 'a nose' (smär'agh A). See mĕrko.

smålk'ra 'a wooden spoon' (smolkera). Irish smalcaire.

smentena 'cream' (smentenna). Romani.

smugal 'an anvil' (smuggle L).

snĕl 'a needle', 'a rush'. *Snĕly* 'rushy'; *carnān* [Irish word] *snĕly* 'a heap of rushes' (γ 3g).

sori 'burial' (sorhi). Irish tōrramh [tōrä].

sorm 'blue'. Irish gorm.

sorš 'resin'. Irish roisīn [ros'ĭn].

sprazi 'a sixpence' (sprazie G). Also aspra, q.v.

spurk 'coïre' 'to flirt', and related meanings, expressing various degrees of immorality. Participle, *spurku*. Irish corbadh: or perhaps Anglo-Irish slang "sparkin'" (=playing the gallant).

spurk'ra 'a fornicator', male or female, though the word may sometimes be used in a milder sense (spurkera).

sragāsta 'breakfast' (sragaster). Irish bricfeasta, from English.

sragon, srāgon 'cloth'. *Mun'i sragon grifin* 'a good cloth coat'.

sraiχa 'a clerk' (γ 2b). Perhaps Irish cleireach, with apocope of first syllable.

sramala 'a robber' (srammurla). *Srumalin the mun'kra* (G) 'robbing the country'.

Sranī 'Mary' (G).

srascoat 'a waistcoat' (G). English. Compare graskot.

sraskīn 'a dish' (G). Irish miosgān.

srat 'a gate' (G). Irish geata. Also sluta (G).

Srat'rin 'Catherine' (G).

srāχ 'a cake' (G). Irish cāca.

Srāχū 'Crosby', a surname. Irish Mac an Chrosāin [χrosån'].

srāpa, sāpa 'string'. *Strāpa munt'es* 'twist tobacco'. Irish rōpa, from English.

srent 'to rave'. Participle *srentu* (β 23).

srēk, srīk 'done', 'finished'. Irish crīoch [kr'ĭχ] 'end'.

Srikel 'Michael' (G).

sringan 'drink' (G). *S. rīl'e* 'intoxicating drink'.

sriš 'a basin' (G). English 'dish' (also **šriš**).

srittle 'a kettle' (G). English 'kettle' (also **šrittle**).

srīdug 'a kingdom', 'a reign'. Irish rioghacht [rīyaχt].

srīd'a 'wine' (srīdya, srīχa).

srīgo 'a king'. *B'ōr' srīgo* 'a queen'. Irish rīgh.

srīlik 'a wheel'. Irish roithleōg.

srīntul 'a friend' (srīnthul). Compare **grīntala**.

srīpa 'a button'. Query, from Irish cnap.

srĭš 'a week' (srīs G).

sroid'an 'morning', 'in the morning' (sroidyan, sroijan, γ 1c). Irish maidin.

Srortan 'Martin' (G). Also **Šrortan**.

srotar 'a key' (srothar G). Also **šroχar, šuχar, šorik**. Irish eochar.

srōmēd' 'a minute' (srōmeid G). See **sumad'**.

Srōn'e 'the River Boyne' (srōinya). Irish Bōinne [in genitive case].

srōpa 'string'. *Srōpa rēglum* 'a chain'. See **srāpa**.

srug 'a jug' (G). English 'jug'.

srunta 'a pint'. English 'pint'.

srurd 'a table'. Irish bord.

stafa 'long', 'far', 'late'. *Stafa tober* 'a long road' (but *tober stafa* 'a main road'); *nīd'eš stafa* 'never'; *nīd'eš krad'i stafa* 'don't stay late'; *stafa dī'lša* 'far from you'; *nīd'eš stafa buga dī'lša* 'I'll never give it to you'; *stafa talósk* 'spring'. **Stoffie** (G) 'quickly' is probably the same word. Irish fada.

stafara, -ri 'a prayer' (s'thaffice G). *Stafaris* 'prayers', 'blessings'. *Stafri* as plural appears in γ 2a. Irish paidir (?).

stall 'lodgings' (G).

stama 'a letter', 'paper'.

stamēr' 'a [money] note' (bank- or treasury-note) (stamēir G).

stam'ra 'to spit' (stamara).

stardy 'a hat' (N). Romani stādi.

stāl *Sthāl your whids*, or *sthāl your torrying* (G), translated 'stop talking'. Probably, like 'stall' (L'), cant, not true Shelta (Sampson).

stān 'tin' (G). *Stān šriš* 'a tin basin'. Also **strān**. Irish.

Stān 'John' (G).

stedi 'to stand' (stedhi). Also **šedi**.

stēš 'yes': 'yes is', 'indeed', 'also', 'and'; 'this, that, or here is'; 'I have'; and a variety of related meanings. Used also in opposing a previous statement (like Anglo-Irish 'sure'), 'but in reality' (γ 2a). *Stēš šeltu nid'as* 'here are seven persons'. *Can I inoχ my st'ima at the t'era? Stēš* (G) 'May I light my pipe at the fire? You may'. (In such a question 'can' is almost invariably used for 'may' in Anglo-Irish.) *Stēš mwīlša's nad'ram* 'here is my mother'; *stēš gloχ* 'the same man'. From Irish tā sē, or is ē 'he is': probably the two verbs mixed up together.

stiff 'writing paper'. Cant, not Shelta (Sampson).

stofi See **stafa**.

Stofirt, Stofrik 'Patrick'.

stoχa 'soft'.

straihmed 'a year' (L). Irish bliadhain.

strān See **stān**.

stretch 'a year'. Probably English word, but compare **straihmed**.

strides 'trousers' (G). Probably English cant.

strīpuχ 'a harlot' (strèpuck L'). Irish striopach. See **rīpuχ**.

strod 'a boot' (K). Irish brōg.

strumble 'straw' (G).

sturt 'in', 'into', 'inner'. See **astúrt**. *Gilifon sturt* 'an inner waistcoat'. Irish isteach [is't'aχ] 'inside'.

st'ēmon 'a rat' (styēmon L).

st'īma 'a pipe', 'bagpipe', 'tobacco-pipe' (stī'ma A, steamer G, stioma, stiomagar K). Irish piopa. Also **št'īma**.

st'īm'ra 'a piper' (stimera, styümera: stiomara K: shliéma L, but the l must be a t left uncrossed). *St'īm'ra dī'lša, a st'īma aga dī'lša* 'If you are a piper, have your own pipe'. *Šorikinlub st'īm'ra* 'a key-hole whistler', a technical term for a ragged begging vagrant. Also **št'īm'ra**.

1 **st'īmon** 'a neck'. Irish pīobān 'windpipe'. Also **št'īmon**.

2 **St'īmon** 'Michael' (styīmon, stchümon).

suba Uncertain word, explained as 'not much account'. See the sentence under **šang**, below. Perhaps Irish seabhōid [s'awōd'] 'nonsense'.

subaχ 'a boar'.

subōl 'a bottle' (suburl). *Subōl a' skai* 'a bottle of water'. Irish buidēal.

sud' 'to mix'. Irish suaithim.

sud'ata 'company'. Irish cuideachta [cud'aχta].

sugad' *Gloχ sugad'* 'a doctor'. Irish liaigh (?).

1 sugū 'war'. Irish cogadh [cogū] 'war'.

2 sugū 'sly', 'fun'. *Grēdin sugū* 'making fun'. Irish magadh [magū]; or perhaps sūgach 'funny'.

sugūn 'bacon' (sugurn). Irish bagūn.

sul'an 'a baby' (suillean W, suilin, suilean K).

sumad' 'a minute', 'moment' (simaja, srumad, sumaj). Irish nōimid [nōmid'].

sumōl 'a robber': 'to rob'. See **sramala**.

sup 'a few' (G).

surdu 'trade'. *Gloχ surdu* 'a tradesman'. See 3 **surgu**.

surgon 'a bargain'. Irish margadh, or English 'bargain'.

1 surgu 'a thorn'.

2 surgu 'sea'. Irish fairrge.

3 surgu 'market'. See **surdu**. Irish margadh.

surk 'to hang'. *Gloχ surku* 'hangman'. Irish crochadh.

surχa 'tired'. *Mwīlša's nap's surχa* 'my back is tired'; *nurth bug surχa* (written surhū) 'now he is getting tired' (γ 1d). Irish cortha.

surtul 'plough' (surthul).

sušgad 'a small pot'.

sūbl'i 'brother', 'friend', 'fellow', 'a man', 'a boy' (subri, sōbli, sūibli, swibli [γ 2a], swubli: soobli L, soobri L', sobyé L, sōbli C'). Like Romani 'pal', used in addressing a friend or equal.

sūbl'in Diminutive of **sūbl'i**.

sūl'a 'around' (γ 1a).

sūni 'to see', 'to look' (or **sŭni**. The Liverpool evidence is on the whole in favour of the short u, but the evidence for ū is strong. Sooney G, sauni, sonni L', sūnain L). *I sonnied him* (L') 'I saw him'; *slun'a swūner* 'a looking-glass'; *gloχ sunal* 'a showman'; *sūnis* the 'looks' of anyone; *sunal* 'like'; *sŭnal* 'seeing' (β 76), 'resembling' (β 84).

sūpla *Sūpla talósk* 'a few days'. Irish cūpla 'couple'.

sūrk, swūrk 'hair'. Irish grūag.

swudal *Gloχ swudal* 'a gentleman'. Also **swuda** [swuder]: *b'ōr' swuda* 'a lady'; *Dal'ōn swuda* 'God Almighty'. See **swurt**.

swurk 'to sing' (swurko). *Swurkal* (sorcán G) 'singing'; *swurkal grēt'in* 'a singing bird'.

swurkin 'a song'. *Glōri the swurkin* 'listen to the song'.

swurk'ra 'a singer'. *Stēš a mun'i swurk'ra* 'he's a good singer'.

swurt 'on', 'upon', 'up', 'above' (swurth). *Swurt a munk'ri* ['up country'=] 'Munster'. *B'ōr' a k'ena nīd'eš grāsta solk grit' gloχ swurt the mam'rum* 'The woman of the house won't be pleased to take a sick man up to the room'. *Swurt a mun'iaθ* 'up in Heaven' (α); *luš swurt* 'drink up!', i.e. drink quickly. Probably Irish *suas* 'up'.

Š

šakar 'four'. See **šarka**.

šako 'to sin': 'a sin'. Irish peacadh [p'ako].

šal'wa 'dumb' (salawa). *Šlug šal'wa* 'a tongueless bell'. Irish balbh [balw].

šam 'a boy' (G). *Are you g'ami, šam?* 'Are you sick, lad?' Apparently a perversion of **kam**, q.v.

šan 'steam' (K).

šang 'to think', 'to understand'. Also spelt **shüng**. *Mwĭlša šangs the gloχ täri·in suba* 'I think the man is speaking not much of account'. Query, from Irish *meas*.

šangar 'a snake', 'an eel'.

šant 'a pint'. *Šant a gāter* 'a pint of ale'. English Shelta only.

šarag 'a kiss' (C).

šaragi 'a soldier' (Gleoch sharragy G). Irish saighdiūr [said'ūr].

šarig 'to vex'. Irish crādh.

šark 'to cut', 'a cut'. *Šark a dura* 'a slice of bread'; *I'll šark your n'uk when I misli aχím* 'I'll cut your head when I go out'; *šark brauen* 'to reap'. Irish gearradh.

šarka, šarkr 'four'. *Šarkr skaihōp* 'a quart of whisky'. Properly **šākr**.

šarker 'a cutter', 'an axe', 'scissors'. *Od šarker* (lit. 'two-cutter') 'a pair of scales' (β 76); *sharcúrs* (G) 'shears'.

1 **šarog** 'red', 'red-haired'. *Šarog fē* 'raw meat'. Irish dearg [d'arg].

2 **šarog** 'vexed'.

šarpōg 'a boy' (G). Irish gasūr.

šaru 'a quarter' (β 27). Irish ceathramhadh [k'ahru].

1 **šākr** 'a brother' (šarkar; also sikar, sicdar, šikar G). Irish bráthair.

2 **šākr, šāka** 'four' (seácer G). Irish ceathar.

šārk' 'clever' (sáirc G).

šeb, šib 'to call', 'to name'. G writes *séb*, as though **šēb**. Etymology doubtful.

šedi 'to stand', 'to mend' (sedhi). As preposition, 'on', 'upon' (α). Irish stad (?).

Šeldrū 'Shelta', the tinker's cant (Sheldhrū, Sheldhruχ, Shīldrū, Shīldhrū, Shelta, Shelto, Shelderoχ, Shelru). *Nōb'ri Šeldru* 'bog-Latin', 'bog-Shelta'. Irish bēlra, bēarla 'language', 'jargon'.

šelk 'to sell' (L': also spelt shē·ēlk L, sílc G). Irish reac?

šeltu 'seven'.

šē 'six' (sai, sy L'). *Šē n'uk* 'sixpence'. Irish sē (s'ē).

šēd 'police' (shade G). *Are there šēds in the grag'? Is there a šēds-k'en in the grag'?* (G) 'Are there police—Is there a police-barrack—in the town?' Shadyog (L) 'policeman' = šēd-g'ūk. Query, slang from English shade (cf. 'to shadow').

šēkar 'a sister' (šelkar, šērkr). *B'ōr' šēkar* 'a nun'. Irish siūr, genitive seathar 'sister'.

šērkū 'daughter'. *Šērkū na slī* 'daughter-in-law' (γ 1d). Etymology doubtful. Welsh merch (?).

šib See šeb.

šingomai 'a newspaper' (L).

šišer 'Irish'.

šidrug 'a soldier', 'policeman' (shaidyog, shadyog L). See **šēd**.

šīkr, šīka 'three' (šēka). *Šīkr n'uk* 'threepence'.

šīrk 'grass'. *Gušin ned'as a' šīrk* 'sitting down on the grass'. Irish fēar [fēr].

šīrt 'down', 'downward'. *Šīrt gāter to kam* 'down from father to son'; *šīrt a munk'ri* 'down the country'. Irish síos [s'īs].

šī·u 'to sow'. Irish síol [s'īl] 'seed' (?).

škimis 'to drink'. *Air a sgeamas* 'drunk' (W). Irish meisge 'drunk'.

škimišk 'drunk' (škimašk, škimeršk, skimišts: ishkimmisk L, sgeamhas, isgeamhas K, scimeis G).

škimišter 'a drunkard'.

škráχ 'a tree'. *Šarkin škráχs* 'cutting trees'. Irish sgeach 'a bush', especially a whitethorn.

šk'ibl'ĭn 'a barn'. See sg'ibŏl.

šlāka 'a cloak'. Irish clōca, from English.

šlĭ·a 'leather'. *Šlĭ·a sālta* 'a leather belt'. Irish leathar [l'aḥar]. This word should almost certainly be spelt sl'ĭ·ar.

šlōh'a 'ashes' (γ 3d). Irish luaith [lōḥ'].

1 šlug 'a bell' (also slug). *Šlug šal'wa* 'a dummy of a bell'; *šlug māl'a* 'a hand-bell'. Irish clog [klug].

2 šlug 'slow', 'weak', 'slowly': 'to fall'. Also slug. Irish lag 'weak'.

šl'an 'ale' (A). Irish leann.

šl'ĕm 'to leap'. Irish l'eim.

šl'ĕma 'a frog'.

šl'ĭ·uχ 'to read' (shlĭχ, shlūχ). *Gloχ šl'ĭ·uχ* 'a schoolmaster'. Irish leigheadh (l'ē·aχ) 'reading'.

šl'ĭ·uχter 'a scholar'. *D'arp šl'ĭ·uχter* 'a real scholar'.

šl'uχ 'rain'. Irish fliuch [fl'uχ] 'wet'.

šl'uχu 'wet'. *Šl'uχu talósk* 'a wet day'.

šorik 'a key'. *Šorikin-lub* 'a keyhole'. See šroχar.

šorknes 'cursing' (šorknesing G). Etymology doubtful.

šoru 'a wake', 'funeral'. Irish tōrramh [tōrã] 'a funeral'.

Šreik, Šreikel (rhyming with 'strike') 'Michael' (Shrike, Shrikel G).

šriš 'a basin' (G). English 'dish'.

šrittle 'a kettle' (G). English 'kettle' (pron. 'kittle' in the country districts of Ireland).

šroχar 'a key' (G). Irish eochair (oχar').

Šrortan 'Martin' (G).

šrug 'a jug' (G). English 'jug'. Also srug.

šrugu 'spotted', 'speckled'. *Skĕv šrugu* ['a spotted fish'=] 'a trout'. Irish breac 'speckled'.

št'ĭma 'a pipe'. See st'ĭma.

1 Št'ĭmon 'Michael'.

2 št'ĭmon 'a neck'. Irish muinēal (?).

št'ĭm'ra See st'ĭm'ra.

šud'ēl 'a bottle' (shudéil G). Irish buidēal [bud'ēl].

šukar 'a jar' (sieucar K). Irish crūsga.

šuχar 'a key' (shuchar G). See šroχar.

šum 'to own' (shum L). Doubtful. Perhaps Irish tā sē uaim ('I want it') misheard and misunderstood.

šuri 'to run' (Suri G). *Šural* 'running'; *kam'ra šural* 'a grey-hound'; *kuri-šural* 'a racehorse'. Irish rith.

šurier ['a runner'=] 'a wheel'. Also **surier**. *Lorc-šurier* 'a cart-wheel'.

šušei 'rabbit' (N). Romani.

šūkr, šūka 'five'. *Šūka numpa* 'five pounds'; *šūka g'et'a* ['five-score'=] 'a hundred'.

T

talop 'belly' (thulop, thalop). *Talop tån* or *talopd* 'enceinte'. Irish bolg.

talósk 'day' (thalosk, tarosk). *Mun'i talósk* 'a fine day'; *talósk min'úrt* 'to-day'; *t. awárt* 'one day'; *t. ērpa* 'another day'; *stafa talósk* 'spring'; *grīnta talósk* 'fair-day'; *kurbug talósk* 'market-day'. In L 'weather'. Irish lāithe 'day'.

tarpŏn 'porridge' (thirpon). Irish bracān.

tarsp 'to die', 'dead', 'death' (tharsp: thawsp G). *Tarspin lī* 'death bed'; *that gloχ's nīd'eš tarsp, he's tåp min'úrt* 'that man's not dead, he's alive now'. Transitively: *that the mīdril may tarsp you* 'that the devil may cause your death'; *tarsp gut may luber him* 'may black death strike him (down)'. Irish marbh.

tar'in 'rope' (tarryin L). Irish srian 'rein' (?).

taši 'to read' (L). Very doubtful: perhaps part of an imperfectly understood Irish sentence beginning tā sē 'it is'.

tād'ir 'strong', 'hard' (thadyur, thardr, thadyol, thardyur, tād'ōl). Irish lāidir.

tād'iraθ 'strength' (thardyūrath) (α).

tāral 'talk', 'saying', 'mode of speech', 'language'. *Tāral a lut'ra* 'north-country talk'; *tāral grīt'in* ['a talking bird'=] 'a parrot'.

tāri 'to talk': 'talk', 'language' (thâ'ri A, thari L; thàri L'; a-tharyin 'talking' L). *Nīd'eš tāri·in* ['let there be no speaking'=] 'don't talk'. G writes thawreen, shewing the two i's of tāri·in coalescing. *Tāri·in* = 'a talking', 'a manner of speech'; *tāri·in a mīdril* ['talk of the devil'=] 'blasphemy' (γ 1d). *Tārier* 'a speaker' (γ 2a). *Tārīm* (G) 'talk'; *tārīn* (G) 'language'. Irish rāid 'he said'.

1 **tån** 'full'. Irish lān.

2 **tån** 'a day' (tawn G). *A buri, a g'ami tån* 'a fine', 'a bad day'.

3 **tån** 'small' (G). Etymology doubtful.

tåp, tåpa 'alive'. Irish beatha [b'aḥa] 'life'.

tirpa (thirpa) *Tirpa gloχ* 'a ragman'. Irish ceart 'a rag'.

tirpōg 'a rag'. *Tirpōg grīto* ['wind-rag'] or *t. mislo* ['going-rag'] 'a sail'; *t. k'ena* 'a rag-shop'.

tōim, tāim 'white' (K).

tom, tōm 'big', 'great', 'many'. *Tom gured* ['big money'=] 'gold'; tom yok, i.e. *tom g'ūk* (L) 'a big man', 'a magistrate'; *tom slesker* 'a farmer'; *tom numpa* (L) 'a bank note'. As adverb, 'violently'; *miš it tom* 'hit it hard'; *tomier* 'bigger'; *atomier* 'rather'. The o is marked long or short indifferently; but it seems to be always long in **tōmān**, q.v. Irish mōr.

tomiaθ 'bigness'.

topa 'brave', 'fine' (thopa, thopan). *Topa t'imi* 'a fine stick'. Etymology doubtful.

tōber 'a road' (thōber). *Kriš tōber* ['an old road'=] 'a lane'; *b'in'i tōber* ['a small road'=] 'a path'; *tōber swurt* 'a high road'; *tōber šīrt* 'a lower road'; *tōber stafa* 'a main road'. *Do the šēds misli this tōber?* (G) 'Do the police patrol this road?' Irish bothar [bōḥər].

tōmān 'much', 'great'. *Bug tōmān* 'give a lot!'; *tōmān l'agun* 'a great loss'; *toman gured* may mean 'too much money' or 'how much money' (γ 1d). Irish mōrān.

tōri 'to come'. *Tōri nasdēš* 'come here'. Irish tar.

tōrog 'a tramp' (C').

trĕ-n'uk 'a threepence' (L').

tribli 'a family'. In γ 1a used apparently to denote a large number of people. Irish teaghlach [t'alaχ], genitive teaghlaigh [t'a-lī].

trīp 'a sup', 'drop' (thrīp). *Trīp a gāter* 'a sup of drink'; *trīp a skai* 'a sup of water'. Etymology uncertain; one of a class of quasi-onomatopoeic words like drīog, srubh, flip, etc. all meaning 'drop'.

trīpus 'a fight': 'to fight' (γ 1d, γ 3j). Etymology doubtful.

tug 'a shawl' (G). Etymology doubtful.

tul 'worth', 'price' (thwuol, thol). *N'uk's tul* 'a pennyworth'. Irish luach.

turan 'a loaf' (W). Perhaps Irish arān 'bread', but doubtful.

turpōg 'a rag'. See tirpōg.

tū 'thou'. Irish.

tūr 'anus'. Also 'bottom' (of a river), γ 1d. Irish tōn.

1 **tūrk** 'up'. Irish suas.

2 **tūrk** 'time'. *Nid'eš tūrk* 'never'; *goiχil tūrk* [every time], 'always'; *šīkr tūrk* 'three times' (γ 1b). Irish uair.

T'

t'al 'half' (chal). *T'al g'et'a* ['half-score'=] 'ten'; *t'al grēt'in* ['a half-bird'=] 'a linnet', 'canary'; *t'al kuri* ['a half-horse'=] 'a mule', 'jennet'; *t'al mīltōg* ['a half-shirt'=] 'a dickey', 'shirt-front'; *t'al nimpa* 'a half-pint'; *t'al numpa, t'al inoχn'ap* (G) 'a half-sovereign'; *t'alsōn, tāirsūrn* (G) *charrshom, cherrshom, tusheroon* (L') 'a half-crown'; *t'al slun'a* 'a half-glass'. *Swurt t'al the skai* 'half out of the water'. Irish leath [l'aḥ] 'half'.

t'ant 'a gill' (chant). Also **kant.**

t'an'uk 'a halfpenny'. Contracted from **t'al-n'uk.**

t'ålra See **cålra.** G gives *talrōg* 'knife'.

t'elp 'to boil' (chelp G). See **t'ėrp.**

t'era 'fire', 'fuel' (chera G, therra, thirra, theddy L, thédy A, tur W, teori K, terri 'coal' L; terry 'a heating-iron' L). Irish teine [t'en'ə]. The forms with *d* indicate an alternative t'ēdi.

t'erp 'to lie'. See **k'erp.**

t'ėrp 'to cook', 'to boil' (cherp, cherrp). Irish berbhim [b'ervim].

t'ėrpin 'a finger, toe' (chēvpīn, chėpīn, chēspīn, chėrpīn : chē'rpīn A, chairpīn G). *T'. a' mål'a* 'finger'; *t'. a' kōli* 'toe'; *tom t'.* 'thumb' or 'great toe'; *t'. slug* 'a finger-bell'.·Irish meur [m'ēr] 'a finger' 'toe' (?).

t'ėt A generic word like inoχ 'thingamy'—used when the specific name is unknown or does not present itself. Used in many senses and combinations: see Russell's vocabulary, s.v. **tshat** and references there. Probably not true Shelta.

t'ini 'fire' (chini A). Irish teine. See **t'era.**

t'inoχ 'a thing': variant of inoχ. *T'inoχ a dura* 'frying-pan'; *t'inoχ awárt . . . t'inoχ a-ola* 'the one [person or thing] . . . the other'; *t'inoχ awart mink'er* 'one of the tinkers'; *t'inoχ kriš in the grēdan* ['an old thing in the face'=] 'a wrinkle'; *t'inoχ karib* ['the killing thing'=] 'poison'.

t'oli 'to follow' (cholli: tolsk, tori G). Irish leanaim [l'anaim] (?).

t'ūχ 'clothes' (chīuχ). Irish ēadach 'clothes'.

U

ugum (uggum, γ 3e). Irish agam 'at' or 'with me'.

uχ 'necessity', 'need'. Also **ucaid.** Irish uchaim.

umpi Doubtful word in the sentence *Sūbl'i umpi stafa nīd'eš,* translated 'Boy, don't be long'.

V

vonger 'money' (N). Means 'coals' in Anglo-Romani.

W

waddler 'a duck' (G). English.

wart 'one'. Cf. **awárt**, which is the proper form. *T'inoχ awárt* 'one thing'; *l'īman wart* 'one year'. Irish amhāin [aŵãn'] 'alone, single, one'.

wed' 'money' (wedge N). Doubtful.

wĭd 'tea' (weed G). English 'weed'.

wobbler 'a goat' (G). Not English, but a perversion of Irish gabhar [gaw'r].

Y

yar, yor 'penis'. See **g'or'**. *Ned'as a yar* 'brothel'.

yergan 'tin'.

yĕdug 'a lady' (γ ɪd). Rhyming slang. See **lĕdōg**.

yišgad See **l'išgad**.

yĭrk 'wit'. See **l'irk**.

yĭrt 'again' (yĭrth, γ ɪb). See **ayĭrt**.

Yĭtus 'Peter'.

yŏrum 'milk' (G).

yūk 'a man'. See **g'ūk**.

yūk'ra 'a beggar'. See **g'ūk'ra**.

yūr 'a clock' (yewr N). Probably cant, derived from Yiddish; but cf. Romani yora, ora, 'a watch or clock; hour'.

CHAPTER VII

BĒARLAGAIR NA SĀER

Prof. Kuno Meyer shewed (*Revue Celtique*, vol. XIII, p. 505) that the word *bēarlagair* does not mean, as had been supposed, 'language of craft'; nor should it be translated 'jargon': it is merely an adaptation of the English word 'vernacular'.[1] The 'Vernacular of the Masons' is therefore the proper translation for the name of the language now to be studied.

There are no such rich materials for the analysis of Bēarlagair na Sāer (which we may henceforth abbreviate into B-S) as for Shelta. It was first introduced to the world in a series of 'Observations on the Gaelic Language' by P. McElligott of Limerick, in the single volume of *Transactions* which records the activity of the Gaelic Society of Dublin (published 1808). At p. 11 McElligott gives a vocabulary of some twenty words, promising further particulars in a separate treatise; this, however, never saw the light.

A fuller vocabulary was published by Mr E. Fitzgerald, architect, of Youghal, about fifty years later.[2] Unfortunately Mr Fitzgerald's acquaintance with Irish appears to have been of the slenderest, and his ear for phonetics was quite undeveloped. He wrote down his words in a haphazard spelling, without any explanation of the orthographical principles, if any, which he followed. It is therefore sometimes impossible to make a choice between several different pronunciations which his orthography will bear. Some etymological speculations added to this vocabulary by its compiler, and by an ingenious friend of his, Mr William Williams of Dungarvan, may be allowed without loss to slip into the limbo of things forgotten.

Mr D. Lynch of Ballyvourney, Co. Cork, contributed to *The Gaelic*

---

[1] As in Fick's 'Glossary to Donlevy's Catechism', in *Archiv für Celtische Lexikographie*, vol. II, p. 28.

[2] 'On ancient Mason Marks at Youghal and elsewhere: and the secret language of the Craftsmen of the Middle Ages in Ireland', *Journal*, Kilkenny Archaeological Society, New Series, vol. II (1858–9), pp. 67, 384, especially pp. 390 ff.

Journal a few sentences and words. He was followed in the same periodical by the Rev. E. Hogan, who gave some further words and sentences compiled from the information of one Hyde, a mason. Tomās Seōns (Mr Thomas Jones) and Lynch made further contributions to later numbers.[1]

A short MS. vocabulary was found among Dr Sampson's papers: it is unsigned, and I do not recognize the writing. Another short vocabulary has been published by Domhnall ō Mathghamhna (Daniel O'Mahoney) from the words of a mason called Shakespeare.[2] This completes the available material.

Analysis of the sentences scattered through these vocabularies, given in detail below, shews that B-S, unlike Shelta, is based on an Irish syntactic framework. The prepositions and other particles, as well as the accidence, are as Irish as the corresponding elements in Shelta are English. It is therefore on the whole less 'spurious' than Shelta, and it is much to be regretted that our material is so scanty as compared with the Shelta harvest. For the present there are considerable lacunae in our knowledge, and I have been obliged to leave much unexplained. On the whole there seems to be proportionally less mechanical manufacture of words (inversion, rhyming, etc.) in B-S than in Shelta, and of 'oghamizing' there is not the smallest trace. There is on the other hand less affinity between B-S and the Bog-Latin vocabulary than is to be observed in Shelta.

I have found the task of analysing, and even of reducing to alphabetical order, the B-S vocabulary, one of no small difficulty; on account of the divergent methods, or want of method, adopted by the reports of different collectors. As in the Shelta vocabularies, I have done my best to arrive at the 'highest common factor' of the different spellings, and have employed the same phonetic symbols as for Shelta. The forms adopted by the different contributors are also recorded, with initials to indicate each:

A Anonymous MS.	J Jones
F Fitzgerald	L Lynch
H Hyde (*per* Hogan)	M McElligott
	S Shakespeare (*per* O'Mahoney)

---

[1] They will be found in vol. VIII, p. 212 (Lynch); vol. IX (paged continuously with vol. VIII), pp. 225 (Hogan), 272 (Jones), 345 (Lynch); vol. X, p. 31 (Lynch). Published in Dublin, 1898-9.

[2] *Bēaloideas*, vol. III, p. 518.

Some of the collectors I suspect of carelessness in proof-correcting, adding to the difficulties by printers' errors.

I give first all the sentences that I have been able to find, with a grammatical analysis. (B-S words are printed, in the analysis, in small capitals, Irish words in italics.) Then follows a vocabulary of all the recorded words.

I. SENTENCES

(1) *Coisdre óm chaí* (M) 'Get out of my way'.

> KOŠTRĬ *ōm 'chaoi*. KOŠTRĬ is the imperative of a verb meaning, generally, 'to move', transitive or intransitive: for other recorded forms see the vocabulary, s.v. *Ōm chaoi* [ōm χĭ] Irish, 'from my way'.

(2) *Cawheke a limeen* (F) 'What o'clock is it?'

> KA-HĬK *a* L'IM-*ĭn*. 'Cawheke' appears only once elsewhere, in another sentence of F's (10). He there spells it 'caw-heke', so that it is to be analysed thus, not 'ca-wheke'. Caw [KA] presumably = Irish *cā* (similarly pronounced) 'what': but HĬK is obscure. *A* is the particle found in the Irish equivalent of the same sentence (*cad o chlog ē?* 'what of-the clock is-it?'): it is really a worn-down form of *de'n* 'of the'. L'IM-*ĭn*, in which the second syllable is most likely the ordinary Irish diminutive suffix, is explained by F as meaning 'a trowel', 'a watch' (as here) or 'tools' in general.

(3) *Cou shous da vow* (F) 'Good morrow kindly'.

> A difficult sentence: even the etymological resourcefulness of F's friend Williams was unequal to the enterprise of explaining it. The vowels are perplexingly ambiguous: are they = ow (as in 'vow') or ū (as in 'boo')? 'Shous' may possibly be the Irish *seamhas* [saũas] 'luck', in which case 'cou' might be meant for the *cā* of the preceding sentence. F's translation in any case is too free to help. As for 'da vow', it can hardly be dissociated from 'mavousa', which F gives for 'myself'. This can be analysed into *mo* VŪS-*sa*, VŪS being aspirated (after the possessive pronoun *mo*) from MŪS, a word recorded by J. In J's sentence (36) 'this ĒŠ's MŪS' means 'this man'; compare Shelta, *this gloχ's d'il*. MŪS therefore may be taken as the equivalent of the Shelta *d'il*, used with possessive pronouns to form personal pronouns. The loss of the -s from 'vow' in this sentence may be explained by the influence of the Irish emphatic affix -*sa*, which may or may not be used according to the desire of the speaker. In an ordinary enquiry after health it would naturally be left out: *cad ē mar atā 'tū'?*

is the simple 'how are you?'; *cad ē mar atā 'tu-sa'?* would be 'how are *you?*' [as contrasted with *him*]. And this syllable being left out, it might carry off the radical s of MŬS along with it. Even yet the sentence is not grammatically satisfactory, and some linking particle must be lost. The simplest emendation would be to insert a d'—*Cā seamhas do[d'] vŭ[s]?* 'What luck to thee?' 'What luck have you?'

(4) *Conus a mar ludhe thu vouludhe* (F) 'How do you come on in the world?'.

Here the last is the only B-S word: the rest is Irish, *cionnas a mar luadhaidh tū*, literally 'How do you move'. 'Vouludhe' must be the same as 'mouleadth', a word given by F for 'day'. MAULƏD (AU pronounced as 'ow' in 'power') seems to be the phonesis on which these spellings converge: prefixing *i* 'in' (which sometimes aspirates) we get *i* VĀULƏD 'to-day' I cannot suggest any etymology for this word, though it seems to be formed similarly to SKŬ-ƏD 'night'.

(5) *Thau she erin shek* (F) 'He is dying'.
(6) *Thu le vow sheka* (F) 'He is dead'.

ŠEK has the primary meaning of 'stoppage': ŠEK *air* means 'stop [something]', 'a stoppage upon': see below, sentences (15), (25). Dying is the most effective kind of stoppage, and the word enters into phrases meaning passively 'to die' or actively 'to kill': see sentences (32), (36). The rest of sentence (5) is Irish: *tā sē ar an* ŠEK 'he is on the stoppage', and exemplifies what has just been said as to the transferred meaning of the word. In sentence (6) 'sheka' is a verbal noun (ŠEK-*adh*, pron. šeka), and 'e vow' is the MŬS construction which we have seen in sentence (3): *a* vŭ[s] 'his personality'=he. 'Thu l'' must then be associated together: it can hardly be anything but *do thuill* [do hil] 'he has earned'. *Ag tuilleamh bhāis*, literally 'earning death', is an established phrase for 'at the point of death'. The two sentences therefore are *Tā sē ar an* ŠEK 'he is on "stoppage"' and *Do thuill a* vŭ ŠEK-*adh* 'he has earned "stoppage"'. It is possible that ŠEK is simply an adaptation of the English 'check'.

(7) *She kuing da vousa* (F) 'To beat a person'.

F's translations are even more untrustworthy than his spellings. After what we have seen in sentences (3), (5), (6), this is obviously ŠEK-ing *do* vŬS-*sa* 'stopping (=killing) you'. This is an unusual case of an English participial form. J has an English macaronic sentence (36) but this is rare. In F's vocabulary I find 'gabing' for 'idling'. I suspect that F,

with his hazy notions of how to report an unknown tongue,
has put these hybrids into the mouths of his informants: just
as I can imagine a traveller talking of his discovery of the
strange jargon current in France, and telling his friends that
'They speak of mongj-ing their dinner'. These forms in -ing
never appear in H's sentences, which are the best yet recorded.

(8) *Custrig agudine alp* (F) 'Hurry to town'.

'Agudine' is the Irish prepositional phrase *go dti an* [god'īan].
For Custrig [KOŠTRĪ] see sentence (1). ALP 'town' is back-
slang for baile [bal'ə] with the same meaning.

(9) *Ne to hu lun naw-gre boul-dre mon the heke* (F) 'A mad cuckold
of a fellow'.

Whatever this gibberish may mean, it is obvious on the surface that F's translation can have only a slender relation to it.
It is impossible to translate, as there is nothing comparable
with it in the rest of the recorded vocabulary. But it reads
like a couple of lines out of a (probably obscene) song:

> *Ne to hu lun nawgre,*
> *Bouldre mon the heke.*

We note the Celtic-looking assonance in 'nawgre', 'bouldre',
when the words are set forth thus. Further it may be suggested
that 'ne-to-hu-lun' ought to be 'ne-tro-hu-lun', and to mean
neamh-triathamhail [n'aũtr'ahūl], a word which we shall meet
with again in sentence (28), and meaning 'un-excellent'.
Triathamhail, as we shall see, is a stock adjective of commendation. The *un* in 'lun' would then be the Irish article, *an*.
'Bouldremon' may be one word, like COSDRAMÁN, which in
one spelling or another is variously explained as 'a beard',
'chimney', 'soot', and a 'road'. 'Heke' may or may not be
the same word as we have seen in F's 'cawheke'. The preceding 'the' is presumably the English article. For the present
we must leave the translation in this unsatisfactory form:

> Un-excellent is the 'nawgre',
> 'Bouldremon' is the 'heke'.

Possibly 'nawgre' should be 'awgre', the n being transferred
from the preceding article. In that case the word might conceivably mean *ōg-rī* 'young fellow' (literally 'young king'—
see the words in the vocabulary).

(10) *Caw-heke in rudghe scab-an-thu na therka na libogue* (F)
'What is smaller than the eye of a midge?'

Apparently a riddle, though F, like jesting Pilate, does not
seem to have waited for the answer. 'Cawheke' we know.

'Therka' is doubtless the same as 'derco', given by F else-where in his vocabulary for 'eye' (Irish *dearc*). 'Libogue' is apparently de-nasalized black-slang for *mioltóg* 'a midge'. This word is feminine, as it takes the genitive singular feminine of the article (*na*). The earlier 'na' is, however, *nä* 'than' after comparatives. In 'scabanthu', which must mean 'smaller', we recognize GAB 'small', back-slang for Irish *beag*: the s-therefore must be disconnected and joined to the preceding 'ghe': for 'in rud' (*an rud*) is Irish for 'the thing'. GHES (however it is to be pronounced) must be used like the Irish *níos*, a particle preceding adjectives in the comparative degree, and -ANTHU (which ought to be written -ANTU) must be a B-S comparative termination. We may therefore rewrite the sentence *cā-HĪK an rud* GĒS G'ABANTU *nä dearc*A *na* LĪB-ōg, lit. 'What the thing which-is-more smaller than eye of-the midge?'

(11) *Muintriath, airig—muintriath aonachar, a chara bi* (H) 'God save you, mason'—'God save you kindly, good friend'.

'Muintriath' I explain as a compressed form of *go mbeannui-ghidh an Triath* 'may the Lord bless' [go m'aní an tria]—no more telescoped than 'goodbye'=God be with you. *Triath* 'Lord' is given by F as used for 'God'. The courteous response usually intensifies the wish, by invoking the further blessing of 'Mary' and 'Patrick'. These names do not appear here, however: 'aonachar' may perhaps mean 'singly, especially' (*aon*=one). *A chara*=my friend. 'Bi' is most likely rhyming slang for *díl* 'dear'.

(12) *Coistrig, aois; coistrig ó chiath; coistrig, aois go cin digabha* (H) 'Come in, young man: walk far away; come, young man, to the public (or eating) house'.

For 'Coistrig', see sentence (1). 'Aois' (pron. ĭš) is the regular word for 'man' (not necessarily *young* man, as given in the translation). 'Ó chiath' (pron. ō chīª) is probably, as in sentence (1), 'out of the way'. 'Cín' (compare the Shelta *k'en*) is 'house'. 'Dígabha' (pron. dīgāūa) is, I suspect, a misprint or mis-noting for *dígala*. L has 'cíne díogla' [=K'ĪN a' DĪGLA] for 'public house'. S has the same expression, spelt 'cín a duigili'. F gives 'deegla' for 'intoxicating drink': and H has two expressions for whisky, 'digabha friúich' and 'díagala friúich'. These I take to be variants of one form. I therefore would amend these phrases to KUŠTRI ĚŠ, KUŠTRI ō chaoi, KUŠTRI ĚŠ go K'ĪN diagla. The word *diagla* means 'drink', or specifically 'ale' or 'beer'.

(13) *Coistrig go dtí an núnlig* [*or* múnlig] *triath. Coistrig go dtí in coperó seô. Triathamhuil mairig ían* (H) 'Come to Mass. Come to the sport [*or* fair, *or* market]. Very well, be it so'.

There is some confusion in the translation here. L gives 'cabró seó' as meaning 'chapel' (i.e. R.C. Church). Therefore the second of these sentences must mean 'Come to Mass' or something similar. 'Múnlig' is given by H as meaning 'a working day', i.e. the hours of light; 'Múnlig Triath' would therefore appear to mean 'God's day, Sunday'. It must be extended to mean 'the *rites* of Sunday'; and this corroborates a suspicion that the B-S vocabulary, as it has survived, is not extensive—just large enough to puzzle unauthorized eavesdroppers—and that its words have to bear wider ranges of meaning than their 'official' equivalents in Irish or in English, in order to convey the sense understood by initiated speakers and auditors. *Triathamhuil* 'excellent', the usual adjective of commendation. 'Mairig' is presumably *mairidh* 'let it remain'; but 'ían' is puzzling. It appears to be that rare thing, a B-S particle, meaning 'so'. The whole sentence, or group of sentences, may be rewritten thus: KUŠTRI *go dtí an* NŪNLIG *Triath*, KUŠTRI go dtí an KŌPERŌŠÔ. *Triathamhail, mairidh* ĪAN 'Move to the Lord's Day [ceremonies], move to the Chapel. Good, let it remain so'.

(14) *Coistrig an sgaochluing am cháid go mineoghad air mo stímire cuthi é* (H) 'Reach me the candle towards me till I redden my pipe of tobacco with it' [but more correctly, 'till I redden it upon my tobacco-pipe,' i.e. light my pipe with it].

Here we have 'Coistrig' in a transitive use. 'Scaechnuid', meaning 'sun', seems to suggest that 'scaech' (SKĒχ) means something like 'light'. As 'long-shuain', apparently 'ship of slumber', is used for 'bed', so SKĒχ-long may mean 'lightship' (-luinge is accusative). 'Cáid' (KĀD'), as the next sentence shews, must mean 'presence' (to be distinguished from caidh (kī), one of the spellings of *caoi*, a 'way'): 'am cháid' therefore means 'in, or unto, my presence'. 'Mineoghad' (the spelling mineochad would be preferable) is as it stands the first singular subjunctive of minighim, which means properly 'to make fine', not 'to redden'. STĪMIRE is also found in Shelta (but 'piper', not 'pipe') but not cuthí [KUHĪ] 'tobacco'. KUŠTRI *an* SKEχ-*long am'* χĀD *go mineochad air mo* STĪMIRE KUHI 'Move the light-ship into my presence till I redden upon my pipe of tobacco it'.

(15) *Sec air do bhinnighthe: sec air, a scuifreacháin: sec air, a gheabaois na múine sead, nach tuaite dhuit bé ná cae: na gclapuach an mhíandubh.* *Secídh an mhiandubh (or* bhiandubh) *an bhô na ciné* (H) 'Stop your talk: stop, you dog: stop your talk, young rascal, you do not understand this or that: you would steal the devil. May the devil stop the woman of the house'.

For 'sec air' see above, sentence (5). 'Binnighthe' BINĬHI, the *b* aspirated after *do*, is the same as A's 'binihe' 'words', F's 'binna' 'to speak', also 'binnue caha' 'begging'. 'Geabaois is G′AB-ÊŠ, literally 'small man', and is used for 'a boy', or 'an apprentice'. SCUIFREACHĂN, vocative *-áin*, is confirmed by F's 'cifrehawn' 'dog'. 'Na múine sead' is evidently something abusive: 'sead' (ŠAD) is alleged to mean 'dirty'; if the u of muine were not marked long, we might render it 'of the dirty neck'. 'Nach tuaite dhuit bé ná cae' should be translated 'who hasn't been taught B nor C'. TUAT-uighim means 'to give', as we learn from the following sentence (16): here again we see a case of extension of meaning to make up for deficiency in the vocabulary. 'Na gclapuach an mhíandubh' hardly means such nonsense as 'you would steal the devil'. In the first place it is in interrogative form—*na*' (for *nach*) gCLAP-óchthá would be the orthodox Irish spelling—'would you not "clap" the devil?' There is no other evidence for a word 'clap' meaning 'to steal'; I should conjecture that it is an adaptation of English 'club', and that the phrase means 'wouldn't you beat the devil' (compare 'That bangs Banagher, and Banagher bangs the divil'). It is noticeable that the masons appear to believe in a feminine devil: the aspiration of the initial in the nominative and accusative shews that. Secidh is imperative third singular in form: clearly the translation of the last sentence should be 'may the devil kill the woman of the house'. 'An bhô na cíne' may be good B-S, but it is bad Irish: two words in genitive relation cannot both have the article. We have already seen a breach of the same rule in Shelta. These sentences should be written thus: ŠEK *ar do* VINNIHĬ, ŠEK *air, a* SKUFR′AχĂN′. ŠEK *air, a* GhAB-ÊŠ *na muine* (?) ŠAD, *nach* TUAT-*uigthe dhuit* BĒ *ná* KĒ; *nach* gCLAP-óchthá *an* MhĬANDUV. ŠEK*idh an* MhĬANDUV *an* BhŌ-*na*-KĪNƏ.

(16) *Geabaig, airig. Luadaig airig, agus tuatóig aes na cíne sgrábán puinc ar gcáid. Túiteoig aois na cíne sgrábán triath* (H) Work easy, mason. Be quick, mason, and the man of the house will give us a pound. The man of the house will give a crown'.

The reporter's spelling is careless. We can hardly believe that Hyde pronounced the word for 'give' in two such diverse ways as are indicated by 'túiteoig' (tūt'og) and 'tuatóig' (twatōg'). 'Geabaig' is imperative of G'AB-*uighim*, of which we have already seen a macaronic participle in F's 'gabing'='idling'. 'Luadaig' is a similar imperative, from the verb which we have already seen in sentence (4). TUAT-*uighim* seems to be a verb with the sense of giving, imparting. 'Ar gcáid' [år gåd'], i.e. '[into] our presence'. Compare 'am' cháid' [am χåd'] in sentence (14). There is some confusion in the names of the coins. 'Sgrábán' [SKRÅBÅN] is diminutive of SKRÅB, which must be F's 'scraub', by him rendered 'a shilling'. 'Puinc' must be F's 'pynke', meaning 'money'. 'Sgrábán triath', which H translates 'crown', is F's 'scraub treah', which he translates 'pound'.

(17) *Bog suas tú féin as soin* (H) 'Hurry out'.

Literally 'Move yourself up out of that'. Entirely Irish.

(18) *Seabhruigh an cnápach* (H) 'Look at the cat'.

'Seabhruigh', misprinted 'slabhruigh' in *The Gaelic Journal*, phonetically ŠĀŪRĪ, is F's 'shouroo' 'look out'.

(19) *Tá sé ag cáiniughadh carruinn* (H) 'He is eating dinner'.

The last two words are B-S with Irish inflexions, meaning literally 'eating meat'. The first part of the sentence is elementary Irish.

(20) *Is gosamhuil do bhille lé bille méanla nú le reac bhfearbhuighe bhíoch ag cáineadh chíobhuir* (H) 'Your mouth is like the mouth of a sow, or like an ugly dog eating dung'.

'Gosamhuil' should be *cosamhail*, the ordinary Irish word for 'similar'. I suspect that the 'g' is simply a transcriber's mistake: there would be no point in disguising this word, and even if there were, so thin a disguise would be futile. BILLE 'mouth' (aspirated after do) is also attested by F in the form of 'belle': it is Irish bēal 'mouth'. I once heard an old Welshman in the village of Llanwrtyd Wells calling out 'shut your bill' to a noisy dog: this may possibly have been the same word, though it is equally likely to have been an intentionally grotesque misuse of the English word. 'Méanla' is F's 'maunlish', meaning 'a pig'. I do not believe in 'reac bhfearbhuighe' = 'ugly dog'. 'Fearbhog' (F'ARVŌG) means 'a cow': 'fearbhuighe' is the genitive; and its initial is eclipsed, which means that the preceding word is a noun in the accusative case, so governed by the preposition *le*. It is interesting to find this survival of a Middle Irish use (eclipsis after the accusative) in B-S, which has been lost in orthodox modern Irish. The

translation of the end of the sentence is a very bad 'howler':
the translator has mixed up F's 'ciabar' (with hard b) meaning
'dung', and the Irish *cíobhar* with aspirated b, pronounced
k'íwar, and more commonly spelt *cíor* 'the cud'. 'Your mouth
is like the jaw of a cow that would be chewing the cud' is still
offensive, but at least it has some sense in it. The rendering
'jaw' for 'reac' is a guess, but evidently reasonable.

(21) *Séarpach gaid na fearbuighe seadmanach ó chia* (H) 'Long are
the horns of cows from afar'—a common Irish proverb,
though the above translation hardly does it justice. Another
translation of the same sentence appears in A: *Is trihooil
iad femīnī na farabuch shadōchee*; and the two can be
analysed together.

'Sead(manach) ó chia' evidently = 'shadōchee', that is ŠAD
(rhyming slang for *fad* 'long') ó *chaoi* 'from the way' as in
sentence (1). The interpolated 'manach' in the first version
of the proverb is presumably some kind of adjectival or
adverbial formative. Compare 'custramaun' (F) 'a road',
which analyses with KUŠTRĪ-MÁN, the walking-place (or something similar). ŠAD being 'long', ŠAD-MÁN might be 'length',
and ŠAD-MÁN-ach (with the usual Irish adjectival formative)
'lengthy'. ŠAD and ŠADMANAχ would thus have the same
meaning. 'Fearbuighe' might be genitive singular, 'farabuch'
genitive plural; but we cannot attach much importance to
such irresponsible differences of spelling. 'Gaid' and 'Femīnī'
are not found elsewhere. 'Gaid', singular 'gad', means a
withe, and 'feimīn', plur. 'feimīnī', means, if anything, the
tail of an animal: so that the proverb as it appears in B-S
would seem rather to say that oversea cows have long *tails*.
'Trihooil' in A is, of course, *triathamhail*. 'Séarpach' in H
analyses into 'Is ēarpach', in which the adjective, otherwise
unrecorded, must have some similar meaning.

(22) *Do sheabhraigheas-sa céapaire cuilēne tnúthughad* [read -adh]
carrainn ag Ealp O'Laoighre (H) 'I saw [better, have seen]
pigeons bringing fire to boil meat at Dublin'—apparently
a crude piece of rustic irony invented for the purpose of
snubbing a boaster.

'Seabhraigheas' is the first person preterite of the verb that we
have already seen in sentence (18), above: *s* aspirated according
to rule, after the preverbal particle *do*. 'Carrainn' is the
'corin' of F, meaning 'meat, flesh', and 'Ealp O'Laoighre',
pron. Alpolīr'ə, is rhyming slang for Baile Atha Cliath
[Bal'akl'ī·ə]. It has nothing whatever to do with the name
of the seaport, Dūn Laoghaire (formerly called Kingstown),

as suggested in *The Gaelic Journal*. The three words 'ceapaire cuilene tnuthughadh' have, I feel sure, been wrongly noted or rendered. 'Thnohid' is given by F as meaning 'fire': 'tnūthughadh' is in the form of a verbal noun, and might mean 'to cook'. We may assume that 'ceapair' means 'pigeon', though there is no other evidence: we can have only one pigeon, however, for the apparent plural ending -e is wanted for the preposition before the next word. The most obvious analysis of 'cuilene' is 'cuil'-*teineadh* 'carrying of fire', assuming a word 'cuil' meaning 'carrying'. But with the material at present available any explanation of these words must be mere guesswork. Indeed, we have no security that the alleged translation is accurate.

(23) *Sead é an cian* (L) translated by him 'Long is the fast'. As the Editor of *The Gaelic Journal* points out in the next number, it really means 'Dirty is the house'. See the vocabulary.

(24) *Gab an lúd* (L) 'Small is the work'. L's translation seems here to be correct.

(25) *Seic air do búith* (L), translated by him 'bad character' (!). It clearly means 'stop your ——': 'búith' (which after *do* ought to be 'bhúith') is unexplained. 'Hold your noise', or something of that sort, is probable.

(26) *Gabéis gabanta na mbulcáin sead* (L), rendered by him 'flippant blackguard of the unseemly words'.
'Gabéis' is the 'gheabaois' of sentence (15) meaning 'boy, apprentice'. 'Gabanta', an adjective formed, on Irish models, from the word underlying F's 'gabing'='idling', therefore meaning 'idle'. 'Sead'='dirty'. We need not quarrel with L's 'words' for 'bulcān': it ought, however, to be so written, not '-āin'. It is genitive plural, in which case the initial is nasalized ('eclipsed') after the article *na*. GABĚŠ GABanta na mBULCĀN ŠAD 'Idle boy of the dirty words', is a rendering nearer to the sense. This particular 'Gabēš' must have been like an accomplished youth in Co. Westmeath, of whom a tramp was heard to remark admiringly, 'Well, I thought I knew *all* swearin', but that young lad has words I never heard in me life!'

(27) *Searaid ad dháil na cruinne caine clútach* (L) 'Take thou the hen eggs'.
This should be corrected by printing 'cruinnecāine' as one word. Otherwise the sentence is easy and the translation

correct, though perhaps it might preferably be rendered 'look
out for', 'take care of' the eggs that are near you. See the
separate words in the vocabulary.

(28) *Ni tuada dham gur searais aon éis ó cian bheatha mo luis có
neamh-thriathúil mar an éis thoilínn am dháil ansgaoid so* (L),
whose awkward rendering is 'I never saw any servant as
bad during my life as thou the person standing before me
at present'.

The first three words are probably 'I do not think' (compare
'tuaite' in sentence (15)). Then: '*that* I-saw *one* man *from
a-while of life* of myself' (the italicized words being renderings
of *Irish* vocables). 'Mo luis' must surely be amended to
'mo muis' or 'mo vuis' (see MŪS in vocabulary, and sentence (6)
above). Then: *so unexcellent like the* man 'thoilínn' *in my
company the-night this*. The available material throws no light
on 'thoilínn', though it must mean something like 'who is
present'.

(29)   *Seō leō a bhearūlām
                     Air ceō na caide
                     Toglu airacin na fiaba
                     A long-shuain* (L).

Evidently a cradle-song, of which crooning nonsense-syllables
like 'seō leō' are a stock beginning. L makes no attempt to
translate it, though he says that 'child' is the meaning of
'bhearūlām'. This is undoubtedly misprinted, and should be
amended to 'bhearūlāin', the vocative of 'bearūlān', a diminutive of some word similar to the Scots *bairn*. The second line
means 'upon the...of stone'. 'Ceō' is obscure: the Irish word
ceō, which means 'mist', is here inappropriate. The last line
means 'his bed': but the third line cannot be translated with
certainty. 'Airacin' may be a playful diminutive of aire
'care', and 'fiaba' a perversion of naoimhe [nīṽ'ə] 'saints'—
'may the saints take care of his bed'. Or 'airacin' may be
analysed into 'air a cīn'—'on his house', and 'fiaba' may
be a perversion of fiacha 'ravens'—'May the ravens take his
bed on to their house'. These are merely indicated as possibilities. Cradle-song literature is full of quaint maledictions
like the second alternative, as in the well-known

         'When the bough breaks, the cradle will fall,
         Down tumbles cradle and baby and all.'

But no satisfactory translation can be offered.

237

(30) *Toghla giomla faisgia bile an chinn* (L).

> An obscure sentence: L offers no translation. 'Bile' is presumably the word for 'mouth' which we have already seen in sentence (20): 'chinn' may be genitive of the Irish ceann 'head', or it may be from κ'ĩΝ 'house'—'mouth of the head' or else 'door of the house' or 'in front of the house'. In these ambiguities it is futile to attempt to interpret the other words, which are not otherwise recorded.

(31) *Custrū na fearbach sead ō caoi mar a gcian* (L).

> No translation: but the meaning is 'drive the cows away from the road (as before?)'.

(32) *Nar a sead go seicir a dháil do chíbir* (L) 'May it not be long till you die on your . . .' is L's translation. Whether the aposiopesis is due to ignorance or a sense of propriety does not appear.

> 'May it not be long till you are stopped (= killed) in front of your. . .' is the literal translation of the phrase. Cíbir seems to mean 'dung': so the malediction means 'may you soon die on your dung-heap'.

(33) *Eis na fearbach eistriū na mbarcann* (L).

> No translation given. At a guess we may suggest 'It is the man of the cows who is a great man for bank-notes', i.e. that cattle are the chief source of wealth in the country, whatever may be the theories of politicians.

(34) *Searacān air do plaicibh fē na sciath(a)ibh sead ō caoi* (L).

> No translation given. Perhaps 'Keep a little watch on farthings when far from the road at night'. See the separate words in the vocabulary.

(35) *Caid ar chaid, caid idir dā chaid, agus caid ōs cionn caid* (Editor, *The Gaelic Journal*, commenting on L's contributions).

> 'Stone to stone, stone between two stones, and stone over stone.' A saying referring to the bond of masonry. The only B-S word is CAID = 'stone'.

(36) *Geab do choistriughadh till I seiciughadh this ēis's mūs* (J) 'You go on till I put a stop to [= do for] this fellow'.

> An interesting sentence, shewing the invasion of B-S by English. Compare the parody of *The Minstrel Boy* following.

(37)   *Geab-ēis an arraic* to the road is gone,
              Giarradh-cine you'll find him,
              His *scit is casar* he has girded on,
              A *cearnōg coistriu*-ing behind him (J).

The tags of B-S mean: The mason's boy—hungry—trowel and hammer—policeman walking.

(38)   *Gā sārōinn cabaisdīn a lūdūdh cuanōg,*
              Tuis gā ratachān i gāid a shamhair,
              Coistiorōinn a bhuadh go cīne dīogla
              Agus bheinn gā luarcū ō sgīod go sgīod (L).

L gives a rendering into Irish, which appears correct enough: the meaning in English is, 'If I were to see a shoemaker working at shoes, the corner of his settle beneath his séant, I would carry his wife to the tavern, and would be kissing her from night to night.'

(39) *In tuadihe dit na binihe* (A) 'Do you understand the words?'

'In' is *an*, the Irish interrogative prefix: the rest is easy.

(40) *Mortmora gian civire pumpa* (A) 'Bring the mortar up on the scaffold'.

The words are wrongly divided: they should be 'Mort morag ian civ ar a' pumpa', literally 'mortar let-it-be so up (?) on the scaffold (?)'. For 'morag ian' compare sentence (13).

(41) *Doorōid na cadauc* (A) 'The stones draw water'.

This sentence is alleged to express a threat that if the mason does not get a drink, the stones will be badly set. 'Door' is a now obsolescent Irish word *dobhar* 'water': 'caid', we have seen, means 'stone', but whether 'cadauc' is a plural form we cannot certainly decide. The roots of the words in this sentence are clear, but their syntactic relationship is less obvious.

The above are all the recorded continuous specimens of B-S. They are scanty, often obscure, and too often badly reported. But they are enough to shew that the language is straightforward modern Irish with a number of jargon words substituted for the orthodox words. The frequency with which certain words recur, even in the scanty sentences which are set forth in the preceding pages, suggests that the vocabulary is not an extensive one. Some of the out-of-the-way words used, and such a grammatical phenomenon as eclipsis after the accusative (in sentence (20)), indicate that B-S took shape when Irish was at a stage of development earlier than the current speech. But these survivals are rare. B-S has changed *pari passu* with the linguistic evolution of Irish, and is now adapting itself to the predominant English, as sentences (36), (37) shew.

The following Vocabulary gives all the words of these sentences, with, in addition, all the separate words that appear in the contributions of the various reporters enumerated above.

II. VOCABULARY

(The numbers in brackets refer to the sentences analysed above.)

A

a causing lenition; particle prefixed to the vocative case (11), (15), (29).

a causing lenition; 3 sing. masc. possessive pron. 'his' (29), (38).

a Relative particle (4).

a Contraction for preposition *de* 'of'. See analysis of sentence (2).

a Contraction for preposition *ag* 'at' (38).

ad Preposition, *i* 'in'+2 sing. possessive pron. *do*; 'in thy' (27).

aes (16). See ēis.

ag Preposition, 'at'. Especially used before verbal nouns to express present participle (as a- in English 'a-dying') (22).

agudine (8). See go dtī.

agus Conjunction, 'and' (35), (38).

aigracawn See ēagracān.

air Often used for **ar**, which see (29), (34).

airacin (29). Meaning unknown.

airig 'a mason', 'craftsman' (HS, arrick F, airic L): genitive arraic (37), vocative airig (11), (16). *A. caide* 'a stonemason'; *a. fiuic* 'a timber-craftsman', 'carpenter'.

aish See ēis.

alp 'a town' (8). Apparently back-slang for Irish *baile* 'a town'. Also (according to F) means 'a job of work', and 'a hill'.

Alpolaoghaire [alpolīr'ə]. Rhyming slang for *Baile Ātha Clīath* 'Dublin' (alpoleera F, Ealp O'Laoighre H).

Alptiarpach [alpt'īarpaχ]. Rhyming slang for *Baile Corcaigh* 'Cork' (ailp- L).

an Article, 'the', in masc. and nom. and dat. fem. sing. (37). *An . . . so* 'this . . .' (28).

an Prefix-particle of interrogative sentences. Appears as in in (39).

aois See **ĕis.**

aon 'one' (28).

aonachar 'singly', 'especially' (?) : (11).

ăr causing nasalization, 1 plur. possessive pron. : 'our' (16).

ar Preposition, 'upon', 'at', 'to' (35). Often written **air.**

arrick See **airig.**

as Preposition, 'out of' (17).

assī 'milk' (assee or isaugh F). *Ass* is an Old-Irish word for 'milk'.

B

barbūdh See **borbū'd.**

barcăn 'a book', 'a pound note' (L, barcawn F, also barcann, gen. pl. (33)).

bĕ The letter 'B' (15).

be 'a woman' (M). See **buadh.**

beatha 'life' (28).

bedhal (F). See **biadal.**

bĕinn 1 sing. conditional of Irish substantive verb : 'I would be'.

belle 'a mouth' (F, bille (20), bile (30)).

bhearūlăn (29). See **mearulăn.**

bhīoch (20). For *bhīodh*, 3 sing. impf. of substantive verb : 'that would be'.

bī Rhyming for *dīl* 'dear' (11).

biadal Reverse for *diabhal* 'devil' (bedhal F, viadul A). See **miandubh.**

bile, bille *Bile an chinn* (30) 'mouth of the head' (?). See **belle.**

binna 'to speak' (F).

binnighthe [b'in'ihi] 'words', 'talk' ((15), binihe (39), binnue (F)). *Binnue caha* F 'begging'. *Bua na binihi tria* (A) 'A woman of the great words ' = 'a nun'.

bō See **buadh.**

bochar 'a mason's square' (F). Irish bacart.

bochna 'sea' (M, bouchling F). Old-Irish word.

bog Reverse of *gabh* 'take' (17).

boo See **buadh.**

borb 'a priest', 'minister of religion' (burub F, borab S). *Borb Triath* (A) 'God's priest' (an R.C. priest); *borb a bhiadail* (J) 'the devil's priest' (a Protestant clergyman). *Cīn a' bhuirb,* see **cīn.**

borbīn 'a labourer' (boribin S, burbeen F).

borbu'd 'married' (literally, 'priested') (burrabood F, borabūd S). But L gives *barbūdh* as a term for a person 'about to be married'.

bouchling See bochna.

bouldremon (9). Meaning unknown.

brīdīn 'a drinking-glass' (brīghidine L).

bruigneōir 'a smith' (bru-ig nore F).

buadh 'a woman' (boo F, buadh ML, bua A). Boo oguntha (F), i.e. *b. ōigeanta* 'a young woman'. *B. ōigeanta cīne an dīogla* (L) 'young woman of a public-house', 'barmaid'. *Buadh na cīne* 'woman of the house'. *Buadh na binnighthe triath*, see binnighthe.

būith 'noise' (?) (25).

bulcān 'a word' (?) (26).

burbeen See borbīn.

burrabood See barbū'd.

burub See borb.

C

cā 'what?' Cou (3).

cabaisdīn 'a shoemaker' (38).

cābh 'a small way or passage' (caugh F). (?) Irish *cabhsa* 'a causeway, alley'.

cabhaill 'a horse' (M, keful F, cowilt A). Irish *capall*. Compare caibhde, caibhire.

cabhro 'to sleep': cowru-ing 'sleeping' (F).

cabrōseō 'a chapel', 'R.C. Church' (L, coperōseô H).

cabrūl 'cabbage' (cabrule F).

cadauc (41). See caid.

cadth See caid.

cae cĕ, kĕ The letter 'C' (15).

caha In 'binnue caha' (F) = 'begging'. Meaning uncertain.

cāhīk 'what' (cawheke (2), (10)). *Cā* is Irish for 'what', but hīk is not explained.

caī See caoi.

caibhde 'a horse' (L).

caibhire 'a horse' (L). These two words are doubtless perversions of the ordinary Irish word *capall*.

cáid A word meaning 'presence' or the like, in such expressions as *ār gcáid* [he will give] 'to us' (16); *am chāid* 'into my presence', 'towards me' (14); *i g(c)āid* 'in the neighbourhood of' (38).

caid 'a stone' (coda, cadth F). Genitive *caide*, as in *airig caide* 'stonemason' (coda, F and (29)): but not declined in (35). Dual, *dā chaid* (35). *Cadauc* (41) is possibly a nom. plur. 'Cadth soukeness' (F) said to mean 'top stone', 'chief corner stone' (incidentally, two very different things!). 'Cadth thno-hid' (F), i.e. *caid tnuthuid* 'stone of fire', 'coal'.

cailid 'a goat' (kalidh F).

cáineadh 'chewing', 'eating' ((20), cāiniughadh (19)).

caistriomān 'a key' (L).

caoi 'a road', 'a way': caī (M). *Ō chaoi* 'from the road' = 'out of the way', 'away'. *Ō m'chaī* 'out of my way' (1). *Ō chiath* (12), *ō chia* (21) are no doubt perversions of this formula.

caora-āirnĕis 'sheep-cattle', i.e. sheep (kehernish F).

cara 'a friend'. Vocative *a chara* (11).

carnore See **cearnōg**.

carra 'drunk' (F).

carrabhān 'a drunken spree' (carrawaun F).

carrakeenah See **giarradh-cīne**.

carran 'flesh-meat', 'a dinner' (carrann (22), corin F). Genitive *carruinn* (19). *C. fearbuighe* 'cow-meat', 'beef'.

casar 'a hammer' ((37), cossar F). Irish *casūr*.

caugh See **cābh**.

cawheke See **cāhīk**.

ceann 'a head'. Genitive *chinn* (30). Dative *cionn* (35).

cĕapair 'a pigeon' (22).

cearnōg 'a constable', 'policeman' ((37), JS). 'Carnore' (F) 'a soldier'.

ceδ (29). Meaning unknown.

cia ((21), ciath (12)). See **caoi**.

cian 'a space of time', 'a while ago'. *Mar a gcian* (31) 'as before' (?); *ō cian beatha* (28) 'from a time of life', 'in all (my) life'.

cīan See **cīn**.

cīanruis 'snuff' (keenrush F).

cībir 'dung', 'manure' (32).

cifeanach 'a weaver' (cifenuch F). Part reversal of *figheadóir*, the Irish word with the same meaning.

cifrehawn See **scuifreachán**.

cin 'a house' (MS, cīne L, keene A, keena F, cian (23)). *Cīn a' bhuirb* (keenabuirb F) 'a house of worship' (lit. 'priest's house'); *cīn a dīogla* (misprinted cīn digabha (H), cīn a duigili (S), cīne dīogla (L)) 'a drink-house' 'public-house'; *cīne na laidiana* 'soldiers' house', 'barracks'; *cīne na mearūlān* 'children's house', 'school'. Genitive cīne: *ēis na cīne* 'man of the house'; *buadh na cīne* 'woman of the house'.

cīna 'food', 'a meal' (kinah F).

cinide 'sheep' (L).

cīobhar 'cud' of a cow. Genitive *cīobhair* (20). Irish *cīor*.

cionnas 'how?', 'in what way?' (conus (4)). Irish.

civ 'up' (?) (40).

clapuach 'you would (beat (?))' (15). For clap-ōchthā, 2 sing. of conditional.

clūtach 'a hen' (clūite H, clutōg L, clutoch F). Gen. plur. *clūtach*; *cruinnecāin clūtach* 'hens' eggs'.

cnăpach 'a cat' (18) (knopuck, F).

cnăpaire 'a cat' (cnapara J, cnawpare A).

cnoc 'a potato' (kunuk F).

co = *go*, prefix turning adjectives to adverbs. *Co neamhthriathamhail* 'uselessly' (L).

co . . . mar In comparisons, 'so . . . as . . .' (28).

cobcowil See **geab-cabhaill**.

cŏ-bhuadh See **comh-**.

coda See **caid**.

cŏ-ĕis See **comh-**.

cŏhi See **cuithi**.

coine 'a body' (F).

coing 'a table' (F).

coiseadramān 'a beard' (coshedremon F).

coistreamān 'a chimney', 'soot' (coshtramon F).

coistriughadh [koštr'ū]. A word used of motion in any direction, intransitively or transitively: 'come' (12), 'go' (1), 'hurry' (8), 'move' [an object] (14), 'drive' [cattle] (31). Verbal noun *coistriughadh* (36) (coshdrea F, coistrig, cuistrig H, coisdre M, custrig A (8), custrū (31)). Anglicized present participle *coistriu-ing* (37), conditional 1 sing. *coistioróinn* (38). Anglicized past participle passive *coshtrū'd* 'gone away' (S). Imperative *coshdrea* (F) 'be off', 'run away'.

coithire See **cuithire**.

colla 'a hat' (F).

comh-bhuadh 'a fellow-woman', 'a sister' (cō-bhuadh L).

comh-eis 'a brother' (co-ēis L).

conus See cionnas.

coonogue See cuanŏg.

coperō-seô See cabrōseō.

corin See carran.

cosamhail 'like'. Miswritten gos- in (20).

cossar See casar.

costramān 'a road' (custramaun F).

cou (3). See cā.

coulth. A man who has not served apprenticeship. Merely the Munster pronunciation of the English word 'colt' (F).

cowilt See cabhaill.

cowruing See cabhro.

criabhōg 'a potato' (crevock F).

crith Probably Irish *cruit* 'a fiddle'. 'Aish crith' (F) 'a musician'.

cruinneacān Anything round, like a ball. *C. fiuic* 'c. of timber', 'an apple'; *c. clŭtach* 'c. of hens', 'an egg'. *Cruinneacān ith*, or *ip* (cronikconith F, cruadh chnuip L 'a head': the meaning of the second word is uncertain; possibly the expression should be *cruinneacān coine* 'knob of the body'. [Ith would be pronounced ī, or īḥ.]

cuanōg 'a brogue', 'a shoe' (coonogue F). Gen. plur. *cuanōg* (38).

cuilene (22). Meaning uncertain.

cuithi 'tobacco' (cuthi H, cuhee F, cōhi S).

cuithire 'a dog' (ML, cuhiree F). *Coithire na aipēise* 'a fox': the last word is obscure.

culahee 'porter' (the drink) (deegla culahee F).

custrū See coistriughadh.

D

dā causing lenition, 'two' (35).

dafadōir: 'dafadōr' (S) 'a useless person'; 'dhofudhore' (F) 'a tell-tale'. Perhaps do-fuadōir would be a better spelling.

dāil 'presence', 'company', in such adverbial phrases as *a dhāil* 'in the presence of' (32); *am dhāil* 'in my company' (28); *ad dhāil* 'before you' (27).

dam Preposition *do*+pronoun *mē* 'to me'. Dham (28).

damhsamān 'dancing' (dousamaun F).

davow See mūs.

dearc 'eye' (M, derco F, therka (10)).

degluing See dīogla.

deid 'teeth' (L).

dercu 'courting' (dherkoo-ing F). Perhaps 'ogling' would more closely express the meaning of the word.

des 'land' (M).

dho- For words beginning thus, see **do-**.

dingir 'a rat' (A).

dīogla 'drink' (intoxicating) (deegla F, duigili S). *Cīn a' dīogla* 'a tavern'. *Deglu-ing* (F) 'drinking'. *Dīgabha* (H) is probably erroneous. 'Deegla culahee' (F) 'porter'; 'deegla fuke' (='timber drink') 'cider'.

dit for **duit**, which see. 'In tuadihe dit' 'Is it given to you?' 'Do you understand?' (39).

diū 'land' (due F).

do causing lenition: preverbal particle of preterite tense (22).

do Preposition 'to'.

do causing lenition: possessive pron. 2 pers. sing. 'thy' (15), (34), (36). In (34) *do plaicibh* should be *do phl-*.

dobhar 'water', 'a river' (M, dobair L, dour, duvar F). Old-Irish word.

dobhar-thriath 'lordly water', 'whisky' (L).

dobharuighim 'to draw water': 'to shower', 'rain': 3 sing. present *dobharuighidh* (written dooróid (41)). Anglicized participle *dhourue-ing* (F).

dofai: dofe (F) 'anything bad'; 'dhofu' (F) 'to speak ill of a person' (see **dafadoir**); 'dhofical luda' (F) 'bad or ugly work'. This latter word is probably *do-feiceāl* 'what should not be seen'. Lūd or lūda is 'work'.

dooróid See dobharuighim.

doun-caucha 'whisky' (F), probably a miswritten form of L's dobharthriath.

dour See dobhar.

dousamaun See damhsamān.

duarcān luirce 'a midwife' (L). See **luirc**.

due See diū.

duigili See dīogla.

dūile 'a mouth' (L).

duit Preposition *do*+personal pronoun *tū* 'to thee' (15).

durke 'an ear' (F). Probably a mistake, as 'derco' is given as meaning 'eye'.

E

ĕ 'it' (23).

ĕagracān 'a fish' (aigracawn A, egnakooing F).

ealp See alp.

ĕarpach 'long' (?) (21).

eash See ĕis.

ĕis 'a man' (L, eash F, aes MH, aois (12), aish A). *Ēis na cīne*,
 or *ēis triath na cīne* 'the man' or 'goodman of the house';
 ēis na bhfearbach (so read (33)) 'man of the cows'; *ēis cīne
 an dīogla* 'a publican'; 'aish crith' (F) 'a musician'; *this ēis's
 mūs* (36) 'this man's personality'='this fellow'; *ēis cuanōg*
 ('eash coonuch' F) 'a brogue-maker'; *ēis na lūda* 'foreman',
 'master' [of work]; *ēis seabhrū* 'watchman'; *ēis gearra cīne*
 ('eash carra keenah' F) 'a hungry man' [perhaps *ēis ag
 iarraidh cīne* 'a man seeking for food']; *ēis clūtach* 'a dunghill-
 cock'; *ēis 'garabuch'* 'a turkey-cock'. 'Eistriū' (33) is probably
 ēis triath 'a good man', an expression which F translates
 wrongly 'Lord of man'.

erem = *ar mo* 'upon my' (F).

erin = *ar an* 'upon the' (5).

euch 'butter' (F).

F

faig 'teeth' (F).

faisgia (30). Meaning unknown.

fatramān 'a father' (L).

fĕ Preposition 'under' (34).

fearbach 'a cow' (L, farabuch, farabee F, farabuc A). Gen. sing.
 fearbuighe (20), (21). Gen. plur. (?) *farabuch* (21); acc. plur.
 fearbach (31).

femīn Said to mean 'horn', but more probably 'tail' (21). Plur.
 femīnī.

fiab (29). Meaning unknown. Nom. plur. *fiaba*.

fiuc 'timber': 'fiuch' (M) 'a tree'. Gen. *fuic*: *airig f.* 'a carpenter',
 cruinneacān f. 'an apple'; *dīogla f.* 'cider'; 'fuke' (F),
 apparently the same word as L's *airic* 'fiathbuidhe' 'a carpenter'.

fiūmadōir 'a painter' (fiūmadōr S). But F gives 'fumadhore'
 'a tailor'.

fōrūch 'a foreman' (J).

fūcama 'smoke' (foukama F).

fūinc 'a penny' (founk F). Compare **pūinc**.

G

gâ=prep. *ag*+possessive pron. 3 pers., the latter indicating the object of the verbal noun. *Gâ luarcū* (38) literally 'a-kissing of her'.

gâ=prep. *do*+possessive pron. 'of his' (38).

gâ=*dâ* 'if', used to introduce a condition expected to be unfulfilled: *ga sâröinn* (38) 'If I were to see'.

gab 'small'. See **geab.**

gab 'idle' (perhaps the same word as the preceding). 'Gabing' (F) 'idling'. *Geabaig* 'work easy!' (16).

gabanta 'idle', 'lazy' (26).

gad 'a horn' (?). Nom. plur. *gaid* (21).

gahegan 'a wrong bond', or wrongly keyed arch (F).

gall-thairiseach Literally a person 'with foreign loyalty'. 'Goulthreeshuch' (F) 'a person of different religion': *gall-trīnseach* (L) 'a gentleman'.

garabuch 'eash garabuch' (F) 'a turkey-cock'.

geab 'small': back-slang for Irish *beag*. In B-S always precedes the substantives to which it is attached. Comparative (?) *gabanthu* (10). *Geab-ēis* (15), (37) 'a small man', 'a boy', 'an apprentice' (gabesh FS, vocative *geabaois* (15)); *geab-borb* (gab borab S) 'a clerical student'; 'gabcarra' (F) 'partly drunk'; 'gab-founk' (F: see *fūinc*) 'a halfpenny'; 'gab-lish' (F) 'a small hand', 'a finger', also 'an inch'; 'gab scabogue' (F) 'a small boat'; 'gab scraub' (F=*geab scrāb*) 'a small shilling', 'a sixpence'; *geab-cabhaill* (cob-cowil A) 'a small horse', 'a mule'.

geab Imperative, 'keep on!' (36).

ghes (10). Prefix of comparative degree (?).

giarradh-cīne (J): 'carra keena' (F) 'hungry'. *Ag iarraidh cīne* 'seeking food'.

giomla (30). Meaning uncertain.

Giosân 'John' (Gissaun F).

glaidīn 'a knife' (gladeen F).

gleamadōir 'a piper' (glaumadhore F, glāmadōr S); but 'glamadōir' (L) 'a smith'.

go 'to', 'till' (32), (38). *Go dtī* 'to', 'towards' (8), (13), rendered 'agudine' in (8).

gosamhuil (20). See **cos-.**

goulthreeshuch See **gall-thairiseach.**

grifinthu 'foxy', i.e. red-haired (F).
gudth 'woman of bad character' (F).
gur *go* = that + *ro*, preverbal particle of preterite (28).

H

hīk 'heke' (9). Meaning unknown.
hueso See mūs.

I

i 'in'. *I gāid* (38), see cāid.
iad 'they' (21).
īan 'so', 'thus' (?) (13).
iarr-cīn 'a pawnshop' (J). Theare-keen F.
idir 'between' (35).
in = *an*, interrogative prefix (39).
ip See cruinneacān.
is Irish verb, 'it is'.
is Abbreviation for *agus* 'and'.
isaugh See assī.
ith See cruinneacān.

K

kalidh See cailid.
keenabuirb See cīn.
keenrush See cīanruis.
keful See cabhaill.
kehernish See caora-āirnēis.
knopuck See cnāpach.
kunuk See cnoc.

L

laidiana 'a policeman' (L). *Cīn na laidiana* 'barracks'.
lais 'a hand' (M, luis L). *Geab-lais* 'a finger', 'an inch'.
lāmōg 'a mason's level' (lamogue F).
lār an ingire 'a plumb-rule' (laureneringa F). *Ingir* is Irish for
    'a plumb-rule': the B-S expression means literally 'middle
    of the plumb-rule' in which the plumb-bob hangs.
le 'with'. After words denoting resemblance, 'like to' (20).
leabhracān Diminutive of *leabhar* 'a book': 'leebrecawn' (F)
    'a book', 'a pound note'.
leith 'a tongue' (F).
lenhuing See long-shuain.
līmīn 'a trowel', 'a watch', or, in general, 'a tool' (limeen F).

lībōg 'a midge': libogue (10). Perversion of Irish mīoltōg.

lirke See luirc.

lisīn 'head' (lisheen F).

lofū 'to steal' (loffoo F).

lofūdōir 'a thief' (loffudhore F).

longain See long-shuain.

long-shuain 'ship of sleep', i.e. 'a bed' (M, (29), lenhuing F, longain M).

lorcshown dawin 'an old woman' (A). See luirc, and sean-dān.

lou-ine See luinnidhe.

luadhaim 'to move', 'to go'. The d is de-aspirated in B-S: thus we have the imperative *luadaig* 'work!' 'be quick!' 'look sharp!' (16); the verbal noun *lūdūdh* 'working' (38); the noun *lūda* or *lūd* 'work' (F, (24)); and the third person singular of the present tense, *luadhaidh*, represented by F's ludhe.[1]

luarcū 'kissing' (38).

lūd, lūda See luadhaim.

luinnidhe 'feet' (L). Lou-ine (F) 'legs'.

luirc 'a hag', 'old woman' (L). 'Lirke' F, 'lorc-shown-dawin' (A)— this latter is a compound of *luirc* + sean-dān 'old person'.

luis See lais.

luis Miswritten in (28) for *mūis*. See mūs.

lūisēad 'a bag' (L).

M

māilide 'a pig' (mailide L, maunlish F, mawnlit A).

mairidh Imperative, 'let it remain': mairig (13), morag (40).

mar Conjunction, 'as', 'how' (4): *mar a*, causing nasalization, 'like' (31).

maralaun See mearulān.

mātal 'mother' (L).

maulu See meabhlughadh.

maunlish See māilide.

mavousa See mūs.

mawnlit See māilide.

meabhlad 'day': vouludhe (4), mouleadth (F).

meabhlughadh 'scolding' (maulu F).

---

[1] In F's phonesis dh and th do not imply aspiration, but are attempts at the thick sound of the Irish non-palatalized gingival d, t (the 'broad' d, t, of Irish grammars). The same expedient is frequent on the pages of stage-Irish humour.

Meanȧn 'Michael' (meanaun F).

mĕanla 'a sow'. Genitive *mĕanla* (20).

mearulȧn 'a child' (maralaun F, mearullān L). Vocative *mhearulȧin*, miswritten bhearūlām (29). *Cin na mearulȧn* 'a school'.

miandubh 'devil': also *biandubh* (15).

minighim In Irish 'to make fine', in B-S 'to redden'. First person subjunctive *mineochad* (14).

mo Possessive pronoun, 'my'. Causes lenition of initial following.

monetrea See muintriath.

moragian (40). See mairidh and ian.

mort 'mortar' (40) (murth F).

mouleadth (F). See meabhlad.

muin 'a neck'. Gen. sing. *muine*, not *mūine* as in (15).

muintriath 'good morrow' ((11), monetrea F). See analysis under sentence (11): literal meaning, 'May the Lord bless'.

murth See mort.

mūs Something like 'personality', used (like *d'īl* in Shelta) with possessive pronouns to form personal pronominal expressions. *Mo mhūs* or *mo mhūs-sa* (mavousa F) 'I', 'me'; *do mhūs* 'thou', 'thee'; *this ēis's mūs* 'this fellow' (36). Shek-eremhueso (F) explained as 'discharged, or sent off from the work' is *seic ar mo mhūs-sa* 'a stoppage on myself'.

N

na The Irish article in gen. sing. fem. (10), (29), nom. plur. (41), dat. plur. (34): causing nasalization in following initial in gen. plur. (33).

nȧ for *nō* 'or', 'nor' (15).

nȧ After comparatives, 'than' (10).

na for *nach*, prefix to interrogatives in a negative form (15).

nach 'that not' (15).

nȧra 'may it not be so' (32).

nawgre (9). Meaning uncertain.

neamh-thriathamhail 'unexcellent', 'useless', 'unpleasing' (net[r]o-hu-l F). Negative of *triathamhail*, q.v.

Neathus 'Ned' (F).

nī 'not' (28).

nū = *nō* 'or' (20).

nūnlig 'a working day', 'the hours of light'. *Nūnlig Triath*, 'Lord's day', 'Sunday'; also Sunday ceremonies, 'Mass' (13).

O

ō 'from'. Causes aspiration, ō *chiath* (12): 'ō caoi' (34) should
be ō *chaoi*, as in 'o chee luda' (F), said to mean 'time for
stopping work'. *Ōm'* = ō *mo* 'from my'. *Ō* . . . *go* . . . 'from . . .
to . . .'.

ōigeanta 'young' (L, ogunthu F).

ōs 'over', 'above': ōs *cionn* 'above the head of' (see **ceann**),
'over' (35).

P

plaic 'a plack', 'farthing', 'small coin' (34), dat. plur. *plaicibh.*

preampach 'a tailor' (proumpach F).

prosimig 'to pull out', 'to work hard' (F).

pūinc 'money' (L, pynke F). Compare *fūinc* 'a penny'.

pumpa 'a scaffold' (40).

R

ratachān Rendered by L into Irish *sūisīn*, i.e. 'a settle', 'a small
bed' (38).

reac 'a jaw'? (20).

riarpōg 'a perch' (*sic*) of work (rerepogue F).

rochān 'clothing'. Rochane F 'a suit of clothes'. *Rochān tūir*
'trousers'.

rodamiomān 'a road' (L).

rud 'a thing' (10).

S

's = *is* 'it is' (21).

-sa Emphatic suffix (22).

samhar *anus* (38). Gen. *samhair.*

scāid 'night' (M, sgīod (38), sgaoid (28), sckueed F). Gen. *scāide*
(M).

scaochlong 'a candle' (14). Accus. *-luing.*

scaochnuid 'the sun' (scaechnuid M, sgaunid F). *Scaochnuid
scāide* (M) 'sun of night', 'the moon'. But F has *sgaunid rea*
for 'moon' (*rae* = 'moon' is Irish).

scevela 'a window' (F).

sciath 'night' (L), dat. plur. *sciathaibh* (34). Probably same word
as scāid.

scirtīn (skirteen F). *S. cnis* 'a shirt'. Skirteen is diminutive of
English 'skirt': *cnis* is genitive of Irish *cneas* 'skin'.

scit 'a trowel' (J).

scrāb 'a shilling' (scraub F). *Scrāb triath* (scraub treah F) 'big shilling', 'a pound'.

scrābān Diminutive of **scrāb**. *S. triath* (16) 'a crown'; *s. puinc* (16) 'a pound'.

scuabōg 'a ship' (H, scabogue F). *S. triath* 'a big ship'.

scuifreachān 'a dog' ((15), cifrehawn F). Vocative *-āin*.

sě 'he' (she (5)).

seabhradōir 'head inspector' (shouradore F).

seabhruighim 'to look', 'look at', 'watch'. Imperative *seabhruigh* (18), and, spelt searaid (27), shourig (F); pret. 1 sing. *seabhraigheas* (22), spelt searais (28); conditional 1 sing. *seabhrochainn*, spelt sārōinn (38). *Searacān* (34) is perhaps a diminutive verbal noun, in ironical sense 'keeping a little watch'.

sead 'dirty' (15), (23), (26).

sead 'long', 'far' (21), (31), (32), (34). *Sead ō chaoi* 'far away'. Rhyming slang for Irish *fad* 'length'.

seadmanach 'lengthy' (21). See the analysis there.

seamhas 'luck' (shous (2)).

sean-dān 'old man' (L, shown-dawin A, shoundhaune F), not apparently the ordinary Irish word *sean-duine*.

sear For words so beginning see **seabhr-**.

seic 'a stoppage' by dismissal, death, or any other cause: English 'check' (?). *On the sheic* (S) = 'struck down'. Used imperatively *seic air* 'a stoppage upon ...!' 'put a stop to ...!'. Verbal forms based on this stem are *seiciughadh* (36) 'act of stopping', Anglicized present participle *shek-uing* (7); Anglicized past participle passive shekude (*seicu'd*) (F) meaning killed, *seiceōd* (S) exhausted. *Sheku* (F) 'to murder', 'to spoil a piece of work'. Present passive *seicir*, 'you are stopped' (32).

seirc 'water' (M).

seō leō Meaningless lullaby-crooning sounds (29).

sg- For words beginning thus, see **sc-**.

sh- For words beginning thus, see **se-** or **si-**.

siadōg 'a policeman' (sheedhouge (*sic*) F).

siske 'a chair' (F).

sneith 'a nose' (F).

soin 'there' (17).

sprisanue 'fighting' (F).

spugnig (F), who says that *s. līmīn* means 'six o'clock', 'time for leaving off work'.

stīmire 'a pipe', 'tobacco-pipe' (14) (stheemaree F).

suas 'up' (17).

T

tā 'is' (19): thau (5).

theare-keen 'a pawn-house', 'a gaol' (F). See **iarr-cīn**.

therka 'eye' (10). See **dearc**.

thoilīnn (28). Meaning doubtful.

tiarpach See **Alptiarpach**.

tīompalān Anything round, a measure of any kind (as a pint, quart, etc.): thimpalaun (F). Perhaps L's trīompalān, q.v., is a mistake for this word.

tnūth 'fire' (M); also *tnuthach* (M). F has thinuche, thnohid 'fire', tnuhuh 'venereal'.

tnūthughadh 'to boil', 'to cook' (22).

toghla 'taking', 'laying up' (?) (30), toglu (29).

triath 'a lord'; used regularly for 'God' (rhyming with Irish word *Dia*). Compare the frequent evasion, in oaths, *fīadh*, commonly rendered into English in the phrase 'the deer knows' [usually misspelt 'dear'].

triath As adjective, 'great': tria (AF). *Ēis triath na cīne* 'the goodman of the house'.

triathamhail A much overworked adjective meaning 'good', 'excellent' and the like. Expresses an affirmative response to a statement or command (13). Precedes the substantive (compare *geab*), as shewn by these examples from F—'trehule eashe' 'a fine man', 'trehule rochane' 'a good suit of clothes'. Trihooil (21).

trīompalān 'whisky' (L). The word in Irish means 'a beetle' (the insect). Perhaps a mistake for *tīompalān* (q.v.) and really meaning 'a measure' of the drink.

trise 'a treat' (trisha F). 'Trisha deegla' (dīagla) was the 'drop of drink', the footing, with which every newly installed craftsman was expected to entertain his future comrades. See **tuis**.

tū 'thou', 'you' (17): thu (4). *Tū fēin* 'yourself'.

tuaitighim 'to give', 'impart'. There are several parts of this verb, with a perplexing variety of spellings. Past part. tuada: *ni tuada dham* 'it is not given to me', 'I do not think' (28), or *tuadihe*, in *tuadihe dit* 'understood of thee' (39) and *tuaite* in *ni tuaite dhuit B nā C* 'you haven't been taught the alphabet' (15). Future *tuatōig* and *tūiteōig* 'he will give' (both in (16)).

tuis 'a drop' or 'sup' (of drink) (tuish S).

tuis (L): translated into Irish *beann*, i.e. 'point', 'peak', 'corner'.

tūr *anus* (thouir F).

U

uagainte 'young' (A). See ōigeanta.

V

vaurimaun 'a mother' (F). Probably a misheard vocative, *a mhāthair ionmhuin* 'mother dear'.

viadul See biadal.

vouludhe See meabhlad.

CHAPTER VIII

SUMMARY

It remains to indicate the probable historical relations between the languages which we have now passed in review.

(1) The Druids and their pupils studied an obsolete form of the Goidelic language, because certain sacred hymns, which they considered it important to know by heart, were composed when that stage of the language was the tongue of common speech. The contemporary colloquial dialects had travelled so far from the language of this traditional literature, that the knowledge of the latter gave to the Druidic caste a convenient and useful means of secret communication among themselves. This secrecy they artificially enhanced by various cryptological devices.

(2) The tradition of the usefulness of a secret language survived the Druids and their system; but as the pagan traditional hymns could not be cultivated under Christian auspices, the Druidic secret language passed out of use. The Christian teachers endeavoured to fill its place by an artificial perversion of Latin ('Hisperic').

(3) The underworld of Irish society, composed to a large extent of the dregs of an aboriginal population, may have preserved some fragments of an earlier speech, which, with the addition of *argot* words such as are current among people of the illiterate classes all the world over, would be a secret possession of not inconsiderable practical utility to these down-trodden castes. This Babylonish hotchpotch (to which we may accord a theoretical existence, although no formal records of it are preserved) we shall for the moment call the 'Serf-speech'.

(4) The works of Isidore, Capella, and Maro; the necessity of studying biblical and other ecclesiastical literature in a foreign tongue (Latin); to say nothing of the difficulties presented by juristic and other recondite literature of native production; stimulated a certain amount of practical and theoretical language-study among the learned, in monastic and other circles. The result of this is seen in such compilations as *The Scholars' Primer* and the glossaries of Cormac mac Cuillenáin and others.

(5) Linguistic affectation being 'in the air', so to speak, school-

boys in the monastic schools developed a jargon of their own
('Bog-Latin'). This is a common phenomenon, in ancient and
in modern times. Every public school has its own language—or
to speak with stricter accuracy, its own vocabulary, foisted upon
and adapted to the accidence and syntax of the mother-tongue
of the pupils. 'Bog-Latin' is much more formal in its construction
than the haphazard modern slang vocabularies, and probably had
a longer life. It is highly probable that some of the words of this
mediaeval schoolboy jargon were borrowed from the 'Serf-speech':
schoolboys of all generations associate with such members of what
used to be called 'the Lower Orders' as possess enviable mechanical,
fishing, trapping, or other accomplishments, and often perturb
their respectable kinsfolk by the vocabularies which they acquire
from them.

(6) All arts and crafts have a technical terminology of their
own, unfamiliar to non-initiates: and their practitioners develop
this artificially, the better to preserve their secrets. Masons and
Tinkers did so in Ireland.

(7) The Mason speech was an Irish tradition, and followed Irish
in accidence and vocabulary. So far as the recorded fragments
permit us to judge, it resembled the language of a modern public
school, in that it consisted of a limited number of alternative
words for common things—especially things pertaining to the
mason's craft, but not exclusively so—substituted for the corresponding words in the legitimate language of the country. An
Irish mason might say something entirely in Irish, about 'a
knife'; only, instead of *sgian*, the Irish for 'knife', he would say
glaidīn. So an English schoolboy at one particular school might
say something entirely in English about 'a bath'; only, instead
of the word *bath* he would (if I am not misinformed) say *tosh*.

By an unfortunate fatality there are very few words in the
recorded Bēarlagair na Sāer vocabulary with meanings for which
we have equivalents in Bog-Latin. If there were many, and these
shewed a number of similarities, we might reasonably take these
to be *borrowings* in Bog-Latin, and *survivals* in Bēarlagair na Sāer,
from the 'Serf-speech'. I can find only three such coincidences:

	Bog-Latin	Bēarlagair na Sāer
cat	caipist	cnāpach
hand	luis	lais
word	bercon	bulcan

(8) At the dissolution of the monasteries, the inmates of the
religious houses were thrown out to fend for themselves. Those

who had cultivated artistic handicrafts during their monastic life, might find themselves obliged, *faute de mieux*, to ally themselves with bands of itinerant tinkers. These vagrants may have used fragments of the 'Serf-speech': and we may reasonably see 'Serf-speech' words in the short list (*ante*, p. 119) of elements common to Bog-Latin and Shelta. The broken-down scholars repaid their hosts by enlarging this casual vocabulary with artificial inventions, which needed scholarship for their contrivance; thus strengthening their hands in the bitter struggle for existence. English gradually ousted Irish, but the artificial vocabulary remained; it merely changed its setting. So we can imagine the schoolboy mentioned above, packed off to France to learn French, and saying to a companion, 'Il me faut prendre mon *tosh*'. It would be psychologically natural for him to express himself in this way. In the first place, to represent 'tosh' by 'bain' would require the mental effort of a double translation (tosh—bath—bain); in the second place, the speaker, consciously or unconsciously, is naturally using a mixture of two languages (English + Jargon) and he feels cramped if he cannot continue to do so (French + Jargon). But as neither he nor his interlocutor knows any second Jargon, they perforce retain the words of the original Jargon. In such a way as this we may explain the complete anglicization of the setting in which the specifically Shelta words now find themselves. They have been transferred untranslated from their original Irish setting.

Thus we may glean—precariously—a few words of the theoretical 'Serf-speech' from a comparison of these vocabularies; but of its accidence and syntax one fact only emerges, and that fact is quite remarkable. This lost language had no personal pronouns, and supplied their place with a possessive pronoun and a substantive. It cannot be a coincidence that this periphrasis is used in all three languages: *mo tuillsi* in Bog-Latin, *mo yīlša* in Shelta, *mo vousa* (*mhūs-sa*) in Bēarlagair na Sāer. 'Tuill' and 'D'īl' are probably corruptions of the same word, whatever it may have been—I do not accept the suggestion that it has anything to do with the Irish *toil* 'will', simply because 'my will' seems a very unnatural expression for 'myself'. The Bēarlagair na Sāer word, *mus*, is incompatible with these; but this need not cause us any perplexity. Just as different speakers may call the same person 'a poor old soul' and 'a poor old body', so there may have been more than one word which could stand for 'self' in the 'Serf-speech'; this, in any case, was doubtless a jargon of many dialects, as formless as any conceived of by the author of *Hudibras*.

APPENDIX

AN ENGLISH-JARGON VOCABULARY, FOR COMPARATIVE PURPOSES[1]

English	Bog-Latin	Shelta	Bĕarlagair na Săer
a, an		a, an	
abbot	eorosnach		
able		gråbalta	
above	tinnechuas	swurt	ŏs
across		hal	
[adverbial prefix]			co
advice		luba	
afraid		agétul	
after		ar	
again		yĭrt, ayĭrt	
ale	roinn, collscoin	šl'an	
alive		atå'p, tåp, tåpa	
all		goiχil	
all the more		at'omier	
also		stĕš	
altogether	henir		
always	dobethagres		
and		a, and, stĕš	is, agus
Anne		Grunles	
another		ala, ela, ĕrpa, ly	
anus	tionnor	tūr	samhar, tūr
anvil		smugal	
anyone	niec, nionac		
apple	bloa	grūla	
arise	tinbuid ('which arises')	grĕ	
around		sūl'a	
arrest		salk, solk	
artisan	cerbele		
as			mar
ashes		šlŏh'a	
asleep		kuldrum	
ass		gasal, grasal, kuri, molson, meilor, nagat	

[1] Compound expressions and periphrases (e.g. Shelta *bog asturt* = assume) are as a rule omitted from this vocabulary. The eleven additional words in the Bog-Latin vocabulary (292–302) are not included, as well as the following words of doubtful meaning: aneolsin, certlus, certrann, fairc, groithial, idluisne.

English	Bog-Latin	Shelta	Bĕarlagair na Săer
at		a, aga	a
at all	henir	abúrt	
at his			gă
aunt		granta	
awaken		grūskal	
away		awást	
axe		šarker	
B, the letter			bĕ
baby		sul'an	
back	drogmall	nup	
backward		aráš, agrĕš	
bacon		sugūn	
bad	ur	g'ami, g'amoχ	dofai
bad woman			gudth
badness		g'amiaθ	
bag		lampa, rubōg	lūisĕad
bald	munchaol		
ball			cruinneacăn
bargain		surgon	
Barlow		N'ikair	
barn		sg'ibōl, šk'ibl'īn	
basin		srīš, šriš	
basket		rīsbat, rūski,	
		skipsy	
bastard		losport	
be, I would			bĕinn
be, it would			bhīoch
be, may it not			năra
beard		grisōg, grēsol	coiseadramăn
beat		slim, lōber	
beat, you would			clapuach
beautiful	ailmin	bura, buri	
bed	sgeng	lī	long-shuain
bed-cover	berrech		
bee	bibe		
beer		răn'al, sinăl	
before		aχíver	
beg		g'ēg	
beggar		g'ēg'ra, yūk'ra,	
		g'ūk'ra, d'ūka	
begging			caha
behind		nup, mwĕn'a	
bell		šlug	
belly	haiscis	talop	
below	tinnichis		
belt		salta, slăska	
beside		l'im	
bible		g'iliχon	
big		tōm, tom	

English	Bog-Latin	Shelta	Bēarlagair na Sāer
bigness		tomiaθ	
binding		n'akul	
bird	luathan	grēt'īn	
bit		milk, kūt'i	
bite		luš	
black	bedhb	medel, gūt	
blacksmith		gūtena	
blanket		lampēid'	
blessing	betchennacht	mun'iaθ, nūs	
blind	goll	lud	
blood		liba	
blue		sorm	
boar		subaχ	
boat		kara	
body	troicit		coine
bog	ruodmarg	nōb'ri, ged	
boil		t'ērp, t'elp	tnūthughadh
bond, wrong			gahegan
bone	coich		
bonnet		enaχ	
book		g'iliχon	barcān, leabhracān
boot		strod, gulima	
bottle		drīper, subōl, šud'ēl	
bowl		brikler	
box		rubōg	
box (tinker's)		gruska, mer'gin	
boy	geitheille	sūbl'i, sūbl'in, šam, grȧkin, šarpōg, siblīn, l'ogaχ	geabēis
Boyne		Srōn'e	
brass		granlum, n'ākiš rēglum	
brave		topa	
bread		pek, dura, dād'e	
break		klisp	
break wind		prask	
breakfast		sragāsta	
breeches		brogies	
bridge		grē·ed	
Bridget		Rībīn, Grisod	
bridle		n'ūkal	
bring	gortinne		
Britain	Ondlosbu		
brogue			cuanōg
brooch		gin, bīn-chit, bīn-l'ūr'	
broth		simi, mantri	

English	Bog-Latin	Shelta	Bĕarlagair na Sâer
brother	bertrosar	šākr	comh-ĕis
bucket	muadailm	n'āka, ruket	
bud		koldni	
budget		lampŏg	
bull		garo, goro, bovi	
burial		sori	
burn		skurlum	
bury	onncaill		
bush		skraχo	
butter	iodamm	lat'rum, oid, aid	euch
buttermilk	brasach	g'ami elima	
button		skoi, srīpa	
buy		kari	
C (the letter)			cae, cĕ
cabbage		kåb	cabrūl
cabin		lobān	
cacare		kun'i	
cake	betroisgenn	srāχ	
calf	buiglen, duraibind, adaurutan	b'in'i blānŏg	
call (name)		šeb, šib	
can		ng'aka, n'āka, χurīn	
candle		blinkam, n'okul	scaochlong
cap		enaχ, hālor, k'ēdi, rabēd'	
car		lork, rāg	
card		roiχa	
carry		med'ri	
cart		skrīv	
cat	caipist	krīpa, krīpuχ, kut'er, maksti	cnāpach, cnāpaire
catching		bagail	
Catherine		Srat'rin	
cease		get	
chain		n'ok'lur, slang	
chair		kaihed, saiher	siske
chapel		grēpul	cabrōseō
charm		gris	
cheese	gortrus	kasin	
chewing			cāineadh
chicken		grēt'īn	
child		gåt'rin, goiχera, kon'īn	mearulān
chimney		griml'ŏr	coistreamān
choke		grata	
christen		risp	
church		ligi, maχal	

English	Bog-Latin	Shelta	Bĕarlagair na Sãer
clean		nalk, nolk, nalki	
cleric, clergyman	caill, clitach, cliath	kom, kombat, krimašt	borb
clerk		sraiχa	
clever		šark'	
cloak		šlăka	
clock		horer, yũr	
close, closing	durunad	kurlim	
cloth		sragon, srãgon	
clothing, clothes		d'ūχ, t'ūχ	rochăn
coal		blaci	
coat		grifin	
coif		b'anag	
coin		gored	
coire		spurk	
cold		gwŏp	
colour		got'a, gȧt'a	
comb	maincir	rĭk, rĭrk	
come, to	toiriadai, toraitne	tŏri	
common	colluicenn		
company		sud'ata	dăil
[comparative, prefix of]			ghes
condiment		granlum	
conduct, to		lag	
Connacht		Mwikamo	
constable			cearnŏg
contain		bwikad	
contest, a	betlim		
cook		t'ĕrp	tnũthughadh
copper	onduenne		
copulation	colluisuid		
Cork (city)			Alptiarpach
corn		brauen	
corner		lũk	
counterfeit		skrĭn	
country		munk'ri	
courtship		rud'uaθ	dercu
cow	bethan	blănŏg, gov'li, mũrĭn, dunik	fearbach
craftsman	cerbele		airig
cream		smentena	
credit		cuk	
Crosby		Srãχũ	
crown (5s.)		bul	
cry out		lugil	
cud (of cow)			cĭobhar
cup	coillsge, eonann	brikler, grupån, maχon	

English	Bog-Latin	Shelta	Bĕarlagair na Sāer
curds	gortgruth	grug'im	
curse	metchennacht	laburt	
cursed		grāfša	
cursing		šorknes	
custom	etaingi		
cut, to cut		šark	
cutter		šarker	
dance, dancing		m'auso	damhsamān
dark of night		dolimi	
daughter		šĕrkū, lad'n'aχ	
day		tån, talósk	meabhlad
day, working			nūnlig
daylight		bīn-lightie	
dead		tarsp	
dear			bī
death			seic
decent		m'aunes, skrål	
deer	orail (osail)		
demolish		sakel	
depart		misli	
devil		mīder, mīdril	biadal
devilment		mīderal	
died	rothinnicht bas		
dine		brāsi	
dinner		grīt'i, grit'ēr, grīnt'ūr	carran
dirt, dirty		ladu, lodaχ, glodaχ	sead
dish		līspa, sraskīn, slāta	
ditch		klaiton	
division	durlus		
do, to		grēdi	
doctor		krōker, misler, gloχ srugad', sugad', sikdūr'	
dog		goithean, kam'ra	cuithire, scuifreachān
done		srĕk, srīk	
donkey (see ass)			
door		rodus, d'iger	
down, downward		šīrt, ašīrt	
drawers		karnag	
dress		grūna	
dresser (furniture)		mišūr'	
drink (draught)	doib	gāter, škimiš, sringan	dīogla
drink, to	edmam (= let us drink)	luš	

English	Bog-Latin	Shelta	Bĕarlagair na Sāer
drop		trīp	tuis
drown		sahu, satu	
drum	ninan		
drunk	muincesg	škimišk	carra
drunkard		škimišter	
Dublin			Alpolaoghaire
duck		cackler, laprŏg, waddler	
dumb		šal'wa	
dung			cībir
dung-heap		karnān	
dusk		dorahŏg'	
dwelling		mukin'e	
dying	bethlosach		
dyke		muni	
ear	cuitheilm	kaine, glŏrŏg	durke
earth	tamor, tinne	ladu	
east, in the	tinneachair		
easy		kluš	
eat, to	loisiom (= let us eat)	luš	cāineadh
ecclesiastic	cetech		
edge		l'im	
eel		šangar	cruinneacān
egg		grŏmug, rūmŏg, cackler	
eight	ochtrosar		
eleven	aoinder ciach		
enceinte		rid'u	
end	coilliuch		
England, English		Palantus, Grasano	
escape		bog ar-mislŏ	
especially			aonachar
evening		dorahŏg'	
ever	roisciam	aχi'ver	
every		goiχil	
excellent		d'arp	triathamhuil
exchange		labĕrt	
excreta	caithen	kun'a	
exhibit		grespan	
eye	dercuill, sabar	d'arelallan, lūrk	dearc
face	eochaille, aga	grĕdan	
fair		grīnta, grīntus, fŏros, gruvog	
fairy		grīwog	
fall		slug, šlug	
false	gin		

English	Bog-Latin	Shelta	Běarlagair na Såer
family		tribli	
far		stafa, stofi	sead
farm		kran	
farthing		skurik	plaic
fat	sailailm	m'aur	
father	anrosar	dātair, gāter	fatramān
fear		gita, getūl	
feather		grūd', klūd'	
feed		brāsi	
fellow		nīd'a	
female		grifi	
fern		galapa, grīnlesk mun'i	
fetter	gortlomnach		
few		sūpla, sup	
field		grārk', sārk'	
fight, fighting		trīpus, kamrailid'	sprisanue
find		bog	
fine		bura, buri	
finger	bisi	t'ērpin	
fire	fuilgen, tinim	t'era, t'ini	tnūth
fish		lagprat, skēv	ēagracān
fitting time	maincirt, munghort		
five		šūkr, šūka, skukar	
five men	collcur		
five-pound note		finnif	
flax		grīnlesk	
flea		grārnog	
flesh	collruim	fē	
flirt		spurk	
floor	daurlar		
flour		lūrp	
flower	betbec	lašūl	
flute	gortran		
foal		graro	
follow		t'oli	
folly		mugataθ	
food	anrad	brās, pras	cîna
fool	daurrusus	mong, mugatân, grin'šeg	
foot	cufar	kōri, kōli	luinnidhe (plur.)
foreign loyalty			gall-thairiseach
foreman			fōrūch
forget		l'ag	
forgive		get'a	
forgiveness		get'al	
form, a fair	gortrailbe		

English	Bog-Latin	Shelta	Bĕarlagair na Sāer
fornicator		spurk'ra	
fort	daurun		
fortune (magic)		gris	
fortunes, to tell		griso	
four		šākr, šāka, šakar, šarka, šarkr	
four men	certrosar		
fourpence		grifin	
fox	sceman		
foxy			grifinthu
fresh		ly	
friend		srīntul, men- throḅ, grīntala	cara
fringe	carosar		
frog		šl'ēma	
from			ō
front, in, of	ardoballaib		
frost		gruχ	
fruit	anros		
fuel		t'era	
full	loscan	tẚn	
fun		sugū	
funeral		šoru	
further		atómier	
gaol			iarr-cīn
garden	gorm	rāgli	
gate		srat, g'et'um	
gentleman		gloχ swudal, swuder	
get		bog	
gill		kant, t'ant	
gimlet		borer	
girdle	crionna		
girl	eongort	lākīn	
give	goirtnide, gortinne	bug, nẚp, gōti, gori	tuaitighim
glass (drinking)		slun'a	brīdīn
go, to		d'onẚdu, misli	luadhaim, coistriughadh
goat	glaedmuine, gairmnech	wobbler, gaverog	cailid
God	teo, tiamudh, daur	dẚl'on	
gold, golden		grẚt	
good	manaith	bonar, slum, mun'i, bīn	triathamhail
goodness		mun'iaθ, buriaχt	
goose		mošona, mašīn, laprōg	

English	Bog-Latin	Shelta	Bēarlagair na Sāer
gown		grūna	
grain		brauen	
grand		bīn	
grandmother		karb, lāsūn	
grass		glask, šīrk	
graveyard		n'edas ladu	
great	muinrois, mabar	bīn, tōmān, bura, buri, tom, tōm	triath
green	breiche	granlesk	
grey	loiscia		
groat		grifin	
guinea		n'ugi	
gull		feadar	
gun		nuga	
hag		karb	luirc
hair	fualasg	fleece, sūrk, swūrk, balast, grīrse, grēd'	
half		t'al	
halfpenny		t'an'uk	
hammer		mašūr	casar
hammerer		d'anadair	
hand	luis	mål'a	lais
handkerchief		mankers, mankerso	
hang		surk	
hare	lornan	pāni	
harlot	muindrech	strīpuχ	
haste		ludni	
hat		stardy, nuta, ribad, grata	colla
haunted		grāfša	
hay		rēb', gwīš, grē·er	
he			sě
head	cud	n'uk	ceann, lisīn
hear	cloinntinne (=heard)	glōri	
heart		grīš	
heaven	nionon		
hen		kraudug, kamag	clūtach
her		a	
herd of cattle	ornuit		
hero	cotan		
herring		luskån, skudal	
hide, to		lābi	
highway		lanach	
his		a	a
hit		lōber, karib, miš	

English	Bog-Latin	Shelta	Bēarlagair na Sāer
hold		bwikad	
hole		lub	
home		hāvari	
honey	mincill, maincil		
hood	coimhgeall		
hoop		grunsa, luskan	
horn	culorn		femīn (?), gad
horner	culaire		
horse	eabadcoll, ebandan	gifan, kuri, blyhunka, g'ofan	caibhde, caibhire, cabhaill
hot		get'	
hound	collar		
house	meinichedh, mennrad	brod, k'en, k'ena	cīn
how			mar, cionnas
hunger		krōlušk	
hungry			giarradh-cīne
hurry		graχu	coistriughadh
I		mwīl, mwilša	
ice		gruχ	
idle			gab, gabanta
if			gā
impart			tuaitighim
impostor		k'erp'ra	
in, into, inner		i, na, sturt, a, astúrt	i
in thy			ad
information, give		k'erp	
inspector, head			seabhradōir
interrogation particle		in, a	
interrogation particle (negative)		noχ	
Ireland	Oinciu	Rilantus, Relantus	
Irish		šišer, Rilantu	
iron	ergrand	rēglum	
is, it is	beitid	stēš	tā, is, 's
it			ē
James		N'ētas, Grētis	
jar		šukar	
javelin	crisgeo, goithni		
jaw			reac
jester	daurrusus		
job		gruber	
John		G'ison, Stān	Giosān
jug		srug, šrug	

English	Bog-Latin	Shelta	Bĕarlagair na Sāer
Kane		Sāhon	
Kate, Kathleen		Sat'līn	
keep		bwikad	geab (= keep on)
kettle	scartlann	rengan, srittle, gušu, šrittle	
key		srotar, šuχar, šroχar, šorik	caistriomān
kill		karib	
king	roiscith	srīgo	
kingdom		srīdug	
kiss		gåp, šarag	luarcū
kitchen	collue	slosk	
knife	sgillenn	cålra, t'ålra	glaidīn
know, to		grani, skol'a	
knowledge		granēl	
labourer			borbīn
lack		n'āk	
lad		grōkin, gråkin	
lady		lĕdōg, yēdug	
lamb		cid	
lame		gafa	
land			diū, des
last night		aχĕr	
late		stafa, stofi	
laugh		rågli	
law		slī	
laziness		grolsin'aθ	gabanta
lazy		grolsa	
leap		šl'ēm	
leather		šlī·a	
leave	gortinne	goχ', goχ'i, get	
leek	gortran		
leg	cufar	kōri, kōli	
lengthy			seadmanach
letter		bulla, stama	
level (masons')			lāmōg
liar		k'erp'ra	
lie, to		t'erp, k'erp	
lie down, to		gwil'i	
life		gradum	beatha
light		ludus, blinklum	
light, to		muni, lāsk	
like		gramail	cosamhail
likewise		arárk, arĕk	
lips		bilsag	
listen		glōri	
listening		glōral	
little		b'in'i	
little, a		b'in'ian	

English	Bog-Latin	Shelta	Bĕarlagair na Sãer
living		mukin'e	
loaf		lūbīn, turan	
lock		slãsk	
locksmith		slãsker	
lodge, to		n'edas	
lodgings		stall	
long		stafa, stofi	ĕarpach, sead
look, look at			seabhruighim
Lord			triath
lording	oirthine		
lose		l'ag, dĕnoχ	
loss		l'agun	
louse		l'īma	
love		grå	
luck		grå	seamhas
lunch		mund'ari	
mad		rilū	
magistrate		gesti, gisteramån, pokkonus	
make		grat'i, grēdi	
man	fern	gloχ, gl'õnsk, yūk, fīn	ĕis
manner		rãk, rark	
mantle	brael		
manure			cībir
mare	ebathan	grifi, kesig	
Margaret		Kerribad	
market		grīnta, grīntus, karbu, surgu	
married		lõspo	
marry		lõsp	borbu'd
Martin		Sartin, Srortan, Šrortan	
Mary		Råb, Råbīn, Sranī	
mason		grašano	airig
me		mwī'l, mwīlša	
mead	muinchidh		
meal		bani, blå, lū·õg	cīna
measure			tīompalån
meat	collruim	fē, karniš	carran
meddle		naper	
mend		šedi	
Michael		Šreikel, Št'īmon, Šreik	Meanãn
micturate		nūp	
middle	muincedan		
midwife			duarcån-luirce

English	Bog-Latin	Shelta	Běarlagair na Săer
mile		l'íman	
milk	ailmis, lemocen	elima, elimloχ, y'ōrum, nap, alamaχ	assī
mill	muadhgalan	l'ivin	
miller		grīlt'ūr	
mind	muinbuid	l'art	
minister (religious)			borb
minute		srōmēd', sumad'	
mix		sud'	
moisture	firial		
moment (see minute)			
Monday		slūn	
money		grip, gored, wed', vonger, krop, l'ūr'	pūinc
monkey		g'ūksta	
month		grimšer	
morning	machain	sroid'an, hawrum	
morrow, good			muintriath
mortar			mort
mother	manrosar	kamair, nad'ram	mātal
mountain	bliadh	gl'īt	
mouse	luipist	slāhog	
mouth	beilflesg	pī, bilsag	bille, bile, belle, dūile
mouthful	muincir		
move			luadhaim, coistriughadh
much		tōmăn	
mud		lodaχ	
mule		t'al kuri	
Munster		Glideroχ	
my		mo	mo
myself	motuillsi		
nail		gran'a, nglū, grādna	
nail (finger)	aicris		
name		munska, munik, linska	
name, to		šeb, šib	
near		nolsk	
necessity		uχ	
neck	baicead	št'īmon, st'īmon	muin
Ned			Neathus
need		uχ	
needle	sailscon	snēl, kartson	

English	Bog-Latin	Shelta	Bĕarlagair na Sāer
neighbour		granlum	
nevertheless	certne		
new		grūt	
news		grīson	
newspaper		šingomai	
night	almaig	olomi, kon	sciath, scāid
nine	naerosar	ayen	
nit		gl'åg	
no		nīd'eš	
noise		grolan	būith
nor			nå
north	tinnechuaidh (in the north)	lud'ra	
nose	sropur	smarag, mĕrko, mĕrkŏg	sneith
not		nīd'eš	nī
note		bulla	
note, pound bank-		stamĕr	barcān, leabracān
nothing		nīd'eš	
now		min'úrt, n'urt	
oatmeal		blå, grunim	
of		a	a
of his			gå
of the		a, an, na	na
oh, alas		aχ	
old		kriš	
old person, old man		krišena, g'ūk, g'ūksta	seandān
on, upon		nap (?), swurt, aswúrt, ådi	
one	aoinndir (= one man)	awárt, ain, wart, ēn	aon
onion		grit'ūn	
open, to open	onnbealascan	skŏp, graskal	
or			nå, nū
orchard		mugel	
our	ār		ār
out, outside, out of		aχím	as
oven	amloicit		
over		horsk, olsk	
own		šum	
ox	daurailm		
painter			fiūmadŏir
pair		rīšpa	
pan	artoichenn	fē-t'ĕrp, grĕsub	
paper		stiff, stama	

English	Bog-Latin	Shelta	Bēarlagair na Sāer
passage			cābh
past (*see* over)			
Patrick		Stofirt, Stofrik	
pawn, to		l'ag	
pawnshop			iarr-cīn
pay, to		kari	
peach, to		k'erp	
peak			tuis
pen		niba	
penis	bethul	g'ōr, yar, yor	
penny		n'uk	fūinc
people	muinrosar	fōki, l'it'en	
perch			rīarpōg
person	dairtinne	d'asag, d'oχ, nīd'a	
personality			mūs
Peter		Grītus, Yītus	
petticoat		gredicoat	
Philip		Libisk	
physician		gloχ srugad'	
piece		kūt'i, milk	
pig	muinscuill	mwog	māilide
pigeon			cēapair
pin	delesg, durbuid	nimpīn, niba	
pincers		bwikads, koi	
pint		nimpa, sinta, srunta, šant	
pipe		št'īma	stīmire
piper		st'īm'ra, št'īm'ra	gleamadōir
pitcher	coiclenn		
pitiful	bruipill		
place	loscog	grat', goχ', goχí, n'edas	
plain	muinsgith, muingort		
plant	snuad		
plate	bruinioch	slāta	
please		grāsi	
plenty		gošta	
plough	feimen	surtul	
plumb-rule			lār an ingire
pocket		gōpa	
poem	bailir		
point			tuis
police, policeman		batoma, glōkot, gloχgūt, šēd, šīdrug, muskro, mit'ni	laidiana, siadōg, cearnōg
police-barrack		šēd's k'en	
poor		gop	

English	Bog-Latin	Shelta	Bĕarlagair na Sāer
porridge		lūt, tarpōn	
porringer		gušul, lagūn	
porter (drink)		luš	culahee
portion (of food)	collait		
pot	boige	sušgad, blaiki, gopa, rengan	
potato		kun'el, molem	cnoc, criabhōg
pound		numpa	
power	collumac		
prayer		stafara, stafari	
pregnant		gran'en	
presence			cāid
pretty		lašūl	
price		tul	
priest		kūn'a	borb
prison		bladunk	
prostitute		rīpuχ, lutram	
protestant		blōrna, pornuc, dolsk	
public-house		k'en-gāter	
pull out			prosimig
punch, a		grūskil	
purse		ruspān	
put, to		goχ', goχ'i	
quarrel		kamrailid'	
quarter		šaru	
queer		ly	
quench		graχt	
quick		grent'a	
quiet		sacānta	
quilt		riltōg	
rabbit		šušei, morghen, mut'i, mungin	
race (tribe)	cicinel		
rag		tirpa, tirpōg, turpōg, k'ērk	
rain, raining		robikin, šl'uχ, misla·in, skai a bagail[1]	
raise		grē	
rat		st'ēmon, slāhog	dingir
rave		srent	
razor	lethten	rīsk	
read		šl'ī·uχ, taši	
real		d'arp	
reaping	bruicnet		
red	brech	g'al, šarog	minighim (redden)

[1] See bagail in the Vocabulary.

English	Bog-Latin	Shelta	Bēarlagair na Sāer
reign		srīdug	
[relative particle]			a
remain, let it			mairidh
resin		sorš	
respectable		sak'rente	
ring		grān'e	
rise		grē	
road		tōber	caoi, rodam-iomān, cos-tramān
robber, to rob		sramala, sumōl	
rogue		n'āk	
roguish		n'ākiš	
Roman Catholic		Rilantus	
room		mam'rum	
rope	loarn	tar'in	
rotten		sloχa	
rump	fedseng		
run		šuri	
rush (plant)		snēl	
Sabina		Sibi	
saddle		krīs, gušu	
safety	comroisge		
said	foratmillsi (I said), atroibethe (he said)		
sail, to		skai	
sailor		skaihan	
sails		binsi	
salmon	bedban		
salt	sceglan	laskon	
salt meat	gech		
sand		kretum	
sandals	deilenn corb		
sated, satisfied	sailbledhach	gråsta	
satirist	nionta; (female) brainionta		
sauce		granlum	
saucer		gråser	
scaffold			pumpa
scales		od šarker[1]	
scholar		skol'ami, šl'i·uχter	
school			cīn na mearūlān
schoolmaster		gloχ šl'i·uχ	
scissors		šarker, mīšur	
scolding			meabhlughadh
Scotland		Grasano	

[1] See šarker in Vocabulary.

English	Bog-Latin	Shelta	Běarlagair na Sāer
sea	bar, loircis, liber	skai, surgu, χaran	bochna
seal	roscon		
see, to	fiac	sūni, suni	
self		brahan, d'īl, d'ī'l	
sell		šelk	
sense		l'īrk	
settle (seat)			ratachăn
seven	sechtrosar	šeltu	
shake		getūl	
shame		n'ēfin	
shawl		mīrsrūn, tug	
shears	bisi		
sheep	cetaimni, rosca	klītug, megit, bleater, krī- mūm, kolum	cinide, caora-āirnĕis
sheet		riltōg, rabl'īn, mīltōg	
Shelta		Šeldrū	
shield	sebath		
shift		mīltōg	
shilling		kuler, mid'og	scrăb, scrābăn
ship		bēro,[1] skōbug	scuabōg
shirt	luisnech niam- nach	karmuš, mīltōg, bl'antaχ	scirtīn
shoe	ailmsi, oindsi	lur'an	cuanōg
shoemaker			cabaisdīn
shoot		gruχ	
shop		gropa, opagrō	
short	iomcollamar		
shoulder		grala	
showman		gloχ sūnal	
shut, to shut	derclithe	grūti	
sick		grīt'	
sickness		grīt'aθ	
side		l'im	
sieve	creithne		
sieve-maker		rinškal	
silk		grī·ed	
silver	arbar	skåfer	
similarly		arárk, arḗk	
sin, a; to sin		šako	
sing		swurk	
singer		swurk'ra	
singly			aonachar
sister	salur	šēkar, siskår	comhbhuadh
sit		guš, gūš	
six	sealsor	šē	
sixpence		aspra, sprazi	
skillet		l'išgad, yišgad	

---

[1] A Romani word: see *binsi* in Vocabulary.

English	Bog-Latin	Shelta	Bēarlagair na Sāer
skirt		grifin	
slaughter	muncorbad		
sleep	collterniud	kuldrum	cabhro
slow	mainiciall	šlug	
sly		sugū	
small	betenghort[1]	tằn, b'in'i	gab, geab
smallness		b'in'iaθ	
smell, a; to smell		n'erp	
smith		gloχ krū	bruigneõir
smoke		grat	fūcama
smoke, to		luš	
snake		šangar	
snow		groχta	
snuff			cīanruis
so, thus			īan
so...as...			co...mar
soap		grõpa, lad'ram	
sod		grằd	
soda		grõda	
soft		stoχa	
solder		grằder	
soldier		šaragi, gloχ radam	
some		sik	
son	muincoll	kam	
song		swurkin	
soot		slūya, lodaχ	coistreamān
sorrow	roimincailg		
soul		gris, gradum	
sound	blaistiud		
south	aninches (from the south), tinnices (in the south)		
sow, to		šī·u	
sow, a		g'ofag	mēanla
space (of time)			cian
spade		naper	
speak			binna
spectacles		lūrkõg slun'a	
spit		smaχ, stam'ra	
spoon		nūspõg, mūskõg	
spoon, wooden		smằlk'ra	
spotted, speckled		šrugu	
spree			carrabhān
square, masons'			bochar
stairs		mēri	
stand		šedi, stedi	
stay, to		krad'i	
steal		karib, b'ēg	lofū

[1] Accepting Stokes's emendation: see the article (p. 105) under the heading fo this word.

English	Bog-Latin	Shelta	Bēarlagair na Sāer
steam		šan	
stick		k'ima, d'ima	
stitch		nāk	
stocking		mūti, mūtōg, glogē	
stone	aeile, cluipit, coparn	kad'ōg	cadauc, caid
stool		lāsk, lākūn, losk	
stop		krad'i, stāl	
stoppage			seic
story	sceb	l'esko	
stranger		grānša	
straw		gwĭš, grīsk, strumble	
street		grāg'	
strength		tād'iraθ	
strike		lōber	
string		krauder, srōpa, srāpa, sāpa	
strong		tād'ir	
sugar		grūker	
summer		graura	
sun			scaochnuid
Sunday		d'umnik, bīn-lightment	
supper		griper	
swallowing	srolan		
swear		d'umik	
sweep		fīk'īr, grīwa	
sweet		m'ali, l'ibis, lašūl	
sweetheart		rud'u	
swindle		glader	
sword	slacc, collann		
table		burik, bord, srurd	coing
tail		sgrubul, madel	femīn (?)
tailor		lākr	preampach
take	gem	salk, solk	bog; toghla (=taking)
take off		nap	
talk, to		tāri, mang	
talking, speech		tāral	binnighthe
tambourine	piplennan		
taste		lasp	
tea		grĕ, wĭd, sklåtaχ, skai-t'elpi	
teapot		giligopa	
tell		l'esk	
tell fortunes		k'erp	

English	Bog-Latin	Shelta	Bĕarlagair na Sãer
ten	leited nietrosar	t'al g'et'a	
tenant	ondach		
tent		lobān, lubān	
tent-cover		lumĭ	
testicle	losuill	kauvi	
than (after comparatives)			nã
that not			na, nach
the		an	an
thee		dĭl(ša), dĭ'l(ša)	
there	eoindir		soin
they			iad
thief			lofūdôir
thing		inoχ, enok, enoχ, ainoχ, t'et, t'inoχ	rud
think		šang	
Thomas		Môtas	
thorn		surgu	
thou		tū, hū	tū
thread		graisk	
three		šĭkr, šĭka	
three men	atreisiur		
threepence		trēn'uk	
thus			ĭan
thy			do
tie		n'akul	
till			go
time		grimšer, tūrk	
tin		stān, strān, d'orker, yergan	
tinker		naker, mink'er	
tired		d'aχag, surχa	
to		od	do, go
to him	dairi		
to me	dom'thuillsi cuncullum		dam
to thee	dairet, cunculut, duruit		dit, duit
to them	dairib		
to you	daurub		
tobacco		fôrgarĭ, munt'es	cuithi
to-day	anduiriu	min'úrt	
toe		t'ērpin	
to-morrow	imbethrar	aχáram	
tongs		mongas, nongas	
tongue	ligair	mĭšôg	
to-night	inionghort	aχónšk	
tool			lĭmĭn
tooth, teeth	feirchinn	grēχol	faig, deid

English	Bog-Latin	Shelta	Bĕarlagair na Sãer
top		n'uk	
towards		graχul	
town		āvali, āvari,	alp
		helm, elum,	
		oura	
trade		surdu	
trail		kart	
tramp		tõrog	
treat			trise
tree	cremad	skraχo, škrȧχ	fiuc
tremble, trembling		getūl	
troop	eptem		
trousers		klīspis, strides	
trowel			līmīn, scit
true, truth	ferim	d'arp	
tub	baisi		
tunic	crosar		
turkey		granko, kranko	garabuch
turnip		nap, nanti, kogi	
twelve	daernoerciach		
twenty		g'et'a	
two		ȧd, od, d'asag, do	da
two men	anduiris		
umbrella		gõpan	
uncle		grunkel	
under			fē
understand		šang	
unexcellent,			neamhthria-
unpleasing			thamhail
untrained youth			coulth
useless			dafadõir,
			neamhthria-
			thamhail
up		tūrk, swurt	suas, civ
upon		swurt, nap	ar
		aswúrt ȧdi	
upon my			erem
upon the			erin
vessel	loisgestar		
vex		šarig	
vexed		šarog	
[vocative particle]			a
voice	garta	gresko	
vulva		kõrig	
waistcoat		gilifon, srascoat,	
		graskot	
wait		get	

English	Bog-Latin	Shelta	Bēarlagair na Sāer
wake (funeral)		šoru	
walk		misli	
walker		misli·er	
wall		muni	
want, to		grani, n'ok, misli	
war		sugū, radam	
warrior	cotan		
wash, to		unált, nalk	
watch, a		slūpen	līmīn
watch, to		grat'	seabhruighim
water	usguile	skok, pāni, skai	seirc, dobhar
water, to draw			dobharuighim
Waterford		Skaitwurd	
weakness, lasting	scillber		
weaver			cifeanach
week		graχton, srīš	
welcome	foicert	grālt'a	
well		skrubol	
west	tinnichiar (in the west): ¹aninchiar (from the west)	mwik	
wet		šl'uχu	
what	cert		cāhīk, cā
wheel		srīlik, šurier	
when		nulsk	
where		kē	
whey	muincedhg		
whilst		grūsku	
whisky		skaihōp	dobharthriath, trīompalān
white	luan, socon	nap, lod	
whither		kar	
will	achobar		
wind	bue	grīto	
window		grin'ōg, blinkie	
wine		srīd'a	
wings		binsi	
Winifred		Grūtīn	
wire		gut, bulscur	
wish		n'ok	
wisp		grup	
wit		l'īrk, yīrk	
with		l'e, g'e	le
with him	losca		
with me	losum, uncullum		
with thee	lei(s)cet, un- cullut, roisciut		
with them	loisi		

¹ Adopting the emendation suggested s.v.

English	Bog-Latin	Shelta	Bēarlagair na Sāer
with you	losob		
withe	goithiallad		
without		rāks	
witty		l'īrko	
woman	biairt	mul, b'ŏr	be, buadh
woman, young		bl'ūr	
woman, old		karb	luirc
woo, to		rud'u	
wood	ged	slūfa, sluχul, sruχul	
wool		glūtug, klūt'a	
word	bercon	luba	bulcān, binnighthe
work			prosimig
worth		tul	
wound	giusalath		
wrong bond			gahegan
year	bellit	l'īman, straih-med, stretch	
yellow		g'al, nīp	
yes		stēš	
yesterday	anduire	m'ena	
young		gåt, got	ōigeanta
young person		gåt'na	

INDEX

Lightning Source UK Ltd.
Milton Keynes UK
UKOW05f1850220114

225098UK00001B/91/P